T0399414

GLOBAL EQUITY IN ADMINISTRATION

Governments around the world face the challenge of espousing principles of fairness but practicing inequity in their administration. Issues of equity and justice are fundamental concerns of government, and thus to public administrators, who constantly struggle to evaluate a country's social climate and ensure equity in governance. Such evaluation is unlikely to occur in a serious way, however, if government actors are fundamentally too uncomfortable to directly engage the topic. The result, this book argues, is a context of "nervousness," which unless squarely acknowledged and addressed, can become debilitating and thwart progress toward achieving social equity.

This volume explores and expands our understanding of the concept of nervousness in the administration of government services around the world, demonstrating the ways in which such an emotional and physical reaction can debilitate government actions that are needed to promote social equity and justice. Each of the chapters in this edited volume focuses on a single country and examines a specific nervous area of government, highlighting important historical and political considerations, as well as specific evidence of promising progress. It considers the complexity of nervous areas of governments around the world, while identifying encouraging approaches and initiatives. *Global Equity in Administration* is required reading for all practicing and aspiring public servants concerned with fair and equitable provision of public services around the world.

Susan T. Gooden is dean and professor of the L. Douglas Wilder School of Government and Public Affairs at Virginia Commonwealth University. She is an internationally recognized expert on social equity. Gooden is an elected fellow of the congressionally chartered National Academy of Public Administration and is past president of the American Society for Public Administration. Her books include *Why Research Methods Matter, Race and Social Equity: A Nervous Area of Government*, and *Cultural Competency for Public Administrators*. Her research has been funded by several organizations including the Russell Sage Foundation, the Kellogg Foundation, the Smith Richardson Foundation, MDRC, and the Manhattan Institute for Policy Research.

GLOBAL EQUITY IN ADMINISTRATION

Nervous Areas of Governments

Edited by Susan T. Gooden

Routledge
Taylor & Francis Group

NEW YORK AND LONDON

First published 2020
by Routledge
52 Vanderbilt Avenue, New York, NY 10017

and by Routledge
2 Park Square, Milton Park, Abingdon, Oxon, OX14 4RN

Routledge is an imprint of the Taylor & Francis Group, an informa business

Library of Congress Cataloging-in-Publication Data
Names: Gooden, Susan, editor.
Title: Global equity in administration: nervous areas of governments / Edited by Susan T. Gooden.
Description: New York, NY: Routledge, [2020] |
Includes bibliographical references and index. |
Identifiers: LCCN 2020010990 (print) | LCCN 2020010991 (ebook) |
ISBN 9780367519841 (hardback) | ISBN 9780367519780 (paperback) |
ISBN 9781003055945 (ebook)
Subjects: LCSH: Equality—Government policy—Case studies. |
Social justice—Government policy—Case studies. | Public administration—Social aspects—Case studies. | Globalization—
Case studies. | Comparative government—Case studies.
Classification: LCC HM821 .G564 2020 (print) |
LCC HM821 (ebook) | DDC 352—dc23
LC record available at https://lccn.loc.gov/2020010990
LC ebook record available at https://lccn.loc.gov/2020010991

ISBN: 978-0-367-51984-1 (hbk)
ISBN: 978-0-367-51978-0 (pbk)
ISBN: 978-1-003-05594-5 (ebk)

Typeset in Bembo
by codeMantra

CONTENTS

FIGURES

TABLES

CONTRIBUTING AUTHORS

Anna M. Agathangelou teaches at York University. As a fellow in the Program of Science, Technology & Society at the School of Government, Harvard (2014–2015), she has worked on bioconstitutionalism and global innovation humanitarianisms. She is the co-editor of (with Kyle D. Killian) *Time, Temporality and Violence in International Relations (De) Fatalizing the Present, Forging Radical Alternatives* (2016); the co-editor of (with Nevzat Soguk) *Arab Revolutions and World Transformations* (2013); the co-author (with L.H.M. Ling), of *Transforming World Politics: From Empire to Multiple Worlds* (2009); and the author of the *Global Political Economy of Sex: Desire, Violence, and Insecurity in Mediterranean Nation States* (2004).

Anbu Arumugam is a senior assistant professor with the Department of Politics and Public Administration at Annamalai University, Tamil Nadu, India. Her first book titled *An Introduction to the Noon Meal Scheme in Tamil Nadu* was published in 2017. She received the Chester A. Newland Presidential Citation of Merit in 2018 and 2017 for service to ASPA. She played an important role in bringing the sixth Young Scholars Workshop (2017) to India and was part of the organizing committee that year. She served on the PA Times Editorial Board during 2015–2016. She was selected for the 2013 Young Scholars Workshop in China and awarded the Founders' Fellowship by ASPA in 2014. She received the Junior Research Fellowship from University Grants Commission, New Delhi, in 2006.

Susan Appe is an assistant professor at Rockefeller College at the University at Albany, NY, USA. Her research focuses on government-nonprofit relations and the dimensions and evolution of the nonprofit sector. She examines how government policy influences and shapes civil society and nonprofit organizations; how and why nonprofit organizations respond to government regulation and policy; and the relationship between civil society, foreign aid, and development. She has published articles related to government-nonprofit relations and foreign aid, and teaches courses on nonprofit management, philanthropy, public administration, and public policy. She has been awarded several research fellowships in Latin America, including Fulbright Scholar awards in Colombia and Ecuador. She is co-editor-in-chief of *VOLUNTAS: International Journal of Voluntary and Nonprofit Organizations,* one of the leading academic journals in third-sector studies, publishing on topics related to civil society, nonprofit organizations, volunteering, and philanthropy.

Jelena Arsenijevic obtained her PhD in Public Health at Maastricht University. She works currently as an assistant professor at the Utrecht University School of Governance. Her research interests include equity in healthcare, social protection policy, and poverty induced by healthcare costs.

John Barry is a professor of Green Political Economy in the School of History, Anthropology, Philosophy and Politics at Queen's University Belfast. His main research interests include the ethics of sustainability/sustainable development, green moral and political theory, green political economy, civic republicanism and green politics, Irish/Northern Irish politics, and sustainable energy politics and policy. His extensive publications include the books *Environment and Social Theory* and *The Politics of Actually Existing Unsustainability: Human Flourishing in a Climate-changed, Carbon-constrained World.* He is civically active in organizations ranging from school board to the Green Party in Northern Ireland.

Fátima Bayma de Oliveira is a professor at the Brazilian School of Public and Business Administration at Getulio Vargas Foundation, Rio de Janeiro, Brazil. Her primary research focus is educational policy about which she has authored several books and articles. Dr. Bayma de Oliveira is a member of the Rio de Janeiro State Educational Council. She was previously the Executive Secretary of the Worker Protection Fund Board (CODEFAT), and the Jobs and Wages Director at Brazil's Ministry of Labor and Employment. She holds a PhD in Education from Rio de Janeiro Federal University (UFRJ).

Brendan F. Burke is an associate professor at Suffolk University, Boston, Massachusetts. His research and teaching interests include organizational theory, administrative reform, executive leadership, and comparative public administration. He has published in Publius: *The Journal of Federalism, State and Local Government Review,* and other journals. Prior to his academic career, he served local government managers in North Carolina and Virginia; he currently holds advisory board positions with the Massachusetts Department of Mental Health.

Kalliopi Christoforou obtained her MA in Gender Studies at the University of Cyprus. She currently works as a Mathematics teacher at a public school in Nicosia, Cyprus. She is civically active in the NGO Urban Gorillas which undertakes projects, events, and activities that enrich community building and creative collaboration.

Loren Gatch is a professor of Political Science at the University of Central Oklahoma.

Sofia Georgiou obtained her MA in Gender Studies from the University of Cyprus and MEd in Counselling from the University of Bristol. She currently works as a counselor in public high schools in Cyprus.

Susan T. Gooden is dean and professor of the L. Douglas Wilder School of Government and Public Affairs at Virginia Commonwealth University. She is an internationally recognized expert on social equity. Gooden is an elected fellow of the congressionally chartered National Academy of Public Administration and is past president of the American Society for Public Administration. Her books include *Why Research Methods Matter, Race and Social Equity: A Nervous Area of Government*, and *Cultural Competency for Public Administrators*. Her research has been funded by several organizations including the Russell Sage Foundation, the Kellogg Foundation, the Smith Richardson Foundation, MDRC, and the Manhattan Institute for Policy Research.

John Hitz is adviser for the Master of Arts Program in Teaching English as a Second Language at the University of Central Oklahoma. He lived and taught English in Turkey for six years.

Angela Kline is an assistant professor in the Department of Public Policy and Administration at West Chester University, and received her PhD in Urban Affairs and Public Policy from the Joseph R. Biden, Jr., School of Public Policy and Administration at the University of Delaware. Her research interests include nonprofit management and accountability, open data, and social equity. Kline currently has served as the District II Representative on the National Council of the American Society for Public Administration. Before joining academia, Kline worked for several nonprofit organizations doing resource development and evaluation.

Samantha June Larson is an assistant professor in the Department of Public Administration at the University of Wisconsin—Oshkosh. Her research examines policy implementation, program evaluation, and performance measurement through a social equity lens. Her work has been published in such scholarly journals as *Public Administration Review, Public Integrity,* and the *Journal of Public Affairs Education.*

Simone Martin-Howard is an Assistant Professor of Healthcare Administration at Long Island University-Brooklyn. She holds a Ph.D. in Global Affairs from Rutgers University-Newark, a Master's in Public Administration and a Master of Arts in International Relations from the Maxwell School of Citizenship and Public Affairs at Syracuse University. Dr. Martin-Howard's multidisciplinary background has formed her research interests which include domestic and global healthcare administration and policy, maternal and child health, addressing violence as a public health issue, and nonprofit service delivery. Simone's work has been published in the Journal of Health and Human Services Administration, the Journal of Public and Nonprofit Affairs, Contemporary Perspectives in Family Research, and Criminal Justice Review.

Sean A. McCandless works as an assistant professor of Public Administration and an associate director of the Doctorate in Public Administration Program at the University of Illinois at Springfield. His research concerns how accountability for social equity is achieved, specifically how different societal groups interpret the meaning of social equity in practice and how they debate over how best to achieve it. He is the chair of the Section on Democracy and Social Justice of the American Society for Public Administration and an associate editor of *Administrative Theory & Praxis*. He is fluent in French.

Wendy M. Nicholson received her BS in Psychology from Tufts University, and her MPA from John Jay College of Criminal Justice, where she is currently an adjunct professor in the MPA Program, and is currently pursuing her Doctorate in Public Administration at the Rutgers School of Public Affairs and Administration. Her research interests include the role of race and racism at the nexus of educational, criminal justice, and governmental budgeting policies; diversity, equity, and inclusion; Critical Race Theory; and Racial Battle Fatigue. Through her work, she seeks to improve the quality of life for underserved and marginalized communities.

Elizabeth Overman is a professor and a co-coordinator of the Master of Public Administration at the University of Central Oklahoma and the director of Internships and Irregular Enrollment, where she teaches Public Policy Analysis, Public Program Evaluation, and Nonprofit Management. She is the author of "Education in Oklahoma" which appears in *Oklahoma Government & Politics* (2020) and "Reframing as a Pathway to Democratic Deliberation, Dialogue & Deliberation: Leveraging Best Practices from State College and Universities" by *American Association of State College and Universities* (2017).

Yali Pang is a PhD candidate in Public Administration and Policy at L. Douglas Wilder School of Government and Public Affairs, Virginia Commonwealth University (VCU). Her research interests focus on nonprofit management and social equity. Yali is also an adjunct instructor at the Department of Political Science and a research fellow at the Partnership for People with Disabilities at VCU. Prior to her PhD program, Yali received a Master's degree in corporation management and a Bachelor's degree in Business Administration at Southwest University in China.

Nadia Rubaii is a Professor of Public Administration and Co-Director of the Institute for Genocide and Mass Atrocity Prevention at Binghamton University, State University of New York. Her research has long focused on issues of diversity, inclusion, and cultural competence in both academic and practitioner settings in the US and globally. She is currently engaged in a multi-year project with the Latin American Network for Genocide and Mass Atrocity Prevention to assess and facilitate improvements in national and regional policies and programs to protect and promote indigenous rights. She is a past president of NASPAA and member of the Executive Committee of INPAE. She is a founding co-editor of *Gobernar: The Journal of Latin American Public Policy and Governance,* and is an associate editor of the *Journal of Comparative Policy Analysis.*

Erna Ruijer obtained her PhD in Public Policy and Administration at the Virginia Commonwealth University. She is currently an assistant professor at the Utrecht University School of Governance. Her research interests include social equity, open government, open data, and transparency.

Marilyn Rubin is distinguished research fellow at Rutgers-Newark School of Public Affairs and Administration, and professor emerita of Public Administration and Economics at John Jay College of the City University of New York. Dr. Rubin has published many books, articles, and professional reports on public administration and has had 40 years of experience working as a consultant to government officials in the US and abroad on fiscal policy, economic development, and strategic planning. She is a fellow in the National Academy of Public Administration and holds a PhD from New York University's Robert F. Wagner Graduate School of Public Service.

Ezechiel Sentama is Rwandan by nationality. He holds a PhD in Peace and Development Research from the University of Gothenburg, Sweden. He has 19 years of teaching and research experience in peacebuilding, conflict, and reconciliation. Sentama has been a lecturer at the University of Rwanda; a senior lecturer at Linnaeus University, Sweden; and a Guest Researcher at the University of Gothenburg, Sweden. Sentama is currently an assistant professor and Marie S. Curie research fellow at Coventry University in the United Kingdom.

Crystal Soderman is a recent graduate of the Masters of Public Administration program at the University of Wisconsin—Oshkosh. She is continuing her education as a doctoral student in the field of Public Affairs. Her research interests include climate change, environmental policy, and social equity.

ACKNOWLEDGEMENTS

In many ways, this book represents life—it is full of the unexpected. Growing up in a rural area of Virginia, and never traveling internationally until I was well into adulthood, I never expected to experience a life that allowed me to travel to so many countries and to experience the beauty of people, community, and culture. I also never imagined becoming a Dean, learning much about university administration, and having the opportunity to work closely with The Honorable L. Douglas Wilder, 66th Governor of Virginia, first elected African-American Governor of the United States, and namesake of our School of Government and Public Affairs at Virginia Commonwealth University. Many years ago, when I earned my undergraduate degree from Virginia Tech in 1990, Governor Wilder was my commencement speaker when I was in the sea of faces earning a degree and energized by future opportunities that lay ahead. And, I certainly never, ever imagined that my father, Rev. John W. Tinsley, who taught me so much about life and was such a great supporter of his community, and an amazing husband, father, and provider, would tragically commit suicide while I was in the early stages of working on this book.

A few years ago, I authored a book, *Race and Social Equity,* which introduced the term "nervous area of government" into the lexicon of public administration. There are many areas of social equity—such as race, gender, sexual orientation, religion, class, and ability status—that governments are uncomfortable addressing because of an historical record of discrimination, bias, and exclusion. This historical record is immutable, but the future is an open canvas, full of endless positive possibilities. But these possibilities will not be realized without confronting truth and difficult history, and demonstrating an unwavering commitment to redress previous inequities. Like life, these governmental truths yield a combination of great accomplishments and tragic shortcomings.

This edited volume of essays, authored substantially by individuals who have a deep knowledge base of each respective country, examines nervous areas of government around the globe. Each chapter offers a matter-of-fact discussion of a country's social equity challenge, examining historical and social context, and providing evidence of a promising intervention. Instead of "standardizing" chapters along a U.S. academic yardstick, each chapter respects the voice and approach of a variety of interdisciplinary international scholarly perspectives.

I am thankful to my colleagues at the International Association of Schools and Institutes of Administration (IASIA) for a vibrant exchange of ideas and perspectives on social equity; to my editor at Routledge, Laura Stearns, for her support of this volume; and to the copyeditor at codeMantra, Erin Arata. I am also grateful to the assistance of David Hayter and Dante Rankin at VCU, in preparing the manuscript for submission.

My deepest gratitude is to my family—my husband, Basil; our daughter, Caper; our cousins Donnie and Cameron; and the beautiful life God has blessed us to live together. This book is dedicated to my father, the late John W. Tinsley, and to my mother, Shirley S. Tinsley. Thank you for providing me with a loving home; a wonderful childhood; and the skills, humor, independent thinking, fortitude, and courage to address the nervous areas of life.

1

NERVOUSNESS IN A GLOBAL CONTEXT

Susan T. Gooden

Global Nervousness

Governments around the world face the challenge of espousing principles of fairness while practicing inequity in their administration among particular groups. This zone in which they operate is best understood as the "nervous area of government." "The nervous area of government is how an organization considers, examines, promotes, distributes, and evaluates the provision of public justice in areas such as race, ethnicity, gender, religion, sexual orientation, class, and ability status" (Gooden, 2015, 9). Nervousness is an emotional and physical reaction that can interfere with one's ability to perform critical tasks. Both individuals and organizations can experience nervousness. In government, it becomes harmful when it debilitates actions that are needed to promote social equity and justice.

The nervous area of government often involves considerable discomfort because it addresses difficult systemic inequities. Nervous areas of government are commonly described as uncomfortable, difficult, challenging, or sensitive. Such descriptions, however, fail to recognize a more important concern. The first consideration should not be how comfortable (or not) individuals, organizations, or systems view these areas, but rather how essential, vital, and necessary successfully engaging nervous areas of government is to affected marginalized groups, as well as to the ultimate thriving of the polity at-large.

Issues of equity and justice are fundamental concerns of government, and thus to public administrators, who constantly struggle to evaluate the country's social climate and ensure equity in governance (Akram, 2004). Such evaluation is unlikely to occur in a serious way if government actors are fundamentally too uncomfortable to directly engage the topic. The result is an important, taken for granted, but unacknowledged context of nervousness, which unless squarely acknowledged and addressed, can become debilitating and thwart progress toward achieving social equity. Simply put, working effectively within the nervous area of government is the only way to shorten the distance between equity in principle and equity in action. Equity in principle makes us feel good. Equity in action confirms that our governments are actually doing good.

As detailed in my earlier book, *Race and Social Equity: A Nervous Area of Government*, the nervous area of government is grounded in an extended application of organizational justice. Issues involving organizational justice involve some person or group benefitting or harmed in a manner that is unfair. The dominant concern is how the organization provides public justice rather than solely individual justice. Public justice is the larger organizational value within which issues of social equity reside. Although public justice is similar to social equity, the latter is more concerned with the delivery of public services, whereas the former is more value-oriented. In some instances, achieving equity requires treating everyone the same; in other cases, it means treating groups differently based upon current and/or past inequities. Importantly, the implementation of equity is context based—determining what is fair is dependent upon understanding a complex array of historical, political, and social factors.

> Despite the long-standing commitment to fairness as an administrative principle, administrators must be humbled by the realization that they contributed to the discrepancy and in many places helped to institute inequality in the past by enforcing discriminatory laws and using their broad discretion to advance exclusionary social mores.
>
> *(Smith, 2002)*

"A primary managerial means to achieve social equity includes a managerial commitment to the principle that majority rule does not overturn minority *rights* to equal public services"
(Frederickson, 1980, 47 original emphasis). As Frederickson later explained,

> It is time for public administrators of all kinds to ask the so called second question. The first question is whether an existing public program or proposed program is effective or good. The second question is more important. For who is this program effective or good?
>
> *(2005, 36)*

Hence, social equity is "the fair, just, and equitable management of all institutions serving the public directory or by contract, and the fair and equitable distribution of public services, and implementation of public policy, and the commitment to promote fairness, justice, and equity in the formation of public policy" (National Academy of Public Administration, 2000). As Shafritz and

Russell (2002) explain, "Fairness in the delivery of public services; it is egalitarianism in action—the principle that each citizen, regardless of economic resources or personal traits, deserves and has the right to be given equal treatment by the political system" (395).

United Nations and an International Equity Framework

How are international standards for social equity determined, particularly given the vast differences in history, social norms, and cultural values? Herein, I contend that the United Nations (UN) offers the best (albeit far from perfect) international social equity framework. Following World War II, the UN was established in 1945 as an international organization designed to promote international peace and security. Currently comprised of 193 member states around the world, the mission of the UN is guided by purposes and principles contained in its founding charter. Article I of this charter details four primary purposes of the UN. Item 3 is fundamental to social equity: "to achieve international co-operation in solving international problems of an economic, social, cultural, or humanitarian character, and in promoting and encouraging respect for human rights and fundamental freedoms *for all without distinction as to race, sex, language or religion*" (United Nations Charter, 1945, emphasis added). Executing the mission of the UN involves intentional work by all member states toward these core principles—each operating within its own particular historical and social context which operates as a nervous area of government.

Importantly, there are critical trade-offs to fulfilling the mission of the UN. All countries maintain their sovereignty, and there is hierarchy within UN member states, with the five permanent members of the UN Security Council—China, France, Russia, the United Kingdom and the United States—having important veto power. And, ultimately given each member states' recognized sovereignty, the UN has limited ability to enforce principles and sanctions. Despite these limitations, however, the actions of the UN remain critical in providing a global social equity framework, exposing humanitarian inequities, and aiding in countries improving their equity performance.

Universal Declaration of Human Rights

Within an international context, social equity is advanced through the Universal Declaration of Human Rights (UDHR) of the UN.

> The Universal Declaration of Human Rights (UDHR) is a milestone document in the history of human rights. Drafted by representatives with different legal and cultural backgrounds from all regions of the world, the Declaration was proclaimed by the United National General Assembly in Paris on 10 December 1948 as a common standard of achievements for all

peoples and all nations. It sets out, for the first time, fundamental human rights to be universally protected and it has been translated into over 500 languages.

(United Nations, Universal Declaration of Human Rights)

Currently, there are 193 members of the UN, all of which have signed in agreement with UDHR.

The UDHR is comprised of 30 articles designed to recognize equal and inalienable rights of all members of the human family and is the foundation of freedom, justice, and peace in the world. As stated in Article 2,

Everyone is entitled to all the rights and freedoms set forth in this Declaration, without distinction of any kind, such as race, colour, sex, language, religion, political or other opinion, national or social origin, property, birth or other status. Furthermore, no distinction shall be made on the basis of the political, jurisdictional or international status of the country or territory to which a person belongs, whether it be independent, trust, non-self-governing or under any other limitation of sovereignty.

(United Nations, Universal Declaration of Human Rights)

Gender and the UN

In 1979, the Convention on the Elimination of All Forms of Discrimination against Women (CEDAW) was adopted by the United Nations General Assembly. "Although the CEDAW Convention is an antidiscrimination instrument for the elimination of sex and gender-based discrimination against women, its proclaimed overall goal is the practical realization of substantive equality between women and men" (Šimonović, 2014).

Article 1(1) defines discrimination against women as

any distinction, exclusion or restriction made on the basis of sex which has the effect of purpose of impairing or nullifying the recognition, enjoyment or exercise by women, irrespective of their marital status, on the basis of equality of men and women, of human rights and fundamental freedoms in the political, economic, social, cultural civil or any other field.

(OHCHR, n.d.)

The Convention considers three primary dimensions relative to the equity for women: civil rights, reproductive rights, and the influence of culture and tradition on women's human rights. Relative to civil rights, the legal status of women receives the broadest attention with specific attention "to guaranteeing women (irrespective of their marital status) the right to vote, to hold public office and to exercise public functions" and to "affirm women's rights to non-discrimination in education, employment and economic and social activ-ities" (OHCHR, n.d.). The Convention's emphasis on women's reproductive rights with "provisions for maternity protection and child-care proclaimed as essential rights and are incorporated into all areas of the Convention, whether dealing with employment, family law, health care or education" (OHCHR, n.d.). And, the Convention's emphasis on cultural and tradition focuses on the obligation of member states to

> work towards the modification of social and cultural patterns of individ-ual conduct in order to eliminate 'prejudices and customary and all other practices which are based on the idea of the inferiority or the superiority of either of the sexes or on stereotyped roles for men and women'.
>
> *(OHCHR, n.d.)*

As Šimonović (2014) explains, "Consequently at the heart of the Convention is the obligation of state parties to not only formally embody the principle of equality between women and men, but also to assure its practical realization of substantive gender equality" (592). Importantly, the Convention recognizes the importance of special measures such as affirmative action to positively promote equality.

> CEDAW addresses the realities of institutionalized inequality by calling on countries to undertake corrective measures to achieve equality. . .Under CEDAW, governments cannot simply adhere to principles of equality going forward, but must redress the systemic problems that created the inequality in the first place.
>
> *(Friedman, 2005, 483)*

Although the CEDAW is the second most accepted of the nine core UN inter-national human rights treaties, an important limitation of the Convention is that it does not contain a separate provision for violence against women (Šimonović, 2014) which remains an important issue. To the credit of the CEDAW,

> In 1989, relatively early in its work, the CEDAW Committee adopted General Recommendation No. 12 on violence against women, in which it stated that Articles 2, 5, 11, 12, and 16 of the Convention obliged state parties to protect women from violence and invited them to include information about laws and other measure relating to protection from violence under their reports under the Convention. . .General recom-mendation No. 12 was then superseded by General Recommendation No. 19 of 1992, which substantially elaborated on the issue of violence against women.
>
> *(Šimonović, 2014, 600)*

Ultimately, as Šimonović (2014) summarizes,

> One could question whether the lack of an express provision on violence against women is an inadequacy of the Convention which requires its revision by amendment or even an Optional Protocol on violence against women. So far the Convention's undisputed application to violence against women as a form of discrimination under the Convention indicates that the system can work as a form of discrimination under the Convention indicates that the system can work as it is, yet the remaining pertinent question is whether the system would work better with more detailed guidance.
>
> *(601)*

While gender is addressed directly by the UN in the 1948 UDHR and the 1979 Convention on the Elimination of All Forms of Discrimination Against Women, sexual orientation is not. Although UN international human rights laws apply to everyone and UN human rights experts have confirmed that international law prohibits discrimination based on sexual orientation, gender identity, and sex characteristics (United Nations for LGBTI Equality, n.d.), sexual orientation does not have the same UN policy protections as either gender, race, or religion. "More than a third of the world's countries criminalize consensual same sex-relations" (UN Free & Equal, n.d.). In 2013, the Office of the United Nations High Commissioner for Human Rights (OHCHR) launched a global information campaign to promote equal rights and fairness for LGBTI people. In 2016, the United Nations Human Rights Council adopted a resolution on "Protection against violence and discrimination based on sexual orientation and gender identity" to mandate the appointment of an independent expert on the subject. This historic UN resolution tasks the expert with

> assessing the implementation of existing international human rights law, identifying best practices and gaps, raising awareness of violence and discrimination based on sexual orientation and gender identity, engaging in dialogue and consultation with states and other stakeholders, and facilitating provision of advisory services, technical assistance, capacity-building, and cooperation to help address violence and discrimination on these groups.
>
> *(Human Rights Watch, 2016)*

Race and the UN

Described as "the international community's tool for combating racial discrimination which is at one and the same time universal in reach, comprehensive in scope, legally binding in character, and equipped with built-in measures of implementation" (UNESCO, 1978), the International Convention of the Elimination of All Forms of Racial Discrimination (CERD) is a fundamental instrument of the UN charter. "The Convention drew its primary impetus from the desire of the United Nations to put an immediate end to discrimination against black and nonwhite persons" (Meron, 1985, 284). Article 1(1) defines racial discrimination as:

> any distinction, exclusion, restriction or preference based on race, colour, descent, or national or ethnic origin which has the purpose or effect of nullifying or impairing the recognition, enjoyment, or exercise, on an equal footing, or human rights and fundamental freedoms in the political, economic, social, cultural, and any field of public life.
>
> *(UNESCO, as cited by Meron, 1985, 286)*

CERD offers an important international framework. Four of its principles particularly apply to race and social equity: (1) the elimination of racial discrimination is the core goal; (2) a government's previous historical record relative to discrimination matters; (3) public organizations are responsible for ending racial discrimination; and (4) remedies to racial discrimination may be race conscious, rather than race blind.

A dominant goal of the CERD is to end racial discrimination, not to minimize or reduce it. "Parties condemn racial discrimination and undertake to pursue by all appropriate means and without delay a policy of eliminating racial discrimination in all its forms and promoting understanding among all races" (Meron, 1985, 292). Article 2(1)c of the convention requires "each state to take effective measures to review governmental, national and local policies, and to amend, rescind or nullify any laws and regulations which have the effect of creating or perpetuating racial discrimination wherever it exists" (UNESCO, 1978). The perpetuation of racial discrimination is directly linked to a nation's historical record. Often, current structural racial inequities were preceded by a legal discriminatory past. As Meron explains,

> Past acts of discrimination have created systemic patterns of discrimination in many societies. The present effects of past discrimination may be continued or even exacerbated by racially neutral policies or practices that, though not purposely discriminatory, perpetuate the consequences of prior, often intentional discrimination.
>
> *(Meron, 1985, 289)*

Historical records provide significant guidance in terms of how governments should prioritize their social equity work. Addressing contemporary structural inequities should not only involve the elimination of discriminatory policies, but also involve the establishment of new structures to promote racial equity among specifically historically disadvantaged groups.

The provisions of CERD have particular relevance for public administrators, as noted in the specific mention of "public life." Governmental entities are responsible agents in eliminating racial discrimination. Addressing racial discrimination is not a matter of choice or preference, but rather a public interest: "There is a compelling state interest in eliminating discrimination and assuring access for all to publicly available goods and services, which includes not only tangible ones, but also privileges and advantages" (Meron, 1985, 294). Structural inequities that result in a pattern of white privilege and advantages are in direct contradiction to the larger state interest of eliminating discrimination relative to public services. Public administrators, though their respective agency missions, can examine and develop aggressive policies to address such structural advantages.

Additionally, CERD is clear that remedies are not required to be race-neutral. As Meron states, "The bona fide affirmative action programs cannot be challenged under the Convention, as they could be if the Convention mandated color blind policies" (1985, 305). Rather, Article 2(2) obligates states to operate in a race-conscious manner:

> Parties shall, when the circumstances so warrant, take, in the social, economic, cultural and other fields, special and concrete measures to ensure the adequate development and protection of certain racial groups or individuals belonging to them for the purpose of guaranteeing them the full and equal enjoyment of human rights and fundamental freedoms. These measures shall in no case entail as a consequence the maintenance of unequal or separate rights for different racial groups after the objectives for which they were taken have been achieved.
>
> *(UNESCO, 1978)*

The very important discretionary language of Article 2(2) is the phrasing "when the circumstances so warrant," as it does not provide specific guidance in terms of when such measures are warranted. Merton suggests that a government's obligation to utilize affirmative action "should be determined by the group's degree of access to political and economic resources" (1985, 308). Applying Meron's criterion, data that report access to political and economic resources by racial groups can provide useful guidance in developing and targeting specific affirmative action policies. "The test is whether the group in question requires the protection and aid of the state to attain a full and equal enjoyment of human rights" (Meron, 1985, 308).

Religion and the UN

In addition to explicit protection of religion in the 1948 UDHR, one of the primary sources of international protection of religion is the 1981 Declaration on the Elimination of All Forms of Intolerance and of Discrimination Based on Religion or Belief. As detailed in Article 1, "Everyone shall have the right to freedom of thought, conscience, and religion. This right shall include freedom to have a religion or whatever belief of his choice, and freedom, either individually or in community with others and in public or private, to manifest his religion or belief in worship, observance, practice, and teaching" (OHCHR, n.d.).

Since the late 1990s, there has been substantial concern from many Muslim-majority countries regarding "defamation of religions." As Rehman and Berry (2012) explain,

> For well over a decade, several resolutions under the banner of 'defamation of religions' were sponsored within the UN by members of the Organisation of Islamic Cooperation (OIC)—the second largest inter-governmental organization in the world after the UN, which officially represents modern Islamic states.
>
> *(432)*

The 1999 Defamation of Religions resolution urged

> all States, within their national legal framework, in conformity with international human rights instruments to take all appropriate measures to combat hatred, discrimination, intolerance and acts of violence, intimidation and coercion motivated by religious intolerance, including attacks on religious places, and to encourage understanding, tolerance and respect in matters relating to freedom of religion or belief.
>
> *(Commission on Human Rights, 1999)*

Between 1999 and 2010, UN bodies enacted about 20 resolutions relating to the defamation of religion (Scharffs, 2013). Critiques of these resolutions cite concerns with limiting both freedom of expression and freedom of religion (Rehman & Berry, 2012; Kayaoglu, 2014).

> There are unintended ill effects of prohibitions on defamation of religion as well. While these laws are ostensibly aimed at protecting Islam, they may have the opposite effect, intimidating reform-minded Muslims, providing grounds for persecuting sectarian opponents within the Islamic faith, and encouraging vigilante justice.
>
> *(Scharffs, 2013, 68)*

While defamation of religion remains an unsettled, nervous area of government for the UN, it also highlights the conflict and ambiguity of terms such as free speech and incitement to hatred.

Sustainable Development Goals

The previously discussed actions by the UN provide a strong foundation for promoting social equity around the globe and explicit language regarding fundamental universal rights for humanity. More recently, in 2015, the UN Sustainable Development Goals (SDGs) were adopted by all UN member states as a universal call to integrated action to combat poverty, protect the planet, and promote peace and prosperity. These goals, which replace the Millennium Development Goals (MDGs), recognize the importance of focusing on systems to promote desired improvements among humanity by 2030.

These 17 goals include the following[1]:

1. End poverty
2. No hunger
3. Good health and well-being
4. Quality education
5. Gender equality
6. Clean water and sanitation
7. Affordable and clean energy
8. Decent work and economic growth
9. Industry, innovation, and infrastructure
10. Reduced inequities
11. Sustainable cities and communities
12. Responsible consumption and productivity
13. Climate action
14. Life below water
15. Life on land
16. Peace, justice, and strong institutions
17. Partnership for the goals

While these goals are laudable and ambitious, they showcase the fundamental importance of social equity at the global level. A glimpse of the problem includes, for example, 836 million people who live in extreme poverty; poor nutrition causes 45% of deaths in children under five years old; 103 million youth lack basic literacy skills—more than 60% are female; 2.4 billion people lack access to basic sanitation services, such as toilets; one in five people lack access to modern electricity; and more than 75% of the population live in societies where income is more unequally distributed than it was 25 years ago.

Overview of the Book

Contemporary inequities are often the result of previous state-caused discrimination. Each of the chapters in this edited volume focuses on a single country, examining a specific nervous area of government. Together, this volume expands our understanding of nervousness in the administration of government services around the world, offers important historical and political considerations, and provides specific evidence of promising progress. It considers the complexity of nervous areas of governments around the world, while identifying encouraging approaches and initiatives.

Implementing the social equity principles guided by the UN framework suggests the importance of governments analyzing not only their legal policies, but their practices as well to consider several fundamental questions. For example, how does equity in practice align with equity in principle? What practices do governments have in place to routinely monitor, report, and correct policies that have a discriminatory effect (whether intentional or not)? What criteria are governments using to gauge their progress in ending discrimination? What additional actions will governments employ to accelerate progress or to provide historical redress? The answers to these questions directly involve government policies and actions by public administrators.

The following chapters include an examination of nervous areas of governments in 11 countries including Brazil, China, Cyprus, France, Germany, India, Mexico, Rwanda, South Africa, the Netherlands, and the United Kingdom (Northern Ireland). The social equity issues considered in this book include gender and sexuality, race and ethnicity, and religion and community, although as several chapters discuss there is important intersectionality of these issues. A variety of countries were intentionally targeted, in order to show the range and complexity of social equity issues being addressed by considerably different countries. Table 1.2 provides the GDP per capita, median household income, median income, Gini index, and population for each of these countries as well as the United States. Table 1.3 provides health and livelihood indicators including life expectancy, the human development index, and population. Table 1.4 provides the proportion of seats held by women in each country's parliament (or equivalent).

As these tables illuminate, these countries vary considerably. The Gini index provides a measure of equality (relative to the distribution of income among individuals or households within an economy deviates from a perfectly equal distribution). As Table 1.2 indicates, for example, while the Netherlands ranks most equal and South Africa as least equal, among the included countries, the Gini index measures of China, the United States, and Rwanda are relatively close, even though the median household income of the United States is substantially higher than that of either China or Rwanda. And, as Table 1.4 indicates, the three countries with the highest percentage of women in parliament are Rwanda, Mexico, and South Africa, respectively. Comparatively, among this group, the three countries with the lowest percentage of women in parliament are Brazil, India, and Cyprus.

This volume offers the reader a brief international social equity tour by examining a nervous area of government for each country. For consistency, each

TABLE 1.1 Universal Declaration of Human Rights

Preamble

Whereas recognition of the inherent dignity and of the equal and inalienable rights of all members of the human family is the foundation of freedom, justice and peace in the world, Whereas disregard and contempt for human rights have resulted in barbarous acts which have outraged the conscience of mankind, and the advent of a world in which human beings shall enjoy freedom of speech and belief and freedom from fear and want has been proclaimed as the highest aspiration of the common people,

Whereas it is essential, if man is not to be compelled to have recourse, as a last resort, to rebellion against tyranny and oppression, that human rights should be protected by the rule of law,

Whereas it is essential to promote the development of friendly relations between nations,

Whereas the peoples of the United Nations have in the Charter reaffirmed their faith in fundamental human rights, in the dignity and worth of the human person and in the equal rights of men and women and have determined to promote social progress and better standards of life in larger freedom,

Whereas Member States have pledged themselves to achieve, in cooperation with the United Nations, the promotion of universal respect for and observance of human rights and fundamental freedoms,

Whereas a common understanding of these rights and freedoms is of the greatest importance for the full realization of this pledge,

Now, therefore, The General Assembly, Proclaims this Universal Declaration of Human Rights as a common standard of achievement for all peoples and all nations, to the end that every individual and every organ of society, keeping this Declaration constantly in mind, shall strive by teaching and education to promote respect for these rights and freedoms and by progressive measures, national and international, to secure their universal and effective recognition and observance, both among the peoples of Member States themselves and among the peoples of territories under their jurisdiction.

Article 1.

All human beings are born free and equal in dignity and rights. They are endowed with reason and conscience and should act towards one another in a spirit of brotherhood.

Article 2.

Everyone is entitled to all the rights and freedoms set forth in this Declaration, without distinction of any kind, such as race, colour, sex, language, religion, political or other opinion, national or social origin, property, birth or other status. Furthermore, no distinction shall be made on the basis of the political, jurisdictional or international status of the country or territory to which a person belongs, whether it be independent, trust, non-self-governing or under any other limitation of sovereignty.

Article 3.

Everyone has the right to life, liberty and the security of person.

Article 4.

No one shall be held in slavery or servitude; slavery and the slave trade shall be prohibited in all their forms.

Article 5.

No one shall be subjected to torture or to cruel, inhuman or degrading treatment or punishment.

Article 6.

Everyone has the right to recognition everywhere as a person before the law.

Article 7.

All are equal before the law and are entitled without any discrimination to equal protection of the law. All are entitled to equal protection against any discrimination in violation of this Declaration and against any incitement to such discrimination.

Article 8.

Everyone has the right to an effective remedy by the competent national tribunals for acts violating the fundamental rights granted him by the constitution or by law.

Article 9.

No one shall be subjected to arbitrary arrest, detention or exile.

Article 10.

Everyone is entitled in full equality to a fair and public hearing by an independent and impartial tribunal, in the determination of his rights and obligations and of any criminal charge against him.

Article 11.

1. Everyone charged with a penal offence has the right to be presumed innocent until proved guilty according to law in a public trial at which he has had all the guarantees necessary for his defence.
2. No one shall be held guilty of any penal offence on account of any act or omission which did not constitute a penal offence, under national or international law, at the time when it was committed. Nor shall a heavier penalty be imposed than the one that was applicable at the time the penal offence was committed.

Article 12.

No one shall be subjected to arbitrary interference with his privacy, family, home or correspondence, nor to attacks upon his honour and reputation. Everyone has the right to the protection of the law against such interference or attacks.

Article 13.

1. Everyone has the right to freedom of movement and residence within the borders of each State.
2. Everyone has the right to leave any country, including his own, and to return to his country.

Article 14.

1. Everyone has the right to seek and to enjoy in other countries asylum from persecution.
2. This right may not be invoked in the case of prosecutions genuinely arising from non-political crimes or from acts contrary to the purposes and principles of the United Nations.

Article 15.

1. Everyone has the right to a nationality.
2. No one shall be arbitrarily deprived of his nationality nor denied the right to change his nationality.

(Continued)

Article 16.

1. Men and women of full age, without any limitation due to race, nationality or religion, have the right to marry and to found a family. They are entitled to equal rights as to marriage, during marriage and at its dissolution.
2. Marriage shall be entered into only with the free and full consent of the intending spouses.
3. The family is the natural and fundamental group unit of society and is entitled to protection by society and the State.

Article 17.

1. Everyone has the right to own property alone as well as in association with others.
2. No one shall be arbitrarily deprived of his property.

Article 18.

Everyone has the right to freedom of thought, conscience and religion; this right includes freedom to change his religion or belief, and freedom, either alone or in community with others and in public or private, to manifest his religion or belief in teaching, practice, worship and observance.

Article 19.

Everyone has the right to freedom of opinion and expression; this right includes freedom to hold opinions without interference and to seek, receive and impart information and ideas through any media and regardless of frontiers.

Article 20.

1. Everyone has the right to freedom of peaceful assembly and association.
2. No one may be compelled to belong to an association.

Article 21.

1. Everyone has the right to take part in the government of his country, directly or through freely chosen representatives.
2. Everyone has the right to equal access to public service in his country.
3. The will of the people shall be the basis of the authority of government; this will shall be expressed in periodic and genuine elections which shall be by universal and equal suffrage and shall be held by secret vote or by equivalent free voting procedures.

Article 22.

Everyone, as a member of society, has the right to social security and is entitled to realization, through national effort and international co-operation and in accordance with the organization and resources of each State, of the economic, social and cultural rights indispensable for his dignity and the free development of his personality.

Article 23.

1. Everyone has the right to work, to free choice of employment, to just and favourable conditions of work and to protection against unemployment.
2. Everyone, without any discrimination, has the right to equal pay for equal work.
3. Everyone who works has the right to just and favourable remuneration ensuring for himself and his family an existence worthy of human dignity, and supplemented, if necessary, by other means of social protection.
4. Everyone has the right to form and to join trade unions for the protection of his interests.

Article 24.
Everyone has the right to rest and leisure, including reasonable limitation of working
  hours and periodic holidays with pay.
Article 25.
1. Everyone has the right to a standard of living adequate for the health and well-
   being of himself and of his family, including food, clothing, housing and medical
   care and necessary social services, and the right to security in the event of
   unemployment, sickness, disability, widowhood, old age or other lack of livelihood
   in circumstances beyond his control.
2. Motherhood and childhood are entitled to special care and assistance. All children,
   whether born in or out of wedlock, shall enjoy the same social protection.
Article 26.
1. Everyone has the right to education. Education shall be free, at least in the
   elementary and fundamental stages. Elementary education shall be compulsory.
   Technical and professional education shall be made generally available and higher
   education shall be equally accessible to all on the basis of merit.
2. Education shall be directed to the full development of the human personality and
   to the strengthening of respect for human rights and fundamental freedoms. It
   shall promote understanding, tolerance and friendship among all nations, racial
   or religious groups, and shall further the activities of the United Nations for the
   maintenance of peace.
3. Parents have a prior right to choose the kind of education that shall be given to
   their children.
Article 27.
1. Everyone has the right freely to participate in the cultural life of the community,
   to enjoy the arts and to share in scientific advancement and its benefits.
2. Everyone has the right to the protection of the moral and material interests
   resulting from any scientific, literary or artistic production of which he is the
   author.
Article 28.
Everyone is entitled to a social and international order in which the rights and
  freedoms set forth in this Declaration can be fully realized.
Article 29.
1. Everyone has duties to the community in which alone the free and full
   development of his personality is possible.
2. In the exercise of his rights and freedoms, everyone shall be subject only to such
   limitations as are determined by law solely for the purpose of securing due recognition
   and respect for the rights and freedoms of others and of meeting the just requirements
   of morality, public order and the general welfare in a democratic society.
3. These rights and freedoms may in no case be exercised contrary to the purposes
   and principles of the United Nations.

Article 30.
Nothing in this Declaration may be interpreted as implying for any State, group
  or person any right to engage in any activity or to perform any act aimed at the
  destruction of any of the rights and freedoms set forth herein.

TABLE 1.2 Economic Indicators by Country

Country	GDP Per Capita	Median Household Income	Median Income	Gini	Population
Brazil	8,920.80	7,522	2,247	53.3	211,049,527
China	9,770.80	6,180	1,786	38.6	1,433,783,686
Cyprus	28,159.30	18,242	4,932	34	1,198,575
France	41,463.60	31,112	12,445	32.7	65,129,728
Germany	48,195.60	33,333	14,098	31.7	83,517,045
India	2,015.60	3,168	616	35.7	1,366,417,754
Mexico	9,698.10	11,680	2,900	48.3	127,575,529
Netherlands	53,024.10	38,584	14,450	28.2	17,097,130
Rwanda	773.00	1,101	235	43.7	12,626,950
South Africa	6,374	5,217	1,217	63	58,558,270
UK	42,491.40	31,617	12,399	33.2	67,530,172
USA	62,641	43,585	15,480	41.5	329,064,917

Sources: GDP per capita (current US$). (n.d.). Retrieved November 15, 2019, from https://data.worldbank.org/indicator/ny.gdp.pcap.cd.

*Median Income by Country Population. (n.d.). Retrieved November 15, 2019, from http://*worldpopulationreview.com/countries/median-income-by-country/.

Notes: Figures are converted by PPP GINI index (World Bank estimate). (n.d.). Retrieved November 15, 2019, from https://data.worldbank.org/indicator/SI.POV.GINI.

The Gini index measures the extent to which the distribution of income (or, in some cases, consumption expenditure) among individuals or households within an economy deviates from a perfectly equal distribution. A Lorenz curve plots the cumulative percentages of total income received against the cumulative number of recipients, starting with the poorest individual or household. The Gini index measures the area between the Lorenz curve and a hypothetical line of absolute equality, expressed as a percentage of the maximum area under the line. Thus, a Gini index of 0 represents perfect equality, while an index of 100 implies perfect inequality.

chapter introduces the specific country and the "nervousness" issue considered. The author(s) proceeds to offer an explanation of why it is a nervous area of government by providing important historical and social context. Each chapter then identifies a promising practice by government designed to promote social equity and concludes by providing a brief assessment of progress to date and remaining challenges.

In Part I, Chapters 2–5 examine issues of gender and sexuality. In Chapter 2, Yali Pang examines China's nervousness in addressing gender equity and discusses the "Care for Girls" campaign adopted by the Chinese government to address the causes and the negative outcomes of gender imbalance. Chapter 3 by Anbu Arumugam highlights the impact of a mid-day meal program in India, designed to promote gender equality and increase educational opportunities for females. In Chapter 4, Nadia Rubaii and Susan Appe examine Mexico's nervousness in addressing opportunities afforded to indigenous women. In Chapter 5, Anna Agathangelou, Kalliopi Christoforou and Sofia Georgiou

TABLE 1.3 Health and Livelihood Indicators by Country

Country	Life Expectancy	HDI
Brazil	75	0.759
China	76	0.752
Cyprus	81	0.869
France	83	0.901
Germany	81	0.936
India	69	0.64
Mexico	75	0.774
Netherlands	82	0.931
Rwanda	68	0.524
South Africa	64	0.699
UK	81	0.922
USA	79	0.924

Life expectancy at birth, total (years). (n.d.). Retrieved November 15, 2019, from https://data.worldbank.org/indicator/SP.DYN.LE00.IN?view=chart.

Human Development Index (HDI). (n.d.). Retrieved November 15, 2019, from http://hdr.undp.org/en/data.

Notes: "The HDI was created to emphasize that people and their capabilities should be the ultimate criteria for assessing the development of a country, not economic growth alone. The HDI can also be used to question national policy choices, asking how two countries with the same level of GNI per capita can end up with different human development outcomes. These contrasts can stimulate debate about government policy priorities.

The Human Development Index (HDI) is a summary measure of average achievement in key dimensions of human development: a long and healthy life, being knowledgeable and have a decent standard of living. The HDI is the geometric mean of normalized indices for each of the three dimensions.

The health dimension is assessed by life expectancy at birth, the education dimension is measured by mean of years of schooling for adults aged 25 years and more and expected years of schooling for children of school entering age. The standard of living dimension is measured by gross national income per capita. The HDI uses the logarithm of income, to reflect the diminishing importance of income with increasing GNI. The scores for the three HDI dimension indices are then aggregated into a composite index using geometric mean. Refer to Technical notes for more details.

The HDI simplifies and captures only part of what human development entails. It does not reflect on inequalities, poverty, human security, empowerment, etc. The HDRO offers the other composite indices as broader proxy on some of the key issues of human development, inequality, gender disparity and poverty.

A fuller picture of a country's level of human development requires analysis of other indicators and information presented in the statistical annex of the report."

examine the Republic of Cyprus' LGBT efforts, identifying the simultaneous nervous area of religion.

In Part II, Chapters 6–9 examine issues of race and ethnicity. In Chapter 6, Marilyn Rubin, Fátima Bayma de Oliveira, and Wendy Nicholson consider the nervous area of government of racial equity in Brazil through their use of quota systems in universities. Chapter 7, authored by Simone Martin-Howard

TABLE 1.4 Women in Parliament by Country

Country	% Women in Parliament
Brazil	11
China	25
Cyprus	18
France	40
Germany	31
India	12
Mexico	48
Netherlands	36
Rwanda	61
South Africa	42
UK	32
USA	20

Proportion of seats held by women in national parliaments (%). (n.d.). Retrieved November 15, 2019, from https://data.worldbank.org/indicator/sg.gen.parl.zs.

and Ezechiel Sentama, examines the reconciliation in post-genocide Rwanda through the National Unity and Reconciliation Commission. In Chapter 8, John Hitz, Elizabeth Overman, and Loren Gatch discuss Germany's nervous area of government in affording educational opportunities to Turkish origin Germans. In Chapter 9, Samantha Larson and Crystal Soderman look at the nervousness in South Africa through their government's Truth and Reconciliation Commission.

In Part III, Chapters 10–12 examine social equity in the areas of religion and community. In Chapter 10, Brendan Burke and John Barry, discuss the religious nervous area of government of Northern Ireland as the government works to reduce the disparities between Catholics and Protestants in the workforce. In Chapter 11, Sean McCandless and Angela Kline examine the issue of Islamophobia in France and how the French government has adopted tactics designed to address issues of bias. Chapter 12, authored by Erna Ruijer and Jelena Arsenijevic, examines nervousness in the Netherlands as the Dutch address inequities in healthcare.

As these chapters illuminate, nearly all inequities are sustained by structural inequities that are reinforced by historical practices and policies that present nervousness. Such practices and policies offer a powerful, but deceptive image: They allow the reality of inequity to appear as normal or equitable, because they are engrained in the fabric of our respective societies. Yet, expanding our thinking and exposure to other nations' conceptualizations of equity helps reveal our own inequities more clearly. Our challenge is to gain the courage and the stamina to look closely in that mirror. This is an important first step in confronting this nervous area of government around the globe and achieving social equity for all.

Note

1 See United Nations Sustainable Development Goals. https://www.un.org/sustainabledevelopment/sustainable-development-goals/.

References

Akram, R. 2004. *Social Equity and the American Dream: Standing Panel on Social Equity in Governance*. Washington, DC: National Academy of Public Administration.

Frederickson, H. George. 1980. *New Public Administration*. Tuscaloosa: University of Alabama Press.

Frederickson, H. George. 2005. "The State of Social Equity in American Public Administration." *National Civic Review* 94(4): 31–38.

Friedman, Andrea. 2005. "Using the Convention on the Elimination of All Forms of Discrimination against Women to advocate for the Political Rights of Women in a Democratic Burma." *Harvard Journal of Law and Gender* 28: 481–490.

Gooden, Susan T. 2015. *Race and Social Equity: A Nervous Area of Government*. Routledge.

Human Rights Watch. 2016. "UN Makes History on Sexual Orientation, Gender Identity" June 30, 2016. https://www.hrw.org/news/2016/06/30/un-makes-history-sexual-orientation-gender-identity

Kayaoglu, Turan. 2014. "Giving an Inch Only to Lose a Mile: Muslim States, Liberalism, and Human Rights in the United Nations." *Human Rights Quarterly* 36(1): 61–89.

Meron, Theodor. 1985. "The Meaning and Reach of the International Convention on the Elimination of All Forms of Racial Discrimination." *American Journal of International Law* 79(2): 283–318.

National Academy of Public Administration. 2000. *Standing Panel on Social Equity in Governance Issue Paper and Work Plan*. Washington, DC: National Academy of Public Administration.

Rehman, Javaid and Stephanie Berry. 2012. "Is 'Defamation of Religions' Passé? The United Nations, Organisation of Islamic Cooperation, and Islamic State Practices: Lessons from Pakistan." *The George Washington International Law Review* 44(3): 431–472.

Scharffs, Brett G. 2013. "International Law and the Defamation of Religion Conundrum." *The Review of Faith and International Affairs* 11(1): 66–75.

Šimonović, Dubravka. 2014. "Global and Regional Standards on Violence against Women: The Evolution and Synergy of the CEDAW and Istanbul Conventions." *Human Rights Quarterly* 36: 590–606.

Smith, J. Douglas. 2002. *Managing White Supremacy: Race, Politics, and Citizenship in Jim Crow Virginia*. Chapel Hill: University of North Carolina Press.

United Nations. n.d. About Us. https://www.un.org/en/about-un/

United Nations. Universal Declaration of Human Rights. 1948. https://www.un.org/en/universal-declaration-human-rights/index.html

United Nations Educational, Scientific, and Cultural Organization (UNESCO). 1978. "Committee on the Elimination of Racial Discrimination." 33 UN GAOR. Supp. (No. 18) at 108, 109. UN Doc. A/33/18.

United Nations Free and Equal. 2018. LGBTI Equality: Frequently Asked Questions. https://www.unfe.org/wp-content/uploads/2018/10/FAQs-English.pdf

United Nations Free and Equal. 2017. About. https://www.unfe.org/about/

United Nations, Office of the High Commissioner for Human Rights (OHCHR). n.d. "Convention on the Elimination of All Forms of Discrimination against Women." New York, 18 December 1979. https://www.ohchr.org/en/professionalinterest/pages/cedaw.aspx

United Nations, Office of the High Commissioner for Human Rights (OHCHR). n.d. "Declaration on the Elimination of All Forms of Intolerance and of Discrimination Based on Religion or Belief." 25 November 1981. https://www.ohchr.org/EN/ProfessionalInterest/Pages/ReligionOrBelief.aspx

PART I
Gender & Sexuality

2

GENDER EQUITY IN CHINA AND THE IMPACTS OF FAMILY PLANNING POLICIES AND ACTIONS

Yali Pang

Since the foundation of the People's Republic of China in 1949, China has undertaken a series of actions to promote women's rights and dignity, for example, legislating against gender discrimination in political, economic and social areas; supporting women's development in government agencies; and establishing a gender statistics system to monitor the progress of equity (The Information Office of the State Council, 2015). "Women hold up half of the sky" is a popular government slogan in China that indicates the widespread awareness of gender equity and the improvement of women's status (Tan, 2017). In spite of these efforts and progress, gender equity is still a nervous area in China and an arduous task for the Chinese government to tackle in the long run. This chapter offers an overview of a nervous area in China, gender equity and its social impacts, and outlines the historical and political contexts for the gender imbalance. The chapter also introduces the correct gender imbalance actions adopted by the Chinese government, the "Care for Girls" campaign and the newly launched universal two-child policy, to address the causes as well as the negative outcomes of the gender imbalance. The policy outcomes, major challenges and policy implications are further discussed at the end of this chapter.

A Nervous Area of Government in China

Gender equity is still a nervous area for the Chinese government today. According to the World Gender Gap Report, China has closed 67.3% of the gender gap by 2018, leaving a remaining gap of 32.7% (World Economic Forum, 2018). While this overall gender gap index has marginally increased 1.7% compared to the level of 2006 (65.6%), the rank has dropped dramatically from

63 out of 115 countries in 2006 to 103 out of 149 countries in 2018 (World Economic Forum, 2006, 2018). Despite the achievements in gender parity with regard to economic participation and opportunity (a 3.2% increase) and political empowerment (a 5.3% increase) since 2006, the gender parity in health and survival has decreased 2.1%, ranking at the bottom of 149 countries across the world. In fact, China had been one of the bottom five countries in regard to its health and survival since 2006 and remained the lowest-ranked country in this area in the past successive four years from 2015 to 2018.[1] The low score in health and survival can be largely attributed to the disproportionate sex ratio at birth (SRB)[2] and the wider gender gap in healthy life expectancy (World Economic Forum, 2008, 2018).

In particular, China is now experiencing a significant gender imbalance, and it has reached a crisis point where a large surplus of males can lead to social problems and social disorders (Jiang, Zhang, & Sánchez-barricarte, 2015; Trent & South, 2011; Zhou, Yan, & Hesketh, 2013, etc.). Since 2015, China had been at the top in the global ranking in regard to the SRB with a rate of 114.94 in 2018, meaning 114.94 boys were born per every 100 girls at birth (World Economic Forum, 2018). In fact, the significant gender imbalance in China started in the late 1980s (See Figure 2.1 in later section). In 1982, the SRB in China had exceeded 107, slightly higher than the world average (UNFPA China, 2018). Since then, the SRB in China increased drastically and was staggering, compared to other countries around the world. The SRB peaked around 121.18 in 2004 and dropped slightly to 118.58 in 2005, implying that roughly 1 million more boys were born than girls in 2005 (Gupta, Ebenstein, & Sharygin, 2010; UNFPA China, 2018). In the meantime, the gap in SRB between China and the world average was increasing. The difference in the SRB between China and the world average was over 9 points in 2000, and this difference increased to about 12.58 points in 2007 and maintained about 9.89 points on average over the past decade (UNFPA China, 2018). In particular, sex ratios are higher among children and young adults. For example, in 2017, population aged 5–9 had the highest sex ratios, reaching 118.55, followed by the age 10–14 (118.46), age 15–19 (117.7), age 0–4 (114.52) and age 20–24 (110.98) (National Bureau of Statistics of China, 2018). These data indicate an increasingly skewed sex ratio among adults in the near future.

Gender imbalance also varies with areas in China. In general, the gender imbalance is higher in rural areas than in urban areas. As shown in Figure 2.2, the SRB was 115.2 in cities and 119.9 in towns, but as high as 122.9 in counties (rural areas) in 2005 (China Population Census, 2005). In 2015, the SRB demonstrated a downward trend but was still high, which was 110.42, 115.23 and 114.48 in cities, towns and counties, respectively (China Population Census, 2016). The gender imbalance variation is also striking at the provincial level. In 2017, the sex ratio for the never-married population aged 15 and above was 144.46 at the national level, meaning there were 32,218 more males than females in this group (National Bureau of Statistics of China, 2018). Out of 31,[3] 11 regions had a sex ratio over 150 for the never-married population aged 15 and above. Over half of these areas were located in Midwest and South-west China such as Hubei (166.81), Hunan (153.36), Guangxi (168.29), Sichuan (151.63), Guizhou (151.27) and Yunnan (164.83). However, Zhejiang province, located in East China, had the highest sex ratio with 187.43 never-married males aged 15 and over per 100 females, while Ningxia, an autonomous region in Northwest China, had the lowest sex ratio with only 86.51 never-married males aged 15 and over per 100 females. About 87% of the regions had a sex ratio over 120 for this group. The severely abnormal sex ratio in China has drawn attention worldwide and become an area of increasing anxiety for the Chinese government.

Why Gender Imbalance Is a Nervous Area of Government

Historical and Political Context for Gender Imbalance

The Early Family Planning Idea and Practice

The son preference culture and family-planning policies, especially the one-child policy, are considered the main causes of the significant and increas-ing gender imbalance in China (Jiang et al., 2015; Shen, Antonopoulos, & Papanicolaou, 2013; Tucker & Hook, 2013, etc.). China has a cultural his-tory of favoring large families and believes that more children suggest a better life (Ebenstein, 2010; Shen et al., 2013). The population in China was about 541.67 million in 1949 when the "New China" was established, and rapidly increased to 614.65 million in 1955 with an average growth rate of 2% each year (Banister, 1992). The fast-growing population caused nervousness in the Chinese government. In 1956, the Chinese government first introduced the idea of family planning that encouraged birth control among families in highly populated areas to reduce the family burden and ensure better education and employment opportunities for the younger generations (NPC Standing Com-mittee, 1957). However, this idea was strongly criticized during the Great Leap Forward movement (1958–1960). Mao Zedong, the first President of the New China, who initially supported the idea, abandoned this scheme and believed that a large population empowered the country (Zhang, 2017).

In the early 1960s, fertility increased significantly with a rate of over six births per woman, and the population maintained a fast growth rate of over 2.5% per year and reached about 818.32 million in 1970 (The World Bank, 2019a). In 1964, the Chinese government established family planning com-missions for the research, regulation and supervision of family planning at the national level (Tian, 2009). Shortly afterward, provincial-level regions succes-sively set up corresponding local institutions for family planning operations.

Even though Mao's Cultural Revolution movement (1966–1976) had halted the early family planning practice, a serious family planning campaign started in full swing in the early 1970s when Mao reemphasized the urgent need for population control. This campaign was featured by the "Later, Longer, Fewer" slogan that encouraged citizens to marry at a later age (23 years old for women and 25 years old for men) and wait over three years after the first birth to have a second child and have two children at most per couple (Zhang, 2017). This campaign accompanied detailed monitoring of women's pregnancies and childbearing ages, and the extensive promotion of birth control technologies (Whyte, Wang, & Cai, 2015). National statistics show that the number of IUD (intra-uterine device) insertions, sterilizations (including male and female) and abortions in 1973 reached 13.95 million, 4.89 million and 5.11 million, respectively (Ministry of Health of China, 2010). And the overall fertility rate dropped from over 6 per woman in 1964 to less than three per woman in 1978 (The World Bank, 2019a).

The One-Child Policy and Implementation

In 1979, the Chinese government officially launched a more restrictive policy, the one-child policy, with a goal of limiting the population to 1.25 billion by 2000 (The World Bank, 1985). This policy allowed only one child for one couple and was strictly enforced across the country (Settles, Sheng, Zang, & Zhao, 2013). The provincial and local authorities used both inducements and penalties to ensure the policy implementation. Couples with only one child would receive financial and material incentives such as longer paid pregnancy leave, salary increases and privileges in education and healthcare services (Richards, 1996; Settles et al., 2013). However, couples with more than one child were not only excluded from these benefits, but were also subject to penalties such as heavy fines for each additional child (ranging from three to six times each parent's annual income), demotion, loss of jobs or even confiscation and imprisonment (Dowling & Brown, 2009; Howden & Zhou, 2015). A lot of women had to use an IUD, undergo medical sterilization (sometimes this applied to men also) or even get abortions for birth control (Croll, 1981; Mosher, 2006). In 1983, the number of IUD insertions, sterilization operations and abortions significantly rose to 17.8 million, 20.65 million and 14.37 million, increased by 27.6%, 322.29% and 181.21%, respectively, compared to the levels of 1973 (Ministry of Health of China, 2010).

The implementation of the strict one-child policy was very successful in urban areas but confronted greater challenges in rural areas where agriculture relied heavily on labor and the preference for male children prevailed (Dowling & Brown, 2009; White, 2006). In 1984, the Chinese government allowed some flexibility within the one-child policy, known as "one-son-or-two-child" policy. The mandated limits varied in different regions during different time periods (Greenhalgh, 1986). In general, a couple was eligible to have a second child if they were from poor and remote areas and their first child was a daughter or had a disability, or if they belonged to an ethnic or specially privileged group (Greenhalgh, 1986; Shen et al., 2013). By 2001, 19 provincial-level regions allowed a rural couple to have a second child if their first child was a daughter; 31 provincial-level regions allowed a couple to have a second child if their only child had a disability; and 27 provinces allowed a couple to have a second child if the couple were the only child of their families (Settles et al., 2013). Research estimates that in the late 1990s, about 35.4% (438.83 million) of the population were subject to the strict one-child policy, 53.6% (664.44 million) were subject to the "one-son-or-two-child" policy, 9.7% (120.24 million) subject to two-child limit and 1.3% (16.12 million) were subject to the three-child limit (Gu, Wang, Guo, & Zhang, 2007).

The one-child policy brought great success in controlling the population growth in China (Settles et al., 2013). The fertility rate dropped from 2.753 per woman in 1979 to 1.868 per woman in 1993 and further decreased to 1.565 per woman in 2005 (The World Bank, 2019a). From 1979 to 2005, population growth fell from 11.6% to 5.9%, implying that the one-child policy prevented about 250–300 million births during this time period (Settles et al., 2013).

Son Preference and "Missing Girls"

While the family planning policies significantly slowed down population growth, it also caused other social problems, gender inequities in particular, in the past decades. China has a long tradition of son preference especially in rural areas, because sons are the ones who carry the family name and prolong the family lineage (Tan, 2017). And in tradition, sons are the major source of social security for elderly parents, while daughters are usually considered subordinate to their husbands and expected to take care of their parents-in-law (Dowling & Brown, 2009). Within this cultural norm, sons become more desirable especially when parents are subject to one child or two child limits. Most families spared no efforts to have at least one son even through multiple births (Johnson, 2016). In order to avoid penalties, some parents chose to abandon "out of plan" female infants, keep them undocumented, place them in orphanages or give them to legal or illegal adopters (Johnson, 2016; Pletcher, 2019). Research estimated that the number of female infant deaths was about 39,000 per year from 1985 to 1987, and the number of adoptions from 1980 to 1987 was about 2.65 million, among which 75.87% of adoptees were girls (Johansson & Nygren, 1991). Some of these unwanted girls became victims of human trafficking. A striking infant trafficking case in 2003 revealed that, of the 117 baby girl victims, 86 were abandoned in trash bins and collected and sold by pickers (Sun, 2007).

The abortions of female fetuses also increased with the introduction of ultrasound technology in the 1980s that made sex selection available (Settles et al., 2013). Data shows that in 2000, boys represented about 62% of the second birth for women with one daughter and up to 70% of the third birth for women with two daughters, while in 1982 boys represented only 52% of the second birth for women with one daughter and 54% of the third birth for women with two daughters (Ebenstein, 2010). All these efforts of "concealing" or aborting unwanted girls contribute to the large number of "missing girls" in China. In 1970, the number of "missing girls" in China was 27.2 million, about 44.59% of the total "missing girls" in the world. In 2005, this number increased to 55.7 million, making up 47.85% (116.4 million) of the total "missing girls" in the world (Bongaarts & Guilmoto, 2015). In 2015, the percentage of "missing girls" in China was over 50% of the total "missing girls" in the world. Due to the large number of "missing girls," the overall SRB in China became skewed towards males since the 1970s and became increasingly abnormal, rising from 106.32 in 1970 to 119.0 in 2006 (UNFPA China, 2018).

Social Problems Caused by Gender Imbalance

The severe gender imbalance results in a large surplus of males. Scholars estimated that the single men of marriageable age (25–39 years old) in China would peak at about 30 million in 2040 and there would be more than one quarter of single men (about 24 million) who cannot find a woman to marry in 2060 (Tucker & Hook, 2013). In the meantime, there will be about 680,000 elderly bachelors (above 50 years old) in 2033 and the number of elderly bachelors will peak 17.84 million in 2054, accounting for 51% of all bachelors, which will pose a great challenge to the social welfare system in China (Huang, 2014). Other social problems caused by the gender imbalance include a marriage squeeze, instable marriage, mercenary marriage, women trafficking, crimes and mental health issues of unmarried males that can interrupt social stability (Golley & Tyers, 2012; Gupta, Ebenstein, & Sharygin, 2010).

Marriage Squeeze

The national shortage of women leads to increased male marriage squeeze that enhances women's bargaining power and status in the marriage market and household (McKenzie & Tullock, 2012; Porter, 2016). However, it also leads to higher prerequisite and expense for marriage, especially in rural areas where the gender imbalance is much more severe (Wang, 2013; Zhang, 2000). For example, a house property and a car were not prerequisites for marriage in the early 1980s but have now become basic necessity for marriage (Wang, 2013). A survey indicated that more than 70% of women agreed that owning a house is a necessity for a man to get married (Liu, 2013). Otherwise, a man will be less competitive in the marriage market (Li, 2012). An increasing number of women today consider a house, a car and increased bank savings as important factors for their decision-making regarding dating and marriage.

The marriage expense also increases rapidly and has become very striking since the early 21st century. Although marriage expenses, generally including housing, bride price[4] and marriage banquet, are incurred by in both the male's side and the female's side, the expense is usually much higher for males than females (Jiang et al., 2015; Zhang, 2000). Because men from families in poor areas are at a disadvantage in the marriage market, they often have to offer a higher bride price or show more possessions to ensure a marriage, causing a continuing rise in the marriage expense (Wei, Xiong, & Xie, 2010; Wei & Zhang, 2011). Literature documents the surprisingly high expense for marriage in rural regions. For example,[5] the marriage expense for a man was about 28,000–50,000 yuan (about 3,415–6,098 dollars)[6] in 2005, equivalent to 14–25 times of a person's annual net income. In 2009, this expense was about 95,500 yuan (13,982 dollars) nationwide; 74,000 yuan (10,835 dollars) in western China (about 22 times of a resident's annual income in the area); and 112,500 yuan (16,471 dollars) in eastern China, which was about 18.8 times of a resident's annual income in the area. In 2011, the expense increased to about 150,000 yuan (23,220 dollars) including housing and other expenses based on a survey in central China, which amounted to 10–20 years of a family's annual household savings (Jiang et al., 2015). Other research also finds that households with a son tend to have higher savings rates compared to identical households with a daughter in the same region and identical households with a son in other regions where the sex ratio is lower (Wei & Zhang, 2011). Because Chinese parents usually take responsibility for paying for their sons' marriage expense, the striking marriage expense not only exhausts the household's savings, but also often burdens the parents with heavy debt, resulting in deeper poverty, as well as familial conflicts (Han & Eades, 1995; Jiang et al., 2015). Other consequences of the heightened marriage expense include deepening marriage as a transaction (Gao, 1994), unequal investments in sons and daughters (Edlund, Li, Yi, & Zhang, 2009), a distorted marriage-broker market, mercenary marriages, marriage frauds and women trafficking (Liu, Jin, Brown, & Feldman, 2014; South, 1991).

Marriage Migration and Marriage Stability

The scarcity of women in the marriage market shifts the tradition of prevailing local marriages in rural areas to long-distance interprovincial marriages (Davin, 2007; Jin, Liu, Li, Feldman, & Li, 2013). Long-distance interprovincial marriages have increased gradually since the 1990s, and women make up the majority of interprovincial marriage migrants (Davin, 2007). Data shows that marriage was the leading reason for female migration, accounting for 28.9% (1.4 million) of interprovincial female migrations between 1985 and 1990

(Fan & Huang, 1998). More and more women in poor areas take interprovincial marriage as a strategy to escape poverty and pursue improved economic security and well-being (Lavely, 1991; Wei & Zhang, 2016). For men in rural areas, interprovincial marriage has become an alternative option if they cannot find a suitable local wife because the bride price for a nonlocal wife is often lower compared to local ones (Liu et al., 2014).

However, research finds that most women in long-distance marriages only move from one rural area to another because of the constraints of the *Hukou* institution[7] and the undesirability of peasant women as brides in urban areas (Tan & Short, 2004; Wei & Zhang, 2016). And, interprovincial marriages in rural regions are often less stable. Migrant wives reported lower satisfaction with their marriages compared to local wives due to low-socioeconomic status; fewer chances to know each other before marriage; and unfamiliar local dialects, culture, and customs (Davin, 2007; Han & Eades, 1995; Liu et al., 2014). In addition, migrant wives are often young, less-educated, and thus vulnerable to deception and abduction contributing further to gender inequity within the household (Fan & Huang, 1998; Liu et al., 2014). A survey of migrant wives in a rural county in eastern China revealed that "75 percent (3,124) of the sample had been 'sold' to husbands in ways involving some degree of deception" (Han & Eades, 1995, p. 860). These migrant wives often receive limited support from their natal family network from afar. They are more likely have low status within the household and experience abuse and discrimination (Liu et al., 2014). Moreover, rural migrant women often suffer from restraints on personal freedom and even contact with their natal families, because their husbands are concerned that they would run away with the bride price, which has been frequently reported in remote interprovincial marriages (Liu et al., 2014). A survey in 2009 showed that of 351 surveyed villages with nonlocal wives, about 40% of villages reported cases of nonlocal wives' running away with an average 2.9 cases each village between 2006 and 2008 (Jin et al., 2013). And these cases happened more frequently in less-developed villages with a more serious marriage squeeze, suggesting the instability of interprovincial marriages in rural areas.

Trafficking of Women and Girls

Trafficking is a large contributor to the nervous area of government, especially with respect to women's human rights and equity. A massive domestic migration, especially an increasing number of female migrants from rural areas to urban areas, intensifies the gender imbalance in rural areas (Bakken, 2005). The increasingly severe shortage of women and the rising local bride price lead to an increasing demand for brides in rural areas, resulting in the reemerging and rapidly growing human trafficking market (Chu, 2011; Zhao, 2003). While there is no way to record all trafficking cases, data shows that there were about 176,000 women and children abducted in Sichuan, a province in Southwest China, between 1974 and 1991 (Zhang, 1993). Furthermore, the number of female trafficking cases received by courts was 9,165 between April 2009 and December 2010, during which time over 18,000 women were rescued (The Information Office of the State Council, 2011). Teenage girls increasingly become victims of trafficking. They are easily deceived with fraudulent job offers but end up being sold into the sex industry or into coercive marriages in poor areas (Chew, 1999; Shen et al., 2013). As the demand for brides rises, the target of trafficking expands from young illiterate women from poor areas to educated women, including university students, from urban areas (Chu, 1996; Zhang, 1993), and from women in China to women from neighboring countries such as North Korea and Vietnam (Stöckl et al., 2017). The buyers of trafficked women are usually involuntary bachelors with poor education and at personal disadvantages in remote and poor rural areas where the purchase of a wife has become a tradition and culture rather than a crime (Zhao, 2003). In some areas, the local villagers even put up collective violent resistance to police officials who try to rescue the trafficked women, making it difficult for the government to eradicate the trafficking market (Cao, 1997; Chu, 1996).

Trafficking and forced marriages often cause physical and mental harm to the victims. Research shows that most trafficked women suffer from violence, intimidation, sexual abuse and deprivation of basic human rights, leading to physical disabilities, mental disorders and, sometimes, even death (Zhao, 2003). A survey of 51 trafficked Vietnamese women and girls revealed that 86% of these victims reported experiencing high levels of sexual violence during trafficking, 52.9% reported having post-traumatic stress disorder and even 3.9% reported attempting suicide (Stöckl et al., 2017). The trafficking also leads to distress, frustration and disruption to the victims' families, causing broader social disorders (Biddulph & Sandy, 1999).

Destructive Behaviors and Well-being of Involuntary Bachelors

The gender imbalance leads to a large number of involuntary bachelors, especially in rural China. A survey administered to 364 villages in 28 provinces during 2009 found a total of 3,268 involuntary bachelors in these villages, of which western villages had a higher density of involuntary bachelors (3.9 per 100 households) than central villages and eastern villages (2.3 per 100 households, respectively) (Jin et al., 2013). With a culture of universal marriage in China, these unmarried men can pose great threats to social security (Cai & Lavely, 2003; Jin et al., 2013). Involuntary bachelors are found more likely to engage in destructive behaviors, abuse drugs and alcohol and commit crimes such as murder, robbery and sexual assault compared to married males (Hudson & Boer, 2002). In particular, unmarried, low-status males are frequently reported as the offenders in sexual assault cases where over 60% of the victims are underage girls, women with disabilities and elderly females (Jin & Liu, 2009). Research reveals that the number of criminal offenses is increased by 13.6% annually between 1988 and 2004, and the abnormal sex ratio contributed to about 14% of this increase (Edlund, Li, Yi, & Zhang, 2007). Every 1% increase in the sex ratio of the age 16–25 leads to about a 3% increase in the number of violent crimes and property crimes (Edlund, Li, Yi, & Zhang, 2007). The severe sex ratio has become a major contributor for social instability, which causes increasing nervousness for the Chinese government.

Involuntary bachelors are not only the offenders and destroyers, but also the victims of the gender imbalance. Research indicates that involuntary bachelors often suffer from familial sexual and emotional frustration and receive low social recognition (Li, Zhang, Yang, & Attané, 2010). They are more likely to engage in commercial sex and are at a higher risk for sexually transmitted infections such as HIV or AIDS (Poston & Glover, 2005; South & Trent, 2010). Evidence shows that poor, uneducated and unmarried men are more likely to pay for low-cost sex workers, and they have made up a new and distinct population with increased risk of HIV infections since the mid-1990s (PSI Research Division, 2005). In 2005, about 50% of new HIV infections were through sexual contact, and the population infected through sex comprised 43.6% of the total infected population (Ebenstein & Sharygin, 2009). Moreover, involuntary bachelors are less confident, more aggressive and at a higher risk of depression and suicide compared to married men (Zhou et al., 2013). Since involuntary bachelors usually have lower educational levels and lower income, they are more likely to live in poverty without financial security as well as support from wives and children when they are getting older (Gupta et al., 2010). Social security for these elderly bachelors is becoming a greater challenge for the Chinese government, a challenge that is expected to worsen over time.

A Promising Government Initiative: Actions to Correct the Gender Imbalance

In order to address the skewed sex ratio and the inequities associated with the gender imbalance, the Chinese government has adopted a series of policies and actions since the end of 1990s. The "Care for Girls" campaign and the universal two-child policy are two promising practices to address the causes, as well as the consequences, of the gender imbalance. The "Care for Girls" campaign focuses on the causes of the gender imbalance, son preference culture and gender inequity in particular, which contribute to the abnormal sex ratio in China under the strict family planning policy. The universal two-child policy concentrates more on addressing the consequences of gender imbalance, especially the low fertility rate and the growing aging population.

"Care for Girls" Campaign

The "Care for Girls" campaign, initiated by the National Population and Family Planning Commission (NPFPC), was to address the highly abnormal sex ratio in China by weakening son preference culture and protecting women and girls' basic rights of survival, development, protection and participation (Song, 2009). This campaign started as a pilot research project, *Improving the Living Environment of Girls*, in five counties of Chaohu City in 2000 with the aim of creating favorable macro and micro living environments for girls (Li, 2007). This project successfully reduced the SRB by 8.8% from 125 in 1999 to 114 in 2002 in the experimental city (Li, Shang, & Feldman, 2013). In 2003 and 2004, the government expanded the "Care for Girls" campaign to another 24 counties across 24 provinces where the SRBs were extremely high (Fan & Gu, 2017). This large-scale pilot campaign had strict regulations on drugs, ultrasonic technology and other methods of pregnancy termination. It prohibited the fetal gender screening without medical justification; illegal sex-selective abortions; abandonment of female infants and illegal adoptions; and improved family planning and reproductive healthcare services including contraception, pregnancy monitoring and postpartum care (Yang & Shang, 2010). Moreover, it called for the formulation of social policies conductive to girls' growth and women's development; promotion and advocacy for gender equity; data collection, monitoring and evaluation; and support from leadership and special funds (Yang & Shang, 2010). In particular, this campaign provided incentives and other supports to families with one daughter or two daughters as their only child(ren). These supports include a tuition waiver for girls' primary and middle school education, college scholarships, healthcare support and social security for parents, financial incentives, tax reductions and free-or-low-interest loans (Fan & Gu, 2017).

This large-scale pilot campaign lowered the average SRB of 24 counties to 119.6 in 2005, a 10.6% decrease compared to the level of 2000 (Li, 2007). The great success of this campaign made the "Care for Girls" campaign a national strategy to address the high SRB in China in 2006. A basic governance model was developed based on the pilot campaign efforts to lead the national "Care for Girls" campaign, which was characterized by "two illegalities", "whole-course services", "benefits and interests–oriented social policies", "advocacy" and "statistics, monitoring and evaluation" (Li et al., 2013, p. 85). At the same time, the Chinese government developed a 15-year long-term plan for addressing the high SRB in the country with a goal of achieving a normal SRB at the national level between 2016 and 2020. Local governments quickly responded to this national campaign. Twenty-nine provincial regions clearly prohibited fetal gender screening without medical justification as well as illegal sex-selective abortions in their family planning regulations by 2005; 30 provinces revised their family planning regulations; and 8 provinces even adopted special regulations based on the national governance of SRB by 2010 (Li et al., 2013).

Universal Two-Child Policy

The universal two-child policy is a family planning policy, effective in January 2016, allowing all couples, regardless of household registration (urban or rural *Hukou*), region and ethnicity, to have two children (CPC Central Committee, 2016). According to this policy, China uses a birth registration service system to keep track on the fertility rate and provide reproductive healthcare support to families. Couples no longer need to obtain birth permissions for their first and second children. However, incentives will not be available to families who decide to have only one child under this policy, while families who received benefits for having only one child before this policy will continue enjoying the same benefits. The enforcement of the universal two-child policy marks the end of the one-child policy that had impacted a majority of the population in China for about 35 years.

Since the 1980s, China began softening the one-child policy that allowed couples in rural areas or from ethnic groups to have two children under certain conditions (Greenhalgh, 1986). At the end of 2013, the Third Plenary Session of the 18th CPC Central Committee decided to relax the one-child policy under which a couple was eligible to have two children if one of the spouses was the only child in his or her family (Wang, Ding, & Wang, 2016). This relaxed policy was enforced across the country in 2014. However, the policy relaxation did not improve the fertility rate as expected. Only 9.72% (1.07 million) of all eligible couples (11 million) in the country applied for the birth permission for a second child by the end of 2014, and 16% (1.76 million) of eligible couples requested a birth permission to have a second child by September 2015 (Attané, 2016). The number of children born in 2015 was 0.8 million under this relaxed one-child policy, far below the expected 2 million additional births annually (Attané, 2016). In 2016, the universal two-child policy (see the policy elements in Table 2.1) was launched to address the aging population and gender imbalance and, at the same time, maintain family planning as the basic national policy for population control in China (CPC Central Committee, 2016). In addition, the Chinese government made amendments to the People's Republic of China Population and Family Planning Law of 2002 to ensure the implementation of the universal two-child policy. For example, the revised law replaces the advocacy of one child for each couple with encouragement of a second child for each couple, allows couples to choose birth control methods for family planning, grants extended leave and other benefits for couples who comply with laws and removes the encouragement for later marriage and childbearing (NPC, 2015). The universal two-child policy also supports and continues the national "Care for Girls" campaign, prohibiting sex-selective fetal gender screening and abortions and protecting women's rights in property inheritance, employment, and maternity leave to improve gender equity. Citizens who violate the universal two-child policy are required to pay a social compensation

TABLE 2.1 The Implementation of Universal Two-Child Policy

Follow four basic principles: people first; innovative development; guidance of law; coordinated development

Implement universal two-child policy: Carry out the revised population and family planning law across the country; reform reproductive service management system; strengthen newly born population monitoring and prediction; reasonably allocate public service resources

Improve family planning service management: Strengthen family planning services to women and children; improve the equality in basic public health and family planning services to migrant population; intensify foundation work at the local level; encourage participation of social agencies

Establish a supportive system for family development: Increase support for families observing family planning policy; improve families'capacity for caring for children and the elderly; promote gender equality

Strengthen organizational leadership: Clearly identify responsibilities for party committees and governments at different levels; strengthen collaboration between departments; deepen the study on population development strategies; promotion and public opinion guidance; intensify task supervision, monitoring and evaluation

Source: CPC Central Committee 2016.

fee for each additional child. However, there is no specific standard and amount set for this fee, and the local governments will decide the fee based on local residents' income and the number of children born outside the policy. The goal of this policy is to facilitate long-term balanced population development by alleviating the adverse consequences from the one-child policy such as the growing aging population, low fertility rate, labor shortage, heavy burden of younger generation to support their aged parents and striking gender imbalance (CPC Central Committee, 2016).

Assessment and Evidence of Progress

The nationwide "Care for Girls" campaign and the implementation of the universal two-child policy together have demonstrated positive outcomes toward reducing the serious gender imbalance as well as its adverse social consequences in China. While it is difficult to exclude impacts from other policies and factors, evidence shows that increasing access to education for girls, weakening son preference culture, declining gender imbalance at birth and growing births and populations occurred after both the large-scale "Care for Girls" campaign and the universal two-child policy were implemented. The nationwide "Care for Girls" campaign, that focuses on protecting women and girls' basic rights, is important to prevent more severe gender imbalance under the universal two-child policy. And the universal two-child policy also emphasizes the continuous implementation of the "Care for Girls" campaign to ensure positive outcomes on population development.

Increasing Access to Education for Girls

The "Care for Girls" campaign advocated equal education for girls and proved effective in improving girls' education in the 24 pilot counties. Research reveals that several years after the "Care for Girls" campaign, there was a 4.61% increase in the number of females with an associate degree or above, a 1.33% increase in the number of females with a bachelor's degree or above, and a 0.792 year increase in girls' education years in the pilot counties (Fan & Gu, 2017). And no improvement was found in female education in other counties without the "Care for Girls" campaign even in the same provinces, which suggests the positive impacts of the campaign on girls' education. At the national level, an increasing number of girls had access to education after the campaign started. The sex ratio of boys to girls (girl = 100) who enrolled in primary education reduced from 103.37 in 1997 to 100.64 in 2006, and this sex ratio decreased below 100 since 2014 with a slight increase to about 101 from 2007 to 2011 (The World Bank, 2019b). For secondary education enrollment (middle and high school), the sex ratio was 113.68 in 1997, which decreased to 100.77 in 2006 and dropped below 100 since 2007 with one exception in 2010 (100.16) (The World Bank, 2019b). While the decrease can also be attributed to the Compulsory Education Law, the sex ratio in postsecondary educational enrollment also decreased from 189.50 in 1994 to 120.93 in 2003, and further fell to 105.87 in 2006 after expanding the "Care for Girls" campaign. This sex ratio has dropped below 100 since 2008 and reached 82.90 in 2016 (The World Bank, 2019b). Because of the increased educational enrollment for girls, the illiterate and semi-literate female population is declining. The percentage of illiterate and semi-literate females aged 15 and over compared to the total female population in this age group was 22.61% in 1998 (as opposed to 9.01% for males) (National Bureau of Statistics of China, 1999). This percentage declined to 13.72% (4.87% for males) in 2006 and further dropped to 7.77% (2.73% for males) in 2010 (National Bureau of Statistics of China, 2007, 2011).

Weakening Son Preference Culture

The son preference culture has been significantly weakened in the past few decades, and an increasing proportion of families demonstrates no gender preference (Hou, Huang, & Xin, 2015; Hou, Gu, & Zhang, 2018). A meta-analysis of 152 surveys from 1979 to 2017 reveals that the ideal number of boys as children reported by families reduced by 19.32% from 0.533 in 1990–1999 to 0.430 in 2010–2017, and the proportion of families who considered boys as ideal children dropped from 34.6% to 27.9% (a 6.7% decrease) (Hou et al., 2018). There was also a decline in the ideal number of girls as children. This ideal number was 0.466 per family between 1990 and 1999 and fell to 0.344 between 2000 and 2009, but it increased slightly to 0.429 during 2010–2017. Families who considered girls as ideal children also decreased from 30.2% in 1990–1999 to 27.8% in 2010–2017 (a 2.4% decrease) (Hou et al., 2018). In general, more and more families had no gender preference for their children. The percentage of families with no gender preference increased from 35.2% in 1990–1999 to 44.3% in 2010–2017 (Hou et al., 2018). While sex ratios are often much higher in rural areas where son preference culture is popular, Hou and other researchers (2018) found that both rural and urban families showed declining boy preference for children and increasingly demonstrated no gender preference. The percentage of urban families with son preference dropped from 33% in 1990–1999 to 18.5% in 2010–2017, and this percentage declined from 34.5% to 25.8% for rural families. About 60.8% of urban families and 51.9% of rural families had no gender preference for children in 2010–2017 with a 25.6% and an 18% increase, respectively, compared to the percentages of 1990–1999 (Hou et al., 2018). In particular, the sex ratio of ideal children dropped to 100.2 in 2010–2017 after about 30 years of increase. These changes indicate the gender preference culture, especially the son preference culture, is weakening in the 21st century. More and more families recognize that girls are valued the same as boys and indicate no gender preference for their children. This is important for ensuring the effectiveness of the newly launched universal two-child policy; otherwise, the son preference culture could worsen the gender imbalance again under this policy.

Declining SRB

The SRB is declining. Research shows that the SRB of pilot counties in the "Care for Girls" campaign decreased by 14.1% on average compared to non-pilot counties in the same provinces, and this campaign contributed to 74.17% of the SRB decrease in the pilot counties (Fan & Gu, 2017). These impacts were more statistically significant in pilot counties with a higher SRB. The sex ratio of the population aged 1–4 reduced by 16.91% in pilot counties with more-severe gender imbalance and 7.71% in pilot counties with less-severe gender imbalance (Fan & Gu, 2017). At the national level, the SRB in China has decreased since 2008, two years after the implementation of the national "Care for Girls" campaign, and it dropped as low as 113.51 in 2015 (see Figure 2.1). Even though the SRB increased slightly in 2016 compared to the level of 2015, it was decreasing after the enforcement of the universal two-child policy. The difference between China and the world average is also decreasing. The difference in SRB between China and the world average was 12.95 points in 2008 and dropped to 10.19 points in 2013. The difference further reduced to 7.86 points in 2016. At the regional level, the SRB has dropped significantly in both

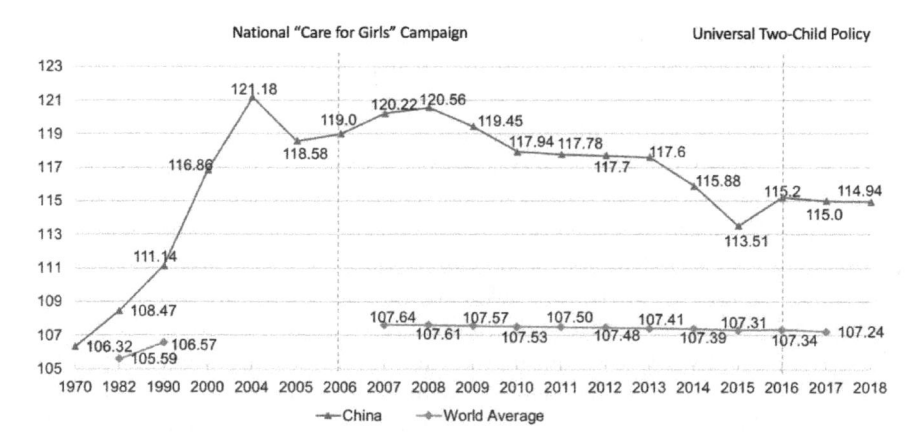

FIGURE 2.1 Trend of SRB in China and World Average.

Data in this figure comes from different sources. The data of China Sex Ratio at Birth (SRB) from 1970 to 2015 is from UNFPA China. (2018, January). UNFPA China policy brief series: Toward a normal sex ratio at birth in China. Retrieved from https://china.unfpa.org/en/publications/ unfpa-china-policy-brief-towards-normal-sex-ratio-birth-china. The data of China SRB from year 2016 to 2017 is from The World Bank. (2019). *Sex ratio at birth (male births per female births)* [Data file]. United Nations Population Division. World Population Prospects. Available from https://data.worldbank.org/indicator/SP.POP.BRTH.MF?end=2017&loca-tions=CN&start=1962. The data of China SRB in year 2018 is from The World Economic Forum (2018, December 17). *The global gender gap report.* Retrieved from https://www.we-forum.org/reports/the-global-gender-gap-report-2018. The data of world average SRB is from The World Bank. (2019, April 24). *World development indicators* [Data file]. Available from https://data.worldbank.org/indicator/SP.POP.BRTH.MF.

Please note that the data before 2004 is not presented annually due to the availability of data and the size of the figure.

urban and rural areas in China since 2005, and the gap between urban and rural areas is narrowing. As shown in Figure 2.2, the SRB decreased by 4.78 points from 2005 to 2015 in cities, 4.67 points in towns and 8.1 points in counties (rural areas). The gap in SRB between towns and counties declined from 3 points in 2005 to 0.43 points in 2015, and the gap between cities and counties also dropped from 7.7 points in 2005 to 4.38 points in 2015. While the SRBs are still high in these areas, the difference in the number of boys and girls at birth is declining, which indicates a downward trend of returning to the normal level.

In provincial regions, the number of regions with a high SRB (over 110) has also decreased in recent years (see Figure 2.3). As shown in Figure 2.3, the gender imbalance in the provincial regions became worse from 2000 to 2005 due to the widespread use of the ultrasound technology and the large number of missing girls as discussed earlier. In 2005, there were 27 regions whose SRBs ran over 110, increasing by 17.39% compared to the level of 2000. Specifically, about half of regions in mainland China had an SRB between 110 and 119.9;

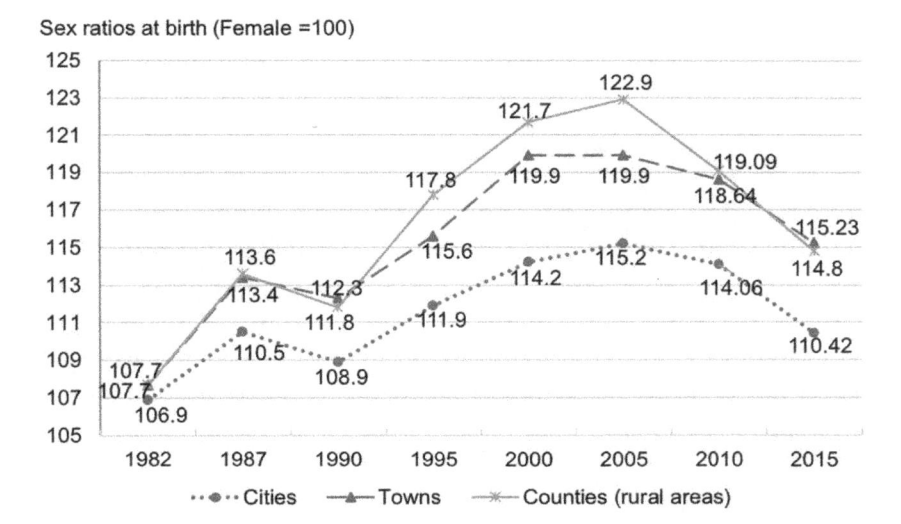

Sex ratios at birth (Female =100)

FIGURE 2.2 SRB in Different Areas in China (1982–2015).
The data in this figure is from China population censuses in 1982, 1990, 2000 and 2010; and China 1% national population sample surveys in 1987, 1995, 2005 and 2015 (See detailed information about these data in reference). A similar data comparison on sex ratio at birth in different areas up to 2005 was performed by Li (2007, October). Imbalanced sex ratio at birth and comprehensive intervention in China. Paper presented at the 4th Asia Pacific Conference on Reproductive and Sexual Health and Rights, Hyderabad, India. Retrieved from https://www.unfpa.org/sites/default/files/event-pdf/china.pdf.

one quarter had an SRB between 120 and 129.9; and about 10% had an SRB over 130. Four years after the national "Care for Girls" campaigns, the gender imbalance diminished. In 2010, while the total number of regions with an SRB over 110 increased by one region, the total area with an SRB over 110 was declining and concentrated in Southeast China. Moreover, 18 out of 31 regions showed a decline in SRB. In 2015, the total area with an SRB over 110 decreased significantly. Nine more regions in this year demonstrated a decrease in SRB, about a 29% increase compared to the number in 2010. In 2015, about 32.26% of regions had an SRB below 110; 58.06% had an SRB between 110 and 119.9. Only three regions had an SRB above 120, and none of these regions' SRBs ran over 130. An increasing number of regions are trending toward normal levels.

Growing Births and Population

While there is now limited data about the outcomes of the newly launched universal two-child policy, evidence shows that the population has been growing under this relaxed family planning policy. The newborn population and birth rate (births per thousand people) have increased since the enforcement of the

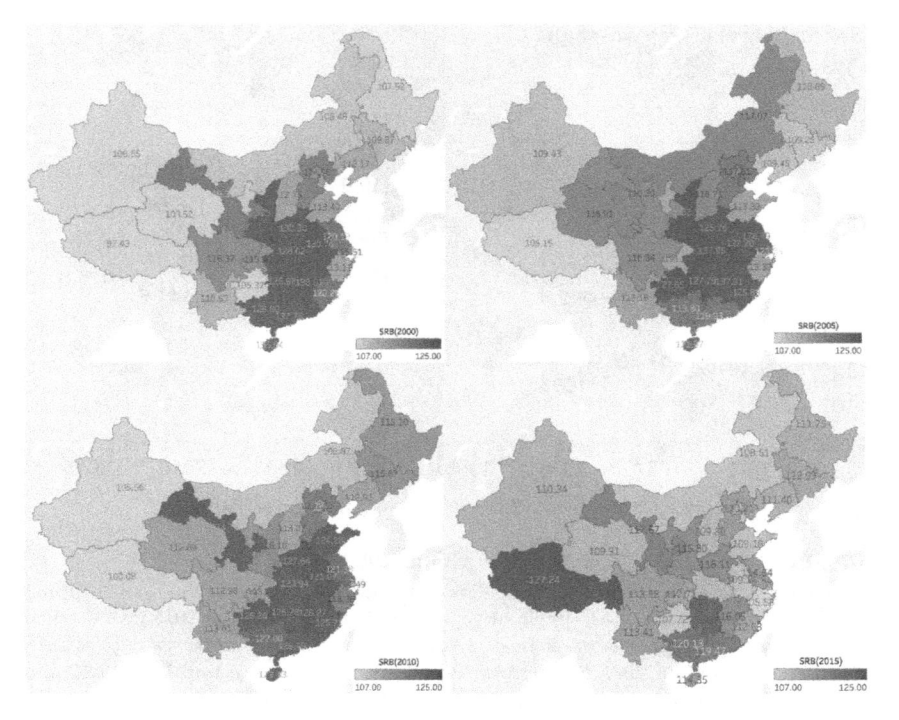

FIGURE 2.3 SRB in Different Regions in China (1989–2015).

Data source: China population censuses in 2000 and 2010; and China 1% national population sample surveys in 2005 and 2015. The map only focuses on Mainland China and does not include areas, Hong Kong, Macao and Taiwan, where this data is not available.

universal two-child policy. The newborn population was 17.86 million in 2016 and 17.23 million in 2017, significantly higher than the average level (16.44 million) during the 12th Five-Year Plan period (2011–2015) (National Bureau of Statistics of China, 2017, 2018). And the birth rate was 12.95 per 1000 in 2016 and 12.43 per 1000 in 2017, increasing 0.84 and 0.32 per 1000, respectively, compared to the average level of 12th Five-Year Plan period. At the provincial level, 29 out of 31 regions in mainland China showed an increase in the birth rate from 2015 to 2017, among which two regions had an increase between 30 and 40%, another two regions between 20 and 20.9%, seven regions between 10 and 19.9% and 18 regions between 1 and 10% (National Bureau of Statistics of China, 2016, 2018). Only two regions experienced a slight decrease in the birth rate with a rate of about 2% from 2015 to 2017. In particular, the newborn second-child population rose to 8.83 million, accounting for 51.2% of the total newborn population in 2017, with a 11% increase compared to the level of 2016 (Li, 2018).

The shift in age distribution from 2008 to 2017 also confirms the population growth and the improvement in the population structure after a more relaxed

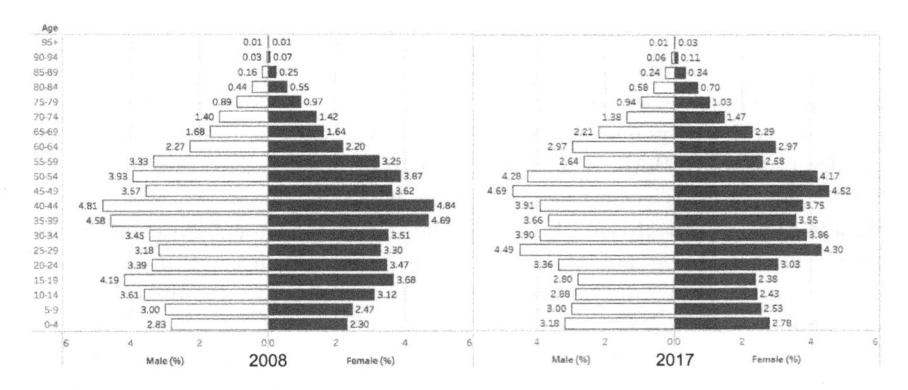

FIGURE 2.4   Population by Age and Sex in China: 2008 and 2017.

Data source: National Bureau of Statistics of China. (n.d.). *China Statistical Yearbook, 2009, 2018* [Data file]. Available from http://www.stats.gov.cn/tjsj/ndsj.

family planning policy. As shown in Figure 2.4, in 2008, China showed a narrow base with a broad middle section, suggesting a negative growth in its population. The number of populations aged 40–44 represented the largest share of the total population (9.65%), followed by the group aged 35–39 (9.27%) and group aged 15–19 (7.87%). However, populations aged 30–34, 25–29 and 20–24 had a smaller share of the total population compared to the top three groups. And there was a decrease in the younger population with 6.73% of the total population for the group aged 10–14, 5.47% for the group aged 5–9 and only 5.13% for the group aged 0–4. However, in 2017, the population structure showed an increasingly broader base. There was also an increase in the number of younger populations with 5.31% of the total population for the group aged 10–14, 5.53% for the group aged 5–9 and 5.96% for the group aged 0–4, which suggests the younger population is growing slowly. While the middle section became a more rectangular shape, the structure of the younger population is improving.

Other benefits of the universal two-child policy identified by scholars include decrease in abortions, reduction in undocumented girls and abandoned girls and a more normal sex ratio in the long run (Zeng & Hesketh, 2016). The policy can also reduce discrimination in nutrition, education and healthcare against girls, especially in rural areas (Svedberg, 2007; Zeng & Hesketh, 2016). This universal two-child policy is expected to create an additional 2–3 million births each year, increase the working age population and reduce the proportion of the aging population in the future (Attané, 2016).

Conclusion

China is now experiencing a sharp gender imbalance, severe marriage squeeze, low fertility rate and growing aging population resulting from the strict birth control policy introduced in the 1970s, its son preference culture and other economic factors (Attané, 2016; Zhang, 2017). The "Care for Girls" campaign and the newly launched universal two-child policy were adopted in different times to tackle the gender inequities and other social problems caused by the gender imbalance. Both policies have shown promising outcomes, especially the "Care for Girls" campaign that has been implemented for more than a decade. The universal two-child policy also demonstrated significant effects on the birth and population growth after its enforcement in 2016. In spite of these promising outcomes, one of the biggest challenges to the universal two-child policy is the low fertility intentions. Most couples delay or do not want a second child due to the heavy economic burden, especially the high cost for a child's healthcare and education. Other factors that contribute to not wanting a second child include limited time and energy for childcare, negative impacts on women's career trajectories and the risks of childbearing for an older mother (Fan & Pei, 2018; Qian & Jin, 2018). In addition, the universal two-child policy may increase fertility pressure on women and cause gender inequity within the household (Qian & Jin, 2018). Additional policy actions are needed to facilitate the effectiveness of the universal two-child policy such as continuing efforts on improving gender equity in the labor force and household, more incentives for couples having a second child, reduction of educational costs and improvement of healthcare outcomes (Zhang, 2017; Zeng & Hesketh, 2016; Zeng, Zhang, & Liu, 2017, etc.). Since the universal two-child policy will not alter the growing aging population in the short term, the social security and pension system should be improved and expanded, especially in rural areas where a large proportion of childless elderly bachelors are concentrated (Zhang, 2017). In fact, the Chinese government has started reforms in some of these areas. For example, the Chinese government started a healthcare system reform in 2009 to increase the accessibility and affordability of the public healthcare services in rural areas, and over 92% of the population were under the insurance programs by 2011 (Yip et al., 2012). In 2014, a reform of the household registration system was launched to relax the restrictions on *Hukou* registration in towns, and small- to medium-sized cities, to facilitate the transference of the village surplus labor force and ensure rural migrant workers' equal access to the welfare benefits and public services in urban areas (Song, 2014). The continuing efforts and effectiveness of these reforms and policies will help tackle this nervous area of the Chinese government by guaranteeing or magnifying the effects of the universal two-child policy and improving gender equity in the long term.

Notes

1 The data is from the global gender gap index of the World Bank. See The World Bank. (n.d.). *TC data 360: Overall Global Gender Gap Index* [Data file]. Retrieved from https://tcdata360.worldbank.org/indicators/af52ebe9?country=BRA&indicator=27959&viz=line_chart&years=2006, 2018.

2 The sex ratio at birth (SRB) means the number of males per 100 females at birth. And all other sex ratios in this chapter is measured based on the number of males per 100 females.

3 There are 34 provincial-level administrative regions in China, including four municipalities, 23 provinces, five autonomous regions and two special administrative regions. The 31 regions here exclude Macao, Hong Kong and Taiwan where the data, sex ratio for never married population age 15 and above, is not available.

4 Bride price means money, property and/or other forms of wealth a man or his family gives to the family of a woman whom the man is going to marry. It is usually a prerequisite for marriage in rural China.

5 The amount of marriage expense in 2005, 2009 and 2011 is from Jiang et al., 2015 (p. 212).

6 All the United States Dollar (USD) equivalents are converted from Chinese Yuan using the average closing price of the China/ United States foreign exchange rate in the same year.

7 *Hukou* institution is a household registration system in China for taxation, conscription and migration regulation (Chan, 2016). There are essentially two kinds of *Hukou* status: agricultural *Hukou* (*nongmin*) or non-agricultural *Hukou* (*shimin*) based on the *Hukou* status of the citizen's parents (Chan & Zhang, 1999). The *Hukou* status is closely related to the holders' access to state-funded social programs and other prerogatives, and the non-agricultural *Hukou* is often considered superior and more desirable because it links to better access to employment opportunities and most state social welfare programs (Wei & Zhang, 2016).

References

Attané, I. (2016). Second child decisions in China. *Population and Development Review* 42(3), 519–536.

Bakken, B. (2005). Comparative perspectives on crime in China. In B. Bakken (Ed.), *Crime, punishment and policing in China* (pp. 64–99). Oxford: Rowman & Littlefield Publishers, Inc.

Banister, J. (1992). A brief history of China's population. In D. L. Poston & D. Yaukey (Eds.), *The population of modern China* (pp. 51–57). Boston, MA: Springer.

Biddulph, S., & Cook, S. (1999). Kidnapping and selling women and children: The state's construction and response. *Violence against Women 5*(12), 1437–1468.

Bongaarts, J., & Guilmoto, C. Z. (2015). How many more missing women? Excess female mortality and prenatal sex selection, 1970–2050. *Population and Development Review 41*(2), 241–269. doi: 10.1111/j.1728–4457.2015.00046.x.

Cao, F. (1997). *The fifth high tide: The crime problem of modern China.* Beijing, China: Today's China Publishing Co.

Cai, Y., & Lavely, W. (2003). China's missing girls: Numerical estimates and effects on population growth. *China Review 3*(2), 13–29.

Chan, K. W. (2016). Five decades of the Hukou system. In I. R. Robyn & F. Guo (Eds.), *Handbook of Chinese migration: Identity and wellbeing* (pp. 23–47). Northampton, MA: Edward Elgar Publishing. doi: 10.4337/9781783476640.

Chan, K. W., & Zhang, L. (1999). The Hukou system and rural-urban migration in China: Processes and changes. *China Quarterly 160*(160), 818–855.

Chew, L. (1999). Global trafficking in women: Some issues and strategies. *Women's Studies Quarterly 27*(1/2), 11–18.

China Population Census. (n.d.). *2005 China 1% national population sample survey* [Data file]. Retrieved from http://www.stats.gov.cn/tjsj/ndsj/renkou/2005/renkou.htm

China Population Census. (n.d.). *Tabulation on the 2010 population census of the People's Republic of China* [Data file]. Retrieved from http://www.stats.gov.cn/tjsj/pcsj/rkp-c/6rp/indexch.htm

China Population Census. (n.d.). *Tabulation on the 2000 population census of the People's Republic of China* [Data file]. Available from http://www.stats.gov.cn/tjsj/pcsj/rkp-c/5rp/index.htm

China Population Census. (1993). *Tabulation on the 1990 population census of the People's Republic of China*. Beijing, China: China Statistics Press.

China Population Census. (2016). *2015 China 1 percent national population sample survey*. Beijing, China: China Statistics Press.

Chu, H. (1996). *Discussion of Management of "Six Evils"*. Beijing: Chinese Procuratorate Press.

Chu, Y. C. (2011). Human trafficking and smuggling in China. *Journal of Contemporary China 20*(68), 39–52.

CPC Central Committee and State Council. (2016, January 1). *Overall implementation of the two-child policy and reforming and improving administration of family planning services*. Retrieved from http://www.gov.cn/xinwen/2016-01/05/content_5030806.htm

Croll, E. (1981). *Endangered daughters of Asia, discrimination & development*. Ithaca, NY: Cornell University Press.

Davin, D. (2007). Marriage migration in China and East Asia. *Journal of Contemporary China 16*(50), 83–95.

Dowling, M., & Brown, G. (2009). Globalization and international adoption from China. *Child & Family Social Work 14*(3), 352–361.

Ebenstein, A. (2010). The "missing girls" of China and the unintended consequences of the one child policy. *Journal of Human Resources 45*(1), 87–115.

Ebenstein, A. Y., & Sharygin, E. J. (2009). The consequences of the "missing girls" of China. *The World Bank Economic Review 23*(3), 399–425.

Edlund, L., Li, H., Yi, J., & Zhang, J. (2007). More men, more crime: Evidence from China's one-child policy. *IZA Discussion Paper No. 3214*. Retrieved from http://ftp.iza.org/dp3214.pdf

Edlund, L., Li, H., Yi, J., & Zhang, J. (2009, February 6). Sex ratios and crime: Evidence from China. *Columbia University Department of Economics Working Paper*. Retrieved from http://cesi.econ.cuhk.edu.hk/wp-content/uploads/Sex-Ratios-and-Crime.pdf

Fan, C. C., & Huang, Y. (1998). Waves of rural brides: Female marriage migration in China. *Annals of the Association of American Geographers 88*(2), 227–251.

Fan, D., & Pei, M. (2018). Research on the influencing factors of residents' second child-bearing willingness: Empirical study based on CGSS2015 Data [In Chinese]. *The World of Survey and Research 9*, 9–13. doi: 10.13778/j.cnki.11-3705/c.2018.09.002.

Fan, Z., & Gu, X. (2017). Rebalance of the sex ratio imbalance: Evidence from "care for girls" campaign [In Chinese]. *Economic Perspectives 4*, 77–89.

Gao, X. (1994). China's modernization and changes in the social status of rural women. In C. K. Gilmartin, G. Hershatter, L. Rofel & T. White (Eds.), *Engendering China: Women, culture, and the state* (pp. 80–97). Cambridge, MA: Harvard University Press.

Golley, J., & Tyers, R. (2012). China's gender imbalance and its economic performance. *The China Story*. Retrieved from https://www.thechinastory.org/chinas-gender-imbalance-and-its-economic-performance/

Greenhalgh, S. (1986). Shifts in China's population policy, 1984–86: Views from the central, provincial, and local levels. *Population and Development Review 12*(3), 491–515.

Gu, B., Wang, F., Guo, Z., & Zhang, E. (2007). China's local and national fertility policies at the end of the twentieth century. *Population and Development Review 33*(1), 129–148.

Gupta, M. D., Ebenstein, A. Y., & Sharygin, E. J. (2010). China's marriage market and upcoming challenges for elderly men. *World Bank Policy Research Working Paper Series No. 5351.* Retrieved from http://ssrn.com/abstract=1632195

Han, M., & Eades, J. S. (1995). Brides, bachelors and brokers: The marriage market in rural Anhui in an era of economic reform. *Modern Asian Studies 29*(4), 841–869.

Hou, J., Gu, B., & Zhang, Y. (2018). The dynamic relationship between gender preferences for children and the sex ratio at birth, 1979–2017 [In Chinese]. *Social Science in China 10*, 86–101.

Hou, J., Huang, S., & Xin, Z. (2015). Changes in the Chinese population's fertility intentions: 1980–2011. *Social Science in China 36*(1), 46–63. doi: 10.1080/02529203.2015.1001482

Howden, D., & Zhou, Y. (2015). Why did china's population grow so quickly? *The Independent Review 20*(2), 227–248.

Huang, K. (2014). Marriage squeeze in china: Past, present, and future. *Journal of Family Issues 35*(12), 1642–1661.

Hudson, V. M., & Boer, A. D. (2002). A surplus of men, a deficit of peace: Security and sex ratios in Asia's largest states. *International Security 26*(4), 5–38.

Jiang, Q., Zhang, Y., & Sánchez-barricarte, J. J. (2015). Marriage expenses in rural China. *The China Review 15*(1), 207–236.

Jin, X., & Liu, L. (2009). Identification of the social risks and anomia in the context of gender imbalance in China [In Chinese]. *Journal of Xi'an Jiaotong University (Social Sciences) 29*(6), 41–50.

Jin, X., Liu, L., Li, Y., Feldman, M. W., & Li, S. (2013). Bare branches' and the marriage market in rural China: Preliminary evidence from a village-level survey. *Chinese Sociological Review 46*(1), 83–104.

Johansson, S., & Nygren, O. (1991). The missing girls of China: A new demographic account. *The Population and Development Review 17*(1), 35–51.

Johnson, K. A. (2016). *China's hidden children: Abandonment, adoption, and the human costs of the one-child policy.* Chicago, IL: University of Chicago Press.

Lavely, W. (1991). Marriage and mobility under rural collectivization. In R. S. Watson & P. B. Ebrey (Eds.), *Marriage and inequality in Chinese society* (pp. 286–312). Berkeley: University of California Press.

Li, S. (2007, October). Imbalanced sex ratio at birth and comprehensive intervention in China. Paper presented at the 4th Asia Pacific Conference on Reproductive and Sexual Health and Rights, Hyderabad, India. Retrieved from https://www.unfpa.org/sites/default/files/event-pdf/china.pdf

Li, S., Shang, Z., & Feldman, M. W. (2013). Social management of gender imbalance in China: A holistic governance framework. *Economic and Political Weekly 48*(35), 79–86.

Li, S., Zhang, Q., Yang, X., & Attané, I. (2010). Male singlehood, poverty and sexuality in rural China: An exploratory survey. *Population 65*(4), 679–693.

Li, X. (2018, January 20). China's 'universal two-child policy' continues to have an impact. *National Bureau of Statistics of China.* Retrieved from http://www.stats.gov.cn/tjsj/sjjd/201801/t20180120_1575796.html

Li, Z. (2012). Rural groom family's marriage payment: Peasants' marital strategy under the background of sex ratio imbalance [In Chinese]. Ph.D. diss. Shanghai University. Retrieved from http://cdmd.cnki.com.cn/Article/CDMD-10280-1013107235.htm

Liu, L., Jin, X., Brown, M. J., & Feldman, M. W. (2014). Male marriage squeeze and inter-provincial marriage in central China: Evidence from Anhui. *Journal of Contemporary China 23*(86), 351–371. doi: 10.1080/10670564.2013.832541

Liu, S. (2013). An analysis of the problem of marriage payment and matching plight: A research based on the new generation of male peasant-workers [In Chinese]. Master's Thesis. Jilin University. Retrieved from http://cdmd.cnki.com.cn/Article/CDMD-10183-1013189472.htm

McKenzie, R. B., & Tullock, G. (2012). *The new world of economics: A remake of classic for new generations of economics students.* New York: Springer.

Ministry of Health of China. (2010). *China Health Statistics Yearbook 2010* [In Chinese]. Beijing, China: Pecking Union Medical College Press.

Mosher, S. W. (2006). China's one-child policy: Twenty-five years later. *The Human Life Review 32*(1), 76–101.

National Bureau of Statistics of China. (n.d.). *China Statistical Yearbook 2018* [Data file]. Retrieved from http://www.stats.gov.cn/tjsj/ndsj/2018/indexch.htm

National Bureau of Statistics of China. (n.d.). *China Statistical Yearbook 2017* [Data file]. Retrieved from http://www.stats.gov.cn/tjsj/ndsj/2017/indexch.htm

National Bureau of Statistics of China. (n.d.). *China Statistical Yearbook 2016* [Data file]. Retrieved from http://www.stats.gov.cn/tjsj/ndsj/2016/indexch.htm

National Bureau of Statistics of China. (n.d.). *China Statistical Yearbook 2011* [Data file]. Retrieved from http://www.stats.gov.cn/tjsj/ndsj/2011/indexch.htm

National Bureau of Statistics of China. (n.d.). *China Statistical Yearbook 2009* [Data file]. Retrieved from http://www.stats.gov.cn/tjsj/ndsj/2009/indexch.htm

National Bureau of Statistics of China. (n.d.). *China Statistical Yearbook 2008* [Data file]. Retrieved from http://www.stats.gov.cn/tjsj/ndsj/2008/indexeh.htm

National Bureau of Statistics of China. (n.d.). *China Statistical Yearbook 2007* [Data file]. Retrieved from http://www.stats.gov.cn/tjsj/ndsj/2007/indexch.htm

National Bureau of Statistics of China. (n.d.). *China Statistical Yearbook 1999* [Data file]. Retrieved from http://www.stats.gov.cn/yearbook/indexC.htm

NPC Standing Committee. (1957, October 25). *The 1956–67 national agricultural development program (revised version).* Retrieved from http://www.npc.gov.cn/wxzl/gongbao/2000-12/23/content_5000392.htm

Pletcher, K. (2019). One-child policy. *Britannica Online Academic Edition.* Retrieved from https://academic-eb-com.proxy.library.vcu.edu/levels/collegiate/article/one-child-policy/490048

Porter, M. (2016). How do sex ratios in China influence marriage decisions and intra-household resource allocation? *Rev Econ Househ 14*(2), 337–371. doi: 10.1007/s11150-014-9262-9

Poston, D. L., & Glover, K. S. (2005). Too many males: Marriage market implications of gender imbalances in China. *Genus 61*(2), 119–140.

PSI Research Division. (2005). *China (2005): HIV/AIDS TRaC study examining condom use among construction workers in Mengzi. First round.* Washington, DC: Population Services International. Retrieved from https://www.psi.org/wp-content/uploads/drupal/sites/default/files/publication_files/522-China_Construction_SMRS.pdf

Qian, Y., & Jin, Y. (2018). Women's fertility autonomy in urban China: The role of couple dynamics under the universal two-child policy. *Chinese Sociological Review 50*(3), 275–309. doi: 10.1080/21620555.2018.1428895

Richards, L. (1996). Controlling China's baby boom. *Contemporary Review 268*, 5–9.

Settles, B. H., Sheng, X., Zang, Y., & Zhao, J. (2013). The one-child policy and its impact on Chinese families. In C. Kwok-bun (Ed.), *International handbook of Chinese families* (pp. 627–646). New York: Springer.

Song, J. (2009, October). Rising sex ratio at birth in China: Responses and effects of social policies. Paper presented at the 26th International Population Conference, Marrakech, Morocco. Retrieved from https://iussp2009.princeton.edu/papers/91145

Song, Y. (2014). What should economists know about the current Chinese *Hukou* system? *China Economic Review 29*, 200–212.

South, S. J. (1991). Sociodemographic differentials in mate selection preferences. *Journal of Marriage and the Family 53*(4), 928–940. doi: 10.2307/352998

South, S. J., & Trent, K. (2010). Imbalanced sex ratios, men's sexual behavior, and risk of sexually transmitted infection in China. *Journal of Health and Social Behavior 51*(4), 376–390.

Shen, A., Antonopoulos, G. A., & Papanicolaou, G. (2013). China's stolen children: Internal child trafficking in the People's Republic of China. *Trends in Organized Crime 16*(1), 31–48.

Stöckl, H., Kiss, L., Koehler, J., Dong, D. T., & Zimmerman, C. (2017). Trafficking of Vietnamese women and girls for marriage in China. *Global Health Research and Policy 2*(1), 28–36.

Sun, X. (2007). Gender imbalance threatens national security. *Forum of Chinese Cadres of Party and Politics 9*, 11–12. doi:10.3969/j.issn.1006-0391.2007.09.005

Svedberg, P. (2017). Child malnutrition in India and China. *2020 Focus Brief on the World's Poor and Hungry People*. Retrieved from https://core.ac.uk/download/pdf/48023975.pdf

Tan, L., & Short, S. E. (2004). Living as double outsiders: Migrant women's experiences of marriage in a county-level city. In A. M. Gaetano & T. Jacka (Eds.), *On the move: Women and rural-to-urban migration in contemporary China* (pp. 151–174). New York: Columbia University Press.

Tan, G. Y. (2017). Missing girls in schools: Gender inequality and educational disparities in rural China. In E. L. Brown & G. Zong (Eds.), *Global perspectives on gender and sexuality in education* (pp. 45–60). Charlotte, NC: Information Age Publishing, Inc.

The Information Office of the State Council of China. (2011, July 14). Assessment report on the national human rights action plan of China (2009–2010). Retrieved from http://www.china.org.cn/china/2011-07/14/content_22989895.htm

The Information Office of the State Council. (2015, September 22). Gender equality and women's development in China. Retrieved from http://english.gov.cn/archive/white_paper/2015/09/22/content_281475195668448.htm

The National People's Congress of the People's Republic of China (NPC) (2015, December 27). Decisions on amending the population and family planning law. Retrieved from http://www.npc.gov.cn/npc/xinwen/2015-12/28/content_1957359.htm.

The World Bank. (1985). *China: Long term development issues and options.* New York: John Hopkins University Press.

The World Bank. (2019a, April 24). World development indicators [Data file]. Retrieved from https://data.worldbank.org/indicator/SP.POP.BRTH.MF

The World Bank. (2019b, April 24). World development indicators: Gender parity index [Data file]. Retrieved from https://data.worldbank.org/topic/gender?locations=CN

Tian, X. (2009). *Sixty Years of China's Population Policies* [In Chinese]. Beijing, China: Social Sciences Academic Press.

Trent, K., & South, S. J. (2011). Too many men? Sex ratios and women's partnering behavior in China. *Social Forces 90*(1), 247–267.

Tucker, C., & Hook, J. V. (2013). Surplus Chinese men: Demographic determinants of the sex ratio at marriageable ages in China. *Population Development Review 39*(2), 209–229. doi: 10.1111/j.1728-4457.2013.00589.x

UNFPA China. (2018). UNFPA China policy brief series: Toward a normal sex ratio at birth in China. Retrieved from https://china.unfpa.org/en/publications/unfpa-china-policy-brief-towards-normal-sex-ratio-birth-china

Wang, D. (2013). Traditional betrothal gifts custom and college students' love and marriage education [In Chinese]. *Journal of Qinghai Normal University (Philosophy and Social Science) 35*(5), 152–155.

Wang, K., Ding, J., & Wang, F. (2016). Influence of the implementation of the universal two-child policy on demographic structure and population spatial distribution in China. *Progress in Geography 35*(11), 1305–1316.

Wei, S., & Zhang, X. (2011). The competitive saving motive: Evidence from rising sex ratios and savings rates in China. *Journal of Political and Economy 119*(3), 511–564. doi: 10.1086/660887.

Wei, G., Xiong, Q., & Xie, L. (2010). Expensive wedding in transition rural China. *Chinese Journal of Population Science 21*(3), 30–36.

Wei, Y., & Zhang, L. (2016). Understanding hypergamous marriages of Chinese rural women. *Population Research and Policy Review 35*(6), 877–898.

White, T. (2006). *China's longest Campaign: Birth planning in the People's Republic, 1949–2005.* Ithaca, NY: Cornell University Press.

Whyte, M. K., Feng, W., & Cai, Y. (2015). Challenging myths about China's one-child policy. *The China Journal 74*, 144–159.

World Economic Forum. (2006, November 23). The global gender gap report 2006. Retrieved from https://www.weforum.org/reports/global-gender-gap-report-2006

World Economic Forum. (2009, June 1). The global gender gap report 2008. Retrieved from https://www.weforum.org/reports/global-gender-gap-report-2008

World Economic Forum. (2018, December 17). The global gender gap report 2018. Retrieved from https://www.weforum.org/reports/the-global-gender-gap-report-2018

Yang, X., & Shang, Z. (2010). Mode recognition for gender imbalance governance in China: Analysis on 24 pilot counties and districts in the national "care for girls action program" [In Chinese]. *Journal of Xi'an Jiaotong University (Social Sciences Edition) 30*(3), 63–69.

Yip, W. C., Hsiao, W. C., Chen, W., Hu, S., Ma, J., & Maynard, A. (2012). Early appraisal of China's huge and complex health-care reforms. *The Lancet 379*(9818), 833–842.

Zeng, Y., & Hesketh, T. (2016). The effects of China's universal two-child policy. *The Lancet 388*(10054), 1930–1938.

Zeng, Y., Zhang, X., & Liu, L. (2017). From "selective two-child policy" to universal two-child policy: Will the payment crisis of China's pension system be solved? *China Finance and Economic Review 5*(1), 14. doi: 10.1186/s40589-017-0053-3.

Zhao, G. M. (2003). Trafficking of women for marriage in China: Policy and practice. *Criminal Justice 3*(1), 83–102.

Zhang, J. (2017). The evolution of China's one-child policy and its effects on family outcomes. *Journal of Economic Perspectives 31*(1), 141–160.

Zhang, S. (1993). *Practical handbook of cases and law on the six evils.* Beijing, China: China University of Politics and Law Press.

Zhang, W. (2000). Dynamics of marriage change in Chinese rural society in transition: A study of a northern Chinese village. *Population Studies 54*(1), 57–69.

Zhou, X., Yan, Z., & Hesketh, T. (2013). Depression and aggression in never-married men in China: A growing problem. *Social Psychiatry and Psychiatric Epidemiology 48*(8), 1087–1093. doi: 10.1007/s00127-012-0638-y.

3

THE STATE OF GENDER EQUALITY IN INDIA AND IMPACT OF MID-DAY MEAL SCHEME

Anbu Arumugam

Its 6.00 am! The alarm screams away as Madhu scrambles to turn it off! She opens the door of her apartment and picks up the newspaper, gives it to her husband, picks up the milk packet and enters the kitchen! Every day is like Monday! Like a cat with nine lives, Madhu in a single day juggles many roles, a dutiful mother, perfect wife and cook, nah ... yet to emulate the mother-in-law though, a cleaner and domestic worker pretty much, goes for work, gets back home, and into another time zone! This is a typical scenario in most modern households across India. Carrying forward the legacy of 'female identity' left by mothers and mothers-in-law is a huge burden for these super-women! The young, educated, liberated women seem to have internalised the 'gendered' attitudes towards their social roles.

"No country can progress if its women are not full partners in the development process" – Narendra Modi, India's current Prime Minister.[1]

A Nervous Area of Government in India

As India nudges ahead in the 21st century, gender equality is a major nervousness area for the government from a national and global standpoint. All the gaits towards development apart India lag massively on gender equality. For example, there is a loss of 26.8% in the country's Human Development Index (HDI) due to inequalities. India ranks a low 127 out of 160 countries on the UN Development Program's Gender Inequality Index (GII) (UNDP 2018). Gender inequalities have had a sustained historical background and socio-political context in India. The clarion calls from the 19th-century reformers of India, to the efforts of governments post-independence, the multitude of issues regarding the state of gender equality have only varied according to the times. Practices such as Sati, female infanticide, child marriages, dowry and celibacy as a widow have existed in India historically.[2] This continued misogyny on one gender in the world's largest democracy is more than a blip on the country. India is a nervous nation when it comes to gender equality even after seven decades of independence. Nervousness stems from centuries of marginalisation which has resulted in a socio-economic-socio-political inequality continuum for its women. Nervousness is generally associated with human beings. Can such an emotion be applied to an organisation or government? The answer is in the affirmative! Gender is one of the major social equity dimensions along with class, religion, disability and sexual orientation (Gooden 2014). According to Gooden, nervousness is directly proportionate to the delivery of equitable public justice towards the stakeholders of a community. The nervousness of the government is definitely visible with regard to the provision of social equity to the women of this country. India will be able to reap the benefits of its socio-economic potential only with further participation by its women.

In this chapter I analyse the current state of gender equality in India which is followed by a brief analysis of the historical and political background. The Mid-Day Meal Scheme (MDMS) is one of the successful targeted social welfare schemes, for the elimination of classroom hunger and promotion of social equity and gender equality in India, that will be discussed later in this chapter. Implemented in India since 1995, it is the largest school feeding programme in the world, at present feeding nearly 91.2 million children hot-cooked lunch in more than 1 million schools across India (Arumugam 2015). Can the government of India shed its nervousness and strongly push ahead structured and targeted reforms for achieving gender equality? India is crafting its policy towards becoming a $5 trillion economy by 2025. The lofty goal is further advanced by the fact that India has entered the 37-year period of 'Demographic Dividend'.[3] Since 2018, India's bulk population is in the range between 15 and 64 years of age, and this bulge will last until 2055. The important observation for India is to harness this potential with the participation and empowerment of its women for any sustainable and long-term development (Figure 3.1).

Why Gender Inequality Is a Nervous Area of Government

Gender is a central factor in the organisation of societies from time to time. The question of parity has political, social and cultural dimensions in a society, whereas the Indian social fabric must be viewed from other important factors such as caste, class, religion and regional divide. These dimensions and factors combined dictate the rules and customs which govern the role of women in our societies. Simply put women go unborn, unwanted, undernourished, unhealthy, unequal and undeserving. Hence, it is imperative to understand the many faces of gender inequality to better analyse the problem of parity in India.

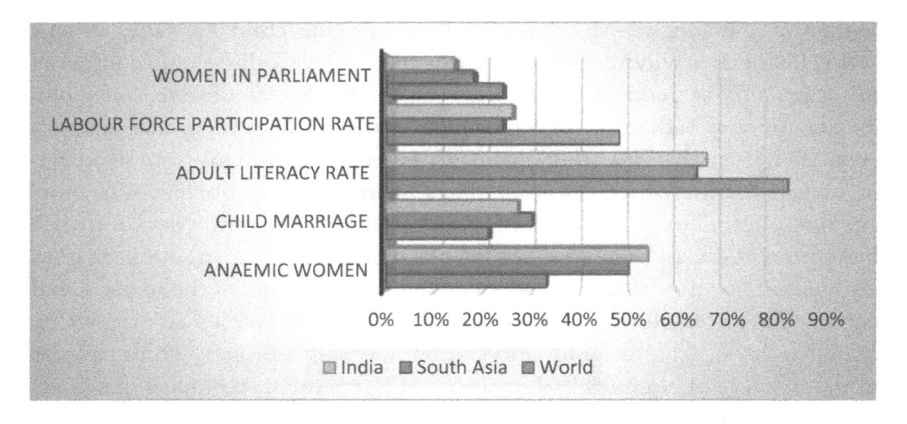

FIGURE 3.1 State of Gender Equality – India.
Source: Gender Statistics (World Bank 2016).

Unborn and Unwanted

I've heard my mother telling me once that there was pressure from my father's family for a boy child after I was born. My strong-willed mother withstood the pressure but indeed delivered a boy next ceding to popular demand from my aunts! Thankfully it was natural selection at work! The tendency is to let the first-born girl live, but the next one doesn't stand a chance. These girls are aborted, abandoned, buried alive, poisoned or starved to death because of a strong preference for a son. Amartya Sen coined the term 'missing women'[4] of India in 1990, and he estimates more than 100 million women were missing due to gender discrimination across the world (Sen, Amartya 1990). This has meant scores of girl children go unborn in India. This is also partly due to the burden of dowry to be given to the groom's family for marriage. The Dowry Prohibition Act of 1961 makes it illegal, yet the practice is widespread cutting across castes and religions. The Pre-conception and Pre-natal Diagnostic Techniques (Prohibition of Sex Selection) Act of 1994 makes gender-based abortions illegal. But in urban areas the families have access to modern methods of sex selection. The case of missing women in India's demography and in turn from its economy is a stark expression of gender discrimination in India.

The sex ratio[5] at birth is 943 females per 1000 males born as per the 2011 Census of India (MoSPI, GOI 2019). The Global Gender Gap Report of 2018 reveals India's dismal ranking of 146 out of 149 countries in the sub-index on sex ratio at birth (WEF 2019). India has in fact increased the gender gap in the last decade on this sub-index. The alarming decline in the child-sex ratio (0–6 years) from 934 down to 918 females per 1000 males between the two census in 2001 and 2011 is a matter of grave concern for India (Census 2011). The state of Kerala has the highest sex ratio in India with 1084 females per 1,000 males, which is well above the national average. Haryana, a north-western state of India, has the lowest sex ratio at 879 females per 1000 males. The Prime Minister Modi feels it's a 'deep shame'[6] on the Indian society, regarding female foeticide, and says all the efforts by the government aside from normalisation may take generations.

Unhealthy and Undernourished

Lack of adequate nutrition and care is reflected in the growth cycle of women in India. Overall 20% of children below five years are wasted and more than 38% suffer from stunting according the Global Hunger Index of 2018. There is a gender dimension for this inter-generational phase in a woman's life cycle. The impact of hunger and malnutrition is a worry because 19.8% girls under age 5 were wasted and 50% girls aged 5–19 were underweight says the Global Nutrition Report (GNR 2018). More than 50% of the women in the reproductive age group are anaemic according to the government (NITI Aayog 2018). The prevalence of early marriages also contributes to the overall health cycle of a woman. The UNICEF estimates that 27% of girls are married before they reach the age of 18 in India (GCR 2019). The incidence of child marriages is another cause for concern despite the legislative provisions.

Gender Gap in Education

India's progress in achieving gender parity in primary education is noteworthy, but there is a need for consistency overall (NITI Aayog 2018). Literacy rates have gone up from a mere 8.86% in 1951 to 64.63% in 2011 according to the Census data (MoSPI, GOI 2019). India is lagging in educational attainment goals because of the gender gap in overall and adult literacy rates (WEF 2019). The gender gap in the adult literacy rate is considerable with the rate at 81.8% and 90% for girls and boys, respectively, as of 2011 (MoSPI, GOI 2019). The regional disparity is also a concern with the rural-urban divide as of 2011, for adult literacy rates were 77.9% for rural women and 90.03% for urban women.

Unequal and Unrepresented

India should be far ahead in advancing the economic participation of women given the stage of its economic development in the last decade. The World Economic Forum report ranks India at 138 of 149 countries in the Labour Force Participation Rate (LFPR) indicator in the Economic Participation and Opportunity sub-index (WEF 2019). Women contribute only 17% to India's Gross Domestic Product (GDP) which is nowhere near the world average of 37% (NITI Aayog 2017). This is because the LFPR for women is 27.4% in comparison with 75.5% for men according to the Fifth Annual Employment-Unemployment Survey for 2015–2016 (NITI Aayog 2018). The McKinsey Global Institute's recent report acknowledges that India has the potential to add 1.4% to its GDP by closing its gender gap (Mckinsey 2018). Unequal wages and unpaid care work are other major impediments for women across sectors in India. The share of women's unpaid care work as percentage of GDP is valued at 3.1% (ILO 2018). According to the government think-tank National Institute for Transforming India (NITI) Aayog women get paid close to 70% of the regular wages of men (NITI Aayog 2018). The share of unpaid care work by women is estimated to be 66% for women in comparison with 12% for men (NITI Aayog 2018) with a gender gap of 40.5% in unpaid care work.

Women representatives form a mere 12% in India's Parliament in the Lok Sabha,[7] and only 8% of seats were allocated for women candidates in the last general elections in 2014 (ECI 2017). Interestingly, this is the highest number of women contesting in proportion to men compared to the previous general elections held in India since 1951. India ranks a dismal 123 out of 149 countries in the Political Empowerment sub-index of the Global Gender Gap Report for the share of women in Parliament (WEF 2019). The story in the State Legislative Assemblies (SLAs) is no better than the national Parliament with women occupying just 8.7% of seats in SLAs as of 2018 (NITI Aayog 2018).

Gender-Based Violence

Violence against women is one of the primary social obstacles to women's empowerment in India. One in three women, who have been married, in the age group of 15–49 has been a victim of spousal violence according to the National Family Health Survey (NFHS 2017). The incidence of rape has increased by 12% in 2016 as compared to 2015 according to the National Crime Records Bureau report. In 2016, 7% of the total crimes committed were against women, and the pattern of crimes and proportion of occurrence varies from Assault on Women at 25%, Kidnapping and Abduction at 19% and Rape at 11% (NCRB 2016).

The state of women in India needs to be observed from a historical and political context to understand the present condition of women in India going beyond statistics and indices. As an author the challenge is to capture the myriad nature of this dynamic spectrum in such a short space albeit with limitations. The colonial rule by the erstwhile East India Company and the British Crown, rise and spread of Indian nationalism, the 19th- and 20th-century Indian renaissance and growth of women's groups have all contributed to the status of women in the modern India. Hence, my attempts here are to mark the important moments in the historical and political space in pre-independent and post-independent India with regard to gender equality.

Social Reforms and Gender Justice in Pre-independent India

Women of yore enjoyed a fair amount of social and personal freedom in ancient India during the Vedic period. They had equal rights and privileges in society.

Monogamy was practised by and large, and widow remarriage was permitted. The medieval period saw the transition of power to the invaders from the Middle East. Women's position also changed and worsened with practices such as purdah system, child marriages, female infanticide and Sati deteriorating their status to almost a non-person. The quest for revival ardently began with the period of reforms in the 18th and 19th century. The plurality and heterogeneous nature of pre-colonial India in the cultural, religious and political life of the people meant the colonialists had to cede authority in certain realms to the customary law of the land (Nair 2000). The popular notion for the legitimacy of Victorian era and colonial sovereignty hinged on the agenda of reforms and civilising the natives, and the colonialists were considered as the harbingers of progress and modernity (Agnes 1999). The overall status of women in the 19th century required political intervention and propagation. A potential transformation of the social fabric of the Indian society was inevitable in the rooting out of social evils that stood firmly challenged in the early 19th century. These efforts restored women from total degradation in the social structure.

Sati – A Funeral Custom

The most important social reform of the 19th century was the enactment of the Abolition of Sati Act (1829). An ancient practice prevalent across various regions in India gradually peaked between the 15th and 18th centuries according to past historian Anant Sadashiv Altekar (Altekar 1938). Sati was the practice of burning Hindu widows on the funeral pyre of their husbands. Even today a visit to the Mehrangarh Fort in Rajasthan will reveal the Sati handprints left by queens before dying. The ritual took two forms: one was 'Saha-marana' or dying in company with the husband; the other was 'anumarana', which permitted the widow to self-immolate themselves on death of her husband (Ray 1978) (Thompson 1928). It was generally practised in Bengal, Rajasthan, and several southern princely states of India (Subramanyam 1984). The movement against Sati was largely due to the efforts of Brahmo Samaj founder Raja Ram Mohan Roy of Bengal, who spearheaded the campaign (Bhattacharjee 1988). He was completely immersed towards the cause after seeing his own sister-in-law being forced to commit Sati. The practice was made a crime and punishable with fine or imprisonment or both (de Souza 1980, Subramaniam 1939).

Female Infanticide – The Endangered Sex

The chilling practice of deliberately killing a newborn female infant was practised widely in India during medieval times (Altekar 1938) and continued during the modern times in all three presidencies of India namely Bengal, Bombay and Madras. This was referred to as 'murder by proxy', usually performed by a woman, the mother or a helper, by way of poisoning, strangulation or suffocation of the new born within hours of birth. Major famines that occurred in India during the 18th and 19th centuries; economic desire to not split land and wealth to heirs; and to avoid payment of dowries to brides, extreme poverty, and taxation policies of the British East India Company have all contributed to this practice during that time. In spite of their policy of non-interference in the social and religious practices of Indians the British rulers were impelled by consideration of humanity advanced by the Indian reformers in removing this practice under the sanction of religion or long-standing usage (Madras Province 1947). The practice was put down by The Female Infanticide Act (1870) which prohibited and outlawed the practice (Gokilavani and Jelestin 2008; Togra 2006).

Widow Remarriage

In the 19th century and first three decades of the 20th century, premature consummation of marriages was not an uncommon practice. Many child wives were done to death or suffered from life-long physical deformity, and a large number of women became widows and suffered from predicaments of enforced widow-hood (Joshi Committee Report 1928). The death of these men left scores of young widows who had to wear white saris as a mark of identity to the community and isolate themselves renouncing all material comforts. The Hindu Widow Remarriage Act of 1856 was due to the strong reformist movement championed by Ishwar Chandra Vidyasagar (Mukhi 1993; Sen 1977).The Act also dealt with the condition of the children born to the widows whose marriage was legalised (Theobald 1856). However, India's first war of independence in 1857, the subsequent transfer of power to the British Crown and the policy of non-interference into personal laws of the civil society hindered the efforts of Vidyasagar against polygamy, polyandry and child marriage.

Child Marriage, Polyandry and Polygamy

The peculiar and immoral customs of polyandry[8] and polygamy[9] have existed in India from ancient times (Coomar and Radha 1987). The Native Marriage Act of 1872 made polygamy a punishable offence. Social reformist Keshab Chandra Sen's efforts in the enactment of the Native Marriage Act of 1872 were instrumental, and the legislation abolished early marriages and polygamy and allowed for widow remarriage and inter-caste marriages (Tandon 1998). The reformists such as Ishwar Chandra Vidyasagar, Keshab Chandra Sen, Behramji M. Malabari and Ranade, and the efforts of other reformers and the pressure of public opinion induced the British Government to act against child marriages. The 1929 Child Marriage Restraint Act besides removing the evils of child marriage promoted female education. The Act clearly indicated that no male below 18 years should marry a girl below 14 years of age (Jagadessan

1990) (Tandon 1998). The Act was also known as the Sarda Act, in the name of Rai Sahib Harbilas Sarda, who moved the Bill in the Legislative Assembly and was referred to the Age of Consent Committee appointed in 1928–1929 under the chairmanship of Sir Moropant Viswanath Joshi (Government of Madras 1930). Such measures in due course helped for women's empowerment or at least arrested the deterioration considerably (Shanthi 1997).

The Right to Property and Women

The right to property and right to profession, which are the basis of economic liberation of women, were yet to be legitimised due to the plurality of personal laws and customs established in pre-colonial India. Deshmukh Act otherwise known as the Hindu Women's Rights to Property Act, 1937, facilitated the removal of the pitiable plight of Hindu widows and assigned property by offering legal right to enjoy the husbands share in the joint family property (Agnes 1999). D.V. Deshmukh was the author of the Hindu Women's Property Right Bill introduced in the Central Legislative Assembly on February 4, 1937. While introducing the Bill, she stated that everything was covered in the name of religion which was alien to the principles of Hindu Law (Gill 1986). The Act was rechristened as the Hindu Widow's Right to Property Act, 1937.

Historically, the British colonial rule, followed by the direct administration of the British Crown, the treatment of the subject population, resentment among the new educated middle-class, rise of nationalist movements and participation of women in the freedom struggle, had contributed to the rise of feminist movements in pre-independent India. A galaxy of eminent scholars and social reformers such as Raja Ram Mohan Roy, Debendranath Tagore, Keshab Chandra Sen, Ishwar Chandra Vidyasagar, Swami Vivekananda, Jyotirao Phule, Govind Ranade, Syed Ahmed Khan, Pandita Rama Bai, Kazi Nazrul Islam, Periyar E.V. Ramasamy, Savitribai Phule, Gopal Hari Deshmukh, Kandukuri Veeresalingam and many more emerged in the 19th-century colonial backdrop and fought for the removal of social obstacles for emancipation of women and their overdue progress. The structural transformation of the Indian social fabric gradually progressed because of this 'Indian Renaissance'.[10]

Changing Status of Women Post-independence

The aftermath of the partition of India and Pakistan in 1947 witnessed one of the largest ever migration and displacement of people.[11] The government-commissioned sub-committee on "Women's Role in Planned Economy" (1947) outlined a proposal for the realisation of women's equality. The report remained only on paper as a political agenda sans constructive action. The focus on economic growth and the geo-political situation of India in the decades after independence was challenging due to economic stagnation, landlessness, unemployment, poverty, hunger and so on. This pulled back the efforts of the reformist and feminist movements of the 19th- and 20th-century India towards the upliftment of women in the society (Menon and Bhasin 1998) (Bhutalia 2000). In this backdrop the status of women took a backseat with the focus on economic development and industrialisation (Government of India 1985).

The enfranchisement of women and provision of civic rights in the Constitution of India was a result of the positive impact of the women's movement alongside the nationalist freedom struggle. Some positive legislative measures during that time included the Marriage Act of 1954, Hindu Succession Act of 1956, Dowry Prohibition Act of 1961 and Maternity Benefits Act of 1961. These legislations dealt with the issues of marriage, divorce, succession, guardianship and adoption to mention a few. For instance, the Hindu Marriage Act penalised polygamy and granted divorce rights for both genders. Inter-caste and inter-religious marriages were given legal sanction. In the 1960s, as a response to the failure of national level organisations and political parties to take up women's problems as issues in their agenda, many action groups relating to women's issues emerged at local levels as well as at the national level (Kasturi 1995). The mid-1970s saw the beginning of a fundamental shift from the domination of the modernisation paradigm of development thinking and intervention to a systematic search for alternatives.

During this period, there were several democratic people's movements, labour strikes, agrarian and student unrest, protests against food shortages, inflation, unemployment and corruption which ultimately culminated in the Total Revolution movement[12] led by the late Sri Jaya Prakash Narayan (Rath 1996). The 1974 Towards Equality Report published by the Status of Woman Commission (Government of India 1975) was a milestone with regard to the push for gender equality. The report highlighted the state of gender equality in India in the decades immediately following the independence of the country. Furthermore, the report emphasised the need for focus on health, political participation and employment status of women. General elections of 1980 brought Mrs. Indira Gandhi back to power. In the same year, women's organisations presented a memorandum to the government titled, "Indian Women in the Eighties: Development Imperative", which influenced the Planning Commission of India to include women in its vision for India. For the first time, the 6th Five-Year Plan[13] period (1980–1985) included a separate chapter for women titled "Women and Development" which was followed by the 7th Plan Period (1985–1989) in which a chapter titled "Socio-economic Programmes for Women" was included in the plan document. The National Education Policy of 1986 included a separate section on education for women's equality (Banerjee 1992). In 1987, the Central Government appointed a Commission to study the problems of self-employed women and women employed in formal sectors and came out with the National Perspective Plan for Women (NPP), 1988–2000. The plan and its 353 recommendations on varied aspects of women's issues remained on paper (Chandra 1989).

The 8th Plan Period of 1992–1997 saw a shift from development and empowerment of women in India. The National Commission for Women was set up in 1992 and is an important organisation for grievance redressal for women in India. The state of women's issues varied from violence against women, domestic violence, price rise, employment for women, political participation for women, etc. The LPG[14] phenomena or the Liberalisation, Privatisation and Globalisation of the Indian economy in the 1990s paved way for the structural deregulation of the economy. This marked the major shift in the nature and direction of the Indian economy due to the balance of payments[15] crisis which the government grappled with during that time. The 73rd and 74th amendments to the Indian Constitution in 1993 provided for the operationalisation of a 33% reservation of seats for women in local governance. The political participation of women in the sub-national level got a big boost because of this amendment. Under the 10th Plan (2002–2007), India's budget was analysed from a gender perspective with the introduction of gender budgeting.

The introduction of the Millennium Development Goals (MDGs) from 2001 allowed for more positive national level convergence and planning for goals and targets for the achievement of gender equality and empowerment of women in all the member countries. The 11th Plan Period of 2007–2012 saw some focus on gender equity, and the Ministry of Women and Child Development was tasked with the gender-responsive budget and mainstreaming process. The 12th Plan Period of 2012–2017 saw the last of the five-year plans in India, and the newly formed NITI Aayog has scrapped this system of planning since 2015 onwards.[16] The impetus was on health, education, urbanisation and governance with regard to improving the state of gender equality in India.

Traversing the centuries from ancient, medieval, and colonial to modern India in just a matter of a few pages provides the reader with a glimpse of the unique nature of the social fabric which relegated its women to a non-persons. Looking back these deep-rooted issues discussed earlier have been challenged and changed. Has the freedom for the country meant the same for the women of this nation? Have the measures taken to ameliorate the centuries of inequalities remained mere "paper tigers"? The answer lies in being able to measure the promise with progress. One scheme that has stood the test of time is the school lunch programme. By providing lunch every school day, the scheme targeted classroom hunger due to high household poverty levels and social equity. I will be discussing how this programme with humble beginnings in the southernmost part of India contributed to gender equality in India.

A Promising Government Initiative: The Mid-Day Meal Scheme

Anaikattu is a sleepy village town, far away from the bustling metropolis of Chennai, located in the Kancheepuram District. I was invited by the

Headmistress to visit the Government High School for my research on the school feeding programme. We walked by the small kitchen shed to the smells of 'sambhar'[17] and 'boiled eggs' prepared for the lunch by the helpers in the school. "Most of them come to school for the lunch otherwise they would earn better as labourers", tells the noon-meal coordinator Bhuvaneswari. She introduced her daughter Selvi, aged 11, who is doing her sixth grade. Selvi told me she wants to become a nurse in the future. During the lunch break, Selvi and the other kids took their plates, washed their hands, got their food served, sat together in the community hall and ate their lunch. To see the smile and content on the face of each child after having a good meal was a sight to behold! One that I never got bored off!

Gender bias can be seen in the household division of food. Girls and women usually eat after the boys and men in the house (Arumugam 2015). The extent of inequalities that persist is reflective of the deep-rooted social bias and transcends religion, caste, creed, poverty, rural-urban divide, etc. The MDMS is one of the best social welfare programmes being implemented in India (Arumugam 2015). The scheme is a key experience in any rural or urban school in most Indian states. The essential support to girl children by way of a hot-cooked school lunch is like scoring a hat-trick in a cricket match! Hunger, nutrition and education are the parameters ticked off by this one scheme. The effects of undernourishment in children which leads to stunting and anaemia in adults stem from hunger. School feeding programmes provide the safety net to children suffering from household poverty. India's tryst with the school lunch programme goes back to the southern state of Tamil Nadu. The scheme was first introduced in 1956 by the then Chief Minister of the state Mr. K. Kamaraj (Arumugam 2015). Lack of funds and challenges in long-term sustainability of the policy led to the stagnation of the programme in a few years.

A Class III dropout in school, Marudur Gopalan Ramachandran or famously known as MGR – founder of the AIADMK[18] party in Tamil Nadu, three-time Chief Minister and recipient of India's highest civilian award the Bharat Ratna – is credited with the success of this scheme in the state. On the eve of inauguration on July 1, 1980, in Pappakurichi Village in the southern district of Trichy he said,

> Let us provide a hot meal with vegetable dishes to the pupils, akin to the lunch served in a middle-income family to the children by their mother.
> *(Kannan 2017)*

By 1982 the scheme covered the entire state of Tamil Nadu and served up lunch to 65.7-lakh children in 31,000 centres. The unique feature of the scheme was the preference in employment given to destitute women. There was a big spike in attendance at primary schools. Attendance jumped to 96.2% in the 6–11 age group and to 66.03% in the 11–14 age group (Arumugam 2015). India hadn't seen a scheme of this enormity until that time. "The foremost reason for students who drop-out and go for work is hunger", said Mrs. Premalatha, an Assistant Head Mistress of the Presidency Girls Higher Secondary School, Chennai. The 235-year-old institution is a model school in the city. She says the programme has benefited many students. Valli, a Class VII student who lives with her disabled mother in a slum[19] near Egmore, is one such student. Her mother is a daily wager and getting two meals a day is a struggle. She said, "I am happy, I get enough food at school". For a nation that grappled with high illiteracy, lack of enrolment and huge drop-out rates of girls from school, bringing children to school was a top priority. The first ever National Policy on Education, released in 1986, put the focus on girls' education. The main objective was the "removal of disparities and to equalize educational opportunity by attending to the specific needs of those who have been deprived of so far" (NPE 1986) (Table 3.1).

By the 1980s many states in India had some sort of school lunch programme being implemented. The success and impact of this scheme eventually led to the rolling out of the National Programme of Nutritional Support to Primary Education (NP-NSPE) on August 15th, 1995. According to Dreze, the MDMS is one of the most successful social welfare schemes with comprehensive benefits in terms of school enrolment, attendance, nutrition among others (Dreze and Khera 2017). As of 2017–2018 nearly 94.6 million children benefit from hot-cooked nutritious food in more than 1 million schools, and 2.5 million cook-cum-helpers are engaged from disadvantaged communities. The World Food Programme (WFP) estimates that almost all countries have some form of school feeding programmes in place (WFP 2013a) and are considered as a common form of social safety net in the world (WB 2018). Such schemes benefit nearly 368 million children in developing and developed nations (WFP 2013a).

The Mid-Day Meal (MDM) provisions are governed by the Ministry of Human Resources Development (MHRD), Government of India. In 2001, the Supreme Court of India stipulated the provision of cooked meals under the MDM. The total cost for the meal provision is around US$100 million last

TABLE 3.1 MDM Programme in Different States

State	Food Supplement	Year of Starting
Tamil Nadu	Cooked Meal	1957
Kerala	Corn Soya Meal	1961
Uttar Pradesh	Corn Soya Meal/Wheat	1952
Andhra Pradesh	Corn Soya Meal	1962
Karnataka	Corn Soya Meal	1964
Bihar	Balahar/Corn Soya Meal	1965
Orissa	Balahar/Milk/Biscuits	1962

Source: www.indiatogether.org.

TABLE 3.2 MDM Provisions

S. No.	Item	Quantity per Child	
		Primary	Upper Primary
A) Nutritional norms			
1	Calories	450	700
2	Protein	12 gms	20 gms
B) Food norms			
1	Food-grains	100 gms	150 gms
2	Pulses	20 gms	30 gms
3	Vegetables	50 gms	75 gms
4	Oil and fat	5 gms	7.5 gms
5	Salt and condiments	As per need	As per need

Source: www.mdm.nic.in.

year. The per head cost for a child is $0.06 for the primary classes and $0.08 for the upper primary classes, respectively. The WFP study indicates that for every US$1 spent on school feeding programmes the return is around US$3–10 by way of improvements in health, education and productivity (WFP 2013b). The MDM rules comply with the provisions under the National Food Security Act (NFSA) of 2013. The nutrition norms are standardised for the beneficiaries aged 6–14, from classes I–VIII, as given in Table 3.2. The food-grains are supplied to the districts by the local depots of the Food Corporation of India (FCI) at 100 and 150gms per child per day for primary and upper primary classes, respectively. The scheme provides for one cook-cum-helper for up to 25 students and an additional cook-cum-helper for more than 26 students.

Apart from the universal entitlements of the scheme many state governments have introduced additional nutritional modifications to the MDM. For example, children are given protein supplements in the form of an egg or banana, especially for those who have vegetarian diet preference in Tamil Nadu (Arumugam 2015). Kitchen gardens have been implemented in schools in the states of Assam, Kerala, West Bengal, Tripura, Sikkim, Arunachal Pradesh, Nagaland and Lakshadweep (Arumugam 2015).

Assessment and Evidence of Progress

Impact of MDMS on Gender Equality

The last decade has seen increasing consensus over the impact of home-grown school feeding programmes across the globe. The multiple benefits of school feeding programmes are discussed in the recent series 'The State of the World' published under the aegis of the United Nations (FAO, IFAD, UNICEF, WFP and WHO 2019). The fully operational scheme has been reported to have a positive impact on enrolment and retention of girl children in school. Significant increase in girls' access to education has also been observed after the implementation of the MDMS. Social equity on the ground was fostered by reducing gender gap in schools, and employment opportunities for women are offered through this scheme (Dreze, J; Goyal, A 2003). The Gender Parity Index (GPI) for primary education was 0.71 in 1991, and India achieved gender parity by 2011 (MHRD 2018). The gender gap reduced by 24.7% between 2001 and 2011 in primary education (MHRD 2018). The scheme had a positive impact in reducing the number of girls dropping out of school as can be seen in Table 3.3.

The MDM can be observed from major perspectives of educational advancement, child nutrition and social equity (Dreze, J; Goyal, A 2003). The Gross Enrolment Ratio (GER) in primary education for females was a mere 65.9% in 1991 and increased to 72.4% by 2001 (MHRD 2018). The MDMS had a positive effect on the health of children (Singh et al. 2014). The high levels of undernourishment were reduced from 54.2% to 37.9% according to the NFHSs of 1998–1999 and 2015–2016, respectively (NFHS-4 2015). The adult literacy rates for females increased from 34% in 1991 to 59.3% by 2011 (Table 3.4).

The localisation of the programme creates income multipliers due to linkages of the school feeding programmes to economic and allied activities and businesses in the local economy (Taylor and Filipski 2014). The scheme also had a positive impact in reducing early marriages in India. The percentage of women in the age group of 20–24, who were married before they were 18 years old, declined from 47.4% in 1998–1999 to 26.8% in 2015–2016 (NFHS-4

TABLE 3.3 Drop-Out Rates in School Education – Classes I to VIII (in per cent)

Category	1960–61	1970–71	1980–81	1990–91	2000–01	2010–11
Boys	75.0	74.6	68.0	59.1	50.3	40.6
Girls	85.0	83.4	79.4	65.1	57.7	41.2
Total	78.3	77.9	72.7	60.9	53.7	40.8

Source: Educational Statistics at a Glance 2014.

TABLE 3.4 Literacy Rate of India (Census 2011)

Census Year	Total (%)	Males (%)	Females (%)
1961	28.3	40.4	15.4
1971	34.5	46.0	22
1981	43.6	56.4	29.8
1991	52.2	64.1	39.8
2001	64.8	75.3	53.7
2011	74.0	80.9	64.6

Source: Official Census, Government of India 1951–2011.

TABLE 3.5 Number of Girls per Hundred Boys Enrolled by Stages of Education

Year	Primary Education (Class I–V)	Upper Primary (Class VI–VIII)
1960–1961	48	31
1970–1971	60	41
1980–1981	63	49
1990–1991	71	58
2000–2001	78	69
2010–2011	92	89

Source: Educational Statistics at a Glance 2014.

2015). The scheme was also effective in increasing the number of girls in primary and upper primary classes as can be seen from the data given in Table 3.5.

The MDMS has contributed to gender equality by empowering girl children with education and nutrition. The available evidence suggests that school feeding programmes stimulate higher returns in four key areas, i.e. accessibility to education for girls; nutrition; provides a safety net to the most vulnerable children in their respective community and, lastly, provides a stimulus of local economies (Bundy et al. 2018). The scheme has served as an incentive for enhancing enrolment and retention of girls in elementary education. The scheme has also had positive impacts on gender equity, poverty and classroom hunger. Being fully operational since 2001, this scheme is one of the best examples of a successful policy initiative that has been mainstreamed by successive governments in a multi-party democracy like India. A time-tested scheme such as the MDMS coupled with other social intervention schemes has contributed to the betterment of women in India in the past decades.

Conclusion: Gender in India's Development Story

Couple of years ago Google doodle featured Rukhmabai Raut on her 153rd birth anniversary for being one of the first women doctors in India. This drew some criticism for ignoring Kadambini Ganguly, who graduated from the Calcutta Medical College in 1886, some eight years before Raut. She was also one of the first physicians in South Asia at that time. I think one can forgive Google for such activity that was the rarity of the case. These path-breaking women would have been proud that the GPI for adult literacy has increased to 0.75 (Census 2011). Progress is being measured in percentiles rather than in exceptions as far as gender is concerned. It was only in 1883 that schools in British India saw the sight of a girl being part of the class. Kamini Roy, who holds that record, joined the Bethune School in Calcutta and eventually went onto become a teacher! Today, India has reached gender parity in primary, upper primary and secondary level of education (MoSPI, GOI 2019) (Table 3.6).

TABLE 3.6 Indicators on Gender Equality

Key Indicators	NFHS-3 (2005–2006)	NFHS-4 (2015–2016)
Child Sex Ratio (Females per 1000 males)	919	914
Adult Literacy Rate for Females (15 years and above) %	55.1	68.4
Women age 20–24 married before age 18 (%)	47.4	26.8
Women age 15–19 who were already mothers or pregnant at the time of the survey (%)	16	7.9
Infant mortality rate (deaths per 1000 live births)	57	41
All women age 15–49 who are anaemic (%)	55.3	53.1
Currently married women who usually participate in household decisions (%)	76.5	84
Ever-married women who have ever experienced spousal violence (%)	37.2	31.1
Women having a bank or savings account that they themselves use (%)	15.1	53

Source: National Family Health Survey (NFHS-4), Ministry of Health and Family Welfare, Government of India.

The scars of colonial plunder formed the bedrock of this cyclic phenomenon connecting the myriad of issues being discussed with regard to the women of this country. The linkages between poverty and gender tend to be simplified and the race for sustenance trumps over the provision of education, healthcare, nutrition, safety of women, etc. According to the United Nations Development Programme's (UNDP) Multi-dimensional Poverty Index of 2019 India has lifted nearly 271 million people from poverty in the last decade alone in comparison with the horrendous nature of human existence in the 1950s with nearly half the population reeling in poverty. For instance, the Mahatma Gandhi National Rural Employment Guarantee Act, enacted in 2005, provides 100 days of paid employment to rural households per year with one-third of the jobs reserved for women. This is the largest public works guarantee programme in the world currently. The wages are paid according to the Minimum Wages Act of 1948 and vary across the states ranging from $1.89 to $3 per day.

Considerable progress has been made to tilt the gender imbalances due to the skewed sex ratio. This complex issue has several heterogeneous socio-economic and cultural dimensions, nevertheless the masculinisation of South Asia as a result of this phenomenon is being closely assessed by national and international agencies. Successive governments have focused on progressive measures in the last two decades; the sex ratio has gone up to 943 per 1,000 births (Census 2011), and the target is to achieve 954 births by 2030 (NITI Aayog 2018). The 'Beti Bachao Beti Padhao'[20] (BBBP) is a flagship national scheme launched in 2014 to improve Child Sex Ratio in select 405 of the 640 districts in India. State governments too have come up with unique policies to push the sex ratio. In 1992 Tamil Nadu initiated the 'Cradle Baby Scheme' to combat the practice of female infanticide.

The unwanted girl babies could simply be dropped into empty cradles kept at Public Health Centres. The 'Ladli' – scheme implemented by the north-western state of Haryana – promotes the second born girl child in families by providing an incentive of Rs. 5,000/- per month for the girl child.

Healthcare and nutrition have seen positive measures in the last seven decades by successive governments. Maternal Mortality Rate (MMR) has significantly come down to 130 in 2014–2016 from 301 in 2001–2003 as per the Sample Registration System (SRS 2016). The country aims to bring down stunting in children to 25% by 2022. The incidence of child marriages too has reduced significantly with the overall decrease in poverty and increase in literacy levels. Judicial activism along with the legislative process has also helped advance gender equality. For instance, the Islamic practice of 'Triple Talaq'[21] or instant divorce by uttering the word 'talaq' three times by husbands was banned by the apex court in 2017 after the landmark Shayara Bano Case.[22] This is noteworthy because of the absence of uniform civil code and having personal laws for religious communities. India aims to completely end spousal violence by 2030 (NITI Aayog 2018). Some of the measures in place are One Stop Centre (OSC), an integrated service centre for catering to women affected by violence, and provide legal, psychological, temporary shelter and a National Women Helpline number '181' established in 2015 for emergency and non-emergency responses. The scheme has been operationalised in 32 states so far across India.

Dr. Muthulakshmi Reddy was India's first female legislator who entered the Madras Legislative Council in 1927 and was also the first woman surgeon in India at that time! India gave the United Nations General Assembly its first female President way back in 1953 itself! Vijaya Lakshmi Pandit holds that eminent record. But in terms of women in power India has a long way to go indeed! The 17th general elections held in May 2019 show a positive trend in having 78 women Parliamentarians at 14.3% which is an increase compared to the 2014 general elections (ECI 2019). The recent elections also saw the major national parties including the incumbent BJP[23] proclaiming their stand to bring in a legislation to provide for 33% gender quotas in the national Parliament. Women form a mere 25.8% of the workforce against the global average of 48% (NITI Aayog 2018). The McKinsey Global Institute estimates that India can up its GDP by 18% by simply increasing the women in the economic space (Mckinsey 2018). There is growing evidence of financial autonomy for women with nearly 33% women owning a bank account, and 31% of financial holdings are held by women (MoSPI, GOI 2019). Not regressing is as essential to advancement! India has put gender in the policy mainstream and is working aggressively to add value to the life of each girl child.

The Quest for Gender Equality

India will be celebrating its 75th year of independence in 2022 as one of the leading and fast-growing economies in the world today. The expectation from the largest and relatively young democracy in the world is to ring in proactive participation of its women in India's success story. There has been gradual progress towards gender equality, and the governments in power have consistently brought in policy measures for the improvement of quality of life for women in India. The measurement of progress also needs to be contextualised and prioritised for a proper understanding of the state of gender equality in India. Colonialism, partition of India and Pakistan, wars with China and Pakistan, regional disparities in growth and development across India, rural-urban divide, globalisation and the economy are some of the important factors that have impacted the country.

Gender mainstreaming has been impacted by a combination of these developments and changes ever since independence as we have seen in this chapter previously. India has taken a few decades to move from 'welfare' to 'development' to 'empowerment' of women in its centralised planning system. The brief analysis from a historical and political context albeit its limitations does reveal that India has faced several social questions before and after independence in the form of uprisings, reform movements, feminist movements, etc. The constitutional, legal and administrative provisions and their impact on women's agency have been assessed by the Indian State once in 1971 and as recently as 2015. The billion plus population interestingly makes India an important partner for all international agencies and collaborations in the 21st century. Hence, India's growth story contributes heavily to the South Asian region. The international collaborations such as MDGs and the ongoing Sustainable Development Goals have pushed the agenda on national, state and local convergence towards progress in gender equality by way of quantitative indicators.

Beyond statistics and indices, my country needs the 21st-century woman to be provided with access and equal opportunities in all aspects of life. To be born free; raised with adequate provisions for childhood; secured in her adolescence; armed economically and with educational attainment; have the choice for career, vocation and marriage; and live with dignity and protection are the basics that India @ 75 needs to be rooting for. This is the woman Mahatma Gandhi wanted to see in a free India, and yet 72 years after independence the Government of India is sitting on a nervous footing with regard to gender equality. As a woman I wish to see this normalisation, in my lifetime in this strong nation of many things yet. This India will grow faster and bigger economically and socially with the participation and contribution of the other half!

Notes

1 As said by Prime Minister Narendra Modi in an interview to Hindustan Times on August 12, 2018.
2 Sati – a practice of women committing themselves to die in their husbands' funeral pyre; Female Infanticide – disposing or killing of newborn girl child; Child Marriage – marrying off young girls after they attain puberty and at a very young age; Dowry – is the opposite of bride price and is paid by the bride's parents to the groom's parents for the proposed marriage.

3 Defined by the United Nations Population Fund (UNFPA) as the growth potential that results from shifts in a population's age structure.
4 The term 'Missing Women' was coined by Amartya Sen in 1990 referring to the shortfall of women measured by sex ratio (Sen, Amartya 1990).
5 Sex ratio is defined as females to per 1,000 males in the overall population in India.
6 Prime Minister Narendra Modi declared female foeticide a 'deep shame' while inaugurating the National Nutrition Mission in Jhunjhunu, Rajasthan, on International Women's Day, 2018.
7 India has a bi-cameral Parliament, like the Westminster Model in Britain, with 'Lok Sabha' (Lower House) and 'Rajya Sabha' (Upper House).
8 **Polyandry** is a practice whereby a woman has two or more husbands at the same time.
9 **Polygamy**, marriage to more than one spouse at a time.
10 The 19th-century social reform movement is famously referred to as the Indian Renaissance.
11 Further reading please see UNHCR (2000).
12 The 1974 Bihar Movement by students in the state of Bihar led by Gandhian sociologist Jaya Prakash Narayan a.k.a. JP became a nationwide against the then Prime Minister Indira Gandhi and her government. The nationwide agitation was against corruption, poverty, lack of development and societal practices.
13 **Five-Year Plans** (FYPs) are centralised and integrated national economic programs.
14 Refers to the economic liberalisation of the Indian economy in 1991.
15 India faced an economic crisis in the 1990s due to fall of Soviet Union, fiscal imbalances, Gulf-war, etc.
16 National Institute for Transforming India (NITI) Aayog is the apex body for planning in India since 2015 replacing the Planning Commission.
17 Sambhar is a very famous and nutritious South Indian lentil-based curry spiced with a unique curry powder mix and tamarind. This contains enough protein due to the Bengal Gram dal or 'Toor Dal' used for the curry.
18 AIADMK – All India Anna Dravida Munnetra Kazhagam, a regional party started by M.G. Ramachandran after he split from the parent party of DMK – Dravida Munnetra Kazhagam.
19 A slum is a densely populated urban settlement usually spread across the city marked by closely packed housing units of dwelling occupied by impoverished sections of the population.
20 'Beti Bachao Beti Padhao' – 'Save the Girl Child' and 'Educate the Girl Child'.
21 Triple Talaq is a customary Islamic practice by Muslim men who can divorce their wives by uttering the word three times orally through any mode of communication.
22 Shayaro Bano & others vs. Union of India case – Shayaro Bano challenged the practices of Triple Talaq, Polygamy and Nikkah Halala (the practice of wanting a woman to marry and divorce another man so that her previous husband can re-marry after triple talaq) as unconstitutional and sought relief from the apex court of India.
23 Bharatiya Janata Party (BJP) is the ruling party heading the Union Government since 2014.

References

Afridi, F. 2009. "The Impact of School Meals on Social Participation: Evidence from Rural India." *Journal of Development Studies* 47 (11): 1636–56.

Agnes, F. 1999. *Law and Gender Equality: The Politics of Women's Rights in India.* Oxford University Press. Accessed May 2019. doi:10.1093/acprof:oso/9780195655247.001.0001.

Ali, A. A. 1938. "Women Suffrage in India." In *Our Cause: A Symposium of Indian Women*, by Shyam Kumari Nehru, pg. 536. Allahabad.

Altekar, A. S. 1938. *The Position of Women in Hindu Civilisation*. Benares: The Culture Publication House.

Arumugam, A. 2015. *"Mid-Day Meal Scheme in Chennai City, Tamil Nadu-A Study"*. Chennai, Tamil Nadu: PhD dissertation, University of Madras.

Banerjee, N. 1992. *Grassroots Empowerment*. New Delhi: Centre for Women's Development.

Bhattacharjee, A. 1988. *A History of Modern India*. New Delhi: Lucas Publications.

Bhutalia, U. 2000. *The Other Side of Silence: Voices from the Partition of India*. Durham: Duke University Press.

Bourdieu, P. 1999. *"The Social Condition of the International Circulation of Ideas" in Shusterman R. (dir), Bourdieu: A Critical Reader*. Oxford: Blackwell.

Bundy, D. A. P., N. de Silva, S. Horton, D. T. Jamison, and G. C. Patton. 2018. "Re-imagining School Feeding: A High-Return Invesment in Human Capital and Local Economies." *Child and Adolescent Health and Development* (World Bank) 8.

Census. 2011. "Census Data." Office of the Registrar General & Census Commissioner, India, Ministry of Home Affairs, Government of India, New Delhi. Accessed April 2019. http://censusindia.gov.in/2011-Common/CensusData2011.html.

Chandra, S. 1989. "National Perspective Plan for Women makes no headway." *India Today*, 30 September. Accessed April 2019. https://www.indiatoday.in/magazine/indiascope/story/19890930-national-perspective-plan-for-women-makes-no-headway-816578-1989-09-30

Chaudhuri, M. 2012. "Feminism in India: The Tale and its Telling." *Revue Tiers Monde* 209 (1): 19–36. Accessed May 2019. doi:10.3917/rtm.209.0019.

Coomar, P. C., and M. K. Radha. 1987. "Polyandry in Ancient India." In *Polyandry in India*, by Palash Chandra Coomar and Manis Kumar Raha, pg. 367. New Delhi: Gian Publishing House.

de Souza, A. 1980. *Women in Contemporary India and South Asia*. New Delhi: Manohar Publications.

Dreze, J., and R. Khera. 2017. "Recent Social Security Initiatives in India." *World Development* 98: 555–72.

Dreze, J., and A. Goyal. 2003. "The Future of Mid-Day Meals." *Economic and Political Weekly* 38 (44): 4673–82. Accessed May 2019. https://www.epw.in/journal/2003/44/special-articles/future-mid-day-meals.html./.

ECI. 2019. Accessed May 2019. https://eci.gov.in/general-election/general-elections-2019/.

ECI. 2017. "Electoral Statistics Pocketbook." Election Commission of India, Government of India, New Delhi. Accessed April 2019. https://www.eci.gov.in/statistical-report/pocket-book-2017/.

FAO, IFAD, UNICEF, WFP, and WHO. 2019. *The State of Food Security and Nutrition in the World*. Rome: FAO. Accessed October 2019. http://www.fao.org/3/ca5162en/ca5162en.pdf.

GCR. 2019. "Global Childhood Report." Save the Children -100 years. Accessed May 2019. https://reliefweb.int/sites/reliefweb.int/files/resources/global-childhood-report-2019-pdf%20%281%29.pdf.

GHI. 2018. "Global Hunger Index." Accessed May 2019. https://www.globalhungerindex.org/india.html.

Gill, K. 1986. *Women's Right to Property in India*. New Delhi: Deep & Deep Publications.

GNR. 2018. "Global Nutrition Report." Accessed May 2019. https://globalnutrition-report.org/.

Gokilavani, S., and G. Jelestin. 2008. *Marriage, Dowry Practice and Divorce*. New Delhi: Regal Publication.

Gooden, S. T. 2014. *Race and Social Equity: A Nervous Area of Government*. 1st Edition. New York: M.E. Sharpe, Inc.

Government of India. 1985. *Women in India-A Country Paper*. Status Report, New Delhi: Department of Women and Child Development, Ministry of Education and Social Welfare.

Government of India. 1975. *Towards Equality-Report of the Committee on the Status of Women in India*. Status Report, New Delhi: Ministry of Education and Social Welfare.

Government of India. 1930. "Government of India's Dispatch on Proposals for Constitutional Reform." Calcutta, pg. 25.

Government of Madras. 1930. "No.F.570/29, Judicial Department, Government of India to the Secretary, Government of Madras." Madras: Judicial Department, 15th October.

ILO. 2018. *Care Work and Care Jobs for the Future of Decent Work*. Report, International Labour Institute (ILO). Accessed April 2019. https://www.ilo.org/wcmsp5/groups/public/---dgreports/---dcomm/---publ/documents/publication/wcms_633135.pdf.

Indian Statutory Commission. 1920. "Report of the Indian Statutory Commission, Vol.I." Surrey, pg. 40.

Jagadessan, P. 1990. *Marriage and Social Legislation in Tamil Nadu*. Madras: Elachiapen Publishers.

Jain, D. 1975. *Indian Women*. New Delhi: Government of India, Publication Division.

Joshi Committee Report. 1928. "Report on Age of Consent:1928-'29." Calcutta, pg. 9.

Kannan, R. 2017. *MGR: A Life*. Chennai: Penguin.

Kasturi, L. 1995. "Development, Patriarchy and Politics-Indian Women in the Political Process 1947–1972." *Occasional Paper*. New Delhi: Centre for Women's Development Studies.

Lok Sabha Secretariat. 2017. *Parliamentary Initiatives in Achieving Sustainable Development Goals*. Lok Sabha Secretariat, Parliament of India, New Delhi: Lok Sabha Secretariat. Accessed January 6, 2019. http://www.sri.nic.in.

Madras Province. 1947. *R.Dis.No.4798/47, Report of the Administration of the Police of the Madras Province 1945*. Madras: Department of Police, Madurai, pg. 7.

Mckinsey. 2018. *The Power of Parity: Advancing Women's Equality in Asia Pacific, Focus: India*. Mckinsey Global Institute. Accessed April 2019. https://www.mckinsey.com/featured-insights/gender-equality/the-power-of-parity-advancing-womens-equality-in-india-2018.

Menon, R., and K. Bhasin. 1998. *Borders and Boundaries*. Piscataway, NJ: Rutgers University Press.

MHRD. n.d. http://mdm.nic.in/.

MHRD. 2018. "Educational Statistics at a Glance." Department of School Education and Literacy, Ministry of Human Resource Development, Government of India, New Delhi. Accessed May 2019. https://mhrd.gov.in/sites/upload_files/mhrd/files/statistics-new/ESAG-2018.pdf.

Ministry of Finance. 2018. *Economic Survery of India*. Survey, Ministry of Finance, Government of India, New Delhi: Government of India. Accessed May 2019. https://mofapp.nic.in/economicsurvey/economicsurvey/index.html.

MoSPI, GOI. 2019. *Women and Men in India 2018*. New Delhi: Social Statistics Division, Central Statistics Office, Ministry of Statistics and Programme Implementation, Government of India. Accessed April 2019. http://www.mospi.gov.in/sites/default/files/publication_reports/Women%20and%20Men%20%20in%20India%202018.pdf.

MoSPI, GOI. 2017. *Millennium Development Goals-Final Country Report of India*. Ministry of Statistics and Programme Implementation, Government of India, New Delhi: Central Statistics Office. Accessed January 15, 2019. http://www.mospi.gov.in.

Mukhi, H. R. 1993. *Indian Society and Social Institutions*. Delhi: Anmol Publications.

MWCD. 2015. "High Level Committee Report on the Status of Women in India." Ministry of Women and Child Development, Government of India, New Delhi. Accessed May 2019. https://wcd.nic.in/documents/hlc-status-women.

Nair, J. 2000. *Women and Law in Colonial India: A Social History*. New Delhi: Kali for Women.

NCRB. 2016. *Crime in India – Statistics*. National Crime Records Bureau, Ministry of Home Affairs, Government of India, New Delhi: National Crime Records Bureau. Accessed May 2019. http://ncrb.gov.in/StatPublications/CII/CII2016/pdfs/Crime%20Statistics%20-%202016.pdf.

NFHS. 2017. *National Family Health Survey (NFHS-4) 2015–2016*. Survey, New Delhi: Ministry of Health and Family Welfare, Government of India. Accessed May 2019. http://rchiips.org/nfhs/NFHS-4Report.shtml.

NFHS-2. 1998. *National Family Health Survey*. New Delhi: MInistry of Health and Family Welfare, Government of India. Accessed May 2019. http://rchiips.org/nfhs/nfhs2.shtml.

NFHS-4. 2015. *National Family Health Survey-4th Round*. New Delhi: Ministry of Health and Family Welfare, Government of India. Accessed May 2019. http://rchiips.org/nfhs/NFHS-4Reports/India.pdf.

NHP. 2018. "National Health Profile." Central Bureau of Health Intelligence, Directorate General of Health Services, Ministry of Health & Family Welfare, Government of India, New Delhi. Accessed May 2019. https://cdn.downtoearth.org.in/pdf/NHP-2018.pdf.

NITI Aayog. 2018a. *SDG India Index Baseline Report*. NITI Aayog, Government of India, New Delhi: NITI Aayog. Accessed January 2019. http://www.niti.gov.in.

NITI Aayog. 2018b. *Strategy for New India @ 75*. New Delhi: NITI Aayog. Accessed https://niti.gov.in/writereaddata/files/Strategy_for_New_India.pdf April 2019.

NITI Aayog. 2017. *India Three Year Action Agenda*. NITI Aayog, Government of India, New Delhi: NITI Aayog, Government of India. Accessed November 23, 2018. http://www.niti.gov.in.

NPE. 1986. "National Policy on Education." Ministry of Human Resource Development, Government of India, New Delhi. Accessed May 2019. https://mhrd.gov.in/sites/upload_files/mhrd/files/upload_document/npe.pdf.

Pande, R. 2009. "Feminism and the Women's Movement in India: A Historical Perspective." *Journal of Women's Studies* 1 (1): 22–39.

Panikkar, K. N. 1975. *"Presidential Address" (Section III) Proceedings of the Indian History Congress, v.36*. Aligarh: PIHC.

Rath, S. 1996. "Feminist Movement in India, Contemporary Issues and Leadership." *Public Policy Research Newsletter*, Winter ed.

Ray, R. 1978. *Role and Status of Women in Indian Society*. Calcutta: Firma KLM Pvt. Ltd.

Sen, A. 2001. "Many Faces of Gender Inequality." *Frontline*, Oct-Nov. Accessed May 2019. https://frontline.thehindu.com/static/html/fl1822/18220040.htm.

Sen, A. 1990. "More than 100 Million Women are Missing." *The New York Review of Books* 37 (20): 61–66.

Sen, A. 1977. *Iswar Chandra Vidyasagar and his Elusive Milestones*. Calcutta: Riddhi Publisher.

Shanthi, K. 1997. *Empowerment of Women*. New Delhi: Anmol Publications.

Singh et al. 2014. "An Evaluation of the Midday Meal Scheme in India." *Economic Development and Cultural Change* 62 (2): 275–306.

SRS. 2016. *Sample Registration System*. Accessed May 2019. http://www.censusindia.gov.in/2011-Common/Sample_Registration_System.html.

Subramaniam, N. 1939. *Self-Immolation in Tamil Society*. Madras: Ennes Pathipagam.

Subramanyam, N. 1984. *The Press and National Movement in South India: Andra 1905–1932*. Madras: New Era Publications.

Tandon, R. K. 1998. *Women Customs and Traditions*. New Delhi: India Publishers.

Tata, H. 1920. *A Short Sketch of Indian Women's Franchise Work*. Bombay: The Pelican Press.

Taylor, J. E., and M. J. Filipski. 2014. *Beyond Experiments in Development Economics: Local Economy-wide Impact Evaluation*. Oxford, UK: Oxford University Press.

Theobald, W. 1856. *The Legislative Acts of the Governor-General in Council, Vol. II. 1852–1858-Hindu Widow Harricaft Act Vol. XV*.

Thompson, E. 1928. *Suttee*. London: George Allen & Unwin Ltd.

Togra, V. 2006. *Jawaharlal Nehru and the Status of Women in India – An Analytical Study*. New Delhi: Reliance Publishing House.

UNDP. 2018. "Human Development Indices and Indicators: 2018 Statistical Updates." United Nations Development Programme. Accessed April 2019. http://hdr.undp.org/sites/all/themes/hdr_theme/country-notes/IND.pdf.

UNESCO. 2014. *Sustainable Development begins with Education*. Paris: UNESCO. Accessed May 2019. https://unesdoc.unesco.org/ark:/48223/pf0000230508.

UNHCR. 2000. "The State of World Refugees 2000- Chapter 3- Rupture in South Asia." United Nations High Commissioner for Refugees, Geneva. https://www.unhcr.org/3ebf9bab0.pdf.

Vastsa, Rajendra Singh. 1971. "The Movement Against Infant Marraiges in India:1860–1914." *Journal of Indian History* XLIX (145–147): 289.

WB. 2018. *The State of Social Safety Nets Worldwide*. Washington, DC: World Bank. Accessed May 2019. https://www.worldbank.org/en/topic/socialprotectionandjobs/publication/the-state-of-social-safety-nets-2018.

WEF. 2019. *Global Gender Gap Report 2018*. Geneva, Switzerland: World Economic Forum. Accessed April 2019.

WFP. 2013a. *The State of School Feeding Worldwide*. Rome: World Food Programme. Accessed May 2019. https://www1.wfp.org/publications/state-school-feeding-worldwide-2013.

WFP. 2013b. *The School Feeding Investment Case*. Internal Document, Rome: World Food Programme. Accessed May 2019. https://docs.wfp.org/api/documents/86593db964f34dada0840ec47d2bad3d/download/.

World Bank. 2016. *Gender Statistics*. https://data.worldbank.org/indicator.

4

CONFRONTING NERVOUSNESS AT THE INTERSECTION OF INDIGENOUS AND GENDER ISSUES

A Case Study of Mexico's Efforts, Accomplishments, and Remaining Work

Nadia Rubaii and Susan Appe

A Nervous Area of Government in Mexico

In 2019, Yalitza Aparicio, a Mexican indigenous woman—of Mixtec and Triqui heritage—from the state of Oaxaca was the first indigenous woman nominated for the Best Actress Oscar for her performance in the film *Roma*. *Roma* is Mexican director Alfonso Cuarón's critically acclaimed film about 1970s Mexico City with political and social issues woven into the story of a live-in domestic worker of a middle-class family. The film itself and particularly Aparicio's performance and nomination brought discussions about indigenous women in Mexico (as well as the treatment of domestic workers) into the Hollywood coverage of the Oscars. And within Mexico itself, *Roma* has started a "national conversation about inequality" (Tillman, 2019). The fame launched Aparicio onto the cover of *Vogue Mexico*, a first time for an indigenous woman. She told the magazine about her cover: "Other faces of Mexico are now being recognized. It is something that makes me happy and proud of my roots" (Argen, 2018). While it has sparked conversation and positive attention—in Mexico and globally—her fame has also brought about negative reactions across online outlets described as "explicitly racist" (Argen, 2018). As is often the case for representatives of historically marginalized groups who break through to mainstream attention, the pressures on Aparicio are great, as reflected on by her comment: "If I do something wrong, they might think we are all that way. So I have to take good care of that image, our image" (Ruiz-Grossman, 2019).

This chapter provides a case study of progress and lingering challenges associated with the Mexican national government's nervousness as it relates to indigenous women like Yalitza Aparicio and the character she portrayed. The intersection of indigenous status and gender is particularly relevant in Mexico given the long history of discrimination against indigenous peoples dating back to the country's colonization and the concurrent deeply embedded culture of machismo which has created inequities for women.

Indigenous women face a multitude of structural inequities in Mexico which extend beyond the summative effect of these two group identities. This chapter examines the intersection of these two phenomena and calls attention to a striking contradiction.

> On the one hand, Mexico is an upper middle income country with an average per capita income of nearly $10,000, is home to the world's wealthiest man and is one of only two countries in Latin America that hold an A investment grade rating.
>
> *(Cross, 2019)*

At the same time, many indigenous communities lack electricity, running water or health clinics, and people struggle to find employment or enough food to eat, and "the poorest, most disenfranchised people in Mexico are indigenous women living in rural areas" (Cross, 2019). Despite Mexico's economic progress on the global scale, close to 40% of indigenous women are malnourished (Coalición por la Salud, 2007). The conditions faced by indigenous women in Mexico mirror Gooden's (2014) characterization of racial inequities in the United States. The inequities faced by indigenous women are "profound, systemic, segregated and cumulative" (Gooden, 2014, p. 23). These inequities are enduring and endemic; they have saturated the full spectrum of policy areas, including policies related to housing, the environment, health, education, economic well-being, and criminal justice, and they have effects that extend beyond a single generation (see Gooden, 2014, Figure 2.1, p. 23). At times seemingly unaware or unconcerned, and at other times well-intentioned but overly cautious, individual public administrators and entire public sector organizations in Mexico have demonstrated nervousness with respect to both groups, and even more so with respect to indigenous women.

This chapter focuses on the Mexican government's recent efforts to confront both issues simultaneously as an example of a noteworthy and important step in the right direction. We highlight a mix of organizations, programs, and policies which collectively comprise the Mexico national government's efforts to confront long-standing nervousness resulting in and stemming from deep inequities for indigenous women. In addition to the aforementioned attention brought to issues of indigenous women in Mexico due to the film *Roma* and Aparicio's new fame, other recent events warrant attention. The 2018 presidential election in Mexico represented the first time an indigenous woman attempted to stand as a candidate for the presidency,[1] the first time that the duly elected President, Andrés Manuel López Obrador, partook in a ceremonial inauguration by indigenous groups, and the first time a sitting President has publicly promised to make indigenous issues a priority of his government (Monroy, 2018). In light of all of these high profile milestones, it is appropriate to look more closely at what the government is doing to acknowledge and change the embedded inequities.

We focus on recent programs and actions explicitly targeted to indigenous women and with the backing—in words, organizational and human capital, and the investment of dollars (or, more accurately, *pesos*)—of the national government of Mexico. We do not examine at all the many and varied initiatives of civil society organizations, affinity associations, political parties, or other groups outside of government, many of which have been instrumental in representing indigenous women's issues and placing pressure on the Mexican government. Drawing upon data from the Mexican government in the form of input, output, and outcome measures, we provide a critical assessment of the effectiveness of these new programs in reducing inequities in access, process, quality of service, and accomplishments. We conclude that despite some signs of progress on the input and output measures related to access and process, there is much less evidence of outcome changes to address the quality of services or true equality of outcomes for indigenous women relative to other members of the Mexican society. We also note that recent organizational consolidation actions provide the potential to more closely monitor, document, analyze, and report data across multiple programs addressing indigenous people generally, but it is unclear whether this change will help or hinder progress for indigenous women. Finally, we call attention to the need for greater attention to dialogues or the so-called race talk (Gooden, 2014), and apologies for past and ongoing discrimination.

Why Indigenous Women Represent a Nervous Area of Government

The intersection of indigenous status and gender is particularly relevant in Mexico given the long history of discrimination against indigenous peoples dating to colonization and the concurrent deeply embedded culture of machismo which has created inequities for women. Mexico's nervousness regarding indigenous women is best understood by first appreciating its history with respect to these two groups separately, and then considering the heightened nervousness at the intersection of these two identities.

Indigenous Status as a Nervous Area of Government in Mexico

At one time indigenous communities flourished throughout the entire Latin American region; now 87% of them reside in just five countries: Mexico, Bolivia, Guatemala, Peru, and Colombia (UNICEF, n.d.). Approximately 522 indigenous groups exist in Latin America, most of them living in Brazil

(241), followed by Colombia (83), Mexico (67), and Peru (43) (UNICEF, n.d.). Several Latin American countries such as Bolivia, Peru, Guatemala, Ecuador, Mexico, and Honduras continue to have a majoritarian indigenous population. In all of the Americas, Mexico is second only to Peru in the number of indigenous people (World Bank, 2015).

The history of indigenous peoples in Mexico shares several tragic characteristics common throughout much of the Americas. An integral part of the conquest and colonization processes undertaken by European nations upon arrival to the Americas was the decimation of indigenous peoples accomplished through genocidal massacres, enslavement, forced religious conversions, displacement from lands, and other means. Colonizing forces intent on extracting the abundant natural resources of the continent used their military power, religion, culture, and language to dominate indigenous groups. Nervousness surrounding this population is grounded in the very concept of indigenous peoples which Coates (2004) observes is inseparable from colonialism and imperialism. International law defines indigenous peoples and nations as those "having a historical continuity with pre-invasion and pre-colonial societies that developed on their territories" and forming "non-dominant sectors of society" who are "determined to preserve, develop and transmit to future generations their ancestral territories," and who seek to do so "in accordance with their own cultural patterns, social institutions, and legal systems" (Martinez Cobo, 1987).

Dating to the Spanish conquest of the Aztec Empire in the 1500s and continuing through the modern era, indigenous peoples in Mexico have been subjected to discrimination in many forms. The manifestations of discrimination have evolved since the colonial era, as outright slavery, servitude, mass killings, or forced religious conversions are no longer practiced, but the devastating effects have lingered. Subtler, although no less insidious, forms of discrimination and efforts at assimilation have continued today. For example, development continues to destroy indigenous lands and, with that, indigenous livelihoods, cultural traditions, and languages. Thus, issues and challenges around indigenous women reflect long-standing nervousness. It has not been directly confronted and, in some cases, has been denied by government officials for many years.

In more recent times, attention around indigenous in particular was launched by the Zapatista Army of National Liberation's (EZLN) declaration of war on the Mexican government in 1994 in an announcement timed to coincide with day the North American Free Trade Agreement (NAFTA) went into effect. This was a catalyst for the adoption of a series of policy reforms in Mexico. Most notable among these were the San Andres Accords of 1996. The Accords outlined indigenous peoples' right to participation and political voice in local governments and asserted, among other things, a State commitment to further social policy focused on indigenous children and women. The Zapatista uprising eventually brought about the 2001 constitutional reform which re-characterized Mexico as a pluricultural nation and allowed for the right of indigenous self-determination. Despite these constitutional provisions, self-determination in practice is severely hampered by conflicts between indigenous cosmovisions and formal Mexican State practices. These conflicts are most apparent in opposing positions regarding the activities of extractive enterprises wherein indigenous values of a harmonious relationship with lands, nature, and natural resources come in direct conflict with state development and investment priorities. Mining activities often threaten the indigenous ways of life based in subsistence agriculture or fishing, have resulted in forced displacement along with deforestation and contamination, and often have sparked violent conflicts. Another area of direct conflict occurs in the realm of criminal justice, as the indigenous principles and procedures for conflict resolution and the corresponding penalties they met out differ greatly from the national system of criminal justice. Indigenous peoples are often denied access to their own justice systems and incarcerated as a result of processes and standards of the state.

The number of indigenous people living in Mexico varies depending on the agency reporting. As of 2018, there were three federal agencies that "measure and monitor" the country's indigenous peoples: the National Population Council (*Consejo Nacional de Población* or CONAPO for its initials in Spanish); the National Commission for the Development of Indigenous Groups (*Comisión Nacional para el Desarrollo de los Pueblos Indígenas*, or CDI), which has since been replaced by the National Institute for Indigenous People (*Instituto Nacional de los Pueblos Indígenas* or INPI); and the National Institute of Statistics and Geography (*Instituto Nacional de Estadística y Geografía* or INEGI). According to Mexico's official census agency, INEGI, at the time of the last census in 2010, more than 16.8 million people in Mexico self-identified as being indigenous, representing more than 15% of Mexico's population (INEGI, 2011). In 2015, INEGI reported an increase to 21.5% of Mexicans self-identifying as indigenous, representing 25.6 million people, 13.2 million of whom are women. In the same year the CDI estimated there were 12.2 million, of whom 6.1 million were women (Global Americans, 2017). Indigenous peoples comprise more than 60 distinct groups and speak just as many languages in Mexico (Martinez Medrano, 2003).

While the exact count of indigenous and indigenous women in particular is not consistent across government agencies, the fact that indigenous people face serious social and political challenge and have been excluded from the country's economic, political, and social development is not contested (CDI, 2017; Matinez Medrano, 2003). According to national government agencies, indigenous people are nearly four times more likely to live in extreme poverty than non-indigenous Mexicans, and speaking their indigenous language only makes them more vulnerable. The National Development Plan (NDP) for the country for the period of 2013–2018 indicates that 40.2% of indigenous people live in extreme poverty compared to 10.4% of non-indigenous Mexicans

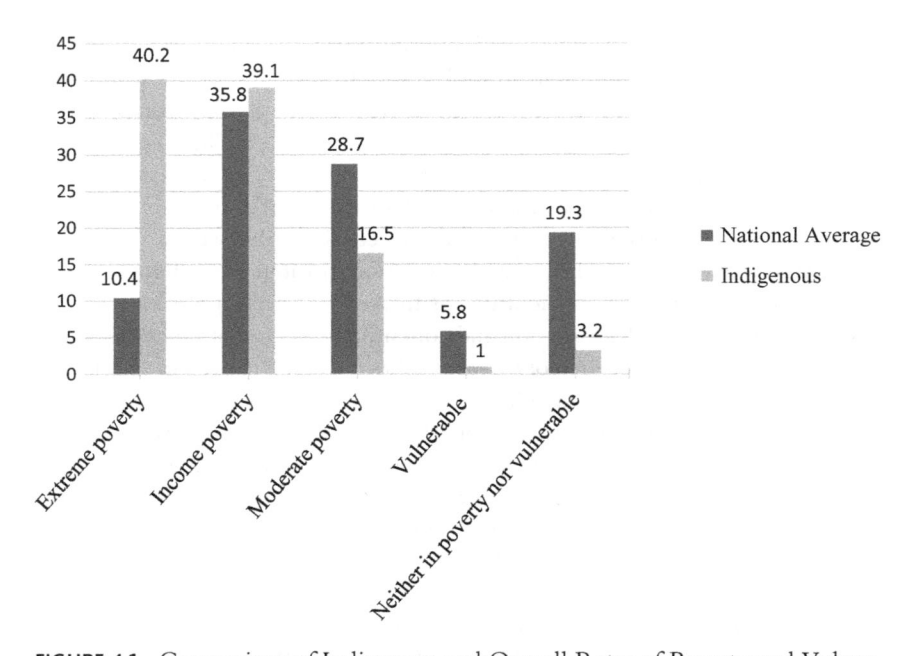

FIGURE 4.1 Comparison of Indigenous and Overall Rates of Poverty and Vulnerability in Mexico, 2010.

Source: Adapted from data reported in the *Mexican National Development Plan: 2013–2018* (Gobierno de la Republica, 2013, p. 48).

(Gobierno de la Republica, 2013). Figure 4.1 illustrates that the gap between indigenous and non-indigenous Mexicans spans all categories of poverty and economic vulnerability. Those who speak their indigenous language are even more likely to live in poverty (77.6% compared to the national rate of 41%) or extreme poverty (34.8% compared to 5.8% nationally) than their indigenous compatriots who speak Spanish (INDI, n.d., p. 11).

While some of the tools of oppression have changed since the colonial era, the pressures to assimilate remain strong. In a 2005 national poll, 43% of respondents thought that indigenous peoples will continue to face discrimination, one-third expressed a belief that the only thing that indigenous people need to do to escape poverty is to stop acting like indigenous people, and 40% objected to having indigenous people live close to their community (Martinez Medrano, 2003).

Nearly half (49%) of indigenous people in Mexico live in urban areas due to internal migration processes based on both push and pull factors. They have been pushed from their native lands by development projects and by abject poverty and absence of basic infrastructure. At the same time they have been pulled to cities in search of better access to education, health, water, sewage, electricity, and employment. In urban areas, indigenous households are located in more insecure and unhealthier environments, thereby systematically anchoring them to poverty and hindering their access to basic services and economic development. These disadvantages are also linked to the unequal access that indigenous peoples have to formal job markets. To the extent that indigenous people are employed mostly in low-income informal activities, they have less access to health insurance, retirement, and other social benefits. Furthermore, their access to new technologies such as the Internet is limited which also has affected their inclusion in globalized economic activities. Only relatively recently has the Mexican national government acknowledged the existence of discrimination in society and taken steps to address it.

Gender as a Nervous Area of Government in Mexico

Alongside the well-documented discrimination and oppression of indigenous peoples, Mexico has a parallel system of entrenched gender inequality grounded in a deeply embedded culture of *machismo*. As Villegas (2017) notes, "[m]achismo has long been widespread in Mexican society. Male entitlement—reflected in telenovelas, movies, work settings, families and romantic relationships—has been tolerated, even celebrated." Like the concept of indigenous peoples, machismo also has colonial roots (Ramos, 1962) in the values, norms, and practices which reinforce a patriarchal system of male dominance and superiority (Segrest, Romero & Domke-Damonte, 2003). Although less widely used in the popular vernacular, the counterpart concept of *marianismo* refers to the stereotypical feminine role in Mexico (Gil & Vazquez, 1996; Stevens, 1973). Also linked to the Spanish conquest, the term draws upon the Catholic faith and the image of the Virgin Maria with the characteristics of saintliness, submissiveness, and frigidity (Gil & Vazquez, 1996). As Mosher and Tompkins (1988) aptly summarize, the gendered relationships in Mexico reflect the dualities of "victor and vanquished, master and slave, the head of the house and woman as his complement, the patriarch and his children."

The culture of machismo is widely credited with contributing to violence against women. Disappearances and killings of women and girls have been labeled by some international watchdog groups as an epidemic in Mexico and are particularly prevalent in Mexico border cities (Binkowski, 2017). In 2015, annual female homicides exceeded 2,500 (Villegas, 2017). In recent years, sexism, misogyny, and violence have been labeled by women's rights groups and by prominent government officials as problems demanding government attention, representing a movement toward recognizing and confronting this nervous area of government. In 2017, the then-President Enrique Peña Nieto called on Mexicans to eliminate "all expressions of machismo" and the "deeply rooted machista culture" which results in "violence against women" (as cited by Villegas, 2017).

Mexico has enacted electoral quotas which have dramatically increased women's representation in Congress and have positioned it as a global leader in gender equality in politics. The country has also invested in educational programs which have brought women's educational attainment in lines with men's, and established more childcare options to allow women access to participation in the paid labor force. Despite this, gender stereotypes and discrimination persist. Mexico has one of the largest gender gaps in labor force participation among the 36 countries which comprise the Organization for Economic Co-operation and Development (OECD). Mexican women continue to perform more than 75% of all unpaid housework and childcare, and they are subject to high rates of violence in private and public spaces with uneven and insufficient access to justice (OECD, 2017).

In its 2018 review of Mexico's implementation of the Convention on the Elimination of All Forms of Discrimination against Women (CEDAW), the United Nations (UN) Committee charged with oversight commended Mexico for efforts in countering enforced disappearances and for increasing women's political participation. At the same time the Committee expressed concerns in a number of areas. Specifically the Committee noted lingering problems in the following areas: vulnerability of migrant women to human trafficking; lack of social services for domestic workers; women's access to land, justice, and economic resources; persistence of child marriage and teen pregnancies; inconsistent state and local laws regarding abortion; lack of gender equality in the armed forces; illegal trafficking of babies for adopting in foreign countries; equality in the workplace and education; sexual violence and exploitation of women; and, most relevant to the discussion in this chapter, discrimination against indigenous women and girls (Committee on the Elimination of Discrimination Against Women, 2018).

The three comparisons shown side-by-side in Figure 4.2 demonstrate Mexico's mixed progress on gender issues. While the gap between women's labor

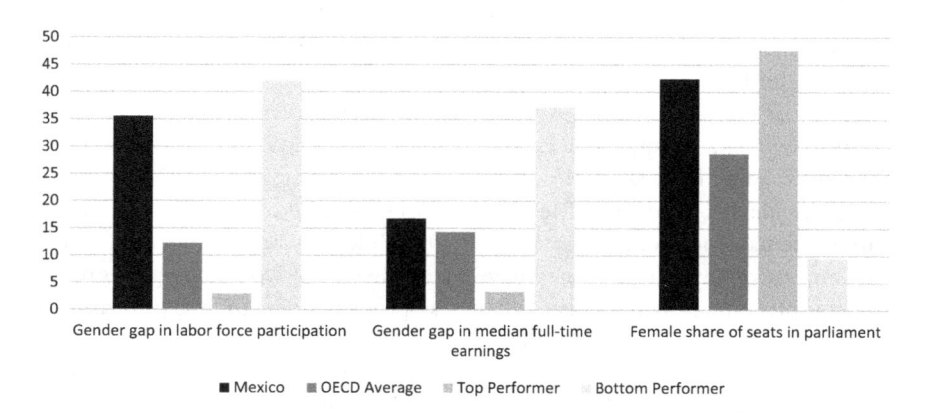

FIGURE 4.2   Mexico's Gender Equity in the Labor Force and Electoral Representation.
Source: OECD, 2017.

force participation and men's participation in Mexico ranks among the worst among countries which comprise the OECD, it is near the average on full-time median earnings, and among the best with respect to electoral representation in the national legislature.

Indigenous Women: An Intersection of Heightened Nervousness in Mexico

While there is sufficient material to develop case studies of nervousness in Mexico in relation to indigenous people or women, we have chosen to focus on the intersection of those two groups. In doing so, we present evidence of the systemic discrimination facing this particularly vulnerable group, and explore the efforts of Mexican policy-makers and public administrators to confront their nervousness and make progress in redressing inequities. The international indigenous rights organization, Cultural Survival, documents how indigenous women face poverty, sexual and physical violence, malnutrition, limited access to services and justice, restrictions on their freedom of expression, and general human rights violations at levels that exceed the already high levels for the indigenous population as a whole (Cultural Survival, 2018). On almost all indices in Mexico, women fare more poorly than men, and indigenous peoples fare more poorly than non–indigenous (Martinez Medrano, 2003). Figure 4.3 illustrates the "double whammy" effect in terms of participation in the paid labor force.

Indigenous women face even more substantial and particularly insidious barriers to full equality, particularly those who speak indigenous languages and do not speak Spanish. As of 2005, 636,720 indigenous women were identified

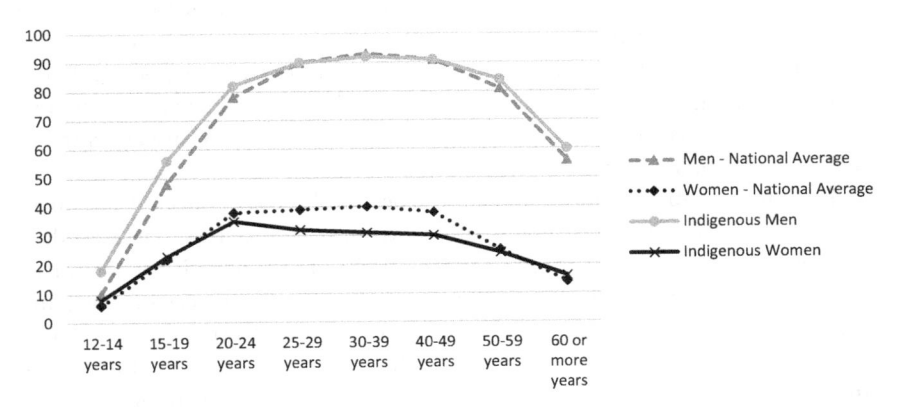

FIGURE 4.3 Employment Rate in the Paid Labor Force by Age Groups, gender, and indigenous status, 2000.

Source: From data reported by INEGI (2000).

as monolingual compared to 371,083 men, and more than half of the women who speak an indigenous language are illiterate (INMUJERES, 2006). In some respects, this is a case study of the intersection of three factors—gender, indigenous status, and language. Indigenous women are less likely than indigenous men to speak Spanish and more likely to depend on their indigenous languages; this adds another layer to the institutionalized inequality on almost all indicators (INMUJERES, 2006).

Several historical examples provide important context for understanding this area of nervousness. We focus on examples related to violence against indigenous women, indigenous women's access to healthcare services, indigenous women's voices in development decisions, and formal participation in elective public office. These four areas are offered simply as illustrative examples and do not reflect an exhaustive discussion of all forms of discrimination faced by indigenous women in Mexico.

Indigenous Women as Victims of Violence

By law since 2013, Mexican women have a right to a life free from violence, and since 2012 the Mexico national government has collected statistics on the crime of femicide or gender-motivated homicide of women. The highest femicide rates in Mexico are in the states with the highest indigenous populations and those along the United States-Mexico border. The border city of Juarez (across from El Paso, Texas) with its thriving *maquiladora*[2] industry is known as the "capital of murdered women" (Cultural Survival, 2018) and is a region where indigenous women migrants are particularly at risk of disappearance and murder (Minority Rights Groups International, n.d.). The crime of human trafficking is receiving greater attention globally, and this is a critical issue in Mexico where an estimated 200,000 people are victims of trafficking each year. Of women trafficked in Mexico, nearly three-quarters (70%) are indigenous women (Velasco, 2013). Some studies suggest that indigenous women and girls who are seeking escape from domestic and sexual violence are particularly susceptible to the false promises made by traffickers of a better future and a stable marriage (Lakhani, 2015).

For other forms of violence against women, the data collected and analyzed by the Mexican government falls short on several criteria. Because data are not collected and services are not provided in indigenous languages or in culturally appropriate ways, they likely exclude the experiences of many indigenous women. Despite multiple reports of increased militarized violence against indigenous women, no official studies have been conducted to examine State-sponsored violence carried about the military with impunity. The cases of Ines Fernandez Ortega and Valentina Rosendo Cantu are illustrative of the problem and the beginnings of a response. Both were raped by Mexican army soldiers, Ines Fernandez Ortega in her home in front of her children and

Valentina Rosendo Cantu when walking to wash clothes at a near stream. They tried for eight years to get justice at the national level before, with the help of high-profile human rights NGO in Mexico called The Tlachinollan Human Rights Center of the Mountain of Guerrero, turning to the Inter-American Court of Human Rights. "The Court's ruling effectively reframed Ines' and Valentina's rapes as a violation of the collective rights of the Me-phaa people" (Sieder, 2016).[3]

Indigenous Women's Limited Access to Healthcare

Living in rural areas where health services are sparse and not speaking the language of the majority of healthcare providers, many indigenous women find it difficult to receive quality, let alone culturally appropriate, healthcare services, particularly with respect to reproductive and sexual health. Indigenous women are especially vulnerable to rape, they have less access to abortion, and they suffer from disproportionately high teen pregnancy and material mortality rates relative to non-indigenous women in Mexico. An estimated 1,400 indigenous women die from complications in childbirth, triple the national average (Coalición por la Salud, 2007). Worse than the absence of healthcare services, or lack of quality services, in some cases the medical treatment that indigenous women receive from the Mexican State has been abhorrent and criminal. Figure 4.4 illustrates both a noticeable gender disparity and a severe disparity based on language (indigenous or Spanish) in access to healthcare even for those indigenous peoples who are in the paid labor force.

Indigenous women in Mexico have for many years been victims of forced sterilization. Through the 1990s, formal State-sponsored programs in Mexico used tactics of intimidation and threats of being cut off from social programs to

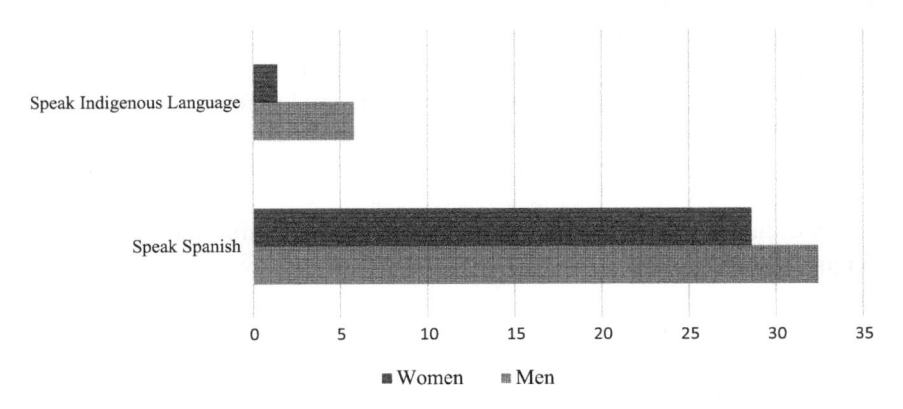

FIGURE 4.4 Percent of Indigenous Peoples in the Paid Labor Force with Access to Healthcare by Gender based on Language, 2000.
Source: INMUJERES, 2000.

get indigenous women to agree to be sterilized whenever they sought reproductive care from the State (Schell, 2014). Although these are no longer the official policies of the Mexican State, a government report from 2013 found that 27% of indigenous women seeking public health services were victims of sterilization without their consent (Wilton, 2018), and the complaints of forced sterilization continue. In 2017, the case of one indigenous woman, Alma, gained notoriety when she revealed that during a two-day hospital stay following the birth of her child, she was harassed and threatened by six different doctors and nurses who sought to sterilize her and who told her she would not be allowed to leave the hospital until she consented to the surgery (Piña & Rodriguez, 2017). In another notable case, Adriana Manzanares faced a series of unjust punishments after becoming pregnant and suffering a miscarriage. She was accused of adultery with no consideration for the fact that her husband had migrated out of Mexico, and she was accused of having an abortion. These accusations were presented by her father to the communitarian assembly, and she was publicly shamed. She was also tried by the State, and throughout the proceedings she was not provided a translator. She spent seven years in prison, before being released following a National Supreme Court decision which ruled that her procedural rights had been violated (Lucio Maymon, 2017).

The Absence of Indigenous Women's Voices on Development

With respect to development and the use of lands and natural resources, indigenous peoples have the right under international law to Free, Prior and Informed Consent (FPIC). Under the International Labor Organization's (ILO) Convention 169 and UN Declaration of the Rights of Indigenous People (UNDRIP), governments have an affirmative duty to consult with indigenous peoples who will be affected by development projects. Roads, hydroelectric plants, mining, and other extractive industry activities all disproportionately benefit the State and the formal economy, and have a correspondingly negative impact on indigenous peoples. The devastating impacts are tangible and psychological, and include displacement from ancestral lands, contamination of drinking water, destruction of habitat for the fish and wildlife upon which indigenous peoples rely.

According to a 2013 opinion of the UN High Commissioner for Human Rights, the component terms of FPIC are defined as follows:

- *Free* implies that there is no coercion, intimidation, or manipulation.
- *Prior* implies that consent is to be sought sufficiently in advance of any authorization or commencement of activities, and respect is shown to time requirements of indigenous consultation/consensus processes.
- *Informed* implies that information is provided that covers a range of aspects, including the nature, size, pace, reversibility, and scope of any proposed

project or activity; the purpose of the project as well as its duration; locality and areas affected; a preliminary assessment of the likely economic, social, cultural, and environmental impact, including potential risks; personnel likely to be involved in the execution of the project; and procedures the project may entail.

- *Consent* includes consultation and participation. This process may include the option of withholding consent (UNHCR, 2013).

Mexico, like most countries, has regularly come up short with respect to all components of FPIC, pressuring indigenous peoples to approve projects, beginning the consultation late in the process after approvals have been granted and work has begun and with a very short time for response, and providing incomplete or highly technical information in written documents only produced in Spanish. Indigenous women, who are more likely than their male counterparts to lack higher education and Spanish language ability, are most excluded from FPIC processes and thus are least likely to have their interests considered or their consent secured before development projects further jeopardize their well-being.

When Individual and Collective Rights Collide Indigenous Women Lose

To add insult to injury, in some cases the individual rights of women and the collective rights of indigenous peoples are in direct conflict, or the federal government's interests in protecting the rights of all individuals are in conflict with the rights of states and municipalities, including indigenous communities, to establish their own policies. The all-too-frequent result is that indigenous women are the ones who suffer. For example, the collective right of indigenous peoples to self-determination and autonomy may result in restricted rights for women in cases in some parts of the country in which traditional indigenous governance is by men only and women are not afforded the right to vote. Similarly, collective rights of indigenous peoples allow for institutionalization and perpetuation of excluding women from having rights to land.

The tension among indigenous collective rights and women's individual rights has created what Sieder (2016) calls "new legal hybrids." That is, state law and community law are not "fixed or static entities" (Sieder, 2015, p. 1129). Indigenous women in Mexico are fighting at both ends, they

> have mobilized to demand recognition of their collective rights as peoples, challenging the racism implicit in universalist frameworks and discourses. At the same time, many have worked tirelessly to challenge and transform their communal institutions and practices to ensure greater gender justice.
>
> *(Sieder, 2016, p. 1135)*

Lopez Cruz (2008) describes the multiple ways in which indigenous traditions and cultural practices (*usos y costumbres*) impede the rights for indigenous women. Among the most problematic practices are those related to (1) an asymmetric division of labor; (2) discriminatory practices which favor men in education, decision-making positions, and access to land; (3) arranged marriages; and (4) social and family tolerance of violence against women. On top of these traditional practices, the neoliberal model embraced by Mexico in the modern era has further burdened indigenous women.

A Promising Government Initiative: New Laws, New Organizations, and Indigenous Women's Houses

While the descriptions in each of the four areas discussed above suggest that the scale of the problem is daunting, there is some evidence of progress. Because some inequities are grounded in discriminatory laws, reversing prior and current inequities on the part of government often begins with adoption of new laws. Mexico has signed on to and ratified nearly every relevant international agreement on issues of general human rights,[4] the rights of women,[5] and the rights of indigenous peoples[6] that have been adopted by the UN, as well as the regional conventions of the Organization of American States (OAS),[7] and has generally been among the first countries to do so. Mexico signed the UN's CEDAW in 1980; ratified the International Labor Organization's Convention 169 Concerning Indigenous and Tribal Peoples in Independent Countries (ILO 169) in 1990, and was a leading actor in promoting the adoption of the UN-DRIP in 2007 and the American Declaration on the Rights of Indigenous Peoples in 2016. These international commitments reflect broad statements of support for equal rights, and they represent an important first step to acknowledging a responsibility to include indigenous women, but they do not directly confront the embedded nervousness.

Key elements of these international agreements are reflected in domestic policy statements, although for many years these policies have lacked adequate mechanisms for implementation or have failed to address explicitly the implications for indigenous women (Lucio Maymon, 2017). For example, the Mexican Constitution was amended in 1992 to state that Mexico is a pluricultural state, however that has not resulted in changes to mainstream cultural and language practices. The Constitution was amended again in 2001, this time to recognize "rights to self-determination, autonomy, and self-governance" of indigenous peoples and to recognize their right to have their own authorities "in accordance with their traditions and customs." Yet, as noted above, in several parts of the country this provision provides constitutional legitimacy to practices which place political and economic power in the hands of indigenous men at the expense of indigenous women. There was some effort to counteract this impact through a provision which states that indigenous peoples are able to "apply their own standards in regulation and solution of their internal conflicts, subject to the general principles of the Constitution, respecting individual guarantees, human rights, and, in a relevant manner, the dignity and completeness of women," and to

> elect, in accordance with their traditional standards, procedures, and practices, authorities or representatives for the exercise of their own forms of internal government, guaranteeing the participation of women in conditions of equality to those of men, in a way that respects the Federal Pact and the sovereignty of the states.

Recognizing that this provision was not adequately protecting the rights of women, in 2015, Article 2 of the Constitution was amended again to explicitly declare a woman's right to vote and hold public office.[8]

Below the level of the Constitution, the Mexican national government has enacted legislation and created organizations to promote gender equality and/or indigenous peoples' rights. A flurry of activity occurred in Mexican politics in 2003, with adoption of the following: the General Law on the Linguistic Rights of Indigenous Peoples which recognizes the indigenous languages as national languages valid for any public matter; the Law on the National Commission for the Development of Indigenous Peoples to promote, monitor, and evaluate all the programs, projects, and policies regarding indigenous peoples; the Federal Law to Prevent and Eliminate Discrimination which established affirmative action policies for vulnerable populations, including indigenous peoples. In 2010, a series of education reforms strengthened the commitment to bilingual education, requiring teachers in indigenous regions to certify that they have bilingual credentials, and sponsoring the production of bilingual education materials. In 2013, the then-newly elected government of the Institutional Revolutionary Party (PRI) included in its NDP 2013–2018 a Special Program for indigenous peoples. One of the strategies of the NDP was the promotion of the social and economic development of the indigenous peoples, fostering their participation in planning for their own development. The Special Program for indigenous peoples specifically recognized that the right to prior consultation (as part of FPIC) has not been fully implemented in Mexico and called for its active implementation (Global Americans, 2017).

Among the public sector organizations established by these and other laws, none are defined by their focus on indigenous women. Instead, we must look for how indigenous women's rights are addressed within the Mexican federal government in four distinct types of agencies, namely those responsible for general human rights, indigenous rights, women's rights, and substantive policy areas. Within the two agencies that address broader issues of human rights and non-discrimination, the National Commission of Human Rights (*Comisión Nacional de los Derechos Humanos* or CNDH)[9] and the National Council to

Prevent Discrimination (Consejo Nacional Para Prevenir la Discriminación or CONAPRED),[10] there are separate units and activities focused on women's equality and on indigenous peoples and communities. Within the National Commission for the Development of Indigenous Peoples (*Comisión Nacional para el Desarrollo de los Pueblos Indígenas* or CDI) and its successor the National Institute for Indigenous Peoples (*Instituto Nacional de los Pueblos Indígenas* or INPI)—which, from 2003 to 2018, and since 2019, respectively, have had overarching responsibility for defining, regulating, designing, establishing, guiding, coordinating, monitoring, and evaluating policies, programs, projects, strategies to guarantee the exercise and implementation of the rights of indigenous and Afro-Mexican peoples—there are programs explicitly focused on women.[11] Within Mexico's agency dedicated to protecting the rights of women, the National Institute for Women (Instituto Nacional de las Mujeres or INMUJERES), there is programing focused on rural and indigenous women.[12] Additionally, within a wide of government agencies at the level of cabinet departments and below, there are specific programs focused on indigenous women. And, finally, at the subnational level, some Mexican states and municipalities acknowledge and address the circumstances facing indigenous women.

The list of entities and policies is impressive, until one realizes that they suffer from chronic lack of sufficient financial or staff resources or strength of leadership. For example, the NDP of 2013–2018 was the first to mainstream gender equality and the corresponding National Gender Equality Policy covering the same five-year period focused on substantive equality within the Mexican federal budget. This included a 157% increase of federal funding in 2015 for equality issues, however, still it makes up only 0.05 of the entire budget (UN Women, n.d.).

The absence of an agency dedicated explicitly to indigenous women's rights may be interpreted to reflect lack of commitment; alternatively, it may reflect a deliberate strategy of addressing the issue throughout all agencies rather than compartmentalizing it. In either case, in a 2018 report based on her visit to Mexico in 2017, Victoria Tauli-Corpuz, UN Special Rapporteur on the Rights of Indigenous Peoples, still characterized the Mexican government's efforts and institutions as weak and called attention to continued inequities for indigenous women (UN Special Rapporteur, 2018). Despite this critical assessment, there are some promising signs of efforts and progress.

Several national government programs initiated by the CDI and now being continued by its successor INPI or are worthy of greater attention. These programs address issues of violence, sexual and reproductive rights, political participation, the criminal justice system, education, and language. CDI/INPI programs in each one of these areas make an important contribution to addressing inequities, but it is together that they demonstrate a commitment to change and the potential to reduce inequities and improve the lives of indigenous women. Here we provide a brief description of each of these initiatives;

in subsequent sections we assess their effectiveness and evidence of progress in addressing the targeted inequities in this nervous area of government.

A signature program of CDI and INPI are its Indigenous Women's Houses (*Casas de la Mujer Indígena* or CAMI). The CAMI are physical spaces comprised completely of indigenous women who are trained to provide specialized support to other indigenous women. The main activities developed by the CAMI are trainings to increase awareness on indigenous women's rights to live free of violence and to have sexual and reproductive freedoms. In some CAMI locations traditional midwifery services are provided as well.

A second set of programs focus on the providing indigenous women with culturally sensitive assistance in the legal processes surrounding cases of violence or sexual and reproductive rights. The CDI coordinated (and now INPI continues to fund) projects to help gather data, raise awareness, and change behaviors. Indigenous people in Mexico, including indigenous women, have been incarcerated at disproportionate rates, often for exercising their rights or simply because no one was available to defend them who spoke their indigenous language. As such, CDI/INPI have developed a series of programs intended to secure the release of wrongly convicted indigenous individuals; to help provide bilingual indigenous training to existing criminal lawyers; and to build the capacity of indigenous lawyers in criminal, agrarian, and human rights law.

Recognizing that a key to long-term equality is the full participation of indigenous women in policy-making positions in government, a third set of programs promote capacity building for indigenous women leaders to encourage greater political participation and understanding of their rights. In this case, the government does not deliver the services directly, but rather provides funding to civil society organizations and higher education institutions to train indigenous women regarding electoral processes, campaigning, and effective advocacy on the policy issues that the women have identified as priorities. Similarly, while the capacity building programs focus on adult indigenous women, another set of programs target indigenous girls and are intended to provide the conditions necessary for educational parity with boys and advancement. These programs offer scholarships for indigenous girls, as well as food and lodging when the girls must travel long distances from their homes to attend school.

Finally, a set of programs exists to preserve indigenous languages and cultural traditions surrounding health practices, and to provide housing and health services to indigenous women in the most rural and poverty-stricken areas of Mexico. These programs support the construction of housing, and construction and equipping of rural medical units able to provide obstetric care.

Assessment and Evidence of Progress

Adopting national laws or agreeing to international conventions which prohibit discrimination toward women and toward indigenous people has proved to be a necessary but insufficient approach to addressing the structural inequities for indigenous women. While institutional provisions have been outlined for indigenous and indigenous women, the evidence shows "that progress in building institutions, embracing international norms, and (in the case of Mexico) affirmative action policies do not translate into less severe exclusion for indigenous peoples" (UN Women, n.d.). This situation has been characterized as a "massive implementation gap" (Global Americans, 2017). Indigenous women continue to face disproportionate levels of violence, poverty, unemployment, and abuse of human rights. Given that institutionalized nature of the inequities, it may be unrealistic to expect that programs which have begun in earnest only within the last two decades could have made much progress.

In assessing Mexico's progress in reducing inequities for indigenous women and confronting nervousness, we first examine quantifiable inputs, outputs, and outcomes. The input and output measures suggest a strong commitment to change as reflected in the number of programs offered and the number of women served. The outcome measures are less dramatic as deep inequities continue. Another way to consider progress is in terms of the four criteria developed by the National Academy of Public Administration's Standing Panel on Social Equity, addressing (1) procedural fairness and due process, (2) levels of access to services, (3) quality of services delivered, and (4) outcomes or impact as measured by equality of accomplishments across groups (as cited in Gooden, 2014, pp. 14–15). When we move beyond the easily measured criteria and look more closely at the underlying aspects of nervousness, there is some indication that Mexico is taking initial steps and clear evidence that a great deal of work remains to be done. Here we critique the extent to which the Mexican government has fostered meaningful dialogue or "race talk" or apologized for the State's role in historical and continued inequities.

More Programs Reaching More Indigenous Women

By a simple measure of the number of programs and the number of indigenous women served, the Mexican government is making great strides in addressing issues facing this population. As of the end of 2017, there were 31 CAMI, up from 18 in 2016, and these were spread across the 16 states with the largest concentrations of indigenous peoples.[13] Figure 4.5 traces this growth from their inception through 2017.

These CAMI served 95,717 indigenous persons, of whom 75,189 were women. In 2017 alone, 10,548 women were served. Between January 2013 and December 2017, the CDI provided support for 371 projects to assess the level of violence against women, prevent the spread of HIV/AIDS, strengthen reproductive rights, and help develop new definitions of masculinity that maintain cultural respect and the rights of women. Over the same five-year period, 259,052 indigenous people have participated in these programs, of whom

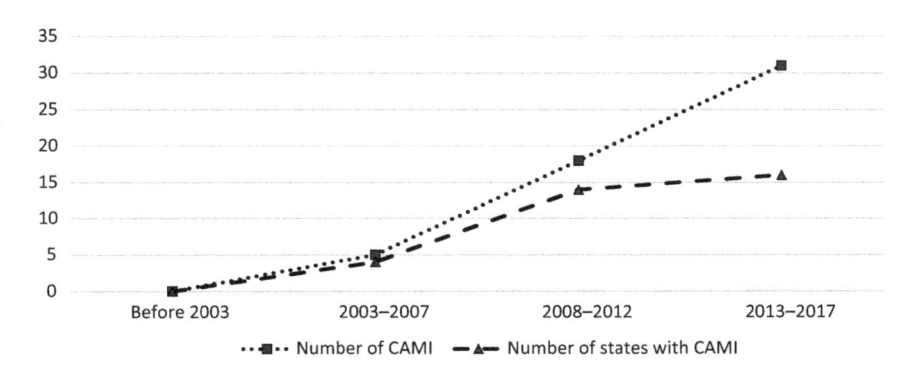

FIGURE 4.5 Increase in Number of Indigenous Women's Houses (CAMI) and their Geographic Dispersion across the Mexican States with the Largest Indigenous Populations, 2003–2017.

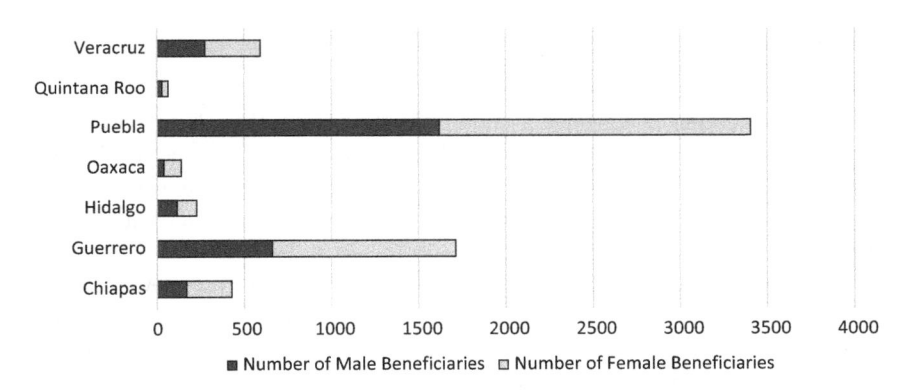

FIGURE 4.6 Beneficiaries, by Gender and State, of Programs Designed to Strengthen the Exercise of Rights with Respect to Human Trafficking, 2017.
Source: CDI, 2018.

190,293 have been women. In 2017 alone, 13,528 indigenous people from 18 states, including 10,804 women, took part in these projects (CDI, 2017b).

In recognition of the severity of the human trafficking problem for indigenous women, the seven states with the highest indigenous populations have been targeted for programs designed to improve understanding of legal rights in this area. Figure 4.6 illustrates that the majority of the beneficiaries of these programs, which involve investments ranging from $125,000 to nearly $800,000 Mexican Pesos in 2017, were women.

Since 2013, when a new program was established, a growing number of women have been trained as interpreters/translators to help in legal proceedings for indigenous persons accused of crimes and they constitute a larger percentage of the total. In 2013, 117 women were trained, representing 20% of the

578 indigenous people to receive the training; by 2017, the number of indigenous women trained in these programs increased to 483 of 1575, representing 31% of the total (CDI, 2017b). With respect to training and capacity building on political rights, the CDI hosted six regional forums on the "Rights of Indigenous Women" (*Los Derechos de las Mujeres Indigenas*), a meeting for indigenous women on "Leadership and Gender" (*Liderazgo y Género*), and a forum designed to increase the participation of indigenous women called "Agenda Building" (*Construyendo Agenda*). Through these programs 1,159 indigenous women were trained in the exercise of their political rights (CDI, 2017b).

While not yet producing measurable changes in outcomes or equality of accomplishments, these programs represent improvements to procedural, access, and quality aspects of equity. A key to knowing if and when programs have had an impact is to have good data and a clear objective, and Mexico is making progress here as well.

Better Data, Clearer Goals

Another indicator of progress is the systematic collection and reporting of data, and the articulation of long-term and comprehensive, rather than short-term or piecemeal, goals and approaches. In the short time since it was established in March 2019, INPI has produced several reports which represent increased commitment and attention to indigenous issues. Two in particular merit attention, one focused on the present and the other on the future.

The first document is a comprehensive report of Government Actions for the Integral Development of Indigenous Peoples (INPI, 2018). This report of nearly 200 pages gathers in one place descriptions of all programs contributing of the Mexican national government which seek to advance indigenous peoples' rights. This report is particularly attentive to providing examples of equity improvements in terms of access, process, and quality of services. In addition to summarizing programs and accomplishments of INPI itself, the report summarizes the relevant activities of eight cabinet departments (*secretarías*), three national institutes, and another national system, as well as government programs at the subnational level in each of the Mexican states. With respect to indigenous women, the report presents both promising and troubling information. For many of the government agencies, the report describes programs that are responding to the particular needs of indigenous women, most notably those focused on the Economy (*Secretaría de Economía* or SE), Health (*Secretaria de Salud* or SALUD), and Welfare (*Secretaría de Bienestar* or BIENSTAR), among others, there are either programs targeting indigenous women or at least the collection of data to document and call attention to the status of indigenous women.

At the same time, reference to indigenous women is noticeably absent from some of the government organizations altogether or data is provided on indigenous women as recipients of departmental services, but none of the supporting narrative suggests an understanding of or deliberate effort to be responsive to their needs. These include the departments of Agriculture and Rural Development (*Secretaría de Agricultura y Desarrollo Rural* or SADER), Communication and Transportation (*Secretaía de Comunicaciones y Transporte* or SCT), Work and Social Welfare (*Secretaría de Trabajo y Prevision Social* or STPS), and Public Education (*Secretaría de Educación Pública* or SEP). A similar pattern occurs at the subnational level, with the report documenting that some Mexican states are directing considerable attention to indigenous women, while others are giving cursory attention to their needs, and still others make no mention whatsoever.

The second INPI product which helps assess Mexico's progress in addressing inequities for indigenous women is the National Program for Indigenous Peoples, 2018–2024 (INPI, n.d.). This document establishes goals for a 25-year timeline, suggesting a long-term commitment on the part of the Mexican government which will be necessary to address such a deeply rooted problem. The National Program is grounded in and makes reference to relevant provisions of the Mexican Constitution and international law, as well as the enabling legislation of INPI and statements from current President López Obrador. The Program outlines 7 guiding principles, 9 specific objectives, 38 strategies, and 110 lines of action. Equality for indigenous women and protection of their rights are addressed as one of the guiding principles, one of the specific objectives, four of the strategies, and six of the lines of action.[14] As a guide for the coming quarter century, the Program prioritizes incorporating the participation and perspectives of indigenous women in regional development plans; promoting their rights; promoting dialogue and providing support to strengthen their participation and representation; and strengthening organizational processes to protect and respond to violence against indigenous women, to strengthen the CAMI, and to promote communal justice processes for indigenous women.

Elevating Indigenous Issues at the Expense of Indigenous Women's Issues

While much of what INPI is doing represents a positive trajectory toward greater equity for indigenous people, this may exacerbate problems for indigenous women. Across multiple years' annual reports of CDI and the initial report from INPI, the priorities have not included indigenous women's rights. In the most recent 2018 report from INPI, the four priority areas include the following: (1) indigenous rights, (2) indigenous infrastructure, (3) improvement of indigenous production and productivity, and (4) support for indigenous education. Noticeably absent from the list is any reference to indigenous women. The gender-focused programs of CAMI and others discussed earlier are positioned largely within indigenous rights writ large.

Also worthy of note in the CDI and INPI annual reports, while programming for indigenous women is featured within the priority of indigenous rights, the language used in the section on indigenous education is less inclusive. The discussion of indigenous education programs focuses on broad access for children which, following traditional Spanish language rules applies the male gender form of the noun, *niños*, as the generic label, thereby omitting any explicit attention to girls' education.

Beyond this there continues to be a tension between the individual rights of indigenous women and the collective rights of indigenous peoples. What Sieder (2016) has found through examining three cases, Mexican

> state authorities intervene selectively against indigenous authorities to champion universal human rights when it is to their political advantage, yet policies of economic development and security promoted by the federal and state governments violate indigenous peoples' fundamental rights and expose indigenous women to greater harm.
>
> *(Sieder, 2016, p. 1149)*

What is lacking are "more nuanced interpretations that situate conflicts surrounding legal pluralism and gender within the broader political and socioeconomic context of relations between indigenous peoples, private interests, and the state-relations that are characterized by racism, violence, and dispossession" (Sieder, 2016, p. 1149).

First Steps in Political Participation: Still a Long Road Ahead

Among the greatest challenges still existing for indigenous women are the barriers to full political participation. Women in Mexico were granted the right to vote in 1947; however, this right has yet to be fully realized by indigenous women and indigenous women are still few and far between in elective office (Worthen, 2015). As of the end of 2015, only 11% of the predominantly indigenous villages in the state of Oaxaca, Mexico, had a woman serving in an official capacity at the municipal level (Worthen, 2015).

Having indigenous women in elective office at all levels in Mexico is important not only for the symbolic representation it would provide, but also for the issues and perspectives they would bring to the policy arena. The 5 members of the 500-seat Mexican Congress who self-identify as indigenous have been responsible for introducing 23 bills related to indigenous issues during their terms (Global Americans, 2017). Among the topics of these bills have been indigenous culture (8 bills), language (6), political representation (3), justice and rights (3), economic development (2), and census (1). More directly relevant to this chapter, the 2014 constitutional amendments guaranteeing indigenous women equal participation in electoral processes were initiated by a Zapotec indigenous woman, Eufrosina Cruz Mendoza, a member of the Federal Chamber of Deputies (Antara, 2015).

One of the challenges to political participation for indigenous women is a debate across individual rights versus collective rights. That is, at the local level, gender equality via legal pluralism required by Mexican law is in tension with indigenous customary law, which is also protected by Mexican law. Beginning in 2016 municipalities in Oaxaca, the Mexican state with the largest number of indigenous people was required to include women and present female candidates within communal governing systems. In some respects, this can be considered a positive action resulting in increased participation by indigenous women. However, many women object on the basis that this requirement does not respect indigenous traditions (Global Americans, 2017), and it reinforces the gendered devaluation of the work that women fulfill within their homes (Worthen, 2015). In contrast to state systems which enfranchise individuals upon attaining a predetermined age, according to indigenous traditions, the right to participate in village elections and hold public office is reserved to those who demonstrate "active citizenship" through service and collective work, but the work that women traditionally perform is not counted (Worthen, 2015). Within indigenous systems, customary traditions (*usos y costumbres*) characterize communal political leadership as voluntary and without a salary. With mandatory participation, indigenous women carry a double burden of being required to perform multiple unpaid tasks involving work for the community and also in the home (Global Americans, 2017).

The candidacy of María de Jesús Patricio Martínez in the 2018 presidential election was path-breaking not only for being the first time an indigenous woman ran for president in Mexico, but also because her campaign deliberately brought these issues and challenges faced by indigenous women into the national discourse that generally are not discussed. In an interview with *The Guardian*, Patricio acknowledged that she had no expectations of winning, stating that "we're not going for votes"; rather her stated objective was "to highlight the problems that those of us at the bottom are experiencing" (Tucker, 2017).

Beyond the Measures: Deeper and More Difficult Challenges to Conflict

With respect to inequities facing indigenous women, the Mexican government has demonstrated some signs of progress according to input and output measures, and according to the criteria of procedural equity, equity of access to services, and equity in quality of services. In terms of results, accomplishments, or equity of outcomes, the consequences of such long-standing inequities have yet to be overcome. This may simply be a matter of time and with patience the programs may generate more dramatic results. Alternatively, real progress in outcomes may require confronting nervousness on a deeper level, through race talk and through public apology.

Where Is the Race Talk at the Individual or Organizational Level?

In discussing race and social equity within the United States context, Gooden (2014) emphasizes the value and necessity of talking about and through individual nervousness. She outlines a continuum of individual level race talk strategies which range from Conversation Avoidance at one extreme to a Multicultural Mosaic at the other. Largely absent from the multitude of policies and programs which comprise the Mexican government's approach to reducing inequities for indigenous women are any which encourage public administrators' dialogue to move past individual nervousness.

Across public organizations in Mexico, there has been an increase in the collection and reporting of data documenting the disadvantaged status of indigenous women, but there has been little formal of what Gooden (2014) refers to as naming, blaming, or claiming to identify, acknowledge, and replace specific organizational policies, practices, or actions which contribute to these inequities. Citing Woodilla's (1998) observations about the importance of conversations within organizations as a means to develop shared meanings and to illuminate contested meanings, Gooden advises that race talk at an individual level and actions taken by organizations need to occur in parallel if they are to fully address nervousness. One promising sign for the future is that INPI's National Program for Indigenous Peoples, 2018–2024, prioritizes "promoting dialogue" as one of the means of strengthening indigenous women's participation and representation.

Acknowledging and Apologizing for the Past

Efforts to remedy current inequities without acknowledging and apologizing for actions of the past may be perceived of as insufficient by the victim groups and can be a barrier to fully addressing nervousness. Formal and public apologies from government to accept responsibility for past injustices, acknowledge the lingering effects, and to formally state an intention to correct past wrongs can be powerful tools. Governments sometimes acknowledge the legacies of past oppression as contributing factors in current discrimination, but they are reluctant "to affirm direct apologies or reparations as remedies" (Myers, Lange & Corrie, 2003, p. 333).

Whether or not apologies include offers of reparations or restitution, they can still help address nervousness. When governments accept responsibility or place it on state actors, it can help to alleviate the tendency—on the part of society as a whole and the victims themselves—to blame the victims for their circumstances (Lerner, 1980, as cited by Gooden, 2014).

The Mexican government's actions in this area are inconsistent. Earlier in this chapter we shared the story of two women who were raped by Mexican army soldiers; denied justice for eight years by the Mexican judicial system; and then finally, Ines Fernandez Ortega and Valentina Rosendo Cantu had their cases decided by the Inter-American Court of Human Rights which declared their rapes a violation of the collective rights of the indigenous tribe to which they belonged. Following the decision, in two separate events in December 2011 and March 2012, the then-Interior Minister Alejandro Poiré Romero publicly apologized to both women and accepted the responsibility of the Mexican State for the violations they had suffered (Sieder, 2016, p. 1145). More recently, however, when a recording of a phone conversation was released of Lorenzo Cordova, the then-Director of Mexico's National Electoral Institute (*Instituto Nacional Electoral* or INE) mocking indigenous peoples and the families of the 43 disappeared indigenous students, his forced apology fell well short of authenticity. His statement of "I offer a frank apology if I offended anyone with my comments" (Telesur, 2015) failed to acknowledge how his actions perpetuate inequities or his responsibility as a public administrator to uphold the value of equity.

While not having offered an apology on behalf of the Mexican government, Mexico's President López Obrador in 2019 asked that Pope Francis and King Felipe VI of Spain apologize to Mexico's indigenous peoples for the human rights abuses suffered by their ancestors 500 years ago at the hands of the Catholic Church and Spanish conquistadors (Sieff, 2019). In fact, Pope Francis had issued somewhat of an apology as part of a speech he delivered in February 2016 in San Cristobal de las Casas, an indigenous community in the southern Mexico state of Chiapas. He said,

> On many occasions, in a systematic and organized way, your people have been misunderstood and excluded from society ... Some have considered your values, cultures, and traditions inferior. Others, dizzy with power, money, and the laws of the market, have stripped you of your lands and then contaminated them. How sad this is ... How worthwhile it would be for each of us to examine our conscience and learn to say, 'Forgive me!' ... Sorry brothers.
>
> *(McCauley, 2016)*

While López Obrador's request received immediate backlash by Spanish politicians in particular, it also demonstrates the sensitivity, and by extension, the importance of having an historical dialogue (Minder & Malkin, 2019). While the request for an apology did not explicitly reference the abuses suffered by indigenous women, it nonetheless represents attention to the historical roots of one aspect of the problem. As Maria de Jesus Patricio Martinez described the situation during her run for the presidency of Mexico, "We have to tear up the roots of what's hurting Mexico. This country needs healing" (Tucker, 2017). In other words, as an indigenous woman Patricio recognizes that Mexico needs to confront its nervousness regarding indigenous women.

Conclusion

If we measure the effectiveness of Mexico's government in confronting nervousness in terms of policies and programs for and participation by indigenous women, the results suggest considerable success. If the standard is demonstrable reductions in inequities, the results are less satisfactory but still somewhat encouraging. If, on the other hand, we look for deeper reflection and dialogue regarding internal organizational policies and societal norms that foster inequities, recognition of the State's historical and continued role in perpetuating inequities, or a sincere apology, there is less progress. The majority of programs featured in this chapter which seek to improve the situation of indigenous women are located within government organizations targeted explicitly to indigenous peoples or explicitly to women. While the programs are helping indigenous women individually and collectively, they are not forcing indigenous men, let alone the entire non-indigenous population of Mexico and the multitude of federal government agencies which do not have an indigenous-focused mandate, to confront their stereotypical beliefs and their deep-seated and long-standing nervousness, and their engrained policies, practices, and procedures which maintain the status quo.

The nervousness surrounding indigenous women is long-standing and well-established, and it will take time to address. The new organizations, programs, and policies are necessary but may be insufficient to achieve dramatic results. It remains to be seen if the current momentum can be maintained or accelerated over time, but it seems that little by little (*poco a poco*) Mexico is chipping away at the problem. In 2017, the then-President Enrique Peña Nieto brought attention to gender as a nervous area of government in 2017 when he called for changes to practices grounded in traditional Mexican values of machismo that continue to victimize women. Much in the same way, President López Obrador is bringing attention to indigenous status as a nervous area of government in 2019 as "the first modern Mexican president who has worked directly with people in the indigenous communities" (Minder & Malkin, 2019). While some have criticized the President's attention to indigenous communities as a "stunt" or an effort "divert attention" from Mexico's economic slowdown and widespread gang violence (Minder & Malkin, 2019), he nonetheless is increasing the country's attention to this traditional area of nervousness. Mexico is yet to have a President who focuses explicitly on indigenous women, but having an indigenous woman candidate for president and a range of policies and programs disbursed throughout many public sector organizations represent important steps.

Notes

1 Maria de Jesus Patricio Martinez, known more commonly as Marichuy, was nominated by the National Indigenous Congress (CNI), a coalition of 58 indigenous groups. Although she did not garner sufficient signatures to be on the ballot, her efforts are expected to encourage more indigenous women to engage in to seek office.
2 *Maquiladoras* are factories in Mexico, often located near the United States-Mexico border and owned by foreign for-profit companies.
3 See other seminal cases involving indigenous women: Adriana Manzanares, Eufrosina Cruz Mendoza, Nestora Salagado Garcia and Jacinta Francisco, Teresa Gonzalez and Alberta Alcantara as cited in Sieder (2016).
4 Including the Universal Declaration of Human Rights (1948); Convention on the Prevention and Punishment of the Crime of Genocide (1948); International Covenant on Civil and Political Rights (1966); International Covenant on Economic, Social and Cultural Rights (1966); International Convention on the Elimination of All Forms of Racial Discrimination (1966); and Convention on the Rights of the Child (1989); among others.
5 Including the Convention on the Elimination of All Forms of Discrimination against Women (1979) and Optional Protocol to the Convention on the Elimination of All Forms of Discrimination against Women (1999).
6 These include the International Labor Organization's (ILO) Convention 169 Concerning Indigenous and Tribal Peoples in Independent Countries (1989), Agreement establishing the Fund for the Development of the Indigenous Peoples of Latin America and the Caribbean (1992), and the Declaration of Rights of Indigenous Peoples (2007).
7 Specifically, the American Convention on Human Rights (1969) and American Declaration on the Rights of Indigenous Peoples (2016).
8 Constitución Política de los Estados Unidos Mexicanos [Constitution, as amended, Diario Oficial de la Federación [D.O.], Art.2, May 22 2015.
9 See: http://www.cndh.org.mx/.
10 See: https://www.conapred.org.mx/.
11 See: https://www.gob.mx/inpi.
12 See: https://www.gob.mx/inmujeres.
13 Mexico is divided into 31 states plus the Federal District.
14 It should be noted that throughout the *Program* most discussions of gender equality refer to both indigenous and Afro-Mexican women, but for the purposes of this case study we focused solely on indigenous women.

References

Antara, L. (2015, March 5). *Overcoming Political Exclusion of Indigenous Women in Mexico*. Institute for Democracy & Electoral Assistance, https://www.idea.int/news-media/news/overcoming-political-exclusion-indigenous-women-mexico%C2%A0

Argren, D. (2018, December 21). We Can Do It': Yalitza Aparicio's Vogue Cover Hailed by Indigenous Women. *The Guardian*, https://www.theguardian.com/film/2018/dec/21/yalitza-aparicio-vogue-mexico-cover-roma-indigenous

Bilmes, M. (1992). Macho and Shame. *International Forum of Psychoanalysis*, 1 (3–4), 163–168.

Binkowski, B. (2017, June 26). Mexico's Epidemic of Missing and Murdered Women. *The Globe and Mail.* https://www.theglobeandmail.com/news/world/mexicos-epidemic-of-missing-and-murdered-women/article25137141/

Coalición por la Salud de las Mujeres. (2007). *Salud Sexual y Reproductiva, Retos Legislativos*, http://coalicionxmujeres.fundar.org.mx

Coates, K.S. (2004). *A Global History of Indigenous Peoples: Struggle and Survival*, Basingstoke: Palgrave Macmillan.

Comisión Nacional para el Desarrollo de los Pueblos Indigenas (CDI). (2017a). *Indicadores Socioeconómicos de los Pueblos Indígenas de México, 2015*. Mexico. https://www.gob.mx/inpi/articulos/indicadores-socioeconomicos-de-los-pueblos-indigenas-de-mexico-2015-116128

Comisión Nacional para el Desarrollo de los Pueblos Indígenas (CDI). (2017b). *Acciones de Gobierno para el Desarrollo Integral de los Pueblos Indígenas*, Informe 2017, https://www.gob.mx/cms/uploads/attachment/file/412757/cdi_informe_2017.pdf

Committee on the Elimination of Discrimination against Women. (2018, July 6). *Committee on the Elimination of Discrimination against Women Reviews Report of Mexico*, https://www.ohchr.org/EN/NewsEvents/Pages/DisplayNews.aspx?NewsID=23344

Constitución Política de los Estados Unidos Mexicanos [Constitution, as amended, Diario Oficial de la Federación [D.O.], Art.2, August 14, 2001.

Constitución Política de los Estados Unidos Mexicanos [Constitution, as amended, Diario Oficial de la Federación [D.O.], Art.2, May 22, 2015.

Cross, G. (2019, March 17). *Empowering the Forgotten: Indigenous Women in Mexico. Center for Sharing*, http://www.centerforsharing.org/empowering-the-forgotten-indigenous-women-in-mexico/

Cultural Survival. (2018). *Observations on the State of Indigenous Women's Rights in Mexico*, Cambridge, MA, https://www.culturalsurvival.org/sites/default/files/CEDAW_Report_Mexico_2018.pdf

Gil, R.M. and Vazquez, C.I. (1996). *The Maria Paradox: How Latinas can Merge Old World Traditions with New World Self-esteem*. NY: G.P. Putnam.

Global Americans. (2017). *Indigenous Political Representation in Mexico*, https://theglobalamericans.org/2017/10/indigenous-political-representation-mexico/

Gobierno de la Republica. (2013). *Plan Nacional de Desarrollo 2013–2018*. Estados Unidos Mexicanos, https://observatorioplanificacion.cepal.org/sites/default/files/plan/files/MexicoPlanNacionaldeDesarrollo20132018.pdf

Gooden, S.T. (2014). *Race and Social Equity: A Nervous Area of Government*, New York: Routledge, a Division of Taylor & Francis.

Instituto Nacional de Estadística y Geografía (INEGI). (2011). *Principales resultados del Censo de Población y Vivienda 2010*, Mexico. https://www.inegi.org.mx/app/biblioteca/ficha.html?upc=702825002042 Instituto Nacional de las Mujeres (INMUJERES). (2016). *Las Mujeres Indígenas en México: Su Contexto Socioeconómico, Demográfico y de Salud*, Mexico, 2006, http://cedoc.inmujeres.gob.mx/documentos_download/100833.pdf

Instituto Nacional de los Pueblos Indígenas (INPI). (2018). *Acciones de Gobierno para el Desarrollo Integral de los Pueblos Indígenas, Informe 2018*, https://www.gob.mx/cms/uploads/attachment/file/461777/inpi-informe-2018.pdf

Instituto Nacional de los Pueblos Indígenas (INPI). (n.d.). *Programa Nacional de los Pueblos Indígenas, 2018–2024*, https://www.gob.mx/cms/uploads/attachment/file/423227/Programa-Nacional-de-los-Pueblos-Indigenas-2018-2024.pdf

Lakhani, N. (2015, April 4). Tenancingo: The Small Town at the Dark Heart of Mexico's Sex-Slave Trade. *The Guardian*, www.theguardian.com/world/2015/apr/05/tenancingo-mexico-sex-slavetrade-america

López Cruz, M. (2008). *Women within the Indigenous Peoples' Movement of Mexico: New Routes for Transforming Power.* Toronto, Ontario: Association for Women's Rights in Development. https://www.awid.org/sites/default/files/atoms/files/changing_their_world_-_women_within_the_indigenous_peoples_movement_of_mexico.pdf

Lucio Maymon, P. (2017). Systems Thinking for Policymaking: The Case of Indigenous Women's Rights in Mexico. *Cornell Policy Review*, http://www.cornellpolicyreview.com/indigenouswomensrightsinmexico/

Martínez Cobo, J.R. (1987). *Study of the Problem of Discrimination against Indigenous Populations*, New York: United Nations. Sub-commission on Prevention of Discrimination and Protection of Minorities.

Martinez Medrano, E.R. (2003). Discrimination against Indigenous Peoples in Mexico: Public Policies to Prevent and Reduce It. *Revista Voices*, 63, 19–22.

Mayo, Y. and Resnick, R. (1996). The Impact of *Machismo* on Hispanic Women. *Journal of Women & Social Work*, 11(3), 257.

McCauley, L. (2016, February 16). Pope Francis Apologizes to Mexican Indigenous for History of Pillage and Abuse. *Common Dreams*, https://www.commondreams.org/news/2016/02/16/pope-francis-apologizes-mexican-indigenous-history-pillage-and-abuse

Minder, R. and Malkin, (2019, March 27). Mexican Call for Conquest Apology Ruffles Feathers in Spain. And Mexico. *The New York Times*, https://www.nytimes.com/2019/03/27/world/americas/mexico-spain-apology.html

Minority Rights Group International. (n.d.). Case Study: Indigenous Women in Mexico, http://stories.minorityrights.org/lifeatthemargins/chapter/36/

Monroy, J. (2018, November 29). Special recognition by indigenous people a sign of confidence in new president. *El Economista*, https://www.eleconomista.com.mx/politica/Habitantes-de-pueblos-indigenas-haran-limpia-a-AMLO-y-le-entregaran-Baston-de-Mando-20181129-0084.html

Mosher, D.L. and Tomkins, S.S. (1988). Scripting the Macho Man: Hypermasculine Socialization and Enculturation. *The Journal of Sex Research*, 25(1), 60–84.

Myers, Jr., S. L., Lange, L. T., and Corrie, B. (2003). The Political Economy of Antiracisom Initiatives in the Post-Durban Round. *American Economic Review*, 93(2), 330–33.

Organisation for Economic Cooperation and Development (OECD). (2017) *The Pursuit of Gender Equality: An Uphill Battle. How Does Mexico Compare?* Paris: OECD Publishing.

Piña, G. and Rodriguez, A. (2017, August 20). Alma, una victima de esteralización forzada en Guerrero, https://lasillarota.com/estados/alma-una-victima-de-esterilizacion-forzada-en-guerrero/171218

Ramos, S. (1962). *Profile of Man and Culture in Mexico*, Austin: University of Texas Press.

Ruiz-Grossman, S. (2019, February 7). Yalitza Aparicio Of 'Roma' Speaks Out On Barriers Facing Indigenous Women. *Huffington Post*, https://www.huffpost.com/entry/yalitza-aparicio-roma-indigenous-women_n_5c5c9692e4b0a502ca339969

Schell, P. Mexico. February 24, 2014, http://eugenicsarchive.ca/discover/tree/530b9ee276f0db569b000016.

Segrest, S.L. (2003). Exploring the Role of *Machismo* in Gender Discrimination: A Comparison of Mexico and the U.S. *Equal Opportunities International*, 22(1), 13–31.

Sieder, R. (2016). Legal Pluralism and Indigenous Women's Rights in Mexico: The Ambiguities of Recognition. *New York University Journal of International Law and Politics*, 48, 1125-.

Sieff, K. (2019, March 26). Mexico's President Wants Spain to Apologize for the Conquistadors, Almost Exactly 500 Years Later. *The Washington Post*, https://www.washingtonpost.com/world/2019/03/26/mexicos-president-wants-spain-apologize-conquistadors-almost-exactly-years-later/?utm_term=.7ed40edfa30c

Stevens, E.P. (1973). Marianismo: The Other Dace of Machismo in Latin America. In A. Pescatello (Ed). *Female and Male in Latin America*, Pittsburgh, PA: University of Pittsburgh Press, 89–102.

Telesur, (2015, May 20). Video of Mexican Official Mocking Indigenous Peoples Goes Viral, https://mexicoinstituteonelections2015.wordpress.com/2015/05/20/video-of-mexican-official-mocking-indigenous-peoples-goes-viral/

Tillman, L. (2019, January 17). Yalitza Aparicio of 'Roma' and the Politics of Stardom in Mexico. *The New York Times*, https://www.nytimes.com/2019/01/17/movies/yalitza-aparicio-roma.html

Tucker, D. (2017, June 12). 'Mexico Needs Healing': The First Indigenous Woman to Run for President. *The Guardian*, https://www.theguardian.com/world/2017/jun/12/mexico-maria-de-jesus-patricio-martinez-indigenous-woman-president

United Nations Children's Fund (UNICEF). (n.d.). *Los pueblos indígenas en América Latina*, https://www.unicef.org/lac/pueblos_indigenas.pdf

United Nations Office of the High Commissioner for Human Rights (UNHCR). (2013). *Free, Prior and Informed Consent of Indigenous Peoples*, https://www.ohchr.org/Documents/Issues/IPeoples/FreePriorandInformedConsent.pdf

United Nations Human Rights Council. (2018) *Report of the Special Rapporteur on the rights of indigenous peoples on her visit to Mexico*. A/HRC/39/17/Add.2. 2018, http://ap.ohchr.org/documents/dpage_e.aspx?si=A/HRC/39/17/Add.2

UN Women. (n.d.). Mexico, http://lac.unwomen.org/en/donde-estamos/mexico

Velasco, E. (2013, June 24). De Cada 100 Mujeres Víctimas de Trata en México, 70 Son Indígenas: ONG. *La Jornada*, http://www.jornada.unam.mx/2013/06/24/politica/015n1pol

Villegas, P. (2017, April 23). Where Machismo Is Entrenched, Focus Moves to the Trenches. *The New York Times*. https://www.nytimes.com/2017/04/23/world/americas/where-machismo-is-entrenched-focus-moves-to-the-trenches.html

Wilton, J. (2013, February 18) Mexican Politics and Economy: Report Reveals Indigenous Women Sterilised without Consent. As cited by Cultural Survival (2018) *Observations on the State of Indigenous Women's Rights in Mexico*, Cambridge, MA, https://www.culturalsurvival.org/sites/default/files/CEDAW_Report_Mexico_2018.pdfWorld Bank. (2015). *Indigenous Latin America in the Twenty-First Century: The First Decade*, Washington, DC: International Bank for Reconstruction and Development, The World Bank.Worthen, H. (2015). Indigenous Women's Political Participation: Gendered Labor and Collective Rights Paradigms in Mexico. *Gender & Society*, 29(6), 914–936.

Worthen, H. (2015, December 8). Indigenous women's political participation in Mexico: Why Legislation Backfires. *Gender & Society Blog*, https://gendersociety.wordpress.com/2015/12/08/indigenous-womens-political-participation-in-mexico-why-legislation-backfires/

5

SEX AND NERVOUSNESS IN CYPRUS AND THE EU

Anna M. Agathangelou, Kalliopi Christoforou, and Sofia Georgiou

A Nervous Area of Government in Cyprus

Queer sexuality is a site of nervousness for the postcolonial state and capitalist systems whose organization of power and political ordering have depended on the fallacy of biological determinism and notions of reproductive capacity granting "absolute privilege" to "heteronormativity" while relegating queer or non-reproductive sexualities to the margins (Edelman 2004: 2). In such states and systems, queerness, or "the side of those not 'fighting for the children'" (Edelman 2004: 3) is "render[ed] unthinkable" (Edelman 2004: 2). Ultimately, the nervousness of the postcolonial state becomes inscribed on its queer subjects; queer self-making is characterized by opposition, overlapping, and sometimes collusion between queer liberalisms and authoritarian/fundamentalist nationalisms. When multiple iterations of liberalism and authoritarian nationalisms collide, it is important to acknowledge how such collisions can transform sexual equity questions and the lives of LGBTQI subjects "negatively" or "positively" or, more accurately, "materially." One space within which to probe these issues and examine the implications of the inscription of postcolonial state nervousness on queer subjects is Cyprus.

Cyprus is divided into two zones, the Republic of Cyprus (RoC) and the "Turkish Republic of Northern Cyprus" (TRNC).[1] Both are nervous about their possibility of reproduction and power within the global "family" of nations, but in this chapter, we discuss only the former except at moments when collaborations between non-governmental organizations (NGOs) on both sides challenge the material effects of dominant sexual discourses and material understandings of the ways queerness is inscribed in the heart of capitalism (Cozzarelli 2019). In 1998, the RoC passed a law decriminalizing homosexuality.[2]

In 2011, the first official LGBT organization, ACCEPT, was created and in 2014, the first Gay Pride march took place, with the assistance of Queer Cyprus, a non-profit organization in the Turkish Republic of Northern Cyprus. In its struggle to "modernize" and transition to neoliberal forms of accumulation (i.e., positing itself as a legitimate global power in the European Union (EU)), the RoC focuses on sexual liberation, bolstered by sexual and racial science to re-constitute its power and the EU order. Its goal is to manufacture the abstract entrepreneurial liberated sexually individual, in armies, schools, service jobs, crucially formative of neoliberal European ways of knowing and materially making dominant capitalist power.[3] In this emerging matrix of sexual contested knowledge-making and its polycentric materiality, the RoC finds itself at a crossroads.

Sexuality is the contested site of the making of this global power and the cause of the nervousness that emerges in its moments of transition. Either the postcolonial state (i.e., Cyprus) will play a pivotal role in making a certain bourgeois sexuality dominant, along with the rest of Europe, thereby sharing the global power of accumulation and exploitation regimes, or it will "lag" behind other European countries. The stakes of the argument are huge. Either we agree to responsibilize sexuality (i.e., a question of equality) or we work through how certain sexual formations are a result of the liquidation of certain lives, the neutralization of the lumpenproletariat in a Fanonian sense, and a result of political formations of violence before calling the property relations (i.e., equity) into question.

Faced with the EU's demands to change its approach to LGBT issues, the RoC has moved to transform colonial laws about sexuality and promote social equality and justice. It has also amended its Constitution to give supremacy to EU law.[4] More recently, it embraced ACCEPT, an advocacy group working to bring equality to the LGBTI community on the island. It has celebrated annual Pride marches by having major political leaders of all parties attend, along with some ex-politicians. At the same time, sexual equality has been contested by some political leaders, such as the former MP (Andreas Themistokleous) and dominant institutions like the state Church, and this has influenced public policy. The Church has declared homosexuality a problem, using strong language which can easily be regarded as hate speech. Discourses that reject homosexuality outright as a perversion and associate it with bestiality, necrophilia, and pedophilia[5] threaten to disrupt the modernity project of the secular state and reveal the material structures and the laws and policies that bolster such institutions and their contingent violences.

On the one hand, the RoC wants to become a legitimate global power in the EU, but on the other hand, it is reluctant to disconnect itself from colonial practices and laws of criminality of sexuality and the positions of the Church. This co-constitutes the state and the political order itself as a site of nervousness (Gooden 2014).

In this chapter we discuss how the state unmakes and makes its own power and identity by endorsing a pro-LGBTQI set of discourses, accepting the EU's desire for a unified Europe guided by certain values, norms, and beliefs. However, the state's nervous reaction interferes with its ability to envision a world beyond the dominant juridico-capitalist arrangements and their production. While it draws on the notion of sex as an important site of deliberation and distributive justice by attending to its LGBTQI community, it simultaneously jeopardizes notions of equity by not challenging the liberal and colonial notions of equality or problematic social division practices of power and terrorizing discourses. We conclude with ideas about the notion of nervousness within a neoliberal global order whose primary sorting mechanism is financial value. It is crucial to pay attention to the ways states leverage this idea, making sex the newest site of struggle, over the provision of public equity and justice in the name of the possibility of the state's reproduction of its power.

Why Sexual Equity Is a Nervous Area of Government in Post-Colonial States

> So they say that the natives want to go too quickly. Now, let us never forget that only a very short time ago they complained of their slowness, their laziness, and their fatalism. Already we see that violence used in specific ways at the moment of the struggle for freedom does not magically disappear after the ceremony of trooping the national colors. It has all the less reason for disappearing since the reconstruction of the nation continues within the framework of cutthroat competition between capitalism and socialism … This competition gives an almost universal dimension to even the most localized demands. Every meeting held, every act of repression committed, reverberates in the international arena.
>
> *(Fanon 1967: 75)*

> The report describes the case of a young, twenty-seven-year old patient who underwent one-hour sessions five times a week, very much in the fashion of Freud's early therapies. The case is surprisingly reminiscent of Freud's famous "Rat Man" …[Fanon] hears not only the desired and negated homosexuality but is equally attentive to the repetitive patterns of signifiers … In the manner of classical analysts, he pays close attention to the denials and the lapses… "I would have liked you to be my father … I cannot be your father, I am your doctor…"
>
> *(Fanon cited in Cherki 2006: 121)*

In the first passage, Fanon speaks of the independence of colonized countries, highlighting how the colonizers' call to slow the process down is strategic and allows them to displace and continue their violence. In the second passage, Fanon is speaking to one of his clients who is grappling with "negated homosexuality" and the desire for Fanon to be his father. Fanon pushes back, as he does not want to take on that role. For Fanon, this kind of paternity is part of the colonial sexual problem. The whole discourse of the centrality of the father in social relations, as well as the role of "white paternity, its symbolic centrality and authority as both an organizing idea and institution" (Marriott 2016), makes possible the colonial sexual relation and prevents a real leap to be made in terms of the political and the social invention of a world that does not depend on conquest and property relations. For Fanon, "it is in this withdrawal that a new *therapeutic* is born as both an institutional project and a politics" (Marriott 2016).

The coloniality of power organizes itself on two axes of power: the "coloniality of power" and "modernity" (Quijano 2000). The coloniality of power and modernity co-constitute themselves by drawing on the notion of a universal and social classification, i.e., racial science. Such a science, in turn, is co-constituted with a hierarchical classification and organization of peoples into those who are superior and those who are inferior. Maria Lugones expands this idea to what she calls the colonial/modern gender system, saying "gender itself is a colonial introduction, a violent introduction consistently and contemporarily used to destroy peoples, cosmologies, and communities as the building ground of the 'civilized' West" (Lugones 2007: 186). She adds:

> To understand the relation of the birth of the colonial/modern gender system to the birth of global colonial capitalism—with the centrality of the coloniality of power to that system of global power—is to understand our present organization of life anew ... How do we understand heterosexuality not merely as normative but as consistently perverse when violently exercised across the colonial modern gender system? How do we come to understand the very meaning of heterosexualism as tied to a persistently violent domination that marks the flesh multiply by accessing the bodies of the unfree in differential patterns devised to constitute them as the tortured materiality of power?
>
> *(2007: 187–188)*

Here, Lugones pushes us to understand that simply liberating a colonized state does not rupture the dominant colonial/modern gender systems. More so, she highlights the multiple modalities of accessing the flesh of the unfree all the while making them as those who threaten this structure but also the "tortured materiality of power," that is, those whose flesh can be the site of violence with impunity.

Similarly, Fanon argues that the displacement of the colonizers by the colonized in the postcolonial state does not rupture the ways through which imperial powers instilled the family, the institution of marriage and sexuality among the bourgeoisie and simultaneously moved to erect it to contain the bodies and lives of the European working class, colonized peoples and sites. Challenging such discourses does not problematize how "sexuality as a eugenicist project to breed a better bourgeoisie" (Chitty 2017: 6) and more efficient body for the capitalist machinery does not bring about genuine liberation.

Both Lugones and Fanon look beyond the scales of the nation. The struggles of coloniality and the reconstruction of the nation reverberate from the flesh, to the body, to the community, to the state, nation-state to the global, with a "cutthroat competition between capitalism and socialism" (Fanon 1967: 75). Fanon argues that the sexual tensions between blacks and whites, colonized and colonizers, have much to do with the "sickness that lies in the family environment" (Fanon 1967: 110). Queer violence, he says, is "etched in the heart of capitalism" and white supremacy's idealization of the notion of infinite virility:

> Still on the genital level, when a white man hates black men, is he not yielding to a feeling of impotence or of sexual inferiority? Since his ideal is an infinite virility, is there not a phenomenon of diminution in relation to the Negro, who is viewed as a penis symbol? Is the lynching of the Negro not a sexual revenge? We know how much of sexuality there is in all cruelties, tortures, beatings. One has only to reread a few pages of the Marquis de Sade to be easily convinced of the fact. Is the Negro's superiority real?
>
> *(Fanon 1967: 122–123)*

If, as Fanon suggests, sexual obliteration and oppression are at the heart of white supremacy and capitalism as a result of the perverse sexuality of white supremacy, the independence of colonized nations does not necessarily mean terror, and queer exploitation and obliteration disappear. As Fanon argues, the violence "in specific ways at the moment of the struggle for freedom does not magically disappear after the ceremony of trooping the national colors" (Fanon 1967: 75).

Both authors suggest the effects of European colonialism, the stealing of indigenous land, and the exploitative conditions characterizing the extraction of Asian, European, indigenous, and African labor, as well as their ways of organizing their responses to their political obligations under colonialism, reverberate throughout postcolonial sites and their struggles for equality and equity. The imperial/capitalist structure co-constitutive with the state as its primary political organization of governing life informs and shapes LGBTQ+ obliteration and oppression of transpeople, blacks, and other marginalized populations, including the poor. But this structure also informs and shapes the contemporary state's possibility of reproduction, including its affects, such as its nervousness about its existential power.

The current struggle in Cyprus over sexuality cannot be understood outside these reverberations and beyond the competition between political projects of socialism and capitalism. Gender and sexuality, as well as the quest for gender and sexual equity and justice, in sites like Cyprus are fraught with dominant notions of capitalist power, ranging from the racism, sexism, and homo/transphobia inscribed in law to anti-colonial and LGBTQ+ struggles against multiple inequities. Put otherwise, explaining equity in terms of sexuality in Cyprus cannot be understood outside the attempts to remake the colonial/modern gender system and to remake global colonial capitalism. And this world that assumes the division of the global into various nation-states and sexualized subjects is a world of capital. It is a world of conquest and division, and its desire is to create a world of sterility as long as it makes profits.

Colonialism and the global order of imperial capital were made possible through re-organizations of social relations and knowledge systems – from expressions of sexual relations to gender and family relations. The "centrality of power to that system of global power," Lugones says, "is to understand our present organization of life anew" (2007: 188). As long as the cis-heteronormative family unit and its structure of gender, that is, the relationship of a heterosexual man and heterosexual woman as the building block of capitalist society remains the hegemonic organizing institution, the perpetuation of obliteration, exploitation, and oppression of queer people will continue. More so, in this structure and political organization of gender and sexuality, another distinction that of between human/non-human is evaded. This distinction is overdetermined by race and racialization as inflected through sex, including the ways axes and structures of power such as class, ability, and nation interact to produce uneven outcomes; thus, it is obscured long enough for the ideal of equitable access to public services to be displaced.

In an attempt to understand Cypriot nervousness and the inequities around sexuality, as well as experiments to render such relations in the contemporary moment dominant or what Gramsci calls hegemonic, we argue that it is important to trace how sexuality becomes dominant in the first place. It is important to read the deliberations of sexuality as "analytical experiments of being and becoming" (Povinelli 2013: 8), that is, as struggles demonstrating the indeterminacy of the history and systematicity of the global and the attempts to conquer and bound sexuality and LGBTQ+ desires into a building block of imperial reproductive and productive structures of the labor market. These deliberations are co-constituted with the emerging power shifts and contestations over the world and the dominant powers – the EU, the US, China, and Russia – who are vying for the leadership of imperialism.

If lesbians and gays are experiencing violence in Nicosia (capital of Cyprus), this struggle calls some but not others to action. Linking this violence to the colonial question immediately demonstrates its linkages to the question of the imperialism and material struggles of oppressed and colonized peoples over equity more broadly.

The supreme violence of capital is manifested in its acts to preserve its power by consistently generating events, products, and institutions capable of "inciting" political, aesthetic, juridical, and ethical aspects of "the field of life (from which labor power is drawn) that are 'suitable' for capitalism's own reproduction" (Walker 2016: 165). As one such institution, the state plays a pivotal role in ensuring that demonstrations of capital's fallacies and promised fictions, along with anything not conforming to society's narrow and imagined roles, are either integrated into the sinews of market power or marginalized within the labor market. Those who put pressure on the empire's telos are pushed outside and even obliterated, even though they are the source of capital's raw power and imperial reproduction and expansion.

While the marginalization of LGBTQ+ people is etched in the productive and reproductive relations of capitalism (Cozzarelli 2019: 8), capitalism denies and displaces this source, this primal energy as being pivotal for its imperial reproduction and expansion. On the one hand, capital desires to remove all limits; on the other, this is impossible, as it requires material bounded relations of power, in "which at least two operations [i.e., the heterosexual vs. the homosexual] mutually implicate and depend on each other, yet cannot be separated precisely because they are mutually constitutive at the same time" (Walker 2016: 181). The tension in capitalism expressed by the dichotomization of heterosexuality and homosexuality reveals how this system is composed based on such segregations, as well as how such forms of violence including their structural boundness make the system possible. In order to think the contemporaneity of this problematic, we need to ask whether and how this tension and the interregnum within which it is generated can be challenged and how the energy can be released for a world otherwise, for a world in which love and desire are truly free.

One of the major theorists to speak of nervous conditions is Georg Simmel. In his *The Metropolis and Mental Life* he mentions a blasé attitude, or inattention and distraction, that is, one whose embodiments are "unconditionally reserved to the metropolis . . . [resulting] from the rapidly changing and closely compressed stimulation of the nerves" (1950: 414). The conditions of modernity, he says, lead the subject to move across the metropolis through "dangerous intersection [where] nervous impulses flow through him in rapid succession, like the energy from a battery" (Benjamin 1969: 175–176). Benjamin's analogy of a battery points to the anxiety of the finitude of human energy and the negative potential for atrophy. This nervousness, as articulated by Benjamin, the anxiety for negative potential and atrophy, is a colonial theory that concerns itself with the imperial power's end. We could also read it to reveal the nervousness at the center of the capitalist imperial system and white supremacy: at what point would the antagonism between the colonized and the colonizers and the anxiety that capital cannot produce life be exposed? At what point would this colonial displaced nervousness and fear of "being penetrated" (i.e., conquered) be undone?

The notion of nervous conditions comes alive in the novel of the same name by Tsitsi Dangarembga. The female characters living in 1960s Rhodesia experience many forms of conquest. Like the Victorian women, the postcolonial subjects are trapped in the domestic sphere and held captive by bodies that define their gender and, as a result, their roles in African life. The Victorian and the 1960s sites have common opinions about the ways women are to be defined; neither site allows women to construct their identities on their own terms. The women in Dangarembga's novel are constrained by a country that is having difficulty coming to terms with its own independence. For Rhodesians, negotiating their postcolonial identity in relation to more supposedly progressive British sites is problematic. Ironically, although their country is newly independent, the 1960s Rhodesian women face the same limitations as the English women, as such, exemplify "the failure of the promise of the liberation struggle to bring freedom equally to men and women" (Shaw 2015: 20).

Many of the characters in *Nervous Conditions* become aware of the global complexities that continue to contribute to making their global gendered, sexualized, and African lives possible. As the book suggests, modernity cannot be understood outside the colonial, and the colonial cannot be understood outside global capitalism's configurations. In focusing on these global complexities, we can capture the variety inherent in equities and struggles about sexuality. From the vantage point of the postcolonial state and queers, as the effects of global dysregulation or displacement, we are able to introduce a new version of how states become nervous in vying for global power and toward the creation of their own positionality in a structure of states.

In what follows, we draw on the deliberations over sexuality in Cyprus and argue that this struggle did not grow out of the mind of Western self-reflection but out of the actual conditions of its possibilities. In the next section, we analytically experiment with this contention by suggesting that the coloniality of power/modernity has queer exploitation and obliteration etched on its heart.

Colonization of Knowledge, Being, and Power

When thinking the ways the postcolonial state emerges as a nervous state in the contemporary moment, we cannot ignore how neoliberal leaders vie for projects to remake their global power and their project remains a scene of racialization (Agathangelou et al. 2008; Duggan 2002; Goldberg 2008; Melamed 2011; Puar 2007). David Theo Goldberg argues that neoliberalism and racial formations are entangled; they reproduce and interpenetrate each other in a hydra-headed fashion (Goldberg 2008). Goldberg highlights that neoliberal formations draw on and derange social relations of power to simultaneously nourish and consolidate racial apartheid globally, sustaining colonial governmentality in postcolonial situations.

We deploy neoliberalism as a political project, that is, a process of economization, which disseminates the model of the market to all spheres of life, even when money is not the issue. This political form of organization and sorting of peoples depends on the ongoing scraping of value out of queers enslaved, the removal of nutrients from the soil, and the extraction of knowledge from Africans, Native Americans, and colonized from all over the world (Povinelli 2019).

Neoliberal economization co-constitutes states and individuals as entrepreneurial actors whose goal is to maximize their value (i.e., on economic, financial, ethical, and affective terms), mainly by stealing value from others. In our study of the relations between the postcolonial state of Cyprus and LGBTQI human rights politics, we point to the contested politics of queerness as a site of unmaking and making the global power of the RoC. By global power, we mean the ways the state orients itself toward imperialism, strengthening itself, ensuring its "regulation" and stability, especially when it has exposed itself and its subjects to violent physical, mental, and social experiences (Hosek, Kavanagh, and Miller, 2006; Pincus, House, Christensen, and Adler, 2001) by drawing on those who are already heralded as "impossible sites" of reproductive capacity and who both "restrain" and expose the Empire's end. These sites can be mobilized to put their subjects and their sexual orientation to work to become sources of a virile potency, both its possibility and its expansion. Its possibility is derived from the power generated in every act of capture, integration, and relegation to exclusion, moves emerging from violence and perversion, from the lived experience of heterosexual conquest.

When capturing sexual orientation, the sovereign may find itself undermined. In *Body Politics*, Alan Sears argues that in the early 20th century, the Ford motor company promoted "masculine pride grounded in providing for dependent family members and the ability to endure difficult, painful and tedious work" (Sears cited in Cozzarelli 2019). As Jean Nicolas, a French Trotskyist, puts it: "[T]he stigma against 'homosexual' people plays the role of throwing queer people out of the labor market and this mechanism is a disciplining effect on 'heterosexual' identified people who repress 'homosexual' desire" (Cozzarelli 2019: 9). More recently, some EU countries, Poland, for instance, have systematically and consistently generated the conditions for attacks and violence against its queers in the name of "family first" and in the eradication of what its political leadership calls the "LGBT dictatorship" (The Economist, 2019).

Cyprus finds itself at a crossroad. On the one hand, it has changed its Constitution to follow EU law, but on the other, it is nervous about what it will mean for it to reorient itself in the direction of the EU – or what Povinelli calls "Rome":

> As Césaire's student, Frantz Fanon noted that the colonial world is not only where colonizers go. It is a system that encloses city and suburb, rural and wasteland, and the roads and waterways that provide or are carved

to provide transport. All roads lead to Rome, because no matter how far from Rome they are built and toward what unknown territory, they are built to move anything of value in only one direction.

(Povinelli 2019)

Yet from the vantage point of Cyprus and its marginalized peoples, the nervousness and the decay of EU look different; the question of sexuality and sexual orientation is more antagonistic. Sexuality or sexual orientation is not just a question of identity or rights; it is a political project of the world and the material redistribution and transformation of life.

We stretch Goldberg's (2008) argument that the neoliberal doctrines of freedom, liberty, and emancipation bypass the material contingencies that produced the invisibility of the colonized other as inflected through sexual orientation. These doctrines also bypass the fact that racialized queer sexualities remain a charged discursive and ontological site that is inherently material to neoliberal governmentality, the making anew the reproductive capacities of the postcolonial state and neocolonialism. Patricia McFadden (2011) argues that neoliberalism has a symbiotic relationship with neocolonial formations, and neoliberal architectures extinguish particular populations while coproducing distinguished and "new privileged subjects." We extend this further. Colonial exploitation and obliteration of queers is etched in the heart of neoliberalism.

Cyprus, a postcolonial state, emerges as a nervous state and draws on homosexuality as a site and potential source of its potency, its masculinity, and its expansion within global arrangements of imperialism and white supremacy. Its possibility, so it imagines, can be derived from the power generated by its act of capturing and integrating homosexuality, that as an axis of accumulation and power. In so doing, the RoC and the capitalist economy cross each other making apparent the coordinates of power and logics that guide them. In its attempts to capture "homosexuality" both as an economy and a figure, the state's potency increases, a power generated in every act of integration. However, this move does not speak to the ways sexuality is at the forefront of either making the world into an absolute sterile laboratory or reorienting us to create the conditions for the invention of immense heterogeneity of bodies, expressions, relationalities, words, affects, sounds, movements, and intensities to emerge and thrive.

It works to rid itself of its anxiety about its own possibility of power within shifting capitalist and white supremacy dynamics by participating in this expenditure or colonization. In drawing on contestations of sexual orientation, it moves to secure the conditions for its possibility as a legitimate and powerful modern state within the EU and the global order. Ultimately, however, the paradoxical appearance of the queer subject on the juridical architectures of Cyprus, as both abject and privileged (Antifanicosia 2017), hinges on the universal racialization of the postcolonial state as homophobic.

What is at stake is just how Western conventional (or radical) studies disentangle the colonial and racialized sexualities from the omnipresence of neoliberalism and the coloniality of sex. Many studies in public administration, international relations, and political science make no mention of racialized sexualities and neoliberalism as it is inflected through the colonial and white supremacy. They evade speaking to how the conquest of sex comes to be imagined to be the primary relation in the entanglement of the birth and the un/making of value both for the state and capital power. They continue to speak of sexuality and sexual relations as if they were independent of the matrices of dominant global power and the coproduction of value and value making and regional orders. Our reading of the postcolonial site of Cyprus and its deliberations over the question of the queer subject demonstrates the limits of these analytics.

The Nervous Postcolonial State and Homoerotics: Contestations of the Postcolonial and the Law

Not only is the queer question for the postcolonial site a nervous area; it is also a global question about the political order. From a queer point of view, queer equity remains a nervous area for the Cypriot government. The legal edifice and struggles around it reveal much about this queer inequity. Until 1923, the Ottoman Turkish law on homosexuality was in force; after 1858, homosexuality was not a criminal offence in the Ottoman Empire (Hussain 2011: 10). With British ownership of the island and the incorporation of the British Criminal Law Amendment Act of 1885[6] into Cyprus Law, the Ottoman tolerance of homosexuality ended; in 1929, male homosexuality was constituted as a criminal act, as in other colonized sites of the British Empire. Interestingly, the law did not recognize or mention female homosexuality as females were not seen as primary subjects of the imperial state.

When Cyprus won its independence in 1960, Cyprus retained British colonial law. The Criminal Law Amendment Act of 1885 became Articles 171 to 174 of Chapter 154 of the Cypriot Criminal Code (Francoeur and Noonan 2003: 294). These articles' inequity toward gays was challenged in 1993 when Alexandros Modinos, a Cypriot architect and *gay rights activist,* brought a legal court case against the RoC, putting its sovereign power to question by bringing the case to a European court. In their ruling on *Modinos v. Cyprus,* the *European Court of Human Rights* said *Section 171 of the Criminal Code of Cyprus* violated Modinos's right to a private life, as protected by the *European Convention on Human Rights,* an international agreement ratified by Cyprus in 1962. While this legal ruling allowed gays to be seen as equal citizens and subjects of the Republic, it did not lead to the revision of the Criminal Code or changes in the equity policies. For instance, one of the Republic's dominant institutions, the military, would not allow homosexuals to serve, arguing that homosexuality was a "mental illness" (Smith 2002). The military wrote the following about a gay man: "Mr. S is unsuitable for military service because he suffers from a sexual perversion, being a passive homosexual" (as cited in Christou 2003). Such notions of queerness sustain in place the possibility of violence in the larger society.

More recently, this ban was removed (National Guard Law 2018), but the discrimination has continued. Trimikliniotis and Karayiannis find the increased visibility of military discrimination has not dissipated the violence:

> The stigma against homosexuals in the army persists, but EU accession has made the Greek-Cypriot army authorities more discrete. It is widely believed that amongst the thousands of persons released for psychological reasons many are gay men. According to figures released by the Ministry of Defence between 1992 to 2006 one in nine new army recruits was released due to psychological reasons: out of 79.376 national guards, 4.279 were released while a further 4.693 recruits were suspended due to psychological reasons.
>
> *(Trimikliniotis and Karayiannis 2008: 28)*

This reductionist alignment of homosexuals to the status of perverse and "mentally ill" humans as a result of sexual orientation is all the more problematic because it not only opens the space for those identified as heterosexual to act as the disciplining machinery against homosexual desires by repressing them and using violence against them. It also misses the agency exercised by the gay community in their many challenges, including their own vision of a Cyprus.

The issue was officially addressed in 1998 as a result of the postcolonial state's anxiety about becoming an EU member. Accession negotiations began that year for Cyprus, Poland, Hungary, the Czech Republic, Estonia, and Slovenia. The EU was unequivocal about its expectations; the "European Parliament issued a warning that it would not consent to the accession of any state that embraces laws that violates the human rights of lesbians and gays" (Bell 2001: 88, cited in Mikulak 2019: 556). Cyprus could not continue to be non-harmonized or dysregulated on the register of sexuality if it wanted access to the global power of the EU, including access to capital such as loans and aid. The increased pressure for change came in different forms, including pressures from the European powers and contestations from its own people who leveraged the transnational discourses or what Kamenou calls "difficult intersections" to harmonize with Europeanization:

> [Europeanization] is broadly defined as a transnationalisation process that includes the emergence and development of European-level structures of governance and institutions and of collective ideas, norms, and values … EU admission and its prospect, and Europeanisation processes initiated from above and below, may both emasculate and reinforce notions of privilege and exclusion based on gender and sexual identities, both within and across national communities.
>
> *(Kamenou 2019: 8)*

Understanding this Europeanization beyond mere political identification with the EU governance structures requires a theory of accumulation and global power dysregulation. To rid itself of its colonial anxiety about its survival, the postcolonial state knows that the only way to access global power in its European iteration is to reorient itself from what some would call fantasies of anti-colonial, socialist, or decolonial projects and put to work any site otherwise marginalized from valuation regimes or ignored for the extraction of value, such as queerness (i.e., queers can now be part of a multi-billion gay market niche). It has to also redress its supposedly outdated policies and juridical practices. Sexual orientation is thus the new site of the contestation for the generation of value of its "dysregulation" or non-captured energies.

The governing fiction of ridding the state of its nervousness involves the resolution of inequalities within the structure itself, to the exclusion of anything that demonstrates the limits and exposes the cracks of the nation-state and empire. Those whose actions refuse to take for granted the idea that the solution to the violence of LGBTQ+ and others can be found in the capitalist and imperialist future promises of the market (see, for instance, Queer Cyprus' mandate) are systematically relegated to non-existence. In this sense, the queer, as Queer Cyprus articulates its project, experiments with demonstrating how the erection and the hypermasculinity of the subject of an equality is entangled with the non-existence or equity of all subjects, irrespective of their sexual orientation, class, and racialized positionality.

The decriminalization of same-sex contact became a question post-Modinos' challenge to the state's power over sexual orientation: "The Council of Europe had warned the RoC that non-abidance with the ECHR ruling could mean expulsion" (Kamenou 2019: 8). As EU membership would extend the life of its fragile sovereignty and accord its authority and power with an emerging global power bloc of capital, the government decriminalized same-sex sexual contact in 1998 (Figure 5.1).

Yet its nervousness about being left out of the accumulation regimes of the EU and its governance structures did not mean the Cypriot state would or could work to end the violence against all LGBTQ+ people or the repression

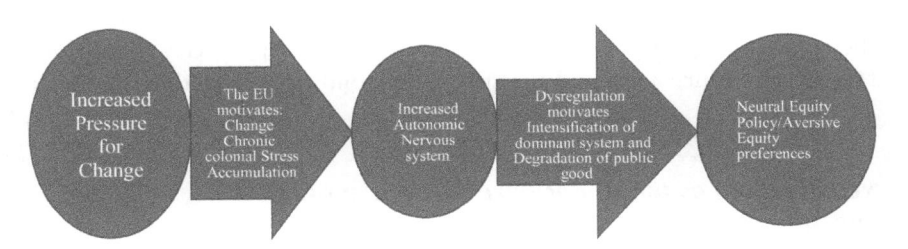

FIGURE 5.1 Theory of Global Power-Related Dysregulation and Sexual Policy Preferences.

of sexuality more generally within that political project. For example, one issue was equalizing the *age of consent*, set at 16 for heterosexual contact and 18 for homosexual. Moreover, according to the Criminal Code, it was a crime to "promote" homosexuality, making it difficult for LGBT groups to organize and protest their human rights violations. The ban was finally lifted in 2000, and the age of consent was equalized in 2002, making the universal age of consent 17.

Other ongoing issues of equalization include the freedom of assembly, the family and its responses to LGBTQI children, and the organizing and ordering of families, such as queer marriages and adoption. Discrimination due to homophobia remains rampant in the areas of labor market, education, military, health services, religion, sports, and the media (Trimikliniotis and Karayiannis 2008: 7–8). Discussions about equality demand a more systemic change revamping of the structure, including ruptures of multiple discriminations against LGBTQ+ people. According to Trimikliniotis and Karayiannis (2008: 25), who have analyzed media texts, documents, and surveys on homosexuality, no measures have been taken against these multiple discriminations by an anti-discriminatory authority:

> No research has been on the subject of multiple discrimination against LGBTs. It can be assumed that LGBT people with ethnic minority backgrounds, LGBT youth, LGBT elders and LGBT disabled people suffer a great deal more than those who suffer from single ground of discrimination … Very few positive practices can be reported, and those targeting sexual orientation specifically or exclusively are minimal. According to the chair of AKOK [Cypriot Gay Liberation Movement (AKOK or *Apeleftherotiko Kinima Omofilofilon Kiprou*)], awareness raising activities generally, do little towards combating social prejudices against homosexuals or even informing the homosexual about their rights.
>
> *(Ibid: 25)*

Despite its lack of "good practices," the RoC's nervousness about being taken seriously in Europeanization, exacerbated by pressure from its own elites and various organizations, ultimately motivated it to take on the gay demands for liberation and equality. One such organization was Cypriot Gay Liberation, a non-profit which pressured the state to respond to the multiple violences against gays.

Neoliberalism as the Financialization of Identities and States? NGO Interventions

Cypriot LGBTQI+ peoples are constituted and distinguished by class, racial backgrounds, educational level, and degree of involvement with transnational

NGOs and related Euro-centric identities. They inhabit a complicated zone, where queer subjects are considered non-normative fashion selves within Cyprus and the EU. Against this backdrop, their self-making strategies challenge our understanding of "normal," drawing from – and complicating – established values and practices of their communities. As such, their identities are fluid and situational, expressed in a variety of ways, according to relationships, violence strategies, and spaces within which they find themselves. These realities have significant implications for the categorical imperatives of transnational LGBTQI rights NGOs.

LGBTQI+ peoples are necessarily influenced by the presence of international LGBT human rights non-governmental organizations (INGOs), whose interventions, which include LGBTQI empowerment programs and projects on access to health, overlook the fluid character of queer self-making and what substantive queer liberation may even look like. Indeed, queer embodied subjects unsettle easy readings of heterosexual and homosexual, racializations and nationalisms, the presumed distinction between racialized-nationalized subjects, and the presumed distinction between Cypriot and un-Cypriot or un-European. For instance, one of the major shifts in Cyprus has been the collaboration of ACCEPT with the RoC and also with Queer Cyprus, the organization based in the North:

> Accept-LGBTI Cyprus from the internationally recognized Greek Cypriot south and Queer Cyprus Association from the breakaway Turkish Cypriot north converged Saturday on the UN controlled buffer zone cutting across the capital Nicosia to mark their partnership by holding a festival replete with a fire juggler. The groups hailed the move as a milestone in helping to break down the east Mediterranean island nation's physical divide and complex politics…. Faika Deniz Pasha with Queer Cyprus Association said Greek Cypriot and Turkish Cypriot gay rights groups were naturally bound by common objectives and had worked together in the past. But the country's division would often raise political and administrative obstacles forestalling tighter bonds.
>
> *(Associated Press 2019)*

These collaborations challenge easy readings of the state and rupture its tendencies to redress its nervousness by sustaining in place bounded notions of the sovereign and sovereign subjects. They experiment with viable conditions for surviving and thriving, beyond the nervousness of the state to reproduce itself in a capitalist transition. These collaborations also challenge certain INGOs to homogenize them as queer at times, while actively rejecting that categorization at others.

More broadly, queer realities and work in Cyprus contradict widespread portrayals in human rights rhetoric of Cyprus as the heart of homophobic darkness, while calling transnational LGBT rights advocates to pay more careful attention to the unexpected ways in which their interventions interact with the Cypriot problem politics in the spaces in which they intervene. Moreover, queer lives allow us to see the extent to which neoliberal projects around health and human rights can foreground conditions of precarity for particular constituencies and exacerbate their vulnerability (Povinelli 2011: 3).

LGBTQ+ peoples and the violence they experience cannot be understood in isolation from wider political and economic projects. The privatization of public services after the recession, austerity, and financial bailout of March 2013 (Dzankic 2015: 8–10) has impacted peoples differentially. Queers of different racialized backgrounds, of the working class or from rural areas, for instance, may be unemployed. Those who are gainfully employed find jobs through their own initiatives or through family relations. Jobs range from hairdressing to tailoring and making and selling foods. In some cities, like Nicosia or Limassol, queers may be able to express homoerotic intimacies more openly than in others. Such presence, however, operates through nuanced networks of secrecy and disavowal. In such sites, transnational imperatives of being "out" can aggravate established strategies of queer self-making in ways that provoke the very homophobic violence NGOs are seeking to combat.

The continuing marginalization of postcolonial nation-states in the global political economy is rooted in the history of unequal power relations founded by enslavement and colonialism. The current anxieties around equality and equity related to queers and transnational LGBT human rights activism cannot be detached from the conditions created by enslaving and neocolonial modernity. For example, the queers of Cyprus are embedded in LGBT human rights projects that attract funds (ACCEPT and Queer Cyprus) to resolve homophobia. These projects, however, elide the other processes that intersect to trigger anti-homosexual violence, such as racialized backgrounds and class, and the harsh regulation of Cyprus' economy by neoliberal institutions based in Euro-American institutions, such as the International Monetary Fund (IMF), the World Bank (WB), and the EU. Thus, queers, supposedly the beneficiaries of the funds, emerge as vulnerable subjects and targets. It is clear that the optimistic practices by the state and the transnational LGBT NGOs, together with the hardships suffered by the queers of Cyprus, produce the homophobia that both queer liberal and Greek Christian authoritarian regimes neglect.

Promising Initiatives: The Work of Grassroots Organizations

The first organization ever in Cyprus to defend gay rights was the Cypriot Gay Liberation Movement (AKOK or Apeleftherotiko Kinima Omofilofilon Kiprou), founded in 1987. The President of this movement was Alekos Modinos whose struggles (mentioned above) led to the decriminalization of homosexuality in 1998. However, "the amended law was more degrading to people of same-sex sexual choice than the previous one. It included ambiguous provisions designed to ensure that living as a homosexual in Cyprus would be harder than pre-1998" (Kamenou 2012). The ensuing debate led to the formation of an organization representing LGBT people.

ACCEPT-LGBT Cyprus is the only organization in the RoC presently focusing on LGBT rights, including the repeal of civilian criminal homosexual prohibitions. It is a liberal bourgeois NGO and was founded in 2011, and has been organizing the annual Pride parades since May 2014. Early on, it missed making connections with the North for nationalist reasons, but it has recently been changing its stance by collaborating with one of the major queer organization in the North.

In the TRNC, discrimination against queers is also equally intense. An initiative was established in 2007 to redress the discriminations against lesbians, gays, bisexual, and transgender people. In April 2008, the group submitted a proposal to the Head of Parliament, Fatma Ekenoğlu (Queer Cyprus), seeking to change the colonial laws in the books:

> Chapter 154 of the Penal Code, which has been in effect since the British administration, has lost its currency and applicability on many levels. Considering the improved and modernized understanding of law and human rights, altering the Penal Code is inevitable. On 25 April 2008, the Initiative Against Homophobia presented their proposal on changing the articles which discriminate on the grounds of sexual orientation to Fatma Ekenoğlu by also requesting that the proposal is discussed at the parliament". In the modern world, considering homosexuality as a disease or fearing homosexuals (homophobia) are unacceptable situations. Homosexual relations are accepted as natural and they are not considered as immoral or illegal by many modern societies. Similarly to women's rights or minority rights, gay rights are also supported by intellectual, democratic individuals and human rights organizations. Nevertheless, article 171 and following articles (172, 173) of the Penal Code categorize homosexual relations as offenses and penalize these relations with heavy sentences. These regulations are completely outdated and are against fundamental and contemporary human rights and liberties.
>
> *(Queer Cyprus https://www.queercyprus.org/en/the-proposal-on-changing-the-penal-code-has-been-presented-to-ekenoglu/)*

The initiative's demands to revise the criminal law in the North are crucial as they point to the nervousness of the TRNC in relationship to Europeanization, even though its relationship to Turkey complicates its vying for global power.

In 2010, *ILGA-Europe* (International, Lesbian, Bisexual, Trans, and Intersex Association) presented the same proposal to the new Head of Parliament, *Hasan Bozer*. However, the arrests of queers based on claims of *"unnatural sex"* did not stop. In October 2011, the *Communal Democracy Party* (TDP) presented the proposal to the Parliament for a third time and demanded the immediate decriminalization of homosexuality in Northern Cyprus. Since March 2012, Initiative Against Homophobia has continued its activities under the name *Queer Cyprus Association* (*Turkish: Kuir Kıbrıs Derneği*).

In the South, while the Modinos case attempted to secure rights to privacy for homosexual men, ACCEPT took on a larger mission, seeking to reform public opinion, fight homophobia and transphobia, raise awareness, empower LGBTIs, and so on. It created visibility for the LGBT community and gave it an official voice. ACCEPT has been an active participant in co-organizing parades and festivals on the island to challenge discrimination and homophobia and to set the grounds for changing public opinion. The first Cyprus Pride Festival, for instance, took place on May 17, 2014 (International Day against Homophobia), and May 31, 2014. (The first day of the event, a Rainbow Walk took place in northern Nicosia with the collaboration of ACCEPT-LGBT Cyprus and the Queer Cyprus Association, among others.) The island's first bicommunal LGBTI festival was held in Nicosia in October 2019 organized by both ACCEPT and Queer Cyprus under the slogan "United by Colours" (Cyprus Mail 2019). Such events go beyond challenging homophobia. They challenge the division of the island as well as discrimination based on racialized backgrounds (i.e., being a Turkish Cypriot vs. a Greek Cypriot or a Cypriot of African, Arab, Armenian, or Latin descent).

On May 28, 2017, a parade festival was co-organized by ACCEPT-LGBT Cyprus, the European Commission Representation, and the European Parliament Office in Cyprus, under the auspices of the President of the Republic, Nicos Anastasiades, and the Mayor of Nicosia. The major slogan for this parade was "Speak Love," as ACCEPT-LGBT Cyprus had decided to integrate it into the global movement against hate speech to all vulnerable minorities, not just LGBTQ+ people.

ACCEPT and Queer Cyprus play a crucial role, because all reports and surveys point to a lack of awareness of LGTBQ issues. According to a recent European Commission Against Racism and Intolerance (ECRI) report (2016), the Republic of Cyprus is characterized by an intolerance of LGBTQ+ people. By the same token, an EU LGBT Survey (2014) found 61% of Cypriot respondents perceived discrimination on the basis of sexual orientation as widespread. As the Hombat report (2016) explains, this climate of homophobia and transphobia has a detrimental impact on how LGBTQ+ people experience themselves within Cyprus and the rest of Europe. Tellingly, in the EU LGBT Survey, most Cypriot LGBTs (nine out of ten participants) chose not to disclose their sexual orientation or gender identity to others to protect themselves.

Assessment and Evidence of Progress in the Integration of LGBTQ+ Peoples

Two victories for ACCEPT have been the amendment of the law on hate speech and the passing of the civil partnership law. In the case of the latter, in November 2015, the Parliament passed a law which "regulates the rights and obligations of couples in civil cohabitation" (Cyprus Mail 2015), including same-sex couples. Up to February 2019, only 100 same-sex couples had formed a civil partnership, however, compared to 467 heterosexual couples (Zoumidou 2019). The law still does not allow same-sex couples to adopt children, a goal ACCEPT has set for the future.

In the case of the former, the amendment of the law on hate speech, a law enacted in 2011 criminalized any person who deliberately and publicly disseminated and incited violence or hatred in any manner against a group of persons or a member of such a group defined by reference to race, color, religion, descent, or national or ethnic origin. It did not contain any reference to sexual orientation and gender identity, but in May 2015, the law was amended to include these two categories. One of ACCEPT's aims is to further amend the law because as it stands now, it does not criminalize discrimination; it criminalizes only incitement to violence or hatred. According to a 2019 report on hate speech prepared by KISA (equality, support, antiracism), discrimination against LGBTQ+ people in Cyprus is common, but hate speech incidents are not identified or recorded properly; if properly recorded, they are not prosecuted, because the authorities claim they are not substantiated (KISA 2019).

Transsexuals can change their sex and gender on their official papers only if they present medical confirmation of gender reassignment surgery. ACCEPT is currently working on promoting a law to provide for the right of any person over 18 whose gender identity does not correspond to the one stated in official documents to request a correction (Cyprus Mail 2015). This is a very controversial issue. As Trimikliniotis and Karayiannis note, "If homosexuality is an unspeakable taboo and if lesbianism is immersed in a numb silence, sex change poses a major challenge and threat to the established order in Cyprus" (Trimikliniotis and Karayiannis 2008). Tryfonidou (2018) also points out that trans persons have, until very recently, been invisible in the Cypriot legal framework, with no progress legal or otherwise, except a handful of legislation on gender identity pioneered by the Ombudsman's office.[7] A discussion of this issue should take place in the Cypriot Parliament in the near future.

Another success for ACCEPT and an indication of LGBT people's increased visibility is the appointment of ACCEPT's former President Costas Gavrielides as an advisor to the President of Cyprus, in a role "promoting multiculturalism, acceptance and respect for diversity" (Cyprus Mail 2018). Moreover, the government is attempting to implement school programs to combat homophobia and transphobia. An Ombudsman report (2012) on homophobia in education underlines the extent of homophobic bullying in schools and emphasizes the psychological impact on children. Children who experience this form of discrimination, it says, often feel isolated, are socially excluded, and have low self-esteem. In 2011, topics related to sexual orientation and gender identity were introduced in the pre-primary, primary, and lower secondary education.

More recently, the Ministry of Education implemented an anti-bullying plan in schools to promote a supportive environment for LGBTI children and organized workshops for teachers of primary and secondary education to create a "shield against homophobia" (Hombat Report 2016).

Social Inequity and Hate Speech: The Church

LGBTQI is an inequity upon which the state draws to dissipate its nervousness about possibly being left behind in the existing socio-economic, ethical, political, and symbolic structures of capital accumulation and global power. Other social institutions do the same, engaging in discourses to contain their anxiety and capture the energy to enable their power. In Cyprus, one such institution is the Greek Orthodox Church. In 1998, when the discussion about homosexuality was brought to the fore in the parliament, Church leaders were outraged. Archbishop Chrysostomos I called on women to revolt against homosexuals, the "depraved sinners," and pledged to "personally excommunicate the perverts" if they refused to "repent their unnatural acts" (Trimikliniotis and Karayiannis 2008: 11). The Church vehemently expressed its opposition to the amendment of the existing colonial law criminalizing homosexuality and tried to intimidate the public by mentioning Cyprus' national security and connecting gay rights with Cyprus' national identity, thus claiming that queer protections render the country as a whole susceptible to the "enemy."

In an interesting sense, the Church was not necessarily expressing an antagonistic universalism to that of the EU, though many have read it in that way. Kamenou (2012) explains that the Church was alarmed by the "peril" of the spread of this new "breed," that is, the homosexual recognized and protected by law. Drawing on the anxieties and nervousness of the question of Cyprus, that is the re-colonization of the island by Turkey in 1974 and the division of the island into two, the Church asked: "How are we going to conduct our fight against [Turkish] occupation … [and] how will marriage and the family (and hence the nation) be protected [if homosexuality is decriminalized]?" Interestingly, this "negative" in a liberal sense or pessimistic position marked by anxiety over the imminent destruction of family life and thereby Greek Cypriot social life goes hand in hand with the positive or optimistic notion of the dominant powers of the EU, that is, the integration and presence of queer life in its structures.

The Greek Orthodox clergy and other Christian groups established an anti-LGTBQI organization, the "Pancyprian Committee for the Fight against the Decriminalization of Homosexuality" (PAHOK). PAHOK organized fierce demonstrations outside the parliament and elsewhere during discussions of the decriminalization law. Group members distributed petitions to Members of Parliament and in churches claiming that the decriminalization of homosexuality was not simply a legal reform; it would give homosexuals license to urge more people to become homosexual (Kamenou 2012). The anxiety about sexual orientation reminds us of Paul Gilroy who argues that "gender differences" are

> important in nation-building activity because they are a sign of an irresistible natural hierarchy that belongs at the center of civic life ... The integrity of a nation becomes the integrity of its cis-heterosexual masculinity. In fact, it can be a nation only if the correct version of gender hierarchy has been established and reproduced.
>
> *(Gilroy 2000: 127, 23)*

Nervousness around sexual orientation has much to do with whether or not the Cypriot nation-state can be socially reproduced and make itself a viable "Europeanized" power (i.e., a viable site for further extraction of value and life).

When Cyprus became a full member of the EU in 2004, it had to comply with the European standards on LGTBQI+ policies and to present itself as a modern European state promoting tolerance of any sexual orientation. However, every landmark state endorsement met with opposition from the Church. In 2014, when the first Gay Pride Parade took place in Cyprus, it received wide support from almost all political parties, but the Church organized demonstrations and used homophobic discourse to reverse the acclaim. As the parade date approached, the Holy Synod issued an announcement calling homosexuality "an affliction and a moral downfall" (Cyprus Mail 2016). On the day of the parade, a group of clerics demonstrated against it just an hour before it started.

Shortly after the Civil Partnership Law was passed in 2015, the Church announced that it would establish its own school to provide the youth of Cyprus with righteous education. In a 2016 television interview, the Archbishop was asked how he would talk to pupils who might actually belong to this social group; he said that he would tell them that homosexuality is a sin and unnatural and they ought to struggle to overcome it. ACCEPT-Cyprus reported the Archbishop's hate speech to the Attorney General, but the matter was not dealt with (KISA 2019).

More recently, Bishop Morphou Neophytos was reported to the Attorney General, because of allegations of hate speech (Cyprus Mail 2019). The Bishop told his audience that gay men give off a nasty smell, and that homosexuality is transferred to a fetus when a pregnant woman has anal sex and enjoys it. However, he claimed homosexuals could be good Christians as long as they subdued their desires through spiritual guidance. His comments triggered a strong public reaction. The government denounced the comments as "insulting the dignity and equality of Cypriots." ACCEPT campaigners called for disciplinary action. An investigation was conducted by the police, in cooperation with the Attorney General's office, to determine whether the comments made by the Bishop could be classed as hate speech. The Attorney General concluded the case did not constitute a criminal offence (Philenews 2019).

1. These may well be read as the ridiculous statements of backward and outdated subjects; however, what is important is that this form of speech is both public and authoritative. The idea that homosexuality is transmitted to unborn children gestures to the understanding of sexuality as a biological phenomenon. Although it is tempting to laugh at the Bishop's statement, many "scientific" studies against queers have made similar arguments (Burton 2015). Such epistemologies based on problematic notions of history and biology remind us that sexuality has been a eugenicist project to breed an efficient conquering and healthy body. Such notions sort and organize peoples based on their sexuality, all the while imprisoning their formation and capacity for infinite realization.
2. Moreover, the violence and terror of the colonial state are displaced in these newer narratives, codes, genres, and genealogies of neo-colonial sexual violence, whose goal is not realization but a reassemblage of a certain meaning of what counts as legitimate "normal" sexual expression and institutions such as the family unit as the site of the possibility of its social reproduction and of dominant capitalist powers.

The Bishop's speech went viral, with organizations and groups challenging it, while highlighting Christianity as one of the major obstacles preventing queer liberation. Elevating queer liberal modernity over Christianity in this paradigm of modernity displaces the co-constitution of these relations or the co-evalness of these modernities (see Fabian 2002) or fundamentalist and entangled universalisms. This depiction of Morphou's speech reinforces the image of a homophobic Cyprus in need of a cure from LGBTQI human rights missionaries in the form of transnational NGOs and the leadership of Brussels. This approach leaves untouched the colonial/imperial structures and their epistemes. It merely allows for a new submission to the norms and regulations of a sexual, asymmetric and often sporadic distribution of rights contingent on secular/EU practices.

The rush to rescue Cyprus from such pessimistic politics, enunciated in responses to the Bishop, parallels what Lauren Berlant (2011) calls the optimistic fantasies that inform the contours of liberal discourse, fantasies embedded in the desire to create a better and just world. Frequently castigating the despicable presence of historically constituted forms of oppression, the liberal ethos paradoxically remains the grounds on which "cruel optimism" proliferates (Berlant 2011: 1).

Many queers, along with the Cypriot state, highlighted that this was "hate speech," but Attorney General Costas Clerides determined there was no indication that the senior Orthodox Christian cleric broke the law. He argued that some "isolated references" by Bishop Neophytos merited criticism and dissent, but in the full context of his remarks, he did not incite hatred or violence, nor did his speech constitute hate speech. Nevertheless, he called for spiritual leaders to avoid "incautious and ill-prepared" views (Associated Press September 2019).

This decision did not dissipate the threats and attacks on the queer community. In fact, it left LGBTQI politics in a space made already precarious by the nation-state's desire to enforce neoliberal policies to harmonize with the EU

(Agathangelou 2004). In effect, the state ended up indirectly enforcing compulsory heterosexuality by distinguishing speech violence from criminal behavior. Its open declaration against the Bishop about his "speech" did not imply that the state was interested in ridding itself of compulsory heterosexuality or the newer notion of a family unit. Rather, it revealed the state's nervousness about the exposition of some of its most ingrained matrices of exploitation, oppression, and even obliteration (Agathangelou 2019) as the conditions of its possibility, its global power, and the imperial order.[8]

The chart shown in Figure 5.2 documents incidents of racism and discrimination from 2005 until 2018. While discrimination related to sexual orientation is not the most prevalent form of discrimination – that of nationality and ethnic origin is much more prominent – there was a significant rise in these incidents or in the reporting of these incidents in 2018. Other positionalities that are equally crucial to incidents of discrimination are community, political views, color, and sexual orientation.[9] The fact that no incident of discrimination on the basis of sexual orientation is documented before 2011 raises questions as to whether LGTBQI+ peoples did not report such incidents, which definitely did take place, precisely because of the widespread societal and public bias. The founding of ACCEPT-LGTB Cyprus in 2011, along with all its actions (Pride

Motive in Incidents and/or Cases of Racial Nature and/or with Racial Motive 2005-2018

(Last update: April 2019)

Motive	2005	2006	2007	2008	2009	2010	2011	2012	2013	2014	2015	2016	2017	2018	Total
Language							1	1							2
Special needs							1						1		2
Nationality / Ethnic origin	2	17	3	6	4	26	12	7	4	1	3	8	15	13	121
Age															0
Religion		1			3	1		1	1	1		3	3	1	15
Community					1	1				3	6	4	10	10	35
Political views	1	16			2	3	2		1				4	1	30
Sexual orientation							1	3	1	3		1	1	9	19
Race		1			1	3		1			1				7
Gender															0
Color	1		1		2	5	9	1	2	4	1	3	1	3	33
Unspecified						1									1
Total	4	35	4	6	13	40	25	15	9	12	11	19	35	37	265

FIGURE 5.2 Motive in Incidents and/or Cases of Racial Nature and/or with Racial Motive 2005–2018.

Source: Office for Combating Discrimination, Crime Combating Department, Police Headquarters, Cyprus Police.

Parades, contributing towards legal amendments) has had a significant impact on attitudes, making it easier for assaults of any kind to be reported.

LGBTQI comprises a series of contested categories and embodiments that challenge the idea that the Republic of Cyprus is a heterosexual nation. It describes an assemblage of subjects bonded by queer identification and homoerotic intimacy and desire. Though homoerotic intimacy has traditionally been part and parcel of Cyprus, and not just the RoC, it is only recently that the state has turned this into a site of explicit contestation and a political project by focusing on the juridical regimes to govern it anew. It must be noted, however, that the boundaries between heteronormative and queer subjects remain blurred, especially as these constituencies are interconnected and interwoven through networks such as families, NGOs, friends, and other community relations.

Such encounters and interactions typify the fluid intersections between queers and heterosexual subjects. These connections must, however, be distinguished as constituting a sexual subjectivity that is both Cypriot and global, transnational and vernacular, Christian and non-Christian. While LGBTQI subjectivities are shaped through their interactions with a state, in the case of the RoC, that is primarily Christian, they are complicated by ongoing histories of colonialism, neoliberalism, global human rights regimes, neoliberal EU projects, and more.

As a Way of Conclusion: Equality in Law Is Not Equivalent to Equity in Life

What, then, is behind the scenes? Shall we read the problematic and violent condition revealed by the Bishop of Morphou as pessimistic and widespread, even endemic, and the response of the state as a hallmark of its desire to save sexual minorities and an embodiment of cruel optimism? However we seek to understand the scenario, the queers of Cyprus posit multiple selves and challenge easy readings of equality with equity which is not equivalent.

ACCEPT and Queer Cyprus navigate this nuanced complexity while grappling with several other issues, such as sexual trafficking, in environments rendered nervous by the cumulative impacts of the European-colonial-Christian domination[10] and of the neocolonial and neoliberal articulations of modernity. Together, these impacts make the state nervous and queer subjects complexly activist.

ACCEPT's vision and mission focuses on equality with regard to sexual orientation. Its agenda includes the following:

> The formation of a society based on respect for each individual and their diversity, free from discrimination and prejudice in particular as regards to their sexual orientation … The cooperation with domestic and international organizations concerned with combating discrimination and

promoting the principle of equality, particularly with regard to sexual orientation and social gender.

(ACCEPT http://acceptcy.org/en/node/242)

A lot of its work is combatting discrimination and creating the space, along with domestic and international organizations, to promote this principle.

> By the same token, Queer Cyprus's agenda includes the following list of imperatives: to support LGBTI rights; to counter discrimination based on gender, gender expression, sexual orientation and gender identity; to organize, participate in, and contribute to activities regarding homophobia, biphobia, transphobia, human rights and freedom, socio-politics, education, health, family, science, art, culture, history, sports, cinema, theatre and similar and/or related fields.
>
> *(https://www.queercyprus.org/en/about-queer-cyprus/)*

Its manifesto goes even further, pushing for a vision beyond equality, thus challenging the misconception that equity and equality mean the same thing—and that they can be used interchangeably.

What's the difference between equity and equality? For ACCEPT, equality means an eradication of the discrimination against subjects on the basis of sexual orientation. For Queer Cyprus, we read equality to mean that all subjects of different sexual orientations have equal access to resources to ensure a safe and high-quality life. Based on their manifesto, it seems that not all queers are evenly positioned in the existing and reassembled hierarchies of power. If that is the case, we argue that equality is not equivalent to equity. Some queers need *more* to have a safe and secure life in Cyprus depending on their class, their racialized backgrounds and environmental spaces of living, or the militarization of the society. In the words of QueerCyprus:

> Queer Cyprus aims at transforming the heterosexist society into one that is equalitarian and accepting of diversity; and also supports the diversity of sexual orientation, gender identity and sexual expression by challenging heterosexism which ignores, degrades and oppresses all other sexual orientations. …Queer Cyprus envisions a society in which individuals are not subject to any form of violence due to their sexual orientation, gender identity or sexual expression and continues their cause to achieve this objective.
>
> *(https://www.queercyprus.org/en/about-queer-cyprus/)*

In laying out a manifesto that is feminist, anti-capitalist, and ecological, we argue that they stretch the notion of equality to mean equity. Thus, it is not enough to argue for equality based on sexual orientation without ridding the conditions that make societies depend on exploitation and obliteration of peoples, the unevenness in power and access to resources, as well as the categories of subjectivity that relegate some to be the privileged ones and others to be the sites of violence with impunity. For queer subjects to be safe, the whole of the society has to become egalitarian and accepting of diversity. Such a transformation requires more of the state's resources to close the social and transnational gaps in standards of living, life conditions, health access, etc.

Changing policies to respond to the discrimination against LGBTQI people to give them a voice in society does not always mean that violence and discrimination do not continue or gaps in life conditions do not remain. Making sure that all LGBTQIs of all classes and national-racialized backgrounds have access to resources and funding to provide high-quality security under "exceptional" institutional conditions will certainly narrow the gaps. However, the overarching nervousness will not dissipate until we move beyond the authoritarian nationalist and liberal understanding of change as "leveling the playing field," that is, until we create conditions that do not reproduce the same kind of violence but provide resources for those who need them. And for that, we need to challenge politics that argue and experiment only with equality. We need to move to grapple with the notion and the practice of equity.

Sexual orientation equity and justice work across Cyprus and, indeed, across the whole of the EU should not be separated from the ongoing project of the decolonization of knowledge and global power. Much of the intellectual work supporting this is pivotal (e.g., ACCEPT and Queer Cyprus), shaping the way forward for the kinds of policies and actions necessary to achieve sexual equity. At the root of conversations of activists/intellectuals in Cyprus (and the rest of the globe) is the need to challenge the way we understand the production of categories such as heterosexual and homosexual, man and woman, nation and region, racialized-nationalisms in circumstances where entrance into and exclusion from each grouping continues to be circumscribed by race, class, gender, sexuality, nation, ability, and other structures of power. And to do so, we need to challenge the property relations that generated such categories and systems of asymmetrical power.

Cyprus-EU-rest of the globe cooperation on sexual orientation equity and justice should begin with a geopolitical unpacking of the way sexual orientation is mobilized as an analytical category in policy, practice, and popular opinion. It should involve a critical examination of how various categories, such as sexual orientation and nationalism, become co-constituted with accumulation of political or globalization order and operate across Cyprus, the rest of Europe, and the globe. It should provide a full account and make appropriate use of the intellectual work of activists/intellectuals/policy makers who, in turn, should engage in a decolonial-sexual orientation analysis.

Fighting for the equal rights promised by capitalism and working to achieve equality in law does not mean equity in life. Conceding formal equality while maintaining exploitation, oppression, and obliteration mechanisms, such as transphobia and homophobia, does not rid us of the sexual misery that accompanies capitalist reproduction. No matter how many laws are passed, the violence against LGBTQ+ people and the repression of sexuality cannot be addressed within a system of property and hypermasculine family unit relations. The world of capital cannot be taken to be the world of equity. It requires that we understand the world as a political project whose goal is not the goal of conquest, nation-states, and capital. Such a world is not ours. Creating the world, from our raw material, our life, that sustains heterogeneity of flesh, bodies, languages, affects, sounds, movements, intimacies, and intensities is and should be our political project.

In the words of Queer Cyprus, let's all be "feminists," "anti-militarists," "anti-capitalists," and ecologists. Challenging the dominant intimacy desire of conquest, they advise us "to establish the organizational practices on ecological production and consumption understandings by adopting a 'consume what you need, as much as you need' approach."

Notes

1 TRNC has been legally recognized only by Turkey and Pakistan.
2 A similar law was enacted more recently in the TRNC.
3 See, for instance, the ILGA Europe Rainbow map (2017) tracking which state is "winning" the sexual race to achieve the legal and policy human rights of LGBTI peoples. Cyprus is not faring very well on this mapping process. On a scale between 100% (i.e., respecting and providing full equality to LGBTI community members) and 0% (i.e., gross violations of human rights, discrimination, bias-motivated violence), Cyprus scored only 23% and was ranked 33rd out of 49 European countries (Rainbow Europe map, 2018), available at https://rainbow-europe.org/
4 The RoC amended its Constitution in 2006 (Ο περί της Πέμπτης Τροποποιησης του Συντάγματος Νομος 2006) (Law 127 (I)/2006)). See also Tryfonidou (2018).
5 See the Cyprus Anti-Discrimination Body Report regarding the prevention and fight against homophobic speech, Complaint No. 55/2010, 56/2010, 57/2010, 58/2010, 61/2010, 29 June 2012, para 3 as cited in Tryfonidou (2018: 205).
6 The UK act of 1880–1899 claims to be "an Act to make further provision for the Protection of Women and Girls, the suppression of brothels, and other purposes." In addition to strengthening existing legislation against prostitution, it recriminalizes male homosexuality.
7 It should be noted that the Ombudsman's office has played a pivotal role in the change of legal architectures around LBGT, specifically trans peoples. See Tryfonidou (2018: 189).
8 In an interesting new twist in the ongoing feud between the LGBTQI community and the Church, ACCEPT Cyprus recently held a workshop on "Church and LGBTQI People: Opportunities for Mutual Understanding and Coexistence." Representatives said that they wished to reconcile their differences, as many of their members are religious (Cyprus Mail 2019).
9 The categories of nationality, ethnicity, community, race, and color are very difficult to separate. For instance, when people speak about race in Cyprus, most likely refer to the color of one's skin or to people of African descent. Ethnicity, nationality, and community tend to refer more to Greeks, Turks, Armenians, Arabs, Eastern

Europeans, etc. However, these categories are themselves all racialized, including nationality, if we take seriously W.E.B. Du Bois when he says the color line is a global one.

10 It should be noted here that the clear separation of Church and state in Europe did not happen in Cyprus. This does not make Cyprus a "backward" state but rather points to the tensions that exist in modernity and capitalism. More so, the split of the Eastern from the Western Christianity (i.e., Catholicism) marks another crucial transition to capitalism and gestures to the many tensions that exist between the Greek Orthodox Church and its political role in the making and unmaking of power. This requires much more research that we currently have available. Also, the relations of the Greek Church, the Ottoman Empire, and Europe are crucial, and it demonstrates how the European empires relegated themselves as the progressive and forward-looking in their vying for their global power and leadership in the world over empires like the Ottoman one.

Bibliography

Agathangelou, Anna, M. 2019. "What Suicide and Greece Tell Us about Precarity and Capitalism" 2019. Globalizations, 16(4): 541–558 https://www-tandfonline-com.ezproxy.library.yorku.ca/doi/full/10.1080/14747731.2018.1464686

Agathangelou, Anna, M. 2004. The Global Political Economy of Sex: Desire, Violence and Insecurity in Mediterranean Nation-States. Palgrave. Agathangelou, A.M., Daniel Bassichis, and Tamara L. Spira "Intimate Investments: Homonormativity, Global Lockdown, and Seductions of Empire." Radical History Review, March 2008, Queer Futures. Issue 100: pp. 120–144

Andreou, Evie. 2015. "A First Step Towards Combating Discrimination". Cyprus Mail. https://cyprus-mail.com/2015/11/27/a-first-step-tdiscrimination/

Antifa. 2017. "Beyond Corporate Pride and Mainstream LGBT politics: Queering our Struggles." https://antifanicosia.espivblogs.net/files/2017/05/Beyond-Corporate-Pride-and-Mainstream-LGBT-politics-Queering-our-Struggles.pdf

Associated Press. 2019. "LGBT Groups from Both Sides of Divided Cyprus Join Forces." https://apnews.com/454770a8a6e745878e14a95bfa8cd8d9

Bell, M. 2001. The European Union—A new source of rights for citizens in the accession countries? In ILGA-Europe (Ed.), Equality for lesbians and gay men. A relevant issue in the EU accession process (pp. 80–89). Brussels.

Benjamin, Walter. 1969. "The Work of Art in the Age of Its Technological Reproducibility," in Illuminations. Edited and with an introduction by Hannah Arendt. Translated by Harry Zohn. New York: Schocken Books. (originally published 1936).

Berlant, Lauren 2011. Cruel Optimism. Durham, NC: Duke University Press.

Cherki, Alice. 2006. Frantz Fanon: A Portrait. Cornell University Press.

Chitty, Christopher. 2017. "Reassessing Foucault: Modern Sexuality and the Transition to Capitalism." Viewpoint Magazine, https://www.viewpointmag.com/2017/04/20/reassessing-foucault-modern-sexuality-and-the-transition-to-capitalism/

Christou, Jean. 2003. "Defence Ministry under fire after gay man denied driving licence on grounds of army discharge papers" The Cyprus Mail (03.07.2003)

Cozzarelli, Tatiana. 2019. "Queer Oppression is Etched in the Heart of Capitalism." Left Voice, https://www.leftvoice.org/queer-oppression-is-etched-in-the-heart-of-capitalism

Dangaremba, Tsitsi 2004. Nervous Conditions. Ayebia Clark Publishing.

Duggan, Lisa. 2003. The Twilight of Equality? Neoliberalism, Cultural Politics, and the Attack on Democracy. Boston: Beacon.

Dzankic, Jelena. 2015. "Investment-Based Citizenship and Residence Programmes in the EU." EUI Working Paper RSCAS 2015/08, European University Institute, Robert Schuman Centre for Advanced Studies, European Union Democracy Observatory on Citizenship, pp. 1–25.

Edelman, Lee. 2004. No Future: Queer Theory and the Death Drive. Durham, NC: Duke University Press.

Fanon, Frantz. 1967. The Wretched of the Earth. Grove Press.

Francoeur, Robert T. and Raymond J. Noonan (eds.) 2003. *The Continuum Complete International Encyclopedia of Sexuality*. London: Continuum.

Gilroy, Paul. 2000. *Against Race: Imagining Political Culture Beyond the Color Line*. Cambridge, MA: Harvard University Press.

Goldberg, David. T 2008. The Threat of Race: Reflections on Racialized Neoliberalism. Wiley-Blackwell.

Gooden, Susan. 2014. *Race and Social Equity: A Nervous Area of Government*. London: Routledge.

Hosek, J., Kavanagh, J., & Miller, L. L. 2006. How deployments affect service members. Retrieved from http://www.rand.org/content/dam/rand/pubs/monographs/2005/RAND_MG432.pdf

Hussain. Ishtiaq. 2011. *The Tanzimat: Secular reforms in the Ottoman Empire*. London: Faith Matters.

Ioannou, C. 2016. "Combating HOMophoBic and Transphobic bullying in schools – HOMBAT: National report Greece". Greece: Athens, pp. 1–41.

Kamenou, Nayia. 2012. "'Cyprus is the Country of Heroes, Not of Homosexuals': Sexuality, Gender and Nationhood in Cyprus." PhD diss., King's College London (University of London).

KISA. 2019. "Hate Speech in Public Discourse Cyprus". Cyprus: Nicosia, pp. 1–32.

Lugones, Maria. 2007. "Heterosexualism and the Colonial / Modern Gender System" *Hypatia* 22 (1): 186–209.

Marriott, David. 2017. On Decadence: *Bling Bling. e-flux*, Journal #79 - February. https://www.e-flux.com/journal/79/94430/on-decadence-bling-bling/

Melamed, Jodie. 2011. Represent and Destroy: Rationalizing Violence in the New Racial Capitalism. University of Minnesota Press.

McFadden, Patricia. 2011. Resisting neocolonial/neoliberal collusion: Reclaiming our lives, our futures. Lecture delivered at the Africa Gender Institute. University of Western Cape.

Mikulak, Magdalena. 2019. Between the market and the hard place: neoliberalization and the Polish LGBT movement Magdalena Mikulak.

Pincus, S., House, R., Christenson, J., & Adler, L. (2001). The emotional cycle of deployment: A military perspective. *U.S. Army Medical Department Journal*, 15–23.

Povinelli, Elizabeth. 2019. "The Urban Intensions of Geontopower." *e-flux*, https://www.e-flux.com/architecture/liquid-utility/259667/the-urban-intensions-of-geontopower/

Povinelli, Elizabeth. 2013. Feminist Theory Workshop. Keynote, Duke University. https://www.youtube.com/watch?v=Bpl56izY2z0

Povinelli, Elizabeth. 2001. "Radical Worlds: The Anthropology of Incommensurability and Inconceivability." *Annual Review of Anthropology*, 30, 319–34.

Puar, Jasbir. 2007. Terrorist Assemblages: Homonationalism in Queer Times. Duke University Press.

Quijano, Anibal. 2000. "Coloniality of Power and Eurocentrism in Latin America." Nepantla: Views from South, 1(3): 533–580.

Sears. Alan. 2017. "Body Politics: The Social Reproduction of Sexualities." Tithi Bhattacharya, (editor) Social Reproduction Theory. Pluto Press, pp. 170–191.

Shaw, Carolyn, Martin. 2015. Women and Power in Zimbabwe Promises of Feminism. University of Illinois Press.

Simmel, George. 1950. The Metropolis and Mental Life. New York: Free Press.

Smith Helena. (26 January 2002). *"Cyprus divided over gay rights"*. *The Guardian. UK.* http://www.sodomylaws.org/

The Economist. 2019. Poland's ruling party confronts the "LGBT dictatorship" May 2, 2019 https://www.economist.com/europe/2019/05/02/polands-ruling-party-confronts-the-lgbt-dictatorship

Trimikliniotis, Nicos and Stavros, Karayiannis. 2008. "The Situation Concerning Homophobia and Discrimination on Grounds of Sexual Orientation". *Simfiliosi*

Towle, Andy. "Cyprus Launches Hate Speech Probe of Bishop Who Said Gays Come from Pregnant Women Who Enjoy Anal Sex." https://www.towleroad.com/2019/08/cyprus-hate-speech-bishop/

Tryfonidou, Alina. 2018. "The Legal Position of LGBT Persons and Same-Sex Couples in Cyprus." *The Cyprus Review*, 29(1), 183–213.

Walker, G. (2016). The sublime perversion of capital: Marxist theory and the politics of history. Durham, NC: Duke University Press.

Zoumidou, Myrto. 2019. "How Many Couple Have Chosen Civil Partnership". *Philenews.* https://www.philenews.com/koinonia/eidiseis/article/656591/posa-zevgria-epelexan-to-symfono-symbiosis-1

PART II
Race & Ethnicity

6

RACIAL EQUITY IN BRAZIL

Marilyn Rubin, Fátima Bayma de Oliveira, and Wendy M. Nicholson

Brazil is one of the largest multi-racial countries in the world. In 2017, of the nation's 207 million residents, 44.2% identified themselves as white; 46.7% as brown or mixed-race; 8.2% as black; and 0.9% as yellow (Asian) or indigenous (World Population Review, 2019). Given this diverse population, racial equity in Brazil presents a complicated panorama viewed differently depending on what type of lens is used.

Looking through a rose-colored lens, some see Brazil as a "racial democracy" defined by harmonious racial relations and an acceptance of multi-racial identities and inter-racial marriages. But those who look through a clearer lens see a Brazil where those with fair-colored skin hold a disproportionate share of wealth and power, and where racial disparities across socio-economic metrics abound. These disparate visions underlie what Edward Telles (2014), a prominent scholar on Brazil, has referred to as the enigma of Brazilian race relations. Parsing this enigma is beyond the scope of the chapter. Instead, the chapter will focus on race in Brazil as a "nervous area of government," a term introduced into the public administration lexicon by Susan Gooden (2015) to describe government's lack of action and interest around issues of race and social equity (McGinnis Johnson, 2015).

In Brazil, even with the absence of laws specifically mandating racial discrimination, de facto actions and policies promulgated by the government, or the lack thereof, have exacerbated racial inequities for centuries, starting in the 16th century with the importation by Portuguese colonists of African slaves. Nervousness regarding government policies to address racial disparities can be seen even until recent times in negative responses by some public officials to affirmative action initiatives adopted to reverse historic racial injustices. These initiatives, specifically those focused on higher education, are discussed in the last sections of the chapter.

The chapter begins with an overview of racial equity as a nervous area of government in Brazil. The next section looks at why racial equity, rooted in the nation's history of slavery, is a nervous area of government. The chapter then turns its attention to affirmative action initiatives adopted by Brazil's central and state governments to redress racial injustices, with a focus on higher education. The chapter concludes with a summary and some observations by the authors on the future of racial equity in Brazil. It should be noted that although indigenous people have historically been subject to discrimination in Brazil, they are not specifically discussed in this chapter.

A Nervous Area of Government in Brazil

A revealing place to start the discussion of race as a nervous area of government in Brazil is with the racial categories delineated in the country's national census of population. As Nobles (2000) writes: "…racial categories on censuses do not merely capture demographic realities, but rather reflect and help to create political realities and ways of thinking and seeing" (p. 1745).

Brazil's history of officially recognizing color distinctions of its residents began in 1776, while it was a Portuguese colony.[1] In compliance with a directive from Portugal requiring that a statistical count be made of the inhabitants of all its overseas possessions, Brazil undertook a census of its residents. Although not required by Portugal to do so, Brazil collected statistics on the color of its residents using census categories: white (*branco*), brown or mixed-race (*pardo*), black (*preto*), and indigenous (*indígena*), in addition to other demographic characteristics, i.e., gender and age (Bucciferro, 2015). [Note: The Portuguese words for color in parentheses will be used throughout the chapter.] Portugal did not require its overseas possessions to collect information regarding the color of their inhabitants; Brazil was its only colony with a significant multi-racial population[2] (de Matos, 2016).

Racial Definitions and the Census of Population

In Brazil, an individual's race is primarily determined by where his or her skin color falls along a color continuum with white (*branco*) and black (*preto*) as the polarities and various shades of brown in between the two. This determination of race is different than that used in other countries, e.g., the United States, where racial identification is based on ancestry, so that an individual is black if at least one of her parents is black; all siblings born to the same parents are also defined as black. In contrast, in Brazil, children with different skin colors, born to the same parents, can fall into different racial categories. That is, in the same two-parent family, a child with light-colored skin and blue eyes can be designated as white; a sibling with darker skin and brown eyes as mixed-race. According to Andrew Francis-Tan (2016), in Brazil, "…within-sibling racial heterogeneity occurs in 17–19% of families" (p. 254).

Race and Brazil's Census of Population

In Brazil, the categories used to define color, and the narrative in the official census related to color reflects the period in which the population count has been undertaken. Nobles (2000) divides the history of Brazil's census into three periods. She says that in the first census period from 1872 to 1910, "...categorization largely reflected elite and popular conceptions of Brazil's racial composition" (p. 1743). In the second census period from 1920 to 1950, "... census texts actively promoted and reported the whitening of Brazil's population" (p. 1743). For example, the introductory section to Brazil's 1920 census, authored by Francisco José de Oliveira Viana, is entitled "Evolution of the Race." Viana, a Brazilian historian known to hold racist views (FGVCPDOC, n.d.), denigrated the intelligence of "blacks" and questioned their willingness to work (IBGE, 1920). This reflected the country's racist efforts to make the population white, an effort catalyzed by the government through its immigration policy subsidizing "white" European immigration, prohibiting "black" immigration, and limiting "yellow" (Asian) immigration.

The third census period identified by Nobles (2000) began in 1960 and continues to the present time. During this period, she says, "...categorization methods have been questioned and contested by statisticians within the Census Bureau and by organized groups within civil society" (p. 1743). In the 1970 census, the color choice was totally eliminated by the Brazilian Institute of Geography and Statistics[3] (*Instituto Brasileiro de Geografia e Estatística* or IBGE), the agency given the responsibility by the Brazilian government to collect official demographic statistics. This action was taken to comply with an "institutional act" passed by the military government[4] to stultify any public discussion of racism or racial inequities (Agier, 1995).

In 1976, in an effort to clarify the color categories used in the census, the IBGE surveyed people living in the northeastern area of Brazil, home to the country's largest concentration of residents with darker skin. The survey asked what *tipos*[5] respondents used to describe their own color. Illustrating the ambiguity of color, IBGE received 136 different responses including "cinnamon," "honey-colored white," "purplish," and "chestnut" (see Appendix 1 for *tipos* given by survey respondents).[6] IBGE ignored the survey results. In fact, four years later, in the 1980 census, the data collection form as originally designed actually excluded a question on color (Daniel, 2006).

In response to pressure from academics and activists (mainly Brazilians with darker skin tones), IBGE reversed its original decision and included a question on color on the 1980 census form. Academics saw that the question would provide data consistent with earlier censuses to allow for research and analysis. Activists believed that a question on color "...would insure that Brazil's racial composition was documented and that social stratification could be analyzed in terms of color" (Daniel, 2006, p. 247).

In the 1990 census,[7] again under pressure from activists and academics, the IBGE reformulated the question about color to include the word "race" for the first time in the history of the country's official population count. The question asked was "What is your color or race?" The wording of this question reflected the growing influence of the Unified Black Movement Against Racial Discrimination (*Movimento Negro Unificado Contra a Discriminação Racial* or MNU) founded in 1978. MNU was in the forefront of the campaign asking people to select a darker color for their self-identification than they might have originally intended. But color was still the predominant way of identifying race in Brazil's census since the "race" descriptor was applied specifically to the indigenous population. According to the IBGE, "Indigenous persons belonged to one race, Brazilians to another race with its many colors" (Nobles, 2000, p. 1744).

For the 2000 and 2010 censuses, IBGE used the same color classifications as it did in the 1990 census, ignoring the growing controversies about its choices. As Loveman, Muniz, & Bailey (2012) state:

> [C]ritics contend that the official distinction between 'black' and 'mixed' Brazilians on the census perpetuates an ideological myth of a fluid racial order; they argue that, in reality, Brazilian racial dynamics are essentially binary, and official categories should reflect this state of affairs.
>
> *(p. 1467)*

Other criticisms of IBGE center on the fact that the color categories it uses are not terms generally applied by Brazilians to identify themselves. This is especially true for the *pardo* category. Bailey and Telles (2002) explain: "Although we translate it as brown, the Portuguese term *pardo* literally refers to an unflattering, arid grayish brown color that in popular parlance would rarely be used to describe one's self…" (p. 5). *Moreno* is an alternative word used by many mixed-race Brazilians to describe themselves and has even been used in hundreds of popular song lyrics. *Moreno* has, however, never been used as a color category in the census. A second issue relating to color categories has been raised by activists who have suggested that the *preto* and *pardo* categories be grouped together as a single category (Telles, 2014) to classify darker-skinned individuals.

As Brazil prepares for its next decennial census in 2020, IBGE's decision to maintain its traditional color categories is again under scrutiny since official census data not only help to shape racial identities, but also have an impact on the implementation of government policies directed at addressing historic racial injustices. This impact is illustrated later in the chapter in the discussion of Brazil's affirmative action policies in higher education.

Socio-Economic Status and Color

In addition to skin tone, socio-economic status affects positioning along the color continuum, often in acknowledgment of the generally accepted aphorism in Brazil that "money whitens." According to Lovell and Wood (1998), at this intersection of race and class:

> ...very dark-skinned persons who are also poor are likely to be thought of – and to classify themselves – as black..., but high-status persons of the same skin tone are more likely to be thought of – and to classify themselves – as brown ... or some other term closer to the white end of the continuum.
>
> *(p. 92)*

The use of color rather than ancestry (which is immutable) to determine race contributes to the fluidity of racial definition in Brazil where people can re-define their color/race over time. This often happens in recognition of the "lighter is better" philosophy that permeates most aspects of Brazilian society (Schwartzman, 2007). Racial fluidity tends to reinforce the existing "money whitens" color lines, with people redefining themselves as higher-status white rather than lower-status black or brown. This redefinition becomes especially important in discussions regarding racial inequities since there continue to be some who argue that what is prevalent in Brazil is class discrimination rather than racial discrimination, reinforcing the notion that Brazil is a racial democracy (Telles, 2014).

It should, however, be noted that there are some instances in which the "lighter is better" philosophy does not hold. This is especially true as the government implements affirmative action programs to address the representational gap for black and brown skin Brazilians. Since these programs are directed at those with darker skin tones, some who might otherwise declare themselves to be *branco* may instead declare themselves to be *pardo*.

Why Racial Equity Is a Nervous Area of Government

Racial equity as a nervous area of government is rooted in Brazil's legacy of slavery – an original racial inequity. Long home to numerous tribes and settlements of indigenous people, Brazil was "discovered" by Portugal in the first decade of the 16th century (see Appendix 2 for time line of government changes in Brazil). Portugal started to traffic slaves from the West African coast beginning in the 15th century (Barrigan, 2017). As Portuguese colonists in Brazil began to establish large sugar plantations, there was a growing need for people to work the fields. At first, colonists enslaved the indigenous population many of whom either ran away or died after contracting diseases from the Europeans. The colonists, following the path Portugal had forged, turned to slave trafficking, transporting captives from Africa to work in the sugar fields and other parts of the growing economy.

From the late 16th century to the middle of the 19th century, at least 4 million African slaves were transported to Brazil,[8] ten times the estimated 400,000

African slaves transported to the United States from the 17th to the 19th centuries. "In Brazil, by 1800 fully one half of the total Brazilian population of 3,200,000 was slave, and by 1818 there were 1,930,000 slaves besides some 526,000 free Negroes and mulattoes, in all about sixty-three percent of the total" (Alexander, 1922, p. 350). Free Negroes and mulattoes were former slaves who were able to purchase their freedom, a much more common practice in Brazil than in the United States. In Brazil, Graham (2016) states that:

> Between two fifths and one half of adult slaves who were freed paid for their freedom in cash or the promise of cash. Slaves secured such funds because of the common practice of allowing them to find their own employment, returning to their masters a fixed sum, and keeping the remainder for themselves. They were called *ganhadores*, "earners".
>
> *(p. 3)*

In addition, some slaves escaped from captivity and established communities, called *quilombos*, often with help from indigenous people. African traditions were continued in the *quilombos*, helping to create a distinct African culture that persists until the present time.

Although male slaves predominated, a significant number of slaves transported to Brazil from Africa were female. Non-consensual sexual unions between Portuguese colonists and African slaves and indigenous women were common, but since inter-racial marriage in Brazil was legal there were also consensual arrangements. Inter-racial marriages reflected the generally held belief that slaves were menial laborers, rather than – as believed in the United States – members of a lesser race (Alexander, 1922) who were "beasts of burden."[9]

Although Brazilians with darker skin were not seen as being of a lesser race, skin color was still a critical factor in perpetuating racial inequities. According to Graham (2016): "[t]he government reinforced the prejudices of white Brazilians, acquiesced in maintaining a hierarchy based on color, and presented obstacles to the ambitions of free African Brazilians" (p. 1). These obstacles would continue long after slavery ended. For instance, Fernandes (1965) saw the predominance of people with darker skin tone in low-status occupations as a legacy of slavery into the 1960s.

The Road to Abolition

It was not until several decades after it won its independence from Portugal in 1822 that Brazil began to pass laws, in a slow piecemeal manner, to halt slave trafficking and to free some slaves. However, conflicting provisions in several of these laws reveal the government's ambivalence about abolition. For instance, the 1871 Law of the Free Womb (*Lei do Ventre Livre*) declared that all children born to slave mothers after the law was passed would be free. But diluting the outcome of the law, one provision stated that "…parents would have to provide for the children until they reached the age of 21. A loophole in the law was that a slaveholder could turn the children over to the government of Brazil and receive payment" (Swift, 2017).

Children turned over to the government were permitted to learn how to read and write; those who stayed with slave-owners generally remained illiterate (Chalhoub, 2006). This would eventually preclude them from voting under the 1881 Savaria Law (*Lei Savaria*) that granted suffrage to former slaves. But, again reflecting government's nervousness about freeing the slaves, *Lei Savaria* also required Brazilians to pass a literacy test to vote (Burns, 1968), diluting the suffrage provisions.

Abolition into the Mid-20th Century

The Golden Law (*Lei Áurea*), enacted in 1888, officially ended slavery, making Brazil the last country in the Western Hemisphere to do so. At the time of abolition, blacks and mixed-race Brazilians outnumbered whites. "Abolition brought panic to the ruling [light-skinned] elite, which hurried to set about constructing public policies aimed at rubbing out the 'black stain' and 'purifying' the nation's racial stock" (Nascimento & Nascimento 2001, p. 121). The government, anxious to keep the support of the elites, instituted "embranquecer," a policy to "whiten" Brazil's population. Wejsa and Lesser (2018) explain:

> In 1891, the government enacted legislation guaranteeing religious freedom to attract European Protestants, whose Whiteness elites believed would help to "de-Africanize" Brazil's population. Politicians simultaneously banned immigrants from Africa and Asia in further hopes of "Whitening" … the country.
>
> *(A New World Order Section, para 2)*

The government's whitening policies continued through the first decades of the 20th century into the 1930s. Ironically, at the same time that racist immigration policies were being implemented, the government was extolling the nation as a "racial democracy," a term generally accredited to Gilberto Freyre. Freyre, a Brazilian sociologist, was the author of *The Masters and Slaves* (Casa-Grande & Senzala), a widely read book published in 1933. Although he never actually used the term "racial democracy" in this book, Freyre later came to accept the term and his "…writings … became the basis of a … semi-official ideology propagated in public proclamations, schools and universities, and the national media" (Andrews, 1996, p. 488). Getúlio Vargas, the Head of Brazil's government from 1930 to 1945,[10] bought into the racial democracy vision, giving his government a way to ignore glaring racial disparities. The government was able to accept this notion of a racial democracy largely because of the absence of segregation laws and the fact that Brazil was home to significant numbers of mixed-race individuals and marriages.

Vargas stepped down in 1945, but was re-elected president in 1950.[11] The government, still promoting the idea that Brazil was a racial democracy, issued a publication in 1951 praising race relations in the country (Skidmore, 1974). Moreover, as Marcos Maio (2001) writes: "...Brazil's seemingly harmonious race relations became famous enough to attract the attention of UNESCO" (p. 120), the United Nations Educational, Scientific, and Cultural Organization. UNESCO, in an effort to learn how Brazil was apparently able to combat racism that was growing in the rest of the world, commissioned a study on race relations in Brazil that was conducted during the early 1950s by a multinational team of social scientists. The study, looking to explain Brazil's racial harmony, "...produced a vast documentation of prejudice and discrimination against Brazilian blacks.... Research findings did not deny the importance of the myth of racial democracy. Rather, they revealed the tensions between the myth and ... Brazilian ... racism" (Maio, 2001, p. 134).

A stark example of racism in Brazil occurred at the same time that the UNESCO study was being conducted when a famous Black ballerina was turned away from a luxury hotel in São Paulo (Andrews, 1996). There was, however, an ironic outcome associated with the publicity surrounding the hotel's action. In 1951 – the same year as the government's publication extolling harmonious racial relations was released – Brazil's Congress passed the Afonso Arinos Act, the country's first law that specifically acknowledged racial discrimination. The law, named after its sponsor, made racial discrimination in public places a misdemeanor (*contravenção*), subject to a short jail stay or a fine. Although relatively few cases would be tried under the law, it opened the door for a legal way to challenge racist actions. Recent government initiatives to address racial discrimination are discussed later in the chapter following a statistical presentation of racial disparities.

Racial Inequities in Brazil

Racial inequities in Brazil can be seen across socio-economic domains. Lovell and Wood (1988) provide a useful construct for looking at these inequities "... by focusing on four critical transitions – surviving childhood, acquiring an education, entering the labor market, and getting paid..." (p. 90). A somewhat modified version of this construct is presented below to provide a sense of the magnitude of racial inequities in Brazil.

Surviving Childhood

Surviving childhood is highly dependent upon getting through the first year of life. For countries, the metric generally used to measure this survival is the infant mortality rate (IMR).[12] In Brazil, the IMR was declining for several decades until 2016 when it increased over the previous year, reflecting the impact of the Zika virus that hit Brazil in 2015. According to the World Health Organization, the virus can "...cause infants to be born with microcephaly and other congenital malformations" (World Health Organization [WHO], 2018).

Women living in Brazil's regions with large populations of darker-skinned residents were most affected by the virus (Lowe, Barcellos, Cruz, Honorio, Kuper, & Carvalho, 2018). This is consistent with earlier findings that

> Many health disadvantages, such as high prevalence of low birth-weight and preterm births, poor nutritional status, and increased risk of death during the first year of life, have been found to be more prevalent among Black infants than among White ones.
>
> *(Matijasevich et al., 2008)*

Moreover, among children under five years of age, "The nonwhite...population has a markedly excessive mortality rate, as do those living in the Northeast region of the country" (Pan American Health Organization, 2012, p. 133), home to the largest concentration of darker-skinned Brazilians.

Acquiring an Education

Gooden (2015) writes that "education is a very important factor in understanding social inequities" (p. 28). In Brazil, there has been a significant increase in enrollment over the past 20 years for children of all races, at all levels of education (see Figure 6.1). However, in both 1995 and 2015, moving through

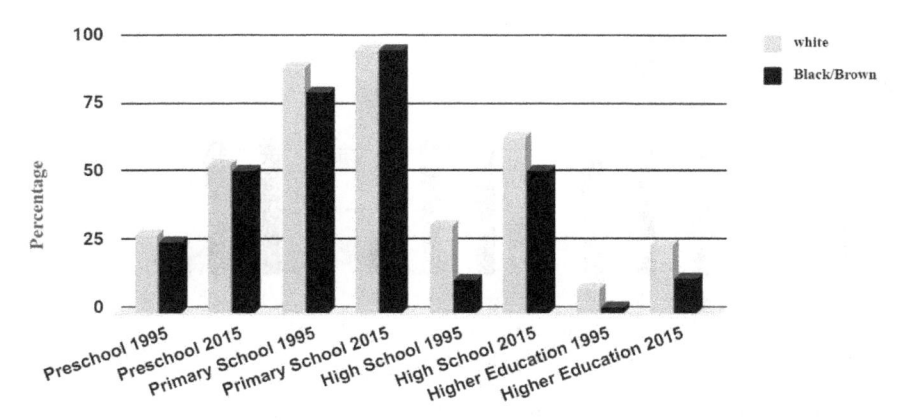

FIGURE 6.1 School Enrollment in Brazil by Color/Race, 1995 & 2015.
Source: Retrato das Desigualdades de Gênero e Raça, Table 3.6.

levels of schooling, racial disparities become apparent. The gap is most glaring in higher education. In 2015, in age appropriate years, 9.1% of whites were enrolled in higher education compared with 2.0% of black and brown individuals. There is even a wider gap among those who actually graduate from a college or university. In 2009, for *pretos*, the completion rate was 4.7%; for pardos, 5.3%; for *brancos*, 15% (IBGE, 2010).

The Labor Market

Although there have been swings in the Brazilian economy since the early years of the 21st century, the trend has moved in a general upward direction. While labor market metrics reflect this growth, when they are disaggregated by race, the gap between *preto/pardo* residents and *brancos* can be seen. *Preto* and *pardo* Brazilians, who together represent more than 55% of the country's population, "…account for nearly two-thirds of the country's jobless" (Sandy, 2018). In 2018, average monthly earnings of *brancos* were 74% above those of *pardos* and *pretos* (IBGE, 2019). Earning differentials hold across industries (see Figure 6.2), although the gap has narrowed somewhat in recent years (Firpo & Renan, 2018). Racial differences in average incomes reflect earnings disparities across all occupations in all industries.

The higher average income for *brancos* across industries reflects, to a large degree, the fact that they generally hold higher positions than do *pretos/pardos*. According to IBGE, in 2018, just 29.9% of managerial positions in Brazil were held by *pretos* and *pardos*. The business ownership metric also demonstrates the racial gap in Brazil. In 2009, among *brancos*, 6.1% were business owners; among *pardos*, 2.8%; among *pretos*, 1.7% (STF, 2012).

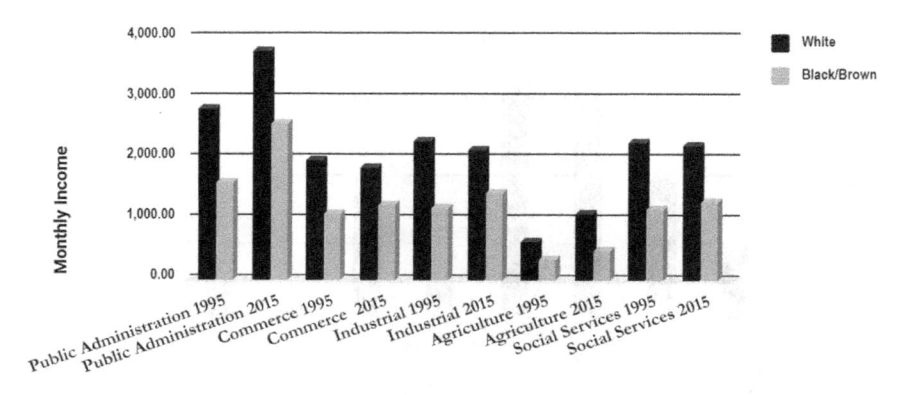

FIGURE 6.2 Average Monthly Income in Selected Industries by Color/Race, 1995 & 2015.

Source: Retrato das Desigualdades de Gênero e Raça, Table 10.1a3.

Other Indicators of Racial Disparities

In addition to the above indicators, there are other markers that document racial disparities in Brazil. For example, looking at family structure, there is significant variation across races in the proportion of families with children under the age of 14 headed by single mothers. They account for 17.7% of all white families, a proportion significantly lower than the 23.3% of all black families, and the 25.9% of all mixed-race families (STF, 2012).

In the criminal justice area, racial disparities also abound. Data on the imprisoned population is one metric that is often used to illustrate this disparity (see Table 6.1). For *pardos*, their percentage of all prisoners was 2 percentage points below their representation in the total population. For *brancos*, their percentage of total prisoners was 10 percentage points less than their proportion of the total population. Conversely, for *pretos*, their proportion of all prisoners was more than double their representation in the population as a whole. Acknowledging that these data are indicative of a serious problem, it is outside the scope of the chapter to delve into the reasons behind the racial disparities in the prison system. It is, however, of interest that the same racial disparities in the proportion of people in the prison system, relative to their proportion in the total population, exist in the United States.

Not only are there racial disparities across socio-economic domains, but so, too, is there a racial gap in the political arena. In the 2018 elections, 125 (24%) of the 513 persons elected to Congress "…declared themselves to be black or brown" (Brazilian Report, 2018), less than half of their representation in the total population.

A Promising Government Initiative: Affirmative Action in Higher Education

In the early 2000s, affirmative action initiatives began to be implemented in Brazil in an effort to address racial inequities either abetted or ignored by government for centuries. This section of the chapter will focus specifically on policies adopted to address racial disparities in higher education. The section begins with a brief description of the context for these policies.

TABLE 6.1 Prison Population and Total Population, by Color/Race, 2017

Race/Color	Proportion of Prison Inmates (%)	Proportion of Total Population (%)
Branco	34.4	44.2
Pardo	44.8	46.7
Preto	16.8	8.2
Amarila	0.7	n.a.
Indígena	0.2	n.a.

Source: Levantamento nacional de Informações Penitenciárias – Infopen, Junho 2017.

Historical Context

As previously discussed, after abolition, through the first decades of the 20th century, government abetted discrimination through its immigration and other policies. This was followed by Getúlio Vargas's two terms in office during which time government extolled Brazil as a racial democracy, ignoring rampant racial disparities. Under the military dictatorship from the 1960s to 1985, government prohibited public discussion of race and racism. After the dictatorship ended in 1985, government policy began to change direction, as demonstrated in the Constitution adopted in 1988.

A country's constitution establishes the rules that regulate the powers of its government and spells out the rights and duties of its residents. For the first time in the country's history, the two constitutions adopted immediately before the one adopted in 1988[13] incorporated some language about equality. The 1946 Constitution stated that "All are equal before the law" (Georgetown, n.d.). The 1967 Constitution is more explicit about race and other demographic descriptors. Drafted under the military dictatorship, during which time public discussion of race and racism was prohibited, the Constitution stated: "All are equal before the law, no distinction based on sex, race, work, religion and political conviction. Racial prejudice will be punished according to the law" (Georgetown, n.d.).

Language regarding race adopted in the 1988 Constitution was more explicit and far-reaching. Article 5, Section XLII of Title II, Fundamental Rights and Guarantees,[14] states: "Racism is a crime for which bail is not available and which is punishable by imprisonment pursuant to law" (Georgetown, n.d.). Other parts of the Constitution affirm a commitment to multiculturalism, including the protection of race-related cultural practices. Another section grants land titles to descendants of *quilombos*, the communities established by escaped slaves.

It would not be until 1995, however, under the presidency of Fernando Henrique Cardoso, that the government would finally admit that Brazil was a racist country. As indicative of Cardoso's recognition of the racism endemic across the country, he established the Interministerial Working Group (*Grupo de Travalho Interministerial* or GTI) for the Development of Public Policies to Valorize the Black Populations (Telles, 2014). However, symbolic of the continuous nervousness in the Brazilian government about redressing racial inequities, "...government ministries actually sought to boycott implementation of the GTIs recommendations" (Telles, 2014, p. 56). Cardoso tried to initiate other actions to correct the historic discrimination against *preto* and *pardo* Brazilians, but he continued to have opposition from members of his own administration including Paulo Renato Souza, the Minister of Education. Souza was a strong opponent of any type of affirmative action initiative that would increase the representation of Brazilians with dark skin in higher education institutions (Htun, 2004).

Despite the objections of Souza and others, "…over the following few years, black activists, politicians, scholars, and students were among the key political forces for the implementation of affirmative action in selected universities across Brazil" (Valente & Berry, 2017, p. 20). These actions took the form of numerical requirements, i.e., quotas, for students with specified demographic characteristics.

Affirmative Action: University Quota Systems

The first state to establish quotas was Rio de Janeiro.[15] In 2002, affirmative action policies were approved by the state legislature mandating that its two state universities set aside 50% of spots in their incoming class for poor public school students and 40% for students identifying as *preto* (Htun, 2004). In 2002, two other states followed suit: Bahia and Minas Gerais. In 2004, the University of Brasilia, a federal university located in Brazil's capital city, instituted a quota system, with 20% of its available admission spaces reserved for students identifying as *preto* (Francis & Tannuri-Pianto, 2009).

These quotas proved to be very contentious. So much so that the controversy over the quota system established at the University of Brasilia ended up being contested in Brazil's Supreme Court. One of the most powerful opponents of quotas was Renato Souza who perceived that the problem of university access was not racial, but rather a matter of insufficient preparation at lower levels of education (Htun, 2004). This was an interesting perspective relating to Brazil's two-tiered education system: public schools and private schools.

Parents who can afford to do so – generally those with lighter skin – send their children to private schools that prepare students to take the Vestibular, the entrance examination required for admission to the highly rated free public universities. Results on the Vestibular are the only criterion for admission to these universities. Children whose parents do not have the means to send them to private schools attend public schools that do not generally provide the quality education found in the private schools. Consequently, a much higher percentage of *branco* students than *preto* or *pardo* students have historically passed the qualifying tests for admission to the public universities.

In April 2012, the Supreme Court found the affirmative action policy at the University of Brasilia to be constitutional, ruling that the quota system was reasonable, appropriate and consistent with constitutional principles (Federal Supreme Court, 2012). In August 2012, Dilma Rousseff, the then Brazil's President, signed into law the act passed by Congress mandating that all federal institutions of higher education allocate 50% of their spots in incoming classes to self-declared *preto, pardo*, and *indígena* students.[16] Additionally, the law required that the total number of vacancies in each federal university be filled according to the percentage of *pretos* and *pardos* living in the state in which the institution is located. Figure 6.3 provides a pictorial representation of how the law was to be implemented at each federal university.

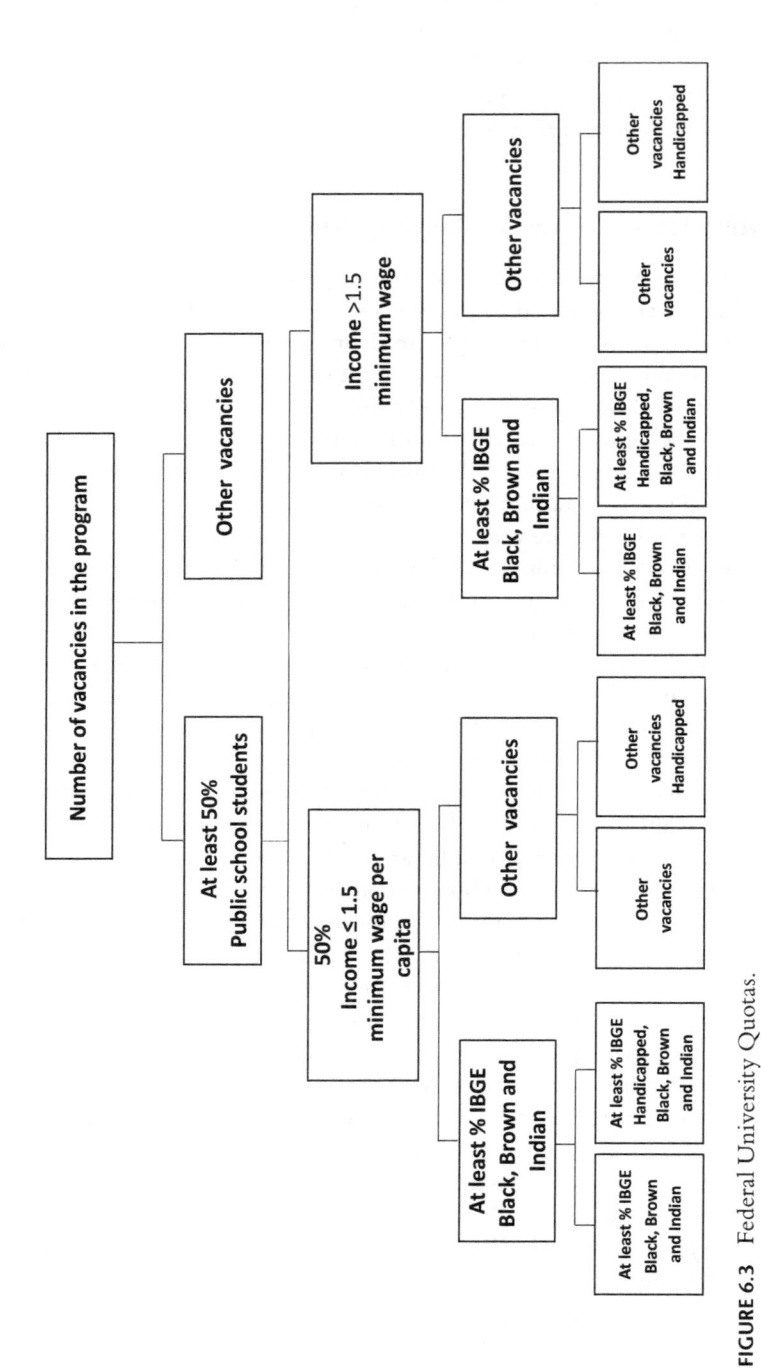

FIGURE 6.3 Federal University Quotas.

Source: http://portal.mec.gov.br/cotas/sobre-sistema.html.

The Debate Over Quotas

Soon after the quota law was passed, challenges to it arose, mostly from white students and their parents, claiming that they were denied university entrance because less qualified black students were being admitted in their stead. The concern of the white students is explained by the fact that Brazilian universities use the European system of limited seats per discipline per year (Lathrop & Dias, 1992). If a proportion of seats are given to non-white students under the quota system, the impact on white students is obvious.

The quotas, especially for the tuition-free top-ranked federal universities, brought the usually veiled discussion about race in Brazil into the open. White students and faculty staged large, angry protests against the quotas. Television news programs showed weeping white mothers describing how their children had prepared their entire lives to follow in their parents' footsteps but were being denied their birthright. The harshest critics of affirmative action insisted that the quotas were introducing racial discrimination into Brazil – rather than working to mitigate it – simply by noting the very existence of a racial hierarchy (Htun, 2004).

One of the biggest controversies associated with quotas centers around the criteria for *preto* designation. All institutions of higher education have developed their own approaches to address this delicate issue. One approach has been to establish race/color commissions or panels. These commissions have been tasked with deciding who is sufficiently *preto*, to be considered eligible for university admission under the quota system. The University of Brasilia, the first federal university to implement quotas, requires applicants to submit photos and to interview with a university panel. The 12 members of the panel rate each person's skin tone on a scale from one (lightest) to seven (darkest) (Vazquez Baur, 2017). The combination of information gleaned from interviews and phenotype is used to decide if the candidate meets basic admissions criteria and is *preto* enough to qualify for admission under the quotas (Da Silva, 2019).

At the Federal University of Paraná (UFPR), applicants are required to submit academic documentation and to write an affirmation declaring their color as defined in the IBGE's official census designations, and stating that they are recognized in society by this designation. Their complete submission package is reviewed by a committee responsible for assessing academic information and evaluating letters of declaration to prove applicant "blackness." UFPR has been severely criticized for this approach (Vazquez Baur, 2017).

Other universities have adopted different approaches to implement the quota law. For example, the Federal University of Pelotas (UFPel) created an Ethnicity Evaluation Committee to verify "blackness" of applicants, by evaluating phenotypical characteristics as mandated by the Public Prosecutor's Office (Vazquez Baur, 2017). Seeking to be more comprehensive in the evaluation process, some universities "enhanced" their admissions criteria. For example, the Department of Education in Para, Brazil's "blackest" state, devised a checklist by which to score applicants that included such check-offs as nose's shape and size, thickness of lips, hair type, and skull shape (Vazquez Baur, 2017). Opinions about these processes have ranged from "they were unfortunately necessary" to "they bring to mind actions of the slave trade" (Vazquez Baur, 2017).

Assessment and Evidence of Progress

Assessments thus far conducted of the affirmative action initiatives have showed somewhat positive results. At the University of Brasilia, for example, an evaluation of the impact of quotas adopted in 2004 showed that they have resulted in changes in the racial and socio-economic composition of students and that there have been positive effects on racial identity and on academic performance of "quota students" (Francis & Tannuri-Pianto, 2009).

Based on inputs, i.e., counts, it appears that quotas are "working" across universities. As shown in Figure 6.4, from 2003 to 2014, the percentage of students identifying as *preto* and *pardo* at federal universities rose from 34% to 48% of all students. By 2018, the proportion had increased to 50.3% (IBGE, 2019).

Thus, input data seem to show that the quotas are working. The more important question is, however, what will be the outcomes, i.e. results, of the quotas? Improving the accessibility of *pardo* and *preto* students to higher education is

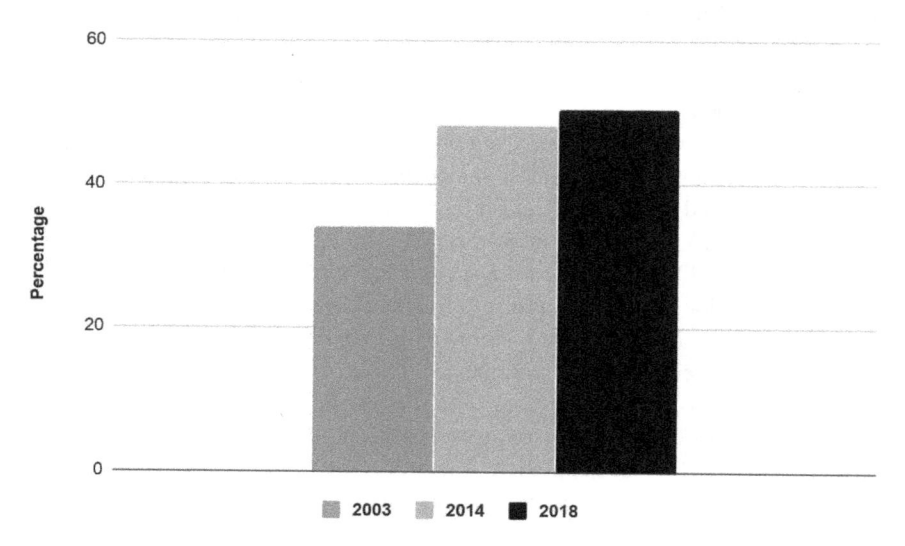

FIGURE 6.4 Percentage of Federal University Students Identifying as Black or Brown.

Source: IBGE (2019); Knoll, T. (2019). "Cost of Opportunity" undergraduates present: Brazilian higher education access spurs both economic and cultural advancement. Does one matter more?

not an end, in itself. Ultimately what will tell if the quotas have been successful is greater accessibility to the job market, higher earnings, and a better quality of life for Brazilians with darker skin tone. It is still too soon after quota implementation to know if this is going to happen. In 2018, *brancos* who held a college degree earned hourly wages 45% greater than those earned by *pardos* and *pretos* (IBGE, 2019). An assessment of the quotas at the UFPel provides cause for concern. It found that some students and professors at the university believe the only thing that has changed with the implementation of quotas is the number of white-looking students self-identifying as *preto* (de Oliveira, 2017).

The quotas have sparked widespread controversy. Many who argue against them believe that easing access to higher education denies the principle of merit that brings excellence to public universities. According to Valente and Berry (2017), however, quota students perform slightly better than non-quota students in private universities, and there is no difference in performance between quota and traditionally admitted students in public universities. How much pressure opponents to quotas can exert, and how responsive lawmakers under pressure will be to their arguments to dismantle quotas, remains to be seen.

Conclusion

"Discovered" by Portugal at the beginning of the 16th century, Brazil's history is rooted in slavery that brought millions of captured people from Africa to work the fields and other parts of the economy. Sexual unions of Portuguese male colonists with indigenous women and female African slaves produced a class of people referred to as "mixed-race," creating the beginnings of what would become one of the largest multi-racial populations in countries across the world.

Brazil won its independence from Portugal in 1822. In 1888, it became the last country in the Western Hemisphere to abolish slavery. Throughout its colonial years until now, racial inequities have existed in Brazilian life, even if there are some who continue to see the country as a "racial democracy." In reality, however, *preto* and *pardo* Brazilians have far lower levels of education and "…make up the majority of the unemployed and poor population…" (OXFAM, 2019). In 2018, *pardos* and *pretos* accounted for 75% of Brazilians in the country's lowest income bracket (IBGE, 2019) but just 27.7% of the top 10% of earners.

For centuries, government either abetted racial inequities or did nothing to redress them. Demonstrating race as a nervous area of government in Brazil, from abolition into the early decades of the 20th century, immigration laws were passed to "whiten" the country's population. During the next several decades, the country's image as a "racial democracy" kept the topic of race and inequity out of public discourse as did a dictatorship that did not want public discussion of race and racism. It was not until 1995 that the then President Fernando Henrique Cardoso publicly acknowledged that Brazil was a racist state. When he tried to change the direction of government to redress racism, there were members of his cabinet who did not want to see this happen. But, reacting to pressure from activists and others, all segments of Brazil's government have since taken steps to mitigate racial discrimination.

In 2012, a significant step was taken by the Supreme Court in its decision that affirmative action – in the form of quotas in universities – is constitutional. Another significant step taken was the 2012 signing by Brazil's then President Dilma Rousseff of a law mandating quotas in federal universities for those with darker skin tones. Quota systems have now been implemented in several state universities as well as in other areas of society including government and the media.

But, the question remains, what does the future hold? There have been substantial gains made by *preto* and *pardo* Brazilians in recent years across socio-economic domains, and incomes have risen across races. "But despite this evolution, the pace has been very slow and the Latin American giant is still listed as one of the most unequal countries on the planet…" (OXFAM, 2019). Much remains to be done if Brazil is to catch up with its neighbors and the rest of the world. According to OXFAM (2019),

> [a]t the current rate inequality is decreasing in Brazil, it will take the country 75 years to reach the United Kingdom's current level of income equality and almost 60 years to meet Spanish standards. Compared to its neighbors, Brazil is 35 years behind Uruguay and 30 behind Argentina.
>
> *(2019)*

Achieving an equitable society will depend, to some degree, on what darker skin Brazilians do, themselves, to remove racist obstacles. Fighting racial injustices will, however, require support from all of Brazil's residents, its president, as well as others in high levels of government. One positive sign is the recent election to Brazil's Congress of black women with progressive platforms promoting justice for all. But it does not appear that Jair Bolsonaro, the current President of Brazil, who sees the country as a racial democracy, perceives the achievement of racial inequity to be a pressing issue (Knoll, 2019). Once there is support from Brazilians across the color spectrum and from all parts of the government, including the president, for equal treatment of people regardless of color, "racial democracy" may actually become a reality.

Notes

1 Brazil was a possession of Portugal from the early part of the 16th century until it won its independence in 1822.
2 Portugal's empire in 1776 consisted of: Brazil, Madeira and Azores, Cape Verde, Guinea-Bissau, S. Tome and Principe, Angola, Mozambique, Portuguese India and Macao.

3 Starting in 1940, the census has been conducted every ten years. In 1967, IBGE became a federal agency linked to the Ministry of Planning, Budget and Management.
4 See Appendix 2 for time line of governments in Brazil.
5 *Tipo* (type in English) is a descriptor of physical characteristics.
6 It should be noted that the great majority of the responses were attributable to relatively few respondents. Most chose the five colors included in the Census.
7 The 1990 Census was actually conducted in 1991.
8 Estimates of how many slaves were brought to Brazil from Africa range from 4–5
million.
9 In the United States, miscegenation was illegal in some states, even before the
country was established, and remained so until ruled unconstitutional in 1967 by
the U.S. Supreme Court.
10 From 1930 to 1934, Getúlio Vargas was Interim President. From 1934 to 1937,
he was the constitutionally elected president, and from 1937 to 1945, ruled as a
dictator.
11 See Appendix 2 for government history timeline.
12 IMR = the number of infants dying before reaching one year of age per 1,000 live
births in a given year.
13 Brazil has had seven Constitutions: 1824, 1891, 1934, 1937, 1946, 1967 and 1988.
14 The 1988 Constitution is made up of nine titles, each of which is divided into chapters and then articles.
15 The State of Rio de Janeiro is the third most populous state in Brazil. One of the
cities in its boundaries is the city of Rio de Janeiro.
16 Also to be included in the quotas are students with disabilities, those who have
completed a public high school education and those whose family income is equal
to or less than 1.5 minimum wage per capita (the measure of poverty in Brazil).

References

Agier, M. (1995). "Racism, Culture and Black Identity in Brazil." *Bulletin of Latin American Research*, 14(3), 245–264. Retrieved from https://www.jstor.org/stable/3339326

Alexander, H.B. (1922). "Brazilian and United States Slavery Compared." *The Journal of
Negro History*, VII(4), 349–364. Retrieved from https://www.journals.uchicago.edu/
doi/pdfplus/10.2307/2713718

Andrews, G.R. (1996, July). "Brazilian Racial Democracy, 1900–90: An American
Counterpoint." *Journal of Contemporary History*, 31(3), 483–507. Retrieved from
https://www.jstor.org/stable/261017

Bailey, S. & Telles, E.E. (2002). "From Ambiguity to Affirmation: Challenging Census
Race Categories in Brazil." *Semantic Scholar*. Retrieved from https://pdfs.semantic-
scholar.org/6290/55c8f510cb4496f417ea2f168c57b4b60184.pdf

Barrigan, Y. (2017). "Uncovering Lisbon's Forgotten History of Slavery." *Black Perspectives*. Retrieved from https://www.aaihs.org/uncovering-lisbons-forgotten-
history-of-slavery/

Brazilian Report. (2018). "Ethnic Representation in Brazil's Congress: A Long Road
Ahead." Retrieved from https://brazilian.report/power/2018/11/20/ethnic-
representation-brazil-congress/

Bucciferro, J.R. (2015). "Racial Inequality in Brazil from Independence to Present."
Retrieved from http://sites.middlebury.edu/ehrgc/files/2015/04/Bucciferro.pdf

Burns, E.B. (1968). *Nationalism in Brazil: A Historical Survey*. New York: Frederick A.
Praeger.

Chalhoub, S. (2006). "The Politics of Silence: Race and Citizenship in Nineteenth-Century Brazil." *Slavery & Abolition*, 27(1), 73–87. doi: 10.1080/01440390500499976.

Daniel, G.R. (2006). *Race and Multiraciality in Brazil and the United States*. University Park: Pennsylvania State University Press.

Da Silva, P.S. (2019). "Skin Color and Educational Exclusion in Brazil: Affirmative-Action Programs in Brazilian Higher Education." *ReVista*. Retrieved from https://revista.drclas.harvard.edu/book/skin-color-and-educational-exclusion-brazil

de Matos, P.T. (2016). "Counting Portuguese Colonial Reparations, 1776–1875." *History of the Family*, 21(2), 267–280. doi: 10.1080/1081602X.2016.1147371.

de Oliveira, C. (2017 April 5). "Brazil's New Problem with Blackness." *Foreign Policy*. Retrieved from https://foreignpolicy.com/2017/04/05/brazils-new-problem-with-blackness-affirmative-action/

Federal Supreme Court. (2012). "STF Declared the Constitutionality of the Quota System at the University of Brasília." Retrieved from http://www2.stf.jus.br/portalStfInternacional/cms/destaquesClipping.php?sigla=portalStfDestaque_en_us&idConteudo=207138

Fernandes, F. (1965). *A integração do Negro na sociedade de classes*. Dominus Editora. São Paulo, 2 vols. 655 págs., 1° Vol. "O legado da raça branca" . 2° Vol. "No limiar de uma nova era."

FGVCPDOC. (n.d.). "Brazilian Contemporary History Research and Documentation Center." Retrieved from http://www.fgv.br/CPDOC/BUSCA/dicionarios/verbete-biografico/francisco- jose-de-oliveira-viana

Firpo, S. & Renan, P. (2018). "The Labor Market in Brazil. IZA World of Labor." Retrieved from https://wol.iza.org/uploads/articles/441/pdfs/the-labor-market-in-brazil.pdf

Francis, A.M. & Tannuri-Pianto, M. (2009). "Using Brazil's Racial Continuum to Examine the Short-Term Effects of Affirmative Action in Higher Education." Retrieved from https://editorialexpress.com/cgi-bin/conference/download.cgi?db_name=ALEA2010&paper_id=49

Francis-Tan, A. (2016). "Light and Shadows: An Analysis of Racial Differences between Siblings in Brazil." *Social Science Research Journal*, 58, 254–265. Retrieved from https://www.sciencedirect.com/science/article/pii/S0049089X16000338?via%3Dihub

Georgetown Political Database of the Americas. (n.d.). "Federative Republic of Brazil / Federative Republic of Brazil (República Federativa de Brasil/ Federative Republic of Brazil Constitución Política de 1946)." Retrieved from https://translate.google.com/translate?hl=en&sl=pt&u=http://pdba.georgetown.edu/Constitutions/Brazil/brazil46.html&prev=search

Gooden, S.T. (2015). *Race and Social Equity: A Nervous Area of Government*. Armonk: M.E. Sharpe.

Graham, R. (2016). "Free Afro-Brazilians in the 19th Century." Retrieved from https://oxfordre.com/latinamericanhistory/view/10.1093/acrefore/9780199366439.001.0001/acrefore-9780199366439-e-287

Htun, M. (2004, February). "From 'Racial Democracy' to Affirmative Action: Changing State Policy on Race in Brazil." *Latin American Research Review*, 39(1), 61–90; University of Texas Press. Retrieved from https://muse.jhu.edu/article/52078/summary

IBGE. (1920). "Text from the 1920 Brazilian Census." Retrieved from *Biblioteca.ibge.gov.br*

IBGE. (2010). "Síntese dos Indicadores Sociais." Retrived from https://biblioteca.ibge. gov.br/visualizacao/livros/liv45700.pdf

IBGE. (2019). "Blacks or Browns are more Educated, but Inequality with Whites Remains." Retrieved from https://agenciadenoticias.ibge.gov.br/agencia-sala-de-imprensa/2013-agencia-de-noticias/releases/25989-pretos-ou-pardos-estao-mais-escolarizados-mas-desigualdade-em-relacao-aos-brancos-permanece

IPEA. (n.d.). Retrato das Desigualdades de Gênero e Raça, table 3.6. Retrieved from http://www.ipea.gov.br/retrato/indicadores_educacao.html

IPEA. (n.d.(a)). Retrato das Desigualdades de Gênero e Raça, table 10.1a3. Retrieved from http://www.ipea.gov.br/retrato/indicadores_pobreza_distribuicao_desigual-dade_renda.html

Knoll, T. (2019). "'Cost of Opportunity' undergraduates present: Brazilian higher education access spurs both economic and cultural advancement. Does one matter more?" Retrieved from https://sites.duke.edu/project_duke_baixada_project/author/tkk5duke-edu/

Lathrop, T.A. & Dias, E.M. (1992). *Brazil: Lingua e Cultura*. Newark (DE): Lingua Text, ltd.

Lovell, P. & Wood, C.H. (1998). "Skin Color, Racial Identity and Life Chances in Brazil." *Latin American Perspectives*, 25(3), 90–109. Retrieved from journals.sagepub.com/doi/10.1177/0094582X9802500305

Loveman, M., Muniz, J.O. & Bailey, S.R. (2012). "Brazil in Black and White? Race Categories, the Census and the Study of Inequality." *Ethnic and Racial Studies*, 35(8), 1466–1483. Retrieved from https://pdfs.semanticscholar.org/ec1a/81d7da295fbb-fb5b4b2f821e27d71fd72923.pdf

Lowe, R., Barcellos, C., Cruz, O.G., Honorio, N.A., Kuper, H., & Carvalho, M.S. (2018 January 9). "The Zika Virus Epidemic in Brazil: From Discovery to Future Implications." *International Journal of Environmental Research and Public Health*, 15(1), 96. Retrieved from https://www.ncbi.nlm.nih.gov/pmc/articles/PMC5800195/

Maio, M.C. (2001). "UNESCO and the Study of Race Relations in Brazil: Regional or National Issue?" *Latin American Research Review*, 36(2), 118–136. Retrieved from https://www.jstor.org/stable/2692090

Matijasevich, A., Victora, C.G., Barros, A.J., Santos, I.S., Marco, P.L., Albernaz, E.P., & Barros, F.C. (2008, April). "Widening Ethnic Disparities in Infant Mortality in Southern Brazil: Comparison of 3 Birth Cohorts." *The American Journal of Public Health*, 98(4), 692–668. Retrieved from https://www.ncbi.nlm.nih.gov/pmc/articles/PMC2376998/

McGinnis Johnson, J. (2015). "Race and Social Equity: A Nervous Area of Government." *Equality, Diversity and Inclusion*, 34(3), 262–264. Retrieved from https://doi-org.ez.lib.jjay.cuny.edu/10.1108/EDI-12-2014-0084

Nascimento, A. & Nascimento, E.L. (2001). "Dance of Deception: A Reading of Race Relations in Brazil." In Charles V. Hamilton, Lynn Huntley, Neville Alexander, Antonio Sergio Alfredo Guimaraes & Wilmot James, (Eds.), *Beyond Racism: Race and Inequality in Brazil, South Africa, and the United States* (pp. 105–156). Boulder: Lynne Rienner Publishers.

Nobles, M. (2000). "History Counts: A Comparative Analysis of Racial/Color Categorization in US and Brazilian Censuses." *American Journal of Public Health*, 90(11), 1738–1745. Retrieved from https://www.ncbi.nlm.nih.gov/pmc/articles/PMC1446411

OXFAM. (2019). "Brazil: Extreme Inequality in Numbers." Retrieved from https://www.oxfam.org/en/even-it-brazil/brazil-extreme-inequality-numbers

Pan American Health Organization. (2012). "Health in the Americas, 2012 Edition." *Pan American Health Organization.* Retrieved from https://www.paho.org/salud-en-las-americas-2012/index.php?option=com_content&view=article&id=9:edicion-2012&Itemid=124&lang=en

Sandy, M. (2018). "Why the Jobless in Brazil Are Disproportionately Black." *Daily Dose.* Retrieved from https://www.ozy.com/acumen/why-the-jobless-in-brazil-are-disproportionately-black/83961

Schwartzman, L.F. (2007). "Does Money Whiten? Intergenerational Changes in Racial Classification in Brazil." *American Sociological Review,* 72(6), 940–963. Retrieved from https://www.jstor.org/stable/25472504

Skidmore, T.E. (1974). *Black into White: Race and Nationality in Brazilian Thought.* New York: Oxford University Press.

STF. (2012). "Arguição de Descumprimento de Preceito Fundamental – ADPF 186/DF." Retrieved from http://www.stf.jus.br/arquivo/cms/noticiaNoticiaStf/anexo/ADPF186RL.pdf

Swift, M. (2017). "Black Then: Discovering Our History. Rio Blanco Law of 1871: A Step towards Abolition in Brazil." Retrieved from https://blackthen.com/rio-blanco-law-1871-step-towards-abolition-brazil/

Telles, E.E. (2014). *Race and Another America: The Significance of Skin Color in Brazil.* Princeton: Princeton University Press.

Valente, R. & Berry, B.J.L. (2017). "Performance of Students Admitted through Affirmative Action in Brazil." *Latin American Research Review,* 52(1), 18–34. Retrieved from https://larrlasa.org/articles/10.25222/larr.50/

Vazquez Baur, A.T. (2017). "Race and Affirmative Action in 'Post-Racial' Democratic Brazil." *CMC Senior Theses.* Retrieved from http://scholarship.claremont.edu/cmc_theses/1702

Wejsa, S. & Lesser, J. (2018). "Migration in Brazil: The Making of a Multicultural Society." *Migration Policy Institute Newsletter.* Retrieved from https://www.migrationpolicy.org/article/migration-brazil-making-multicultural-society

World Health Organization. (2018). "Zika Virus Fact Sheet." Retrieved from https://www.who.int/news-room/fact-sheets/detail/zika-virus

World Population Review. (2019). "Brazil Population." Retrieved from http://worldpopulationreview.com/countries/brazil-population/

7

RECONCILIATION IN POST-GENOCIDE RWANDA

Challenges and Opportunities

Simone Martin-Howard and Ezechiel Sentama

A Nervous Area of Government in Rwanda

The Republic of Rwanda is located a few degrees south of the Equator in the Great Lakes area of central-east Africa. It is a landlocked country with 26,338 square kilometers (Mukashema & Mullet, 2015; NURC, 2014). With a population of approximately 12 million, of which 52% are women and 48% men, Rwanda is demographically a very young country (NURC, 2014; Wallace, Pasick, Berman, & Weber, 2014).

> The median age is just under 19 years and nearly half of the population (43%) are aged 14 and younger (Wallace et al., 2014). For many centuries, three groups have shared the same space: the *Hutu* (about 85 percent), the *Tutsi* (about 14 percent) and the *Twa* (about 1 percent).
>
> *(Mukashema & Mullet, 2015)*

History records emphasize that Rwanda's history has always been marked by a conflict between the main groups of Hutu and Tutsi. This climaxed into one of the most brutal and devastating genocides in the history of humanity, the genocide against Tutsi, between April and July in 1994. It is estimated that around 1 million people were killed within that three-month period (Clark, 2010; Rieder & Elbert, 2013).

The current government of Rwanda, since 1994, has declared its commitment to resolve its dreadful past through reconciliation efforts. The government considers the promotion of reconciliation as a cornerstone to all national efforts and a basis for combating all forms of discrimination and exclusion that have characterized the Rwandans, decades after decades, as well as the only option to survival for Rwanda that is emerging from a divided past, genocide, and moving towards a reconciled and developed nation (NURC, 2014). Rwanda's new government's nervous area—Reconciliation—is thus understood through a desk review-based overview of the country's history and political environment, and the post-genocide reconciliation efforts referring to legal, policy, institutional mechanisms, as well as an assessment of progress, challenges, and critics of these efforts.

Why Reconciliation Is a Nervous Area of Government

Reconciliation in Rwanda results from a long history of division, polarization and hatred between the Hutu and Tutsi people, which culminated in the 1994 genocide. However, in Rwanda, "interpretations of histories change according to the group in power and its ability to decide upon the public transcript" (King, 2014). History records emphasize that before the colonial administration (1897–1962, with first Germany, since 1894–1916, and Belgium, since 1916–1962), Rwanda was an organized society, composed of three classes of people—the agriculturalists (84%), the Tutsi pastoralists (15%), and the Twa hunters and potters (1%), who were always under the leadership of Tutsi Kingship. Heated controversial debates arise particularly when it comes to whether these categories were exclusive, races castes, ethnic or socio-economic groups (Hintjens, 2005; Mamdani, 2001).

Despite the unending debate about the complex relations among Rwandans (Hutu, Tutsi, and Twa), particularly between Hutu and Tutsi majority groups, before colonization, there appears to be broad agreement that the colonial administration built on pre-existing notions of difference between these categories and resulted in their reinforcement and racialization. During Rwanda's colonization by the Germans (1897–1916), the Tutsi were given increasing power, and when the country was under colonization by Belgium (1916–1962), the Belgian administration continued to spread the narrative of Tutsi superiority and domination, which was manifested in access to public service and education. Figure 7.1 illustrates how Tutsi were favored over Hutu.

Since the 1920s, a reference to ethnic origin was required on identity cards and administrative and academic documents (Prunier, 1997). In the early 1930s, all Rwandans were issued identity cards that signified the ethnicity of the holder.

As Rwanda was near to acquire its independence in 1962, a violent conflict between the Hutu-majority and the Tutsi-minority (1959) erupted leading to some Tutsi (notably those from the ruling elite) finding their way to exile. After independence, in 1962, the Hutu this time took over and ruled the country until 1994, with two successive republics: 1962–1973 under President Grégoire Kayibanda and 1973–1994 under President Juvénal Habyarimana. During the two regimes, inequality (particularly in access to jobs in the public sector and

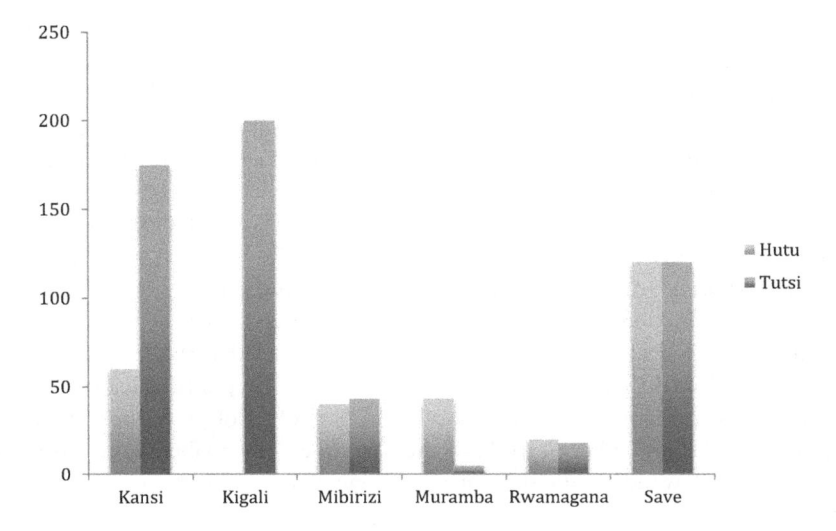

FIGURE 7.1   Hutu and Tutsi's Access to Education and Public Service during Belgian Colonization.

Source: King (2014).

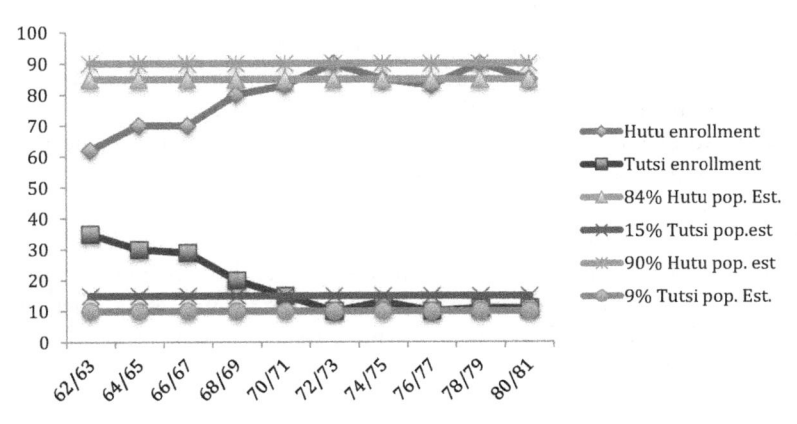

FIGURE 7.2   Hutu and Tutsi's Access to Education during Post–independence First Two Republics.

Source: King (2014).

education) favored the Hutu to the detriment of the Tutsi, under a quota policy. Figure 7.2 illustrates this with regard to people's access to education.

On October 1, 1990, a primarily Tutsi military group, many of combatants being children of Tutsi refugees from earlier violence (1959) had formed the Rwandese Patriotic Front (RPF), launched a war from Uganda, against Habyarimana government. Despite the United Nations' imposed cease-fire that led to the signing of Peace Accords in Arusha, Tanzania, on August 3, 1993, between RPF and the Habyarimana government, the plane that carried President Habyarimana was shot down on April 6, 1994, and he died in the crash. Immediately, the combat between RPF and the government army resumed and, at the same time, the genocide against the Tutsi started (Prunier, 1997).

The anti-Tutsi propaganda, through media outlets and political leaders, had actually begun since RPF launched the war in 1990. "Among the key characteristics of this propaganda discourse was the representation of Tutsi as 'inyenzi' [cockroaches] or 'inzoka' [snakes]; in other words, as vermin to be exterminated" (Fletcher, 2014). Stanton (2003) argues that the Tutsi were the "target race" and their stigmatization in the media by political leaders was a "characteristic phase in the implementation of a policy of genocide." Political figures and the media began to shape the narrative, which labeled the Hutus as belonging in Rwanda while the Tutsis were viewed as outsiders in the country. According to Kellow & Steeves (1998), the Rwandan media, specifically the Radio Télévision Nationale des Mille Collines (RTLM), "has been accused of spreading fear, rumors, and panic by using a kill or-be-killed frame, and of relaying directives about the necessity of killing the Tutsi people as well as instructions on how to do it."

Established in 1993, RTLM was viewed as "hate radio" and pushed a rhetoric of bias against the Tutsi population. "Among the corpus of extant documents attesting to the elaboration of genocide ideology in Rwanda, the speech made by the well-known political figure, Léon Mugesera, on 22 November 1992 to a crowd of approximately 1,000 Rwandans is particularly significant" (Fletcher, 2014). According to Hintjens (1999),

> Mugesera's speech is an important document because it constitutes the earliest evidence of genocidal discourse expressed by a member of the incumbent political party in Rwanda in a public forum and, as such, it has often been regarded as offering a 'blueprint' for the practical implementation of the genocide.

Within the speech, Mugesera emphasized the notion of unity among the Hutus, addressed his listeners as brothers and family members, discussed the importance of patriotism and the relationship between the family, the meaning of the leading political party and Rwanda, and the significance of avoiding "invasion" by the Tutsis.

Furthermore, in his speech, Mugesera put forth images of the Tutsis defecating on the lawns on Hutus and extermination of the Tutsi by Hutu civilians. Mugesera's discriminatory beliefs were further strengthened by the then-President Juvénal Habyarimana. "Habyarimana's regime was one of the more oppressive in Africa, characterized by corruption of political surrogates, ideological and divisive propaganda, brain washing, networks of secret police and . . . the determination to kill any potential opponent" (Gatwa, 1995). Mugesera worked closely with Habyarimana, and his speech in November was recorded and later broadcasted in totality a year later by RTLM, five months before the genocide began in the night of April 6, 1994. On that same evening, the airplane carrying President Habyarimana was shot down by missiles over Kigali airport in Rwanda and his assassination is considered to be the major trigger of the genocide.

According to Lang (2002), almost immediately,

> the claim that rebels from Rwanda's Tutsi ethnic group had assassinated the Hutu president was disseminated widely over Rwandan radio and by other means; within hours, killings, forced displacement, and human tragedy of epic proportions had commenced throughout the country.

In the aftermath of the Rwandan genocide, "1 million Rwandans died, and 2 million refugees left to seek safety in neighboring Zaire, Tanzania, and Burundi" (Kellow & Steeves, 1998). "Most of the killings were carried out by civilian Hutu against their Tutsi neighbors and age, gender, and occupation were no criteria in the massacres" (Kellow & Steeves, 1998). In addition to the extermination of Tutsi, several other Rwandans were also massacred for various reasons: some, for being politicians opposed to the genocidal regime and ideology; and others, for having refused to participate in the killing of, or for having hidden, the Tutsi (NURC, 2014). The genocide ended when RPF took control of the country and drove the government and its defeated army out of the country. Since then, July 1994, the power and ruling of the country have been, and are still, in the hands of RPF as the ruling party.

After the genocide, Rwanda was left with the traumatized survivors, countless orphans and widows, thousands of handicapped people, and generally a very traumatized and vulnerable population. The entire infrastructure of the country, ranging from schools, hospitals, factories, and government departments, had been destroyed or severely looted. Law and order had completely broken down, all national law enforcement agencies and judicial institutions had ceased to exist, and the system of administration of justice had come to a standstill. There was no civil service and the government administrative capacity had collapsed. The aftermath of the genocide against Tutsi was therefore faced with a huge challenge to reconstruct the social, political and economic fabric of the country. The nervous areas of the government were how to bring about reconciliation in a devastated country made up the wounded, disunited, and traumatized people (NURC, 2014).

A Promising Government Initiative: National Reconciliation Policy

Reconciliation Defined in Rwanda's Context

Reconciliation is a complex and context-dependent term (Evaldsson, 2007; Kostić, 2007). Discussions about reconciliation generally make a distinction between the intrapersonal, the interpersonal, and the national reconciliation (Kostić, 2007). The 'intrapersonal reconciliation' refers to the process at personal level by which individuals who suffered from, or conducted, violence need to reconcile with themselves. It is often referred to as trauma 'healing.' The 'interpersonal reconciliation' is concerned with the reparation of relationships between victims and those who harmed them or their loved ones. The 'national reconciliation', also referred to as 'political reconciliation,' refers to the development of a political culture that is respectful of the human rights of all people (Anne, 2006; Stovel, 2006).

In Rwanda, reconciliation is understood as a process that refers to the latter dimension—national or political reconciliation. In this regard, "redefining the Rwandan identity and building a shared sense of Rwandanness is at the center of reconciliation" (NURC, 2009b). The National Policy on Unity and Reconciliation (2014) defines reconciliation as:

> Conduct and practices of Rwandans that reflect the identity of the shared citizenship, culture, and equal rights manifested through interpersonal trust, tolerance, respect, equality, truth, and healing the wounds with the objective of laying a foundation for sustainable development.

Therefore, in Rwanda, the reconciliation model is 'national' oriented (i.e., national or political reconciliation) and bends towards the political/national model, which emphasizes the state's responsibility to "create a culture of rights based upon an inclusive and democratic notion of citizenship" (Anne, 2006). In Rwanda, particularly, the process is mainly aimed at redefining the Rwandan identity and building a sense of a shared citizenship—Rwandanness (NURC, 2009b).

In order to bring about reconciliation, the National Unity and Reconciliation Commission (NURC; 2009b) affirms that Rwanda's model is mainly based on the following six principles: (1) to promote the spirit of Rwandan identity and put national interests first instead of favors based on ethnicity, gender, religion, region of origin; (2) to combat the genocide and its ideology, and strive at creating a nation governed by the rule of law and respect for human rights; (3) to combat any form of divisionism and discrimination, and promote interdependence and synergy in nation building; (4) to multiply strive to heal one another's physical and psychological wounds while building future interpersonal trust based on truth telling, repentance, and forgiveness; (5) to commemorate the 1994 genocide against Tutsi with the aim of making "Never Again" a reality; and (6) to strive for self-determination and passion for work.

Mechanisms for Reconciliation in Rwanda

The process of reconciliation in Rwanda is carried out through various legal and policy mechanisms, as well as educational, judicial, and socio-economic tools, which, as indicated above, are mainly embedded within Rwanda's culture and context.

Legal and Policy Mechanisms. Law has been the leading instrument of post-genocide reconstruction and reconciliation in Rwanda. Shortly after the end of the 1994 genocide, the new government removed the ethnic labels of Hutu, Tutsi, and Twa from Rwandan identity cards and these labels have been officially banned in the public discourse. Major legal changes were however introduced in 2003, with a new Constitution and the Organic Law of 2003. The refashioning of Rwandan political identities was to be carried out by various institutions led by the NURC (Hintjens, 2005). But, before the constitutional reform in 2003, the government of Rwanda had already enacted the Law N° 03/99 of 03/12/1999 establishing the NURC. This law was modified and complemented by the Law N° 35/2002 of 11/14/2002 and Law No 35/2008 of 08/08/2008.

In contemporary Rwanda, it is thus now impossible to identify individuals based on ethnicity under RPF leadership. Past ethnic divisions are no longer acknowledged and are instead officially proscribed. Ethnic labels are no longer found on national identity cards. In the 2003 Constitution, there "is a clause against ethnic divisionism, which includes banning all mention of ethnicity, a policy that is enforced through monitoring and suppression of public speech" (Thomson, 2011). According to Goehrung (2017), "this law removes any civil recourse for ethnic Hutu to oppose the very means of their exclusion from social and political positions, and it prevents them from discussing the system of structural violence that ensures their continued oppression."

The government of Rwanda also enacted the Law No. 40/2013 of 16/06/2013 modifying and complementing the Law No 35/2008 determining the organization and functioning of the NURC. The enactment of Law No. 40/2013 stresses the recognition by the government of Rwanda that reconciliation is a complex and cross-cutting issue and as such must be reviewed accordingly whenever necessary. Also, it is an ample recognition by the government that reconciliation is not only a multi-level but also a multi-actor process, which has to be achieved at individual, institutional, community, and national levels (NURC, 2015a).

In particular, fighting against divisions, and especially the genocide ideology, is the mission at the core in the reconciliation process in Rwanda. It is in this perspective that Article 179 of the 2003 Constitution, as amended to date, created the Commission for the Fight against Genocide that started operating in April 2008. The particular legal measure of implementation is the Law No. 18/2008 of 23/07/2008 relating to the punishment of the crime of genocide ideology (Republic of Rwanda, 2003). In Article 2 of this law,

> The genocide ideology is an aggregate of thoughts characterized by conduct, speeches, documents and other acts aiming at exterminating or inciting others to exterminate people basing on ethnic group, origin, nationality, region, color, physical appearance, sex, language, religion or political opinion, committed in normal periods or during war.
>
> *(Republic of Rwanda, 2003)*

For Uwizeyimana (2014) this law recognized "only Tutsi as legitimate victims of the 1994 Civil War, leaving the category of perpetrators to be filled only by Hutu people." Goehrung (2017) argues that additional amendments to this law "allow for the prosecution of those accused of promoting genocide ideology." For example, those who have spoken about genocide with a focus on the numbers of Hutus who were killed in 1994 have been arrested and imprisoned, independent newspapers have been suspended, foreign national academics have been jailed, and some individuals have been banned from the country indefinitely for promoting pro-Hutu agendas (Goehrung, 2017). Inspired by the Rwandan culture, Art.152 the 2003 Constitution, as amended to date, also established the *Gacaca* courts (discussed about later) in order to engage the community in justice-based reconciliation. It is in this regard that the Law encouraging wrongdoers to admit their wrongdoings, to repent and request for forgiveness (Organic Law No. 10/2007 of 01/03/2007 modifying and completing Law No 16/2004 of 19/6/2004 establishing the organization and competence of the *Gacaca* Courts), was enacted (NURC, 2014).

In August 2007, a National Policy on Unity and Reconciliation for Rwandans was officially publicized. The general objective of the National Policy on Unity and Reconciliation is *"to build a united Rwanda in which all citizens have equal rights and they are free to corporately participate in the governance and development of their country"* (NURC, 2014). The policy serves as a monitoring and evaluation tool designed to measure the achievements made, challenges encountered, and strategies put in place by various organs in fostering unity and reconciliation (NURC, 2014). The policy also underscores the importance of the synergy derived from the participation of every individual as a must for the attainment of unity and reconciliation, as well as the mainstreaming and institutionalizing of unity and reconciliation in Rwanda's day-to-day programs. The guiding principles of the policy are as follows: (1) To promote the spirit of Rwandan identity and put national interests first instead of favors based on ethnicity, blood relations, gender, religions, region of origin, etc.; (2) To combat genocide and its ideology; (3) To strive for creating a nation governed by the rule of law and respect for human rights; (4) To combat any form of divisionism and discrimination; (5) To promote interdependence and synergy in nation building; (6) To mutually strive to heal one another's physical and psychological wounds while building future interpersonal trust based on truth telling, repentance, forgiveness; (7) To commemorate the 1994 genocide with the aim of making "Never Again" a reality; (8) To strive for self-determination and have passion for work (NURC, 2014).

The National Unity and Reconciliation Commission. The NURC is an independent institution established by the government of Rwanda. The commission was established in March 1999 by the Law N° 03/99 of 03/12/1999, which was modified and complemented by the Law N° 35/2002 of 11/14/2002 and Law No 35/2008 of 08/08/2008. The principle of setting up the NURC was reaffirmed by Article 178 of the Rwandan Constitution of 4 June 2003 as amended to date. The NURC engaged in grassroots consultations and national summits to discuss about issues pertaining to reconciliation in Rwanda, introduced a number of mechanisms based on Rwanda's culture, and engaged in research (measuring reconciliation) aimed at measuring the national impact of the introduced reconciliatory interventions (NURC, 2009b).

Consultations, Summits, Seminars, and Assessments. Since its creation in 1999, the NURC (2009b) engaged in *grassroots consultations* all over the country to discuss and debate about issues pertaining to unity and reconciliation in Rwanda, notably the factors that divided Rwandans. These consultations gave birth to various reconciliatory programs (discussed later), as well as the drafting and adoption of the National Policy on Unity and Reconciliation. The consultations further inspired three *National Summits* (since 2000, 2002 and 2004), which were forums that brought together Rwandans from all walks of life, including Rwandans from the Diaspora, as well as important persons from the international community, with the aim to discuss issues pertaining to reconciliation in Rwanda, as well as to evaluate progress and challenges in this regard. The NURC also organized regular *seminars* on the process of reconciliation in Rwanda, which inspired the NURC to develop a relevant Teaching Manual on Civic Education, Conflict Resolution, and a Training Manual on Unity and Reconciliation designed for community mobilization agents, and to develop a reconciliation-based syllabus for civic education, to be used in primary schools of Rwanda. The NURC thus engaged in capacity building on aspects pertaining to reconciliation.

Rwanda Reconciliation Barometer

In a bid to ensure the achievement of its mission, the NURC has privileged multi-dimensional research to explore and analyze the causes and legacies of divisions and violent conflicts, and genocide in Rwanda, and how do address them. This refers to research as part of the strategic tools of the national policy on unity and reconciliation. The process refers to (1) carrying out research on uniting values found in Rwanda's culture with the aim of using them as catalyst for promoting unity, reconciliation, and sustainable peace; (2) carrying out research on prevailing obstacles to unity and reconciliation of Rwandans and to put in place strategies for mitigating conflicts; (3) to disseminate ideas and publications that promote peace, unity, and reconciliation; and (4) to carry out research on the history of Rwanda with the intent of availing well-researched and credible history of Rwanda so that Rwandans may know their past, understand their present, and decide on their future (NURC, 2010).

The Rwanda Reconciliation Barometer (RRB), aimed at measuring (qualitatively and quantitatively) the impact of reconciliatory interventions at the national level, is one of the key programs introduced by the NURC. The first RRB was carried out in 2010, while the second was carried out in 2015 (NURC, 2010, 2015b). Findings of the 2010 RRB had indicated that the genocide ideology and the prevailing poverty, coupled with wounds not yet fully healed resulting from the divisive past and the genocide against Tutsi, were the key challenges to reconciliation (NURC, 2010). The 2015 RRB concluded that the process of reconciliation is at 92.5% and that key challenges were the persistence of (1) ethnic-based stereotypes, (2) the genocide ideology, and (3) the wounds resulting from the divisive past and the genocide not yet fully healed (NURC, 2015b).

Socio-protection programs and reconciliation. A number of studies have indicated that socio-economic development in post-conflict is imperative for peace and reconciliation (Collier & Sambanis, 2002). The government of Rwanda also recognizes that reconciliation process cannot be possible without focusing on poverty reduction strategies (NURC, 2009b). The government of Rwanda focused, particularly, on social protection programs (Ministry of Local Government (MINALOC), 2001) for vulnerable people including genocide survivors, orphans, people with disabilities, historically marginalized people, widows, elderly people, and generally the poor. These programs are notably the *Vision 2020 Umurenge Program* (VUP)[1] and *Girinka*[2] (One Cow per Poor Family) program, as well as the community-driven programs, such as *Umuganda* (community work) and *Ubudehe* (Collective action) (MINALOC, 2002).

Vision 2020 Umurenge Program (VUP): The government of Rwanda, through MINALOC, has embarked on different socio-economic policies to eradicate poverty, especially in rural areas (Brian, 2012). The VUP is one of them. It is directed at poverty reduction in poorest families across the country (Government of Rwanda, 2008). Being both a support and cash transfer program to accelerate social and economic development for the poor, VUP commenced in 2008 and comprises three components: (1) *Direct support*, which targets people who are unable to participate in any employment opportunities within the framework of the program; (2) *Public works*, which offer employment (community work) opportunities to different categories of poor people (extremely poor), who are able to carry out the job opportunities; and (3) *Credit packages*, which provide financial services (credit) to the extremely poor people, through VUP-insured micro loans.

Girinka (One Cow per Poor Family) program: In the Rwandan culture, cows have a special place as a symbol of wealth, love, and unity. This program initiated by President Kagame aims at ending malnutrition, poverty, and strengthening social cohesion. Girinka is thus a national program aimed at providing poor families with cows. It is the community, which decides which recipients have to be provided with a cow. Recipients are also required, as per the social contract, to give the first calf to another recipient to make the program sustainable (RAB, 2013).

Umuganda (community work): This is a community-based program that refers to a traditional practice of mutual help rooted in Rwandan culture of self-help and cooperation (MINAGRI). It is thus a citizen's participation channel where community members of the community would call upon their family, friends, and neighbors to help them accomplish a difficult task. Umuganda is currently regulated by the Community Development Policy adopted in 2001 and revised in 2008 (MINALOC, 2013).

According to the Rwanda Governance Board (RGB), the government of Rwanda drew lessons from this traditional practice so that it could help rebuild Rwanda after the genocide. Umuganda is obligatory, and it is carried out from 8:00 am to 11:00 am on the last Saturday of each month. Residents aged between 18 and below 65 across the country are expected to participate in this community work, and socialize and share information of common interest. As such, the Umuganda achieves both economic and social cohesion objectives (RGB, 2017). The policy of Umuganda was adopted in 2006 and was sanctioned by the Law No 53/2007 governing community works in Rwanda. On 24 August 2009 the Prime Minister's order No 58/03, determining the attributions, organization, and functioning of community works of supervisory committees and their relations with other organs, was established.

Since 2013–2014, Umuganda contribution was integrated into the national budget (RGB, 2017). Nowadays, Umuganda refers to the rallying of communal labor for the reconstruction and repair of basic public development infrastructure under the supervision of village leaders. Roads, bridges, and water channels are to be rehabilitated, schools and health centers built, the vulnerable people given shelter, and the environment protected. *Umuganda* requires everyone to contribute free labor. All Rwandans, including security forces, the President of the Republic, and other political leaders, as well as non-Rwandans, are to participate in *Umuganda* (RGB, 2017).

Educational mechanisms. It is generally argued that education can be an instrument for either conflict or peace (Hilker, 2009; Huyse, 2003; King, 2014). The 1994 genocide and the 1990–1994 civil war resulted in almost total destruction of the education system in Rwanda. The 'official' discourse of the Rwanda's government is that the educational system, since the colonial period up to the 1994 genocide has been a 'divisive and discriminatory instrument.' The task of the post-genocide government was thus argued to be not just reconstruction but also the first-time ever construction of an education system that would be fair, efficient, and capable of combating inequality (RGB, 2017). The narratives contend that the current government, since 1994, corrected the above as it promoted national unity and reconciliation by 'making illegal any form of discrimination,' by 'abolishing the classification of learners and teachers following ethnic affiliation,' and by imbuing school ethos with the philosophy of national unity, reconciliation, and healing, with emphasis on the attributers that bind all Rwandans together, and purposely downplaying dividing factors in order eventually to eliminate them MINEDUC, 2013. In this regard, reforms in formal educational system as well as civic education activities have been key strategies.

Formal educational reforms. As indeed highlighted by the Ministry of Education, one of the major strategies of post-1994 educational system has been to change the curriculum with the objective

> ...to create policies which are in keeping with the new reality ... to correct the errors of the past ... they also aim to build an appropriate educational system, which satisfies the wishes and needs of the population ... to train people free of ethnic, regional, national and religious prejudices, conscious of human rights and responsibilities ... conscious also of their membership to the international community.
>
> *(MINEDUC, 2013)*

To this end, textbooks and curricula that included biased material have been removed. Language policies within education (i.e., use of sole French) have also been changed to accommodate the large number of returning exiles that had been educated in English while living in neighboring Anglophone countries (RGB, 2017). The mission of post-1994 education system has therefore been the following: (1) to prepare a citizen who is free from ethnic, regional, religion, and sex discrimination; (2) to prepare a citizen who is aware of human rights and responsible to society; (3) to promote a culture of peace and emphasize national and universal values such as justice, peace, tolerance, solidarity, and democracy; (4) to promote a culture based on genuine Rwandese culture, free from violence; and (5) to promote freedom of formulation and expression of opinion (MINEDUC, 2013).

The fundamental change in post-1994 education system has thus been to imbue school ethos with the philosophy of national unity, reconciliation, and healing, with emphasis on the attributes that bind all Rwandans together, and purposely downplaying dividing factors in order eventually to eliminate them. A new set of values to be taught included the following: (1) to highlight the similarities among Rwandans and the policy of inclusiveness, (2) to promote individual responsibility, (3) to focus on a progressive future, and (4) to ensure the relevance and applicability of the curriculum to daily life (Obura, 2003). The government of Rwanda affirms to believe that education should be aimed at recreating in young people the values, which have been eroded in the course of the country's history. It is this regard that the formal education was complemented by strategies for civic education known as *Ingando* (solidarity camps) and *Itorero* (civic education school) to which the next discussions turn.

Civic education tools—Ingando and Itorero. Civic education is one of the strategies of the policy on reconciliation in Rwanda. The process focuses on (1) sensitizing every Rwandan on his/her rights, the right of others, and the need to always fight for and defend those rights; (2) inculcating the culture of peace, beginning with the family set up, and then the youth, focusing particularly on schools; (3) entrenching peace education exchanges, as a means of reinforcing the culture of peace and good governance; (4) educating Rwandans on the importance of respecting and defending the Constitution of the Republic of Rwanda; (5) instilling among people of Rwanda the principles embedded in the nation's vision 2020; (6) ensuring that the history of Rwanda is taught at all levels of the community; (7) explaining to the people of Rwanda the meaning of the symbols embedded in the national emblems and values the country attaches to them; (8) empowering people in various positions of leadership to become exemplary servant leaders; (9) ensuring that unity and reconciliation become part and parcel of the school curriculum at all levels of education in Rwanda; and (10) establishing specific unity and reconciliation programs targeting Rwandan Diaspora (NURC, 2009a).

The government's main tools for civic education refer to the traditionally based mechanisms of Ingando (solidarity camps) and Itorero (civic education schools). In practice, the civic education process in Rwanda started with Ingando 'solidarity camps' given the urgency to reintegrate ex-combatants into the national army and society, as well as to reintegrate the returning refugees and provisionally released suspects of the genocide in the community. The process was later expanded to include all citizens. Traditionally, in Rwanda, Ingando referred to a unique moment in which the elders of a village or young people had to leave their village, or their ordinary settlement, to an isolated place for a short or long time for sharing reflections aiming at solving fundamental problems at the community or the nation (i.e. famine, conflict, poverty, etc.) (NURC, 2009a). Ingando entail residential camps, bringing together between 300 and 400 people per program, for between three weeks and two months, depending on the time available and the focus of the sessions. Discussions are mainly about the original narrative of Rwandan history in accordance with national unity and reconciliation (Mgbako, 2005).

In the meantime, separating civic education programs for refugees and ex-combatants (to be provided only in Ingando) from civic education for the rest of citizens, including the Diaspora, was judged as important. It is in this regard that Itorero-civic education school, for the latter segment of the population, was instituted and publicly launched by the President of the Republic on 16 November 2007 (NURC, 2014). This Home-Grown Solution went from being a Taskforce within the NURC to having its own Commission in charge of establishing the vision and mission. The Itorero endeavors to provide a culturally based channel that helps to mentor Rwandans on many different things, including re-educating them in the good practices and behavior that should characterize the Rwandan citizen. Then by using these, achieve real development (NURC, 2009a). Itorero is indeed similar to Ingando in the sense that it also refers to a traditional Rwandan school or center that was used to instill moral values and actions, and capacity to deal with one's problems (NURC, 2014). The process generally culminated in convivial parties (ubusabane); that is, social entertainment activities, whereby people perform cultural songs and dances known as ibitaramo (evening parties) and share food and drinks (Sentama, 2009). Traditionally, Itorero was a civic education channel or school through which the nation could convey the messages to the people regarding national culture in different areas such as language, patriotism, social relations, sports, dance, songs, and the defense of the nation. The Itorero also provided the formative training for leaders of the nation. Itorero participants must understand that cultural values could help them develop their judgment, psychology, work and mutual aid, life, and collaboration with others (NURC, 2009a). In Rwanda, Itorero is especially expected to help instill values in Rwandans especially youth; give back to their communities; and promote patriotism, community cohesion, and social responsibility and volunteerism so as to enhance the socio-economic development of Rwanda, the Rwandan culture and traditions (National Itorero Commission, 2011).

Memory preservation. In Rwanda, memory focuses on the recognition of past injustice and violations of human rights—that climaxed into the 1994 genocide against Tutsi—as well as their impact towards preventive measures under *"never again"* commitment of the Government of National Unity after 1994. The Rwandan government has not thus chosen the amnesia of events that have occurred. Memorials at massacre sites and annual commemorations are used to preserve the memory of the genocide against Tutsi—a climax of the divisive past—and to show the dangerous results of ethnic divisions (Longman & Rutagengwa, 2004).

Monuments, Memorials, and Museums have thus been part of unity and reconciliation process. The same goes to cultural products of various kinds, films, novels, and national holidays. Related activities highlight the maintenance of memorial sites, the promotion of national rituals of commemoration, new national symbols to shape the collective memory of Rwandan history, and the annual-national Day of Heroes, highlighting individuals, who have fought against ethnic division (Richters, Dekker, & Jonge, 2005). The museum also conducts workshops for secondary students: learning from the past, and building the future workshops (Staub, 2014). In particular, every year the national commemoration that remembers, or commemorates for, the victims of the 1994 genocide perpetrated against Tutsi refreshes and fosters collective memory. The official narrative is that preserving memory has been a tool for Rwandans to constantly reflect on what divided them, the consequences of divisions in order to unite, reconcile, and work together for a 'never again' to divisions, violence and genocide (NURC, 2015b).

Judicial institutions—International Criminal Tribunal for Rwanda (ICTR) and Gacaca courts. Within the overall purpose of achieving reconciliation in Rwanda and providing justice to the bursting number of alleged people who were behind bars and prisons (Longari, 2010), traditional forms of justice (ordinary courts) were judged as an effective option. In 2001, the Rwandan government thus adopted the Gacaca courts, designed as a wide-reaching, domestic institution to address the crimes of genocide in Rwanda based on a historical indigenous practice of dispute resolution. The courts were heralded by many as a traditional justice mechanism worthy of emulation, which incorporated Rwandan values with a regard for accountability in line with international norms (UNDP, 2006).

In fact, Rwanda's prisons were full of people who had been charged of crimes and were awaiting trial while the legal system did not have the infrastructures and personnel to deal with them. "It would have to take a hundred years merely to investigate the cases and conduct trial hearings and deliberations for those individuals already in custody" (Longari, 2010). Requests for help from the international community had only resulted in the ICTR seated in Arusha whose proceedings were judged as very slow. Meanwhile, tens of thousands of people were already behind bars and the prisons were bursting (Longari, 2010). Scholars had indeed estimated that if the rate at which genocide detainees were being prosecuted continued in the same manner, nearly one-third would die in prison of old age (Amstutz, 2006). It is in this regard that the government of Rwanda argues that the "only remedy" and "only workable solution" (Republic of Rwanda, 2013) was to use the Rwanda's tradition of communal resolution of disputes, hence the Gacaca jurisdictions.

Gacaca refers to an informal system of justice where people, especially elders, used to sit together in *Gacaca* (the 'grass' or 'lawn') and settle their disputes. It is a pre-colonial justice system that takes place at the village level. It has been modernized with respect to the process over a hundred thousand cases of accused perpetrators of genocide who were languishing in prisons. The *Gacaca* courts had thus to relieve the pressure on the ordinary courts, which were quickly overloaded with the cases of genocide suspects who were filling the prisons. They also had to function within a participatory justice (Richters et al., 2005). A new way of justice that would thus allow communities, including those affected by the genocide, to actively participate in the justice, and within the restorative framework, was thus suggested as 'highly needed' (MINALOC, 2004).

The *Gacaca* courts were thus installed to prosecute and try the perpetrators of the crime of genocide and other crimes against humanity, committed between 1 October 1990 and 31 December 1994 whereby reconciliation was enshrined as one of *Gacaca's* key objectives (Clark, 2010). The overall mission of *Gacaca* was to reveal the truth, to speed up trials, to eradicate the culture of impunity, and to reconcile Rwandans. The Gacaca courts or jurisdictions officially operated for exactly ten years, from June 18, 2002, to June 18, 2012. In the report presented at the closing of the Gacaca courts (June 18, 2012), the National Service for Gacaca Courts (2012) stated that, in ten years, the Gacaca courts had tried 1,958,634 cases, convicting 1,681,648 (86%) and acquitting 277,066 (14%). As indicated by Uvin (1998), with approximately 10,000 tribunals, Gacaca judged all prisoners over a much shorter period of time (ten years). Burnet (2008) had also described Gacaca as the "only possible solution," and that its failure was to be "a threat to the entirety of the reconciliation process."

Assessment and Evidence of Progress

The above legal, policy, and institutional mechanisms are generally considered by the government of Rwanda, and some scholars, as effective strategies that enabled Rwanda to succeed in the process of reconciliation. For example, in 2010, the NURC had already claimed to register tremendous achievements in regard to its mandate and responsibilities in reconciliation endeavors. Indicatively, between 2009 and 2012, it showed great achievements in the areas of civic education consolidation, education for peace and conflict management, capacity building for its staff, strengthening partnership with other stakeholders for the implementation of the national policy of unity and reconciliation. One of the evidence put forward is that as of October 2010, the majority of Rwandans (95.2%) were confident that the country is going into the right direction in terms of reconciliation as well as democratic governance (NURC, 2010). The NURC indeed views itself as the leading engine in reconciliation as it claims to have provided a favorable space and a forum for unity and reconciliation strategies and activities. This refers notably to grassroots and national consultations, research (e.g., the regular RRB) and national summits, and by introducing civic education at all levels of society. The commission also claims to be a haven for safe forums for constructive debates—also extended to the Rwandan Diaspora—for free expression of people's wishes and a Children's Voice, which is an annual event (NURC, 2017). The NURC also claims that civic education, through mechanisms, such as Itorero and Ingando, has contributed to reconciliation as graduates from these schools engage in sensitizing unity and reconciliation values to other citizens, notably at home and in the community, in a way that also fights against divisions and genocide ideology, and in a way that promotes and protects unity and reconciliation (NURC, 2009a).

Social protection strategies such as Girinka program and VUP are also accounted to have contributed to an increase in economic production in Rwanda, which has helped reduce malnutrition and increase incomes. The argument of the NURC, in this regard for example, was that during the 1994 genocide against Tutsi, some genocide perpetrators were poor and their evil actions were motivated by the desire to loot the victims' property, which explains why fighting poverty becomes one of the approaches to combat hatred and rebuild social relations in Rwanda (Kamatsiko & Munyeli, 2009). Social protection programs are also accounted to have promoted good relationships and a sense of community among Rwandans. For example, Brian (2012) contended that programs, such as Girinka, promote human values and behaviors that are critical in socializing, reconciling, and uniting Rwandans. RAB (2013) also argues that Girinka program has contributed to rebuilding inter-personal and intra-personal relations, which is the basic step in reconciling the self-individual and which ultimately leads to unity with other parties. Likewise, some researchers have indicated that community-based socio-economic programs, such as Ubudehe, enhanced social cohesion, unity, inclusiveness, and inclusiveness among Rwandans in their respective communities, re-energized national identity and patriotism (Brian, 2012). Niringiye & Ayebale's study (2012), for example, indicated that Ubudehe program appears to be largely relevant and consistent with the policies of the Rwandan government for fighting poverty and developing the country's economy. Ubudehe has indeed won the prestigious UN Public Service Award due to the participation and ownership of millions of citizens and the strong support of the Authorities of Rwanda for poverty alleviation.

Likewise, Never Again Rwanda and Interpeace (2016) argues that Umuganda has proven to be a major tool for changing the mindsets about national development. Umuganda thus appears to be more than a forum for carrying out community work as it is also perceived as a forum for holding meetings between citizens and local leaders. The 2007–2017 evaluation of the impact of Umuganda on social protection also indicated that Umuganda has made possible access to clean water, hygiene and sanitation, environmental protection, and neighborhood beautification, as indicated by the list of activities that are carried out (MINALOC, 2013; RGB, 2017). Overall, the report emphasizes that 84.8% of citizens are satisfied with Umuganda program implementation and organization (RGB, 2017). The RGB and the Ministry of Local Government accord in arguing that the challenges associated with Umuganda include bad mentality and unwillingness to perform physical labor (for some people who hold the view that community works should be performed by people of lower class, illiterates, and unemployed); poor organization of community works; lack of action plans; exaggerated value of achievements; and degradation

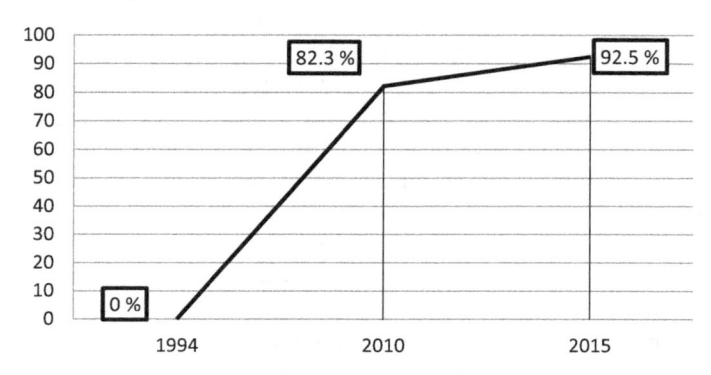

Progress of Reconciliation in Rwanda

FIGURE 7.3 Progress of Reconciliation in Rwanda between 1994 and 2015.
Source: NURC (2010), NURC (2015b).

of the community works realizations and the non-exploitation of youth potential (MINALOC, 2013; RGB, 2017). Illustratively, for example, the NURC engaged in tracking the process of reconciliation in Rwanda since 2010, bearing that Rwandans, had not reconciled in 1994. The 2010 and the 2015 quantitative RRBs indicate that the level of reconciliation among Rwandans arose from 82.3% in 2010 to 92.5% in 2015, as portrayed in Figure 7.3.

In general, the government of Rwanda stresses, however, that in spite of positive progress in the process of reconciliation, the 'ethnic-based divisionism' and 'genocidal ideology' remain key challenges to reconciliation in Rwanda (NURC, 2015b). However, critics of the above-hailed 'success' in the process of reconciliation in Rwanda generally contend that the reconciliation project in Rwanda is surrounded by the 'politically correct' historical narrative of the government. In this perspective, the government's proposed reconciliation mechanisms including the NURC, Gacaca, re-education camps (Ingando and Itorero), community works (Umuganda, Ubudehe), as well as educative and juridical strategies, which serve to instill and reinforce its official narrative of Rwanda's history. MacArthur & MacAulay (2017) also argue that the negative impact on reconciliation approaches in Rwanda is exacerbated by the authoritarian nature of the current government.

Heated debates and critics about the government's promotion of reconciliation thus abound, particularly regarding the legal (i.e., the law against genocide and its ideology) and the judicial mechanisms (i.e., Gacaca) used as a strategy to implement these laws, as well as the history and related government's educational agenda in Rwanda. One the one hand, the government of Rwanda contends that the 2003 Constitution, as amended to date, constitutes a reconciliatory legal framework, especially when it makes it illegal any form of divisions and discrimination among Rwandans. Likewise, the legal institution—Gacaca courts—provided in the Art.152 of the 2003 Constitutions, as amended to date, to promote restorative justice, has been heralded by some for its unique approach to adapting local customs and emphasizing the restoration of social life through confession and public participation. Some scholars such as Clark (2010) and Kirkby (2006) even argue that Gacaca is uniquely designed for dealing with the specific justice and legacy issues emerging from the genocide. Conway (2013) is among few scholars who argued that *Gacaca* is a

> central element in moving towards reconciliation, being a space for public discourse that is open and fair to be the driving factor, and one of few spaces for communication and, for some, it is a way to overcome 'a conspiracy of silence.'

The fact that, in some ways, Gacaca has been successful in emptying prisons and holding to account perpetrators appears to be less debated about. Gasanabo, Simon and Ensign (2014) also argued that, beyond the application of the laudable principle of ending the culture of impunity, and the policy goal of lowering prison populations, the real value of Gacaca was in its creation of a rhetorical space for dialogue about the genocide at the local level where people encountered neighbors with differing experiences on a daily basis, and it is between neighbors that it is most essential for the bonds of a community to become strong. Parent (2010) holds that "*Gacaca* provided a much-needed system of justice for a country with few legal resources." Perpetrators were punished, and victims were allowed to have their say.

Critics, on the other hand, consider the existing laws and the Gacaca courts as politicized instruments to consolidate the control of a de facto single party state (Longman & Rutagengwa, 2004; Loyle, 2018; Ingelaere, 2010; Kohen, Zanchelli, & Drake, 2011; Thomson, 2011; Uvin, 1998). For example, Uvin (1998) argues that the main strength of the regime lay not in its oppression, but in its capacity to legitimize itself, whereby Gacaca was an essential component of that legitimization. Loyle (2018) also argues that based on the principles of accountability and punishment in Rwanda, Kagame's ruling party (Rwandan Patriotic Front or RPF) was able to select and subsequently construct a unique institutional response to the challenges of justice in post-genocide Rwanda whereby Gacaca has gone on to be an effective tool in the consolidation of the political regime in Rwanda through marginalizing political opponents, providing material benefits to the RPF's constituency, and constructing a political narrative.

In fact, through a systematic and iterative analysis, Ingelaere's 2010 study on *Inside Rwanda's Gacaca Courts: Seeking Justice after Genocide* documents how the gacaca "experiment" in transitional justice morphed over time from an emphasis on confession to accusation and from favoring restoration to exacting retribution. Ingelaere's study vividly relays the emotive impact of trials in Gacaca, from the importance of trust to the, at times, overwhelming presence of fear, by arguing that the state played a prominent role in manufacturing the kind of "rehearsed consensus" performed in the courts, particularly through the judges who acted as intermediaries for state power. Ingelaere's study concludes that the dense web of administrative structures in Gacaca proceedings encouraged self-surveillance and self-censorship within the officially sanctioned "regime of truth" and created feedback loops that informed the nature of popular engagement with these state-led projects of reconciliation (Ingelaere, 2010).

Loyle (2018) as well as Thomson (2011) also argue that Gacaca courts were partial and biased, which did not promote reconciliation. For example, Loyle (2018) argues that by prosecuting only those accused of committing genocide while ignoring the crimes against Hutu committed by Tutsi including the alleged crimes of the RPF, Gacaca failed to overcome the very inequities and political marginalization which contributed to the genocide in the first place (Loyle, 2018). Indeed, for Loyle, Gacaca was an essential piece in constructing the pervasive and legitimating narrative regarding the RPF's role in governing post-genocide Rwanda. The political narrative in Rwanda elevates the genocide against the Tutsi as the penultimate violence that the country experienced. This period of conflict is called "the Genocide Against the Tutsi" by the Rwandan government to further highlight the targeting of the Tutsi ethnic group over Hutu political moderates who were killed at the same time (Loyle, 2018).

Debates and critics also refer to memory preservation and educational mechanisms institutionalized by the government of Rwanda toward reconciliation. For example, some observers and those directly involved in the education system in Rwanda argue that the educational policy of inclusion and fair and equal opportunity for every Rwandan irrespective of ethnic identity, political affiliation, or regional quota is fairly implemented and successful (RGB, 2017). Hilker is among the scholars, who argue that Rwanda's educational sector offers important opportunities to diminish tensions and inequalities and to encourage progress toward reconciliation (Hilker, 2009). Likewise, the NURC contends that memory preservation has been a tool for Rwandans to constantly reflect on what divided them, the consequences of divisions in order to unite, reconcile, and work together for a 'never again' to divisions, violence and genocide (NURC, 2015b).

On the other hand, critics point out the distortion of truth-based memory, eclipsing the past (Buckley-Zistel, 2006) and the absence of a history curriculum, as the one taught in schools refers to the 'politically correct' historical narrative of the government. King's study on the educational system (content, structure, and language) in Rwanda indeed concludes that "the education system in Rwanda had and continues to play a more harmful role in intergroup relations" (King, 2014).

While academic historians are debating contested points of Rwandan history, and there is professional recognition that there will never be one definitive history of Rwanda, the government's populist message is more linear and less nuanced. Survivors, perpetrators, Hutu, Tutsi, returnees, the educated elite, and illiterate farmers indicate that there are a multiplicity of social identities and a multiplicity of understandings of the past. The "official" truth, the creation of a single narrative and interpretation, will affect deny or repress the memories of each subgroup within Rwandan society (Freedman et al., 2004). Longman & Rutagengwa (2004) also affirm that the current Rwandan government is founding its reconciliation ideology on selective episodes in Rwandan history that are portrayed as moments of idyllic national unity—representation of the "true" Rwanda unadulterated by colonial or postcolonial dogma. In this regard, some critics argue that this construction of a collective memory of Rwandan national history is undoubtedly politically motivated and ideologically driven. Kohen, Zanchelli, & Drake (2011) indeed argue that while the espoused goals of eradicating "divisionism" and "genocidal ideology" are laudable, the methods undertaken by the Rwandan government to reach these goals are questionable at best.

In fact, the Human Rights Watch (2008) reports that laws now exist regarding "genocidal ideology" and "divisionism," but vague definitions leave them open to interpretation. While these two terms are ostensibly used to label acts that could lead to genocide, they are instead frequently used for political purposes. The political use of these terms to label dissidents, individuals who publicly reference RPF war crimes, and even those who are defense witnesses in trials of prominent participants in the genocide is well documented (Human Rights Watch, 2008). Kohen et al. (2011) eventually argue that by proposing to working with, rather than opposing, the ethnic groups of population, the RPF-driven post-genocide government stands in contrast to the political reconciliation as it implements reeducation programs with the purpose of sending ethnic identity underground. The absurdness of banning and incriminating the reference to ethnic labels, in present Rwanda, is also manifested in the fact that any omission to mention the 'Tutsi' indication in reference to the genocide, hence the 'genocide perpetrated against Tutsi', is a heavily punishable crime as it is referred to as 'genocide ideology'. Yet, as Kohen et al. (2011) hold, the ethnic label of "Hutu" and "Tutsi" presently hold very real meaning to many Rwandans, regardless of the socially constructed origins of the terms all the more so since. In fact, as indicated by MacArthur & MacAulay (2017), more than a million Rwandans have been systematically murdered based on these categories. It follows that, while "history" remains a central point of contention in Rwandan public and private life, how to cope in practical terms with the legacies of mass violence and the judicial crisis produced by the genocide remains a major challenge in post-genocide Rwanda.

Conclusion

Discussions about reconciliation as a nervous area of government in Rwanda since the aftermath of the 1994 post-genocide against Tutsi show that controversial debates and competing narratives about the past of Rwanda and the process of reconciliation make it difficult to promote successful reconciliation in Rwanda. Goehrung (2017) indeed argues that there are now two Rwandas. Since the country elected its fourth President, Paul Kagame in 2000, he has focused on national development, increased the country's GDP, decreased infant and maternal morality ratios, and boosted the number of women in Rwanda's parliament. "In this Rwanda there are no Hutu or Tutsi, ethnicity has been erased, and hostilities forgiven" (Goehrung, 2017). The other Rwanda, according to Goehrung, sees the country pre-genocide and post-genocide as much more complicated.

The civil war and genocide were "an outpouring of anger, frustration, and resentment built up for decades along social, economic, political, and ethnic fissures both real and imagined" (Goehrung, 2017). The new President Kagame, the leader of the RPF, "consolidated power through fear and repression of civil liberties all the while deflecting criticism against his authoritarianism by manipulating the memory of genocide to perpetuate shame and guilt" (Goehrung, 2017). "Just as the Habyarimana government excluded and marginalized ethnic Tutsi, so too now is the Kagame government denying Hutu the opportunity to engage in politics or even voice opposition to the status quo" (Goehrung, 2017). Hitchcott (2013) takes another perspective stating that "inside Rwanda, the post-genocide government has been working hard to reinvent the nation, criminalizing genocide ideology and developing a program of peace and reconciliation." The horizon for reconciliation is thus less promising until a clear roadmap of national truth-based dialogue is initiated toward a reasonable agreed upon consensus among Rwandans of all walks of life about the past of Rwanda and the shared engagement for the future for all Rwandans.

Notes

1 *Umurenge* is the Kinyarwanda name of the *Sector* level of local government in Rwanda.
2 *Girinka* is a Kinyarwanda word that can be literally translated as 'have a cow.' The concept refers to the fact that a cow has always symbolized wealth in Rwanda and the belief is that none can starve when s/he owns a cow.

References

Amstutz, M. R. (2006). Is Reconciliation Possible after Genocide?: The Case of Rwanda. *Journal of Church and State, 48*(3), 541–565.
Anne, B.T. (2006). Truth Telling as a Peace-Building Activity: A Theoretical Overview. In T. A. Borer (ed.), *Telling the Truths: Truth Telling and Peace Building in Post-Conflict Societies*. Notre Dame, Indiana: University of Notre Dame Press, pp. 1–57.

Brian, C. (2012). *Policy Framework for Social Cohesion.* Kigali: Institute of Policy Analysis and Research.

Buckley-Zistel, S. (2006). Remembering to Forget: Chosen Amnesia as a Strategy for Local Coexistence in Post-Genocide Rwanda. *Africa (Pre-2011), 76*(2), 131–150.

Burnet, J. E. (2008). The Injustice of Local Justice: Truth, Reconciliation, and Revenge in Rwanda. *Genocide Studies and Prevention, 3*(2), 173–193.

Clark, P. (2010). *The Gacaca Courts, post-Genocide Justice and Reconciliation in Rwanda: Justice without Borders.* New York: Cambridge University Press.

Collier, P., & Sambanis, N. (2002). Understanding Civil War: A New Agenda. *The Journal of Conflict Resolution, 46*(1), 3–12.

Conway, K. (23, August 2013). The Role of Memory in Post-Genocide Rwanda. Retrieved from https://www.peaceinsight.org/blog/2013/08/the-role-of-memory-in-post-genocide-rwanda/

Evaldsson, A. (2007). *Grass-Roots Reconciliation in South Africa.* PhD Dissertation, School of Global Studies, Department of Peace and Development Research, Göteborg University.

Fletcher, N. (2014). Words that Can Kill: The Mugesera Speech and the 1994 Tutsi Genocide in Rwanda. *Portal, 11*(1), 1-16.

Freedman, S., Corkalo, D., Levy, N., Abazovic, D., Leebaw, B., Ajdukovic, D., & Weinstein, H. (2004). Public Education and Social Reconstruction in Bosnia and Herzegovina and Croatia. In Stover, E., & Weinstein, H. M. (Eds). *My Neighbor, My Enemy: Justice and Community in the Aftermath of Mass Atrocity.* Cambridge: Cambridge University Press, pp. 226–247.

Gasanabo, J. D., Simon, D. J., & Ensign, M. M. (2014). *Confronting Genocide in Rwanda: Dehumanization, Denial, and Strategies for Prevention.* Kigali: CNLG.

Gatwa, T. (1995). Ethnic Conflict and the Media: The Case of Rwanda. *Media Development, 3,* 18–20.

Goehrung, R. (2017). At Issue: Ethnicity, Violence, and the Narrative of Genocide: The Dangers of a Third Term in Rwanda. *African Studies Quarterly, 17*(1), 79–99.

Government of Rwanda. (2008). *Vision 2020 Umurenge Program (VUP) Baseline Survey,* Kigali. Retrieved from file:///C:/Users/s_mar/Downloads/vision2020_umurenge.pdf

Hilker, L. (2009). Everyday Ethnicities: Identity and Reconciliation among Rwandan Youth. *Journal of Genocide Research, 11*(1), 81–100.

Hintjens, H. M. (1999). Explaining the 1994 Genocide in Rwanda. *The Journal of Modern African Studies, 37*(2), 241–286.

Hintjens, H. M. (2005). Nigel Eltringham, Accounting for Horror: Post-Genocide Debates in Rwanda. *Ethnic and Racial Studies, 28*(4), 773–774.

Hitchcott, N. (2013). Between Remembering and Forgetting: (in)Visible Rwanda in Gilbert gatore's le passé devant soi. *Research in African Literatures, 44*(2), 76–90.

Human Rights Watch. (2008). *Law and Reality: Progress in Judicial Reform in Rwanda.* New York: Report.

Huyse, L. (2003). The Process of Reconciliation. In Bloomfield, D., Barnes, T., & Huyse, L. (Eds). *Reconciliation After Violent Conflict: A Handbook* (Handbook Series). Stockholm: International Institute for Democracy and Election Assistance, pp. 19–33.

Ingelaere, B. (2010). Peasants, Power and Ethnicity: A Bottom-Up Perspective on Rwanda's Political Transition. *African Affairs, 109*(435), 273–292.

National Itorero Commission. (2011). *National Itorero Commission Strategy.* Kigali.

Kellow, C. L., & Steeves, H. L. (1998). The Role of the Radio in the Rwandan Genocide. *Journal of Communication, 48*(3), 107–128.

King, E. (2014). *From Classroom to Conflict in Rwanda*. New York: Cambridge University Press.

Kirkby, C. (2006). Rwanda's Gacaca Courts: A Preliminary Critique. *Journal of African Law, 50*(2), 94–117.

Kohen, A., Zanchelli, M., & Drake, L. (2011). Personal and Political Reconciliation in Post-Genocide Rwanda. *Social Justice Research, 24*(1), 85–106.

Kostić, R. (2007). *Ambivalence Peace: External Peacebuilding Threatened Identity and Reconciliation in Bosnia and Herzegovina*. Report nº. 78. Department of Peace and Conflict Research: Uppsala University.

Lang, A. F. (2002). Global Governance and Genocide in Rwanda. *Ethics & International Affairs, 16*(1), 143–150.

Longman, T., & Rutagengwa, T. (2004). Memory, Identity and Community in Rwanda. In Stover, E., & Weinstein, H. M. (Eds). *My Neighbor. My Enemy: Justice and Community in the Aftermath of Mass Atrocity*. Cambridge: Cambridge University Press, pp. 162–182.

Loyle, C. E. (2018). Transitional Justice and Political Order in Rwanda. *Ethnic and Racial Studies, 41*(4), 663–680.

MacArthur, J., & MacAulay, A. (2017). Framing Rwandanness: Studying Rwanda in the Twenty-First Century. *African Studies Review, 60*(3), 221–229.

Mamdani, M. (2001). *When Victims Become Killers: Colonialism, Nativism, and the Genocide in Rwanda*. Princeton: Princeton University Press.

Mgbako, C. (2005). Ingando Solidarity Camps: Reconciliation and Political Indoctrination in Post-Genocide Rwanda. *Harvard Human Rights Journal, 18*, 201–224.

MINALOC. (2002). *National Strategy Framework Paper on Strengthening Good Governance for Poverty reduction in Rwanda*. March, Kigali.

MINALOC. (2004). *Rwanda Five-Years Decentralization Implementation Programme (2004–2008) Poverty Reduction and Empowerment through Entrenchment of Democratic Decentralization*. March, Kigali.

MINALOC. (2013). *National Strategy for Community Development and Local Economic Development (2013–2018)*. Kigali.

MINEDUC. (2013). *Education Sector Strategic Plan (2013/14–2017/18)*. Kigali.

Ministry of Local Government. (2001). *National Social Protection Strategy*. Kigali.

Mukashema, I., & Mullet, E. (2015). Attribution of Guilt to Offspring of Perpetrators of the Genocide: Rwandan People's Perspectives. *Conflict Resolution Quarterly, 33*(1), 75–98.

Niringiye, A., & Ayebale, C. (2012). Impact Evaluation of the Ubudehe Programme in Rwanda: An Examination of the Sustainability of the Ubudehe Programme. *Journal of Sustainable Development in Africa, 14*(3), 141–154.

NURC. (2009a). *Itorero Strategic Plan 2009–2012*. Retrieved from https://www.nic. gov.rw/fileadmin/user_upload/Itorero_strategic_plan_English_2009_-_2012.pdf

NURC. (2009b). *15 Years of Unity and Reconciliation Process in Rwanda: The Ground Covered to-Date*. Kigali: National Unity and Reconciliation Commission.

NURC. (2010). *Rwanda Reconciliation Barometer*. October, Kigali. Retrieved from http://www.nurc.gov.rw/fileadmin/Documents/RWANDA_RECONCILIA-TION_BAROMETER.pdf

NURC. (2014). *Unity and Reconciliation Process in Rwanda: 20 Years after the 1994 Genocide Perpetrated against Tutsi*. Kigali: National Unity and Reconciliation Commission.

NURC. (2015a). *Monitoring Strategies and Tools of Unity and Reconciliation within Institutions based in Rwanda*. Retrieved from http://www.nurc.gov.rw/fileadmin/

Documents/Others/Monitoring_Strategies_and_Tools_of_Unity_and_Reconciliation_within_Institution_based_in_Rwanda.pdf

NURC. (2015b). *Rwanda Reconciliation Barometer*. Kigali: National Unity and Reconciliation Commission.

Obura, A. (2003). *Never Again: Educational Reconstruction in Rwanda*. October, Kigali: International Institute for Educational Planning, UNESCO.

Parent, G. (2010). Reconciliation and Justice after Genocide: A Theoretical Exploration. *Genocide Studies and Prevention*, 5(3), 277–292.

Prunier, G. (1997). *The Rwanda Crisis: History of a Genocide*. New York: Columbia University Press.

RAB. (2013). *Girinka Programme: A Success Story in Rwanda*. Kigali: RAB.

Republic of Rwanda. (2001). *Organic Law n° 40/2000 of 22/01/2001 setting up Gacaca Jurisdictions and Organizing Prosecutions for Offences Constituting the Crime of Genocide or Crimes Against Humanity Committed between October 1, 1990 and December 31, 1994*. Kigali: The Official Gazette of the Republic of Rwanda.

Republic of Rwanda. (2003). *The Constitution of the Republic of Rwanda*. Kigali. Retrieved from https://www.ilo.org/dyn/natlex/docs/ELECTRONIC/64236/90478/F238686952/RWA64236.pdf

Republic of Rwanda. (2013). *Justice, Reconciliation, Law & Order Sector Strategic Plan July 2013 to June 2018*. Kigali. Retrieved from http://www.minecofin.gov.rw/fileadmin/templates/documents/sector_strategic_plan/JRLOS_Strategic_Plan_February_2013.pdf

Rwanda Governance Board. (2017). *Impact Assessment of Umuganda (2007–2016)*. Kigali. Retrieved from http://rgb.rw/fileadmin/Key_documents/HGS/Impact_Assessment_of_Umuganda_2007-2016.pdf

Richters, A., Dekker, C., & Jonge, K. D. (2005). Reconciliation in the Aftermath of Violent Conflict in Rwanda. *Intervention: International Journal of Mental Health, Psychosocial Work & Counselling in Areas of Armed Conflict*, 3(3), 203–221.

Rieder, H., & Elbert, T. (2013). Rwanda – Lasting Imprints of a Genocide: Trauma, Mental Health and Psychosocial Conditions in Survivors, Former Prisoners and their Children. *Conflict and Health*, 7(6), 1–13.

Sentama, E. (2009). *Peacebuilding in Post-Genocide Rwanda: An Exploration of the Role of Cooperatives in the Restoration of Interpersonal Relationships*, PhD Thesis, Gothenburg University, Göteborg, Sweden.

Stanton, G. (2003). "The 8 Stages of Genocide." Online. Retrieved from https://coursecontent.ntc.edu/soc/bootcamp/mcdonald/ti/lp1/the_8_stages_of_genocide.pdf

Staub, E. (2014). The Challenging Road to Reconciliation in Rwanda: Societal Processes, Interventions and Their Evaluation. *Journal of Social and Political Psychology*, 2(1), 2195–3325.

Stovel, L. (2006). *Long Road Home: Building Reconciliation and Trust in Post-War Sierra Leone*. Simon Praser University, Department of Sociology and Anthropology, Dissertation, University of British Columbia.

Thomson, S. (2011). Whispering Truth to Power: The Everyday Resistance of Rwandan Peasants to Post-Genocide Reconciliation. *African Affairs*, 110(440), 439–456.

UNDP. (2006). *The 2006 Human Development Report – Beyond Scarcity: Power, Poverty and the Global Water Crisis*. New York: Palgrave Macmillan.

Uvin, P. (1998). And Where Was the Civil Society? In Uvin, P. (Ed). *Aiding Violence: The Development Enterprise in Rwanda* (Chap 8, pp. 163–179). Retrieved from http://www.ngocentre.org.vn/files/docs/CivilSocietyRwanda.pdf

Uwizeyimana, D. E. (2014). Aspects and Consequences of the Rwandan Law of Genocide Ideology: A Comparative Analysis. *Mediterranean Journal of Social Sciences, 5*(23), 2370–2379.

Wallace, D. A., Pasick, P., Berman, Z., & Weber, E. (2014). Stories for Hope-Rwanda: A Psychological-Archival Collaboration to Promote Healing and Cultural Continuity through Intergenerational Dialogue. *Archival Science, 14*(3–4), 275–306.

8

TURKISH-ORIGIN GERMANS

Temporarily Permanent

Loren Gatch, John Hitz, and Elizabeth Overman

A Nervous Area of Government in Germany

For people of Turkish origin in Germany, everyday existence involves juggling social and structural ambivalences ranging from partial acceptance and minimal toleration, to outright rejection and physical assaults (Paksoy 2018). For example, Mesut Özil, whose family has been in Germany for three generations, and who represented Germany in three FIFA World Cup contests, quit the world-renowned soccer team out of frustration explaining, "I am German when we win, but I am an immigrant when we lose … I am still not accepted into society." Özil pointed out that national team colleagues from a previous era, Lukas Podolski and Miroslav Klose, "are not referred to as German-Polish…" "Why," he asked plaintively, "am I German-Turkish?" (Smith and Eckhardt 2018).

The denial of social acceptance premised on origin across the broad sweep of a society has profound ramifications. In Özil's case, his discontent is both a marker of the general discrimination experienced Germans of Turkish origin and yet emblematic of Germany's aspirations to signal its multicultural bona fides by fielding a German-Turkish player as a representative of Germany at the highest levels of international competition, even if his less famous compatriots at home are not accorded the same degree of acceptance. Most Turkish-origin Germans, even if they are, like Özil, third generation, "grow up marginalized in an economically deprived environment with restricted educational opportunities and a limited command of the German language" (Mueller 2006).

This chapter examines differential outcomes in the German educational system with respect to the performance of children of Turkish immigrants relative to the children of native Germans. A legacy of Germany's *Gastarbeiter* program of the 1960–1970s, Germany's Turkish enclaves have lagged behind the larger ethnic German population in terms of a number of social indicators, including educational outcomes. Despite residing in Germany for over two generations, the Turkish population's inability to integrate fully reflects the enduring discriminatory legacy of the German concept of citizenship which, until recently, bestowed full civic equality only upon those meeting a strict ethnic definition of German-ness. Given that ethnic basis for civic inclusion, German education policy has only with difficulty recognized the particular needs of Turkish students, especially in terms of their German language ability, which influences their likelihood of embarking upon a university-track education. One possible solution to the problem is bilingual and multicultural education, in which Turkish-origin students acquire the linguistic and cultural knowledge necessary to succeed in German society.

Conceptual Political and Historical Context

In all liberal polities, public policy ultimately rests upon equality as a core concept, in the sense that the maintenance and production of some condition of equality is ideologically indispensable to the legitimacy of those polities. Yet the particular sense of equality that is targeted by public policies can vary from the civic (equal access to procedural safeguards like property rights), to the political (equal access to participation, especially the franchise) to the social (equal access to welfare and security) (Marshall 1965). Depending upon their historical relationship to the liberal tradition, polities may stress, and value, one sense of equality over another. In terms of public policy, the prevailing understanding of equality may lead to characteristic ways in which inequality is understood as a policy problem. In other words, the question becomes: when are inequalities as social facts recognized as *inequities*, in the sense of inequalities that require some kind of policy response and remedy?

Given these parallel, and sometimes contending, understandings of equality, "nervousness" in Gooden's (2014) sense arises in public policy debates when inequalities can only with difficulty be recognized as inequities, given the dominant manner in which legitimate equality is understood. In the United States, for example, what Gooden refers to as a resort to euphemism—the language of "diversity," as opposed to race, for example—reflects a sort of discursive aphasia imposed upon those debates given Americans' resistance to discussing substantive, race-based inequalities as if they were inequities at all. This chapter proposes that the inadequate German response to educational disparities between its Turkish and ethnic German populations reflects a peculiarly German "nervousness" in dealing with unequal educational outcomes that correlate with unequal civic status as defined under the country's citizenship laws.

In Germany, equality across the civic, political, and social dimensions has been profoundly shaped by the country's conception of citizenship, especially as this was codified by the citizenship law of 1913. As the classic *jus sanguinis* country, Germany until very recently grounded German identity in lineage. Germany's postwar Basic Law (Article 116, para 1) defined "ethnic German resettler" as qualifying automatically for citizenship. Indeed, prior to 2005, these *Spätaussiedler* could assert citizenship claims even without demonstrating any particular knowledge of the German language. In other respects, however, language proficiency remained both constitutive of German cultural identity, and an essentializing barrier to the citizenship aspirations of non-ethnic German residents of the country. To this extent, language represents a central conundrum that links education and migration policies through their contributions to the creation of a shared German civic consciousness. In particular, the Germans' collective self-conception that they were not a migrant country has accordingly structured their approach (or lack thereof) to the problems of integrating non-German populations and increasing their German language proficiency—problems which, ultimately, are twin aspects of the single challenge of forging a German civic identity, appropriate to a liberal polity, that transcends the exclusionary implications of ethno-cultural markers.

In the history of the Federal Republic, the pedagogical problem of language first emerged not with the forced population transfers accompanying the end of the World War II, but with the manpower demands of Germany's *Wirtschaftswunder*. The country's spectacular postwar economic recovery led, by the late 1950s, to labor shortages that prompted bilateral agreements with a number of other countries, especially Turkey. An exclusively male workforce specifically recruited from the least-developed and -educated regions of Turkey, these unskilled and semi-skilled guest workers were admitted on a "rotation principle" that sought to prevent them from establishing roots in the country.

On these terms, language proficiency in either its educational or civic significance was simply irrelevant, beyond what might be functionally necessary in the workplace. However, employer interests in a stable workforce overrode the temporary nature of these agreements, leading to a permanent, and growing, population of guest workers and their families, whom they brought over to their host country to reside in ethnic enclaves that were largely insulated from the wider German society. In recognition of this new reality, as early as 1964 German law extended compulsory schooling to include migrants' children. Yet this initial step was distinctly limited in terms of its implications for migrants' status. Indeed, a curriculum that taught these children German as a Second Language was paired with instruction in the language of the migrant children's country of origin, an approach that clearly presumed the students' residency was temporary or otherwise limited (Gogolin 2005). Indeed, through the 1950s and 1960s, such assistance as migrant communities would receive came not from the state, but from civil society entities like religious welfare organizations and labor unions, which helped migrants deal with the practical problems of settling in unfamiliar circumstances (Chin 2017: 128).

At the federal level, passage of the Act on Foreigners (1965) allowed for residence permits for non-Germans who were neither guest workers nor ethnic resettlers; it also included a provision for granting permanent residence to asylum seekers. After 1973, the earlier bilateral agreements that had brought in the original guest worker population were terminated. With the return of higher levels of unemployment in the German economy, this population resisted financial incentives offered to leave Germany and return home (Return Assistance Act of 1983). Instead, these workers applied for visas for themselves and their families. Even with the prospect of a permanent migrant population, given their legal status as non-citizens, integration of Turkish residents of whatever generation was not regarded as a policy concern, in the same way that assimilating non-German-speaking "ethnic German settlers" was understood to be. In this respect, Germany differed from its neighbors. Unlike Great Britain and France, which by this time were already struggling with the challenges of integrating postcolonial migrant streams from their respective former empires, the essentially transactional nature of Germany's original relationship with its migrant communities tended to muffle any debate over what the enduring presence of these communities implied about German national identity. Characteristic of this attitude was the very term used to describe the government's approach—*Ausländerpolitik*, or "foreigner policy"—as if to exclude the very possibility of those migrant communities integrating into German society (Chin 2017: 127–131).

At the same time that the *Gastarbeiter* population became a permanent demographic fixture in German society, the postwar Federal Republic acceded to two commitments that further complicated its citizenship framework. First, in order to meet its obligations as a member of the European Economic Community (EEC, later EU), Germany granted freedom of movement and residency status to citizens of other EEC countries through the Law on EEC Residence of 1969. Second, as part of its continuing atonement for the Nazi period, Germany accepted the obligation of serving as an asylum country and enshrined the right to asylum in the 1949 Basic Law (constitution).

These two developments resulted in additional population streams that swelled the number of legal residents who lacked civic equality under German law, and thus the accompanying presumption that their residency status was a prelude to integration into German civic identity. During the 1990s, migration legislation at the federal level sought, in somewhat contradictory fashion, to discourage inflows of migrants from whatever source, and yet to bolster the legal status of those migrants already within the country. In particular, the law embraced the principle of *jus soli* by spelling out the process by which children and young people could be naturalized. This culminated in the Nationality Act, entering into force in 2000, which provided a path to citizenship for minors if one non-German parent had been a legal resident of the country for at least eight years; at age 21, those offspring faced an *Optionspflicht*, choosing at

TABLE 8.1 Legal and Economic Milestones Affecting the Citizenship and Residency Status of Turkish-Origin Germans

Basic Citizenship: *Jus sanguinis* the right of blood	1913
Basic Law Article 116: Citizenship guarantees for nonresident ethnic Germans; Article 16a: right of asylum	1949
Wirtschaftswunder; Bilateral agreements with Turkey; *Gastarbeiter*— Unskilled/semi-skilled male only worker rotation	1950s
1951 Refugee Convention	1951
International treaty; Guest workers applied for family visas; Turkish women allowed	1960
Compulsory schooling for all children, migrants included	1964
Asylum seekers granted permanent residence	1965
EEC Residence Law: free movement within EEC	1969
Bilateral worker agreements terminated; Economic downturn; Termination of labor recruitment	1973
Return assistance act; Stipend to return to Turkey	1983
Unlimited right to asylum curtailed in constitution	1990s
Optionspflicht: Turks at 21 years decide whether to be German or Turkish citizens	
Migration Act: Germany acknowledges that it is a "migration country"	2005

one point whether or not to become German citizens. Only with the Migration Act of 2005 did Germany's citizenship law formally acknowledge that the country was an "immigration country" at all; as with the original rationale for the guest worker programs beginning a half century earlier, this revision of Germany's criteria for citizenship was prompted by the demographic trend towards population decline and an associated shortage of workers in certain high-skilled categories (Gesley 2017).

Table 8.1 summarizes the major legal and economic milestones, starting in 1913, that have defined, and redefined, citizenship and residency statuses in Germany.

Twenty-First Century Imperatives

One sign of an integrated global society is the ability to draw comparisons. In 2003, the Organisation for Economic Co-operation and Development's (OECD) Program for International Student Assessment (PISA) released an international assessment for the first time measuring 15-year-old students' reading, mathematics, and science literacy. The 2003 test focused on mathematics and the second, in 2005, tested science. The findings shocked Germany as it revealed the educational disparities that speak to the challenges of acculturation and socialization for immigrants from Turkey. There were profound differences in minority student performance across OECD countries, but the largest gap was between ethnic German students and non-German minority students. While these non-German minority students came from a wide variety of backgrounds, the largest performance gap within that group appeared specifically between German students and first- and second-generation Turkish students.

In 2005, when the second raft of low PISA scores was released, the Christian Democrats assumed power and Angela Merkel became chancellor. The government immediately began to address the problem at the federal level through personnel appointments and national education summits. Merkel appointed a Commissioner for Migration, Refugees and Integration who hosted an Integration Summit in 2006 bringing 86 political and social representatives from across the country to address issues of German language learning, education, job opportunities, and equity. This was followed by two conferences on Islam sponsored by the Interior Ministry. The focus was on the interaction between Muslim minorities and the national majority around religious topics, German law and values, and policies such as equal opportunity and employment. A youth integration plan was announced in 2007 that examined language, education, local integration, and cultural diversity. This was followed, in the same year, by a national integration plan that developed ten priority areas such as improving integration courses, promoting early German language learning, integration through sports, and diversity in the media.

Following World War II, the national system of education was abolished, as a hedge against the return of Fascism, and replaced with a more decentralized arrangement that allows officials in the 16 *Länder* to determine the delivery of educational and cultural content in the public schools. Despite the fact that German teachers have between five and six years of advanced training, reaching students whose cultures are diverse is problematic. To understand how Germany is addressing the education gap, it is helpful to examine the pedagogical thinking relating to migration-related diversity extant in Germany since the 1960s.

In the 1960s to the 1970s, policy makers and local school teachers assumed that the children of *Gastarbeiter* would return to Turkey, even if they had been born in Germany and never set foot in Anatolia. Resources were provided to assist children in their German language learning, but there were questions as to whether or not the approach truly aided linguistically and culturally diverse students. Since the 1980s, multicultural education with an integrationist and pluralist approach attempted to reinforce an existing cultural identity with mother-tongue alphabetization, an emphasis on cultural heritage and classes that examined all of the major religions. In an effort to respond to a society with a racially hostile environment, curriculum developers fostered antiracist education modalities linked to *interkulturelle Erziehung*. The attitude was that minority ethnic peoples would have to struggle for racial justice and personally defend themselves against any racial discrimination foisted upon them. The schools, for their part, would examine through the study of laws and institutions, the 'racist' structure of society in order to deepen an awareness of social inequities. Since the 1990s, there has been a turn away from the schooled elicitations of the structural discrimination in German society to a promotion of what is called a Eurocentric education that examines the cultural and religious values promoted by the EU countries. Despite these policy and institutional changes, the stress of working and living in Germany for Turkish-origin Germans has not abated (Fass 2008).

Today Germany's immigrant population, 15% of the total population, is the second largest in the world. Yet by November of 2019, on the 30th anniversary of the 1989 fall of the Berlin Wall, the question of who is German remains unsettled. The re-unification of Germany on terms that seem to have solved the "German Question" which had bedeviled Europe for over a century represents an unambiguous triumph. But the issue of who is and who is not a German continues to fester, with the rise in reported incidents of ethnic hatred and violence. In response to the surge of asylum seekers in 2015, a far-right party with a xenophobic platform has scored notable electoral successes in the states of the former East Germany. Indeed, open discrimination against Turkish-origin Germans has been joined by a rising animus directed at Jews. Despite the shift towards a *jus soli* conception of citizenship, public discourse persists in distinguishing between "passport Germans" and "bio-Germans." Even for third- and fourth-generation Turkish Germans whose forerunners came as *Gastarbeiters*, acceptance remains a struggle that cannot be taken for granted (Bennhold 2019).

Why Education Is a Nervous Area of Government

Before promising practices are identified, it is first necessary to discuss the educational barriers faced by Turkish origin students in Germany's educational system. Just as the German political system has been slow to recognize that Germany is a multicultural society, the educational system has only recently begun to develop the curricula and instructional methods appropriate for a multicultural, multilingual population.

Until relatively recently, the German educational system has been striving for homogeneity rather than heterogeneity in its classrooms (Sliwka 2010). Since the 1700s, German educational theorists have attempted to track students in groups in order to reach the "norm" or "the average" in any particular class, rather than focus more particularly on the diverse, individual needs of any one particular student. This mindset has led to the creation of a tracking system with three, four, or even five tiers, depending on the situation of each German *Land*.

At the bottom rung of the educational ladder are *Sonder-* or *Förderschule* for children with physical or mental disabilities; Turkish-origin children have been tracked into the schools at disproportionate rates possibly because of their perceived difficulties with the German language. The *Hauptschule* was traditionally for the blue-collar workers, and most Turkish-origin students find themselves in these institutions. The *Realschule* was established to train workers for white-collar jobs that did not require the academic credentials provided by a university education, and the *Gymnasium*, at the top rung of the educational ladder, prepared an elite for a university education. In some areas, the *Gesamtschule* integrates the *Haupt-* and *Realschule* (Open Society Justice Review 2013). Educators at all levels of this system have been trained not to focus on marginalized groups within the classroom, but on the "average" student within each classroom (Sliwka 2010)—a very challenging educational environment for any Turkish-origin student.

If German migration and citizenship policies are federal responsibilities, education policy is, for the most part, formulated and executed at the *Länder* level. It is through the interaction of these dual policy trajectories—the belated acceptance of permanent migrant populations on a path towards civic inclusion, on the one hand, and the commitment to a highly structured educational system typified by early and permanent tracking, on the other—that the distinctive pedagogical challenges facing Turkish-origin students become apparent.

Given that language acquisition and proficiency are milestones of early childhood development, the formative experiences of migrant- (and especially Turkish) origin children ensure that unequal educational outcomes are structural consequences of basic features of the educational system. Not only does federalism devolve education policy to the German states, but the principle of subsidiarity works to reinforce Turkish social exclusion by limiting their access to educational resources at critical junctures. In particular, responsibility for early childhood education in Kindergarten is assumed not by the state, but by civil society organizations (especially churches). Muslim Turks, whose populations may lack such social infrastructure, are thus unable to mobilize resources available for this purpose (Auernheimer 2005). As Klumpp et al. (2014) report, only 13% of migrant children under the age of three attend day care, and those that do are often segregated with other non-German speaking children.

The German pedagogical tradition regards experiences like Kindergarten not merely as opportunities for narrow skills acquisition useful in later schooling, but as a broader socialization that imparts to children a range of life skills which, while not reducible themselves to a formal educational curriculum, make future encounters with such curricula more successful. Likewise, German schools perform an additional social function by providing facilities for denominationally based religious instruction (conducted, it goes without saying, in the German language). In contrast, for Muslim students, whose faith lacks such a denominational structure, such basic religious training takes place outside of the regular school system and in a language other than German. Finally, the half-day feature of German schools itself disadvantages migrant children by limiting their exposure to German-speaking settings that would be unavailable to them within the broader environment of social segregation (Auernheimer 2005; Søvik 2008).

As a consequence of these features, gaps in German language proficiency between migrant and native German student populations emerge at an early stage, and become self-reinforcing as they encounter the logic of school tracking. Even a lack of access to Kindergarten has justified delaying migrant children's entrance into the formal school system or shunting them immediately into remedial classes (Miera 2007). As the PISA data underscore, the German educational system exhibits a clear correlation between social origins and educational attainment (Klumpp et al. 2014). Once students age out of the *Grundschule* (Primary School), this correlation between origins and attainment is amplified by tracking that exacerbates academic performance differences. Not only does tracking normalize performance expectations with respect to a given school type, but it produces a downward ratcheting effect: while moving from, say, a vocational to an academic track is not possible, transition in the other direction (or simply requiring students to repeat a grade) is a common institutional response to poor student performance. Moreover, the ability to reassign students in this way tends to absolve schools of their responsibility for bad educational outcomes, as they can always ascribe such outcomes to adverse family factors or to the inherent aptitude of individual students (Auernheimer 2005).

Above all, the interaction of migrants' socio-linguistic exclusion with educational tracking has established the *Hauptschule* as the ultimate dumping-ground for low performing students. This became apparent when Turkish-origin students first started enrolling in German schools in the 1960s and 1970s. The educational system's emphasis on homogeneity meant that they were tracked into the lower tiers of the educational system, which did not acknowledge diversity, or see it as a resource that could be used in the classroom. At this point, the prevailing social ethos in Germany endorsed the view that Germany was monocultural and not a country for immigration as expressed in the slogan "*Deutschland ist kein Einwanderungsland.*" The prevailing method of teaching immigrant groups, *Ausländerpädagogik* (Instruction for Foreigners), focused on giving the children of immigrant workers the necessary skills to function in German society before returning to their native countries in segregated, immigrant-only learning environments. Turkish-origin children were also allowed to take classes in their own language after the regular school day concluded so that their repatriation could proceed smoothly. These educational policies ensured that they were overrepresented at the lower levels of the educational system and underrepresented at the upper levels, an undesirable set of circumstances that continues to the present day (Sliwka 2010).

There are signs, however, that the educational system is reforming, if only at a theoretical plane without much practical effect. In part, these changes have resulted from changes to the German citizenship laws that allow migrants to become citizens. For example, the German School Award is given to schools that "deal with diversity" effectively. In this new educational paradigm, diversity is at least tolerated, if not recognized as a prized resource worth encouraging and developing in school curricula and classrooms. Germany has a long way to go before it recognizes diversity in education as a positive influence rather than as a burden to be dealt with, or as an unfortunate cause of conflict and social division (Sliwka 2010).

In what follows, we will show how the educational paradigm that emphasizes homogeneity and fails to recognize heterogeneity effectively discriminates against Turkish-origin children at all levels of their education: *Kinderkrippe* and *Kindergarten*, Preschools; *Grundschule*, Primary Schools; and the *Hauptschule*, *Realschule*, *Gesamtschule*, and *Gymnasium*, all of which are the various tracks in Germany's system of Secondary Schooling.

Kinderkrippe *and* Kindergarten[1] *(Preschools)*

Vast inequalities arise between Turkish- and native German-origin children at a very early age. Becker (2011) administered tests of cognitive and German language skills to Turkish-origin and native German children of three–four years old, and found vast discrepancies in both cognitive and language skills: the native German children consistently scored higher than the Turkish-origin children in both of these areas. Becker explains that the discrepancy results from Turkish-origin parents' lack of German "cultural capital," a result of sub-par educational experiences and German language skills. Without the requisite cultural capital, Turkish-origin parents are less likely to expose their children to educational resources that might include books and other educational media, as well as trips to museums. Becker concludes that the gap between the two groups of children could be narrowed if Turkish-origin children attended high-quality preschools. Crucially, they would have the exposure to German that could greatly facilitate their second language acquisition (Becker 2011).

The importance of Preschool education is borne out by another study showing that 51.4% of immigrant children who attended Preschool were able to enter the *Realschule* or Higher Secondary School tracks, whereas only 21.3% of immigrant children who did not attend Preschool were able to achieve the same level of success (Spieß, Büchel, and Wagner 2003). It is not clear why so few immigrant children attend Preschool, but cost might be a factor because Preschools in Germany are not free. Additionally, Turkish-origin parents may not be aware of the benefits of Preschool due to a lack of German cultural capital, and finally, Turkish mothers may be less likely to work because of gender roles specific to Turkish culture, and therefore can look after their children at home.

Grundschule *(Primary School)*

The German educational system is designed to segregate students into separate groups, and the process starts early. For example, some native German parents try to ensure that their children are not schooled with immigrant children by sending them to Catholic and Protestant schools, and the public schools cater to the native German parents' desire to segregate their children away from foreigners by offering programs and curricula that focus on music or alternative educational approaches. Turkish parents, lacking German cultural capital, may not even be aware of these alternatives. The German penchant for homogenized educational environments demonstrates itself in a *Grundschule* apparently designed for immigrant children, with classes in German as a Second Language. When immigrant children enroll in these schools, they unsurprisingly wind up with few native German children in their classes. Lacking exposure to native German speakers, their second language acquisition of German is negatively affected (Söhn and Özcan 2006).

Turkish-origin children are overrepresented in the *Sonder-* or *Förderschule*, the schools that attend to the needs of the physically and mentally disabled. Although the reasons remain unclear, Turkish-origin children's difficulties with the second language acquisition of German may cause educators to occasionally misdiagnose them as disabled learners: ". . . schools tend to prefer more homogeneous school classes (with regard to academic performance and 'normal' student social behavior and language proficiency) as they are considered easier to instruct in a manner considered adequate" (Söhn and Özcan 2006: 116). Turkish-origin children, who deviate from the "norm," are therefore more likely to be referred to the *Sonderschule*.

Furthermore, once in a *Grundschule*, Turkish-origin students cannot expect much assistance in learning German, or with their coursework: "Training in teaching German as a Second Language is clearly insufficient" (Fernandez-Kelley and Güllüpinar 2012: 98). The cultures of Turkish-origin and other students from immigrant backgrounds receive little or no attention in most classrooms, a practice which is quite different from multicultural educational methods in which the cultures of all children are prized and recognized (Sliwka 2010). Turkish-origin children attend school for only half the day, which in certain cases might deprive them of the valuable natural exposure to German that facilitates acquisition of the second language. Whereas France and Belgium provide mentors to help immigrant children with their homework, Turkish-origin children receive no such benefits (Ross 2009).

After the needs of Turkish-origin students are neglected in their initial years in the *Grundschule*, their teachers determine which educational track they will enter, usually in their fourth year of *Grundschule* when they are nine–ten years old. It is important to emphasize that their mastery of German is the primary determinant of their future educational track: "Three-quarters of children who have one parent who is not fluent in German are assigned to the *Hauptschule*," the lowest educational track (Ross 2009: 696). Without perfect German, entrance into the *Gymnasium* is nearly impossible:

> Likewise, "perfect" German is seen as a precondition for a recommendation to the highest secondary education, while only in the lowest track,

Hauptschule, do schools provide for extra language training. Hence, otherwise gifted children who by the fourth grade have not reached the proficiency of native speakers stand little chance of receiving the instruction their cognitive capacities would actually allow for.

(Söhn and Özcan 2006: 116)

The Hauptschule, Realschule, Gesamtschule, *and* Gymnasium *(Secondary Schools)*

Without adequate exposure to German, adequate second language instruction in German, or adequate appreciation of their culture, in segregated learning environments, Turkish-origin children unsurprisingly find themselves in the lowest track of the educational system, the *Hauptschule*.

It can be seen in Figure 8.1 that Turkish-origin students are overrepresented in the *Hauptschule* as compared to students with no migration background (48.1%–16.6% respectively), and that Turkish-origin students are underrepresented at the middle and upper echelons of the educational system as compared to students with no migration background (*Realschule*: 22.1%–38.6%; *Gymnasium*: 12.5%–33.2%). Data from the first decade of the 2000s show no significant changes, as demonstrated by a survey administered in 2008 by the TIES research group to second-generation Turkish-origin and non-immigrant native German respondents living in Berlin and Frankfurt. In both cities, more Turkish-origin respondents attended a *Hauptschule* than native Germans by a margin approaching 20% (Berlin: 37.4%–18.8%; Frankfurt: 36.1%–19.4%). Again, Turkish-origin students were underrepresented in the *Gymnasium* by a margin of nearly 20% (Berlin: 14.2%–32.0%; Frankfurt: 10.8%–28.9%) (Sürig and Wilmes 2015: 45). The lack of more recent data may be explained by the German government's failure to compile detailed, comprehensive information on the educational attainments of its immigrant population: "It is. . .remarkable that detailed and continuous census data on education in Germany is hardly available" (Söhn, and Özcan 2006: 103), an omission indicative of a lack of concern for the plight of immigrant-origin families. Discrimination takes many forms, and one of them is neglect.

A diploma from a *Hauptschule* often does not lead to acceptable employment: "The certificate of the lowest track (*Hauptschule*), acquired after the ninth or tenth grade, has been greatly devalued over the last decades, putting young adults in an unfavorable position when applying either for vocational training or a qualified job" (Güllüpinar and Kelly 2012: 199). Once in the lower *Hauptschule* track, students find it difficult to change to one of the higher tracks.

Attempts to reform the system have been met with stiff resistance. In an effort to diversify its schools, the Berlin educational administration has stipulated that a *Gymnasium* may choose only 60% of its students, and must allow 30% of its students to be chosen by lottery, with the remaining 10% of allotted places

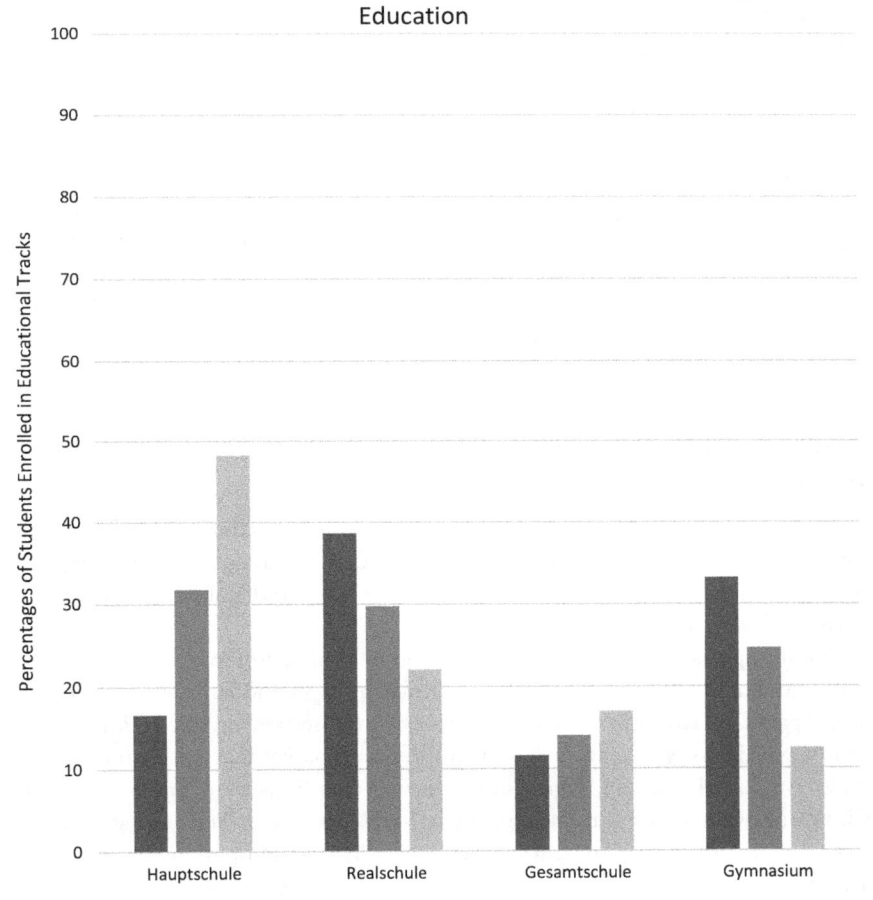

Percentages of Immigrant-, Non-Immigrant, and Turkish-Origin Students Enrolled in the Various Tracks of German Secondary Education

■ No migration background ■ Total number of students with a migration background ■ Turkish Origin

FIGURE 8.1 Proportion of 15-year-old Students in 2000, with/without a Migration Background in Different School Types According to their Countries of Origin or Background (Adapted from Güllüpinar and Kelley 2012: 101).

being set aside for siblings of current students. In response to native German parents' complaints at these integration efforts, school administrators effectively segregated classes on the basis of language skills, so that native German speakers were taught in separate classes from immigrant students, who were denied access to the support necessary for their success (Open Society Review 2013). Again, one sees the German educator's desire for homogeneity in education at work.

In summary, it can be seen that Turkish-origin students at all levels of the educational system are being segregated into lower educational tracks on the basis of their second language skills without being given fair access to the educational resources that would enable them to overcome their language barriers:

> The assignment of migrant students to separate classes based on language skills also constitutes indirect discrimination. There is no evidence to demonstrate a correlation between non-native language skills and academic capacity. Rather, native language is being used as a proxy to separate children based on ethnicity or nationality and to provide children of migrant backgrounds with distinctly different—and in fact, inferior—educational opportunities. Such segregation constitutes unlawful differentiation under international law.
>
> *(Open Society Review 2013)*

A Promising Government Initiative: Bilingual and Multicultural Education

We recommend that Germany adopt educational policies that foster integration and second language acquisition for Turkish-origin students so that they, and all other immigrant students, are treated equitably and not subjected to any form of discrimination.

Most importantly, German educators must be trained to recognize the value of a multicultural education and varied student languages and cultures. The educational paradigm that prizes homogeneity must be revised and replaced with a model that views diversity of languages and cultures as resources that can be used in the classroom, a cultural and mental shift that will take decades to fully implement. Sliwka (2010) makes several helpful suggestions that can facilitate the attainment of this goal, including training teachers to view diversity of opinions, cultures, and languages as resources for successful education, rather than as barriers to it. In order to foster multicultural education, teacher training institutions might try to recruit teacher trainees from immigrant backgrounds, might encourage teachers to do internships at diverse schools, and might encourage teachers to develop their intercultural communications skills by requiring them to travel abroad and learn new languages. The German educational administration must also make a concerted effort to train teachers to teach German as a Second Language (Sliwka 2010).

Becker (2011) showed the importance of Preschool education as the foundation of later educational success, but Turkish-origin families do not take advantage of it because they lack cultural capital to understand its importance or because they cannot afford it. To rectify these problems, the German education ministry could subsidize Preschool education to make it free, and could also embark on a public education program that might include advertisements showing the necessity of Preschool education.

In the *Grundschule*, bilingual education might end the segregation so harmful to immigrant-origin students and could thereby promote the development of second language acquisition necessary to succeed in the top tiers of the German educational system. In one form of bilingual education, two-way immersion, students from two separate linguistic backgrounds take language classes and content-area classes in their dominant language and in their second language. A promising example can be seen in the Aziz Nesin *Grundschule* in Berlin, where Turkish origin students receive bilingual and multicultural education in both German and Turkish together with children of non-migrant German families. This institution sends approximately 50% of its Turkish origin students to the highest tier of the educational system, the *Gymnasium* (Jungius 2006).

Two-way immersion got its start in Germany in 1992, when the Staatliche Europa-Schule Berlin was founded (Meier 2010). The Staatliche Europa-Schule Berlin pairs German with Spanish-, Portuguese-, Italian-, Greek-, Turkish-, and Polish-speaking students. In 2008, 6,000 students benefitted from two-way immersion, and the program is still expanding. In 1993, a German-Italian program was developed in Wolfsburg, followed by a program in Hamburg in 1999 that paired German with Italian, Portuguese, Spanish, and Turkish. The latest two-way immersion program in Cologne, which started in 2001, pairs German with Italian and Turkish (Meier 2010).

In non-bilingual programs, school administrators should resist non-immigrant parents' demands to segregate non-immigrant children from immigrant children, should ensure that teachers with the requisite training teach immigrant children to use German in academic contexts, and should provide mentors to help immigrant children with their homework, as is done in France and Belgium.

The German educational administration must also change when and how the decision to put students into educational tracks is made. Perhaps the decision could be delayed a few years, to the age of 15–16, as is done in France and Belgium. Additionally, second language skills should not figure so prominently in the decision, especially when students are not given the necessary support to acquire German as a Second Language.

In order to facilitate movement between tracks, the *Gesamtschule* could be expanded to include the *Gymnasium* (currently, the *Gesamtschule* encompasses only the *Hauptschule* and the *Realschule*). In the *Gymnasium*, immigrant students should be able to take classes in German as a Second Language; presently, language support classes are only offered at the *Hauptschule*.

Finally, some supervisory body must monitor the German educational system so that segregation and discrimination can be minimized. The German government should "Create an independent oversight body (separate from existing authorities), where parents can take complaints, advocate for their rights and those of their children, and receive support" (Open Society Review 2013).

Assessment and Evidence of Progress

Assessing progress would involve comparisons of the various means of second language education in the various *Grundschulen* in terms of their success when placing students in the *Gymnasium*. A review of the available data seems to indicate that bilingual education with two-way immersion leads to the highest degree of success. Generally, extant studies of two-way immersion indicate that it is effective in developing language skills, academic proficiency, and sociocultural benefits (Meier 2010). Students in two-way immersion benefitted from learning about cultures and from engaging with peers from different cultural backgrounds, all of which led to greater bonding and cohesiveness between classmates. Most studies have examined two-way immersion in its earliest stages of implementation, before its benefits have started to take full effect; only one study of two-way immersion has focused on two-way immersion in its latter stages. Although more research on two-way immersion remains to be done, preliminary results show that it could benefit students from all backgrounds (Meier 2010).

Further indicators of progress would be government-led initiatives to increase the attendance of Turkish-origin children in preschools, plans to develop or expand bilingual and multicultural schooling, or plans to train elementary school teachers in bilingual and multicultural education. In this regard, statistics showing a rise in the number of teachers with immigrant backgrounds as well as exposure to other languages and cultures might indicate that a paradigm shift in German education has taken hold. Second language learners need exposure to German in school, so a lengthening of the school day for these learners might show that their needs are being considered. Also, statistics illustrating a decline in the number of Turkish and immigrant children who are sent to *Sonderschulen* would constitute evidence that their multicultural background and bilingual skills are being prized or at least tolerated. Finally, employment statistics and income figures can show the extent to which Turkish-origin Germans are succeeding in German society.

Other indicators of progress might include a delay in making the *Empfehlung* or recommendation in the tracking system, evidence that the recommendation is not being made largely on Turkish-origin students' mastery of German, movement of students between tracks, an expansion in the number of *Gesamtchule* that include all three tracks, and regular reports from an independent oversight body that monitors discrimination and segregation in the school system.

Conclusion

Ultimately, German education reform must serve both its students and the country's ongoing project of civic redefinition. The educational system in Germany (and in any other country, for that matter) performs at least two important social tasks. First, it creates a workforce that is appropriate and productive for the economic profile of the country. Second, it inscribes German identity onto those oncoming generations whose growth and maturity will, in their time, confer upon them the responsibility for carrying on the necessary task of reimagining the national community.

Given the global economic transformations in which Germany unavoidably participates, an educational system that falls short of imparting to its children the necessary capacities and skills to thrive can be judged, and found wanting, on those terms. In particular, a system whose tracking logic denies to excessive numbers of students the wherewithal to thrive in an information technology environment merits reforms that will introduce more forbearance and flexibility into the operation of that logic.

To the extent that the education system serves to create not merely workers who are German, but *German* workers, the exclusionary implications of differential outcomes for socially marginalized populations reach beyond questions of economic performance or labor market needs. That Germany carries the moral burden of its particularly fraught modern history should not distract from the essential similarity of the civic challenge which it, as a liberal society, shares with all other societies that belong to the same tradition.

In T.H. Marshall's (1965) terms, the moral arc of the liberal tradition has traversed from its original (and narrow) concern with property protection, through a commitment to universal political empowerment, to arrive at an agenda of socio-economic inclusion in the most comprehensive sense. At each stage in this traverse, notions of rights and the very meaning of equality have been objects of political contestation. At these historical junctures, liberalism's challenge has been to redefine the practical and moral content of the equality which constitutes the heart of the liberal worldview. Among other things, in the present day this task requires liberal societies to reconcile their older, cramped understandings of equality with the demands of the newer, multicultural agenda and the role that social institutions like schools should play in furthering this agenda. This reconciliation may not be orderly or pretty, but to the extent that inequalities can be redefined as inequities, "nervousness" as an attribute of public policy actually represents moments of creative tension that may precipitate change.

In the particular framework of German pedagogy, this agenda implies something like the final democratization of the older, Humboldtian tradition of *Bildung*, which otherwise remains an instinctual premise of Germany's educational tracking. The elitism of this pedagogy, and the ambivalent relation between German *Bildungsbürgertum* and the liberal tradition itself (see, e.g., Bollenbeck 2000), is itself an unresolved tension that only becomes harder to ignore as the country becomes more committed to inclusive definitions of civic identity and of citizenship itself.

Note

1 In Germany, *Kinderkrippe* (creche) is a type of Preschool for children aged 0–3, and *Kindergartens* serve children aged 3–6.

References

Anadolu Agency - Berlin. (2019). "Turks in Germany Demand Action against Racism." *World News.* https://www.hurriyetdailynews.com/turks-in-germany-demand-action-against-racism-142099

Auernheimer, G. (2005). "The German Education System." *European Education* 37/4: 75–89.

Baer, M. D. (2013). "Turk and Jew in Berlin: The First Turkish Migration to Germany and the Shoah." *Comparative Studies in Society and History* 55/2: 330–355.

Becker, B. (2011). "Cognitive and Language Skills of Turkish Children in Germany: A Comparison of the Second and Third Generation and Mixed Generational Groups." *The International Migration Review* 45/2: 426–459.

Bennhold, K. (2019). "Wall Is Gone but a Question Divides: Who Is German?" *The New York Times International,* vol. 159, pA4.

Bingöl, A. S. (2013). "Mother Tongue Instruction Policies towards Turkish Migrant Children in Europe, Akdeniz Language Studies Conference 2012." *Procedia: Social and Behavioral Sciences* 70: 1016–1023.

Bollenbeck, G. (Winter, 2000). "German Kultur, the Bildungsbürgertum, and Its Susceptibility to National Socialism." *The German Quarterly* 73/1: 67–83.

Chin, R. (2017). *The Crisis of Multiculturalism in Europe.* Princeton: Princeton University Press.

Cho, H. (2017). "Navigating the Meanings of Social Justice, Teaching Social Justice, and Multicultural Education." *International Journal of Multicultural Education* 19/2: 1–19.

Faas, D. (2008). "From Foreigner Pedagogy to Intercultural Education: An Analysis of the German Responses to Diversity and Its Impact on Schools and Students." *European Educational Research Journal* 7/1: 108–123. doi:10.2304/eerj.2008.7.1.108

Fernandez-Kelley, P. and Güllüpinar, F. (2012). "The Unequal Structure of the German Education System: Structural Reasons for Educational Failures of Turkish Youth in Germany." *Spaces Flows* 2(2): 93–112.

Gellert, C. and Einhard, R. (1992). "Diversification and Integration: The Vocationalisation of the German Higher Education System." *European Journal of Education* 27(1/2): 89–99.

Gooden, S. T. (2014). *Race and Social Equity: A Nervous Area of Government.* New York: M.E. Sharpe.

Green, S. (2003). "The Legal Status of Turks in Germany." *Immigrants & Minorities* 22: 228–246.

Gündüz, M. (2009). "Sociocultural Origins of Turkish Education Reforms and Ideological Origins of Late Ottoman Intellectuals (1908–1930)." *History of Education* http://www.informaworld.com/smpp/title-content-t713599897

Jungius, B. (2006). *Aziz Nesin Grundschule, Berlin: A Bilingual Turkish-German Public Elementary School.* http://www.interculturemap.org/upload/att/200612111022430. CASE%20STUDY%20aziz-nesin-schule_BJOERN.pdf

Klumpp, L. et al. (2014) *Education Policy Outlook: Germany.* ERIC Document Reproduction Service No. 583383. http://www.oecd.org/education/EDUCATION%20 POLICY%20OUTLOOK%20GERMANY_EN.pdf

Kristen, C. and Nadia, G. (2007). "The Education Attainment of the Second Generation in Germany: Social Origins and Ethnic Inequality." *Ethnicities* 7/3: 343–366.

Leibau, E. and Diehl, C. (2015). "Turning Back to Turkey – Or Turning the Back on Germany? Remigration Intentions and Behavior of Turkish Immigrants in Germany between 1984 and 2011." *Zeitschrift für Soziologie* 44/1: 22–41.

Lodigiani, M. (2018). "Turks in Germany: An Evaluation of Socioeconomic Integration." *Colloquium* 11(1). https://ejournals.bc.edu/ojs/indez/php/colloquium/article/download/10242/8926

Marshall, T. H. (1965). *Class, Citizenship and Social Development*. Garden City, NJ: Doubleday & Company.

Meier, G. S. (2010). "Two-Way Immersion Education in Germany: Bridging the Linguistic Gap." *International Journal of Bilingual Education and Bilingualism* 13/4: 419–437.

Miera, F. (2007). German Education Policy and the Challenge of Migration. Paper prepared for the EMILIE research project funded by the European Commission Research DG, Sixth Framework Programme. December. Frankfurt/Oder. http://www.eliamep.gr/eliamep/files/German_ education_policy_and_the_Challenge_of_Migration.pdf.

Mueller, C. (2006). "Integrating Turkish Communities: A German Dilemma." *Population Research and Policy Review* 25(5/6): 419–441.

Open Society Justice Review. (2013). *Submission to the Universal Periodic Review: Germany*. 16th Session of the UPR, 22 April to 3 May 2013. www.justiceinitiative.org

Paksoy, Y. (March 19, 2018). "Turks in Germany Cry Out: We Live in Danger." *Daily Sabah Europe*. https://www.dailysabah.com/europe/2018/03/19/turks-in-germany-cry-out-we-live-in-danger

Ross, C. J. (2009). "Perennial Outsiders: The Educational Experience of Turkish Youth in Germany." *American University International Law Review* 23/4: 685–710.

Rist, R. C. (1979). "On the Education of Guest-Worker Children in Germany: A Comparative Study of Policies and Programs in Bavaria and Berlin." *The School Review* 87/3: 242–268.

Schölnwalder, K. and Söhn, J. (2009). "Immigrant Settlement Structures in Germany: General Patterns and Urban Levels of Concentration of Major Groups." *Urban Studies* 46/7: 1439–1460.

Sen, F. (2003). "The Historical Situation of Turkish Migrants in Germany." *Immigrants & Minorities* 22/2–3: 208–227.

Sliwka, A. (2010): From homogeneity to diversity in German education, in: Effective Teacher Education for Diversity: Strategies and Challenges. Paris: OECD, S. 205-217.

Smith, S. and Eckhardt, A. (August 14, 2018). "Germans of Turkish Descent Struggle with Identity, Seek Acceptance." *NBC News*. https://www.nbcnews.com/news/world/germans/-turkisk-descent-struggle-identity-seek-acceptance-n886961

Söhn, J. (2005). Introduction. In Arbeitsstelle Interkulturelle Konflikte und Gesellschaftliche Integration (AKI), Berlin (Ed.) *Working Paper: The Effectiveness of Bilingual School Programs for Immigrant Children* (pp. 1–3)WZB Discussion Paper, No. SP IV 2005-601, Wissenschaftszentrum Berlin für Sozialforschung (WZB), Berlin

Söhn, J. and Özcan, V. (2006). "The Educational Attainment of Turkish Migrants in Germany." *Turkish Studies* 7/1: 101–124.

Søvik, M. (2008). "Islamic Instruction in German Public Schools: The Case of North-Rhine-Westphalia." In *Islam and Muslims in Germany*, Ala Al-Harmaneh and Jörn Thielmann, eds. Leiden and Boston: Brill: 241–265.

Spieß, Katharina, Felix Büchel and Gert G. Wagner. (2003). "Children's School Placement in Germany: Does Kindergarten Attendance Matter?" *Early Childhood Research Quarterly* 18/2: 255–270.

Sürig, I. and Wilmes, M. (2015). *The Integration of the European Second Generation: Results of the TIES Survey on the Descendants of Turkish and Yugoslavian Migrants*. Amsterdam: Amsterdam University Press.

The Law Library of Congress. (2017). *Global Legal Research Center*. ioc.go/law/help/ migration-citizenship/migration-citizenship-law-postwar-germany.pdf

UNESCO MOST. (2019). *Multiculturalism*. www.unesco.org/new/en/social-and-human-sciences/themes/international-migration/glossary/multiculturalism/

Walkenhorst, H. (2015). "Europeanisation of the German Education System." *German Politics* 14/4: 470–486.

Wilhelm, C. (2013). "Diversity in Germany: A Historical Perspective." *German Politics and Society Issue* 31/2(107): 13–29.

Wirtz, B. (2018). "The German Economic Miracle Depended on Migrants." *Foundation for Economic Education*. https://fee.org/articles/the-geran-economic-miracle-depended-on-immigrants/

9

ACKNOWLEDGING NERVOUSNESS THROUGH TRUTH AND RECONCILIATION

Lessons from South Africa

Samantha June Larson and Crystal Soderman

A Nervous Area of Government in South Africa

This chapter examines a promising approach for acknowledging nervousness associated with historical acts of injustice: the Truth and Reconciliation Commission (TRC) model (Emanuelson Jr., 2018). Such commissions are charged with revealing, documenting, negotiating, and providing recommendations to reconcile past injustices committed by a state. This process has the potential to help government bodies reckon with the inequities they have perpetuated, and therefore process feelings such as nervousness, guilt, and shame that result from their actions. TRCs have been adopted in many countries where marginalized people have shouldered historical trauma. We focus on the renowned example of South Africa immediately following apartheid, a state-sanctioned system of racial segregation that lasted from 1948 to the 1990s. This case offers valuable guidance by illustrating that a government must acknowledge the history of inequities before public justice can be realized.

This chapter proceeds as follows. First, we conceptualize apartheid as a nervous area of government. In South Africa, the transition to a more equitable society began with the foundation of a democracy, where all citizens, regardless of race, ethnicity, gender, or religious beliefs, were given the right to vote and hold office. Those in power often regard this as a panacea for all historical injustices. This often leads to a denial of the full extent of damages caused by state-sanctioned oppression, such as persevering economic disparities. The transition to democracy did not lead to justice writ large. Denial of disparities and the systemic reasons for their existence precipitates a nervous area of government, which is expanded upon in this section.

Next, we propose the TRC model as a promising practice for fostering recognition by government officials. Such acknowledgement is dwindling in today's post-truth era. Selected as their 2016 Word of the Year, *Oxford Dictionaries* defines *post-truth* as "relating or denoting circumstances in which objective facts are less influential in shaping public opinion than appeals to emotion and personal belief" (Oxford University Press, 2019). Diminished confidence in data and the dismissal of personal narratives harms systematically oppressed people the most. When structural racism is denied, people of color remain stuck in subjugation as policies and programs stay the same, perpetuating disparities. Without the truth, wounds of the past cannot heal. The prerequisite for addressing racism as a nervous area of government is thus the act of admitting that the wounds exist in the first place.

Finally, we conduct a systematic literature review of articles published between 1998 and 2018 to assess the extent of progress as a result of the South African TRC process. The review is presented in two phases. First, we apply a deductive approach to investigate two research questions: (a) To what extent do article findings suggest that the South African TRC outcomes were predominantly positive or negative? (b) To what extent did TRC articles focus on predominantly the South African state or society? The second phase includes inductive analysis of three emergent themes: Findings suggest that the TRC most effectively advanced restorative justice between victims and perpetrators, fostering healing in a public space. However, redistributive justice for communities of color has not been realized. In closing, we discuss economic disparities that remain in South Africa and highlight recommendations for commissions interested in undertaking similar reconciliation processes.

Why Apartheid Is a Nervous Area of Government

Apartheid perpetuated a distinctive history of injustice in South Africa. Racism was a residual effect of the colonial past and became part of the political system through laws that restricted the rights of non-white South Africans, as shown in the timeline in Figure 9.1. For instance, the Native Land Act of 1913 allocated only 7% of arable land in South Africa to Africans (South African History Online, 2019). The adoption of discriminatory laws increased after the rise of the Nationalist Party (NP) in 1948. The NP institutionalized a racist administrative state founded on the belief that Black and Coloured South African people were inherently inferior to the white minority population. Appendix A includes descriptions of each law.

This system of oppression lasted for more than 40 years. While resistance grew, state-sponsored violence and discrimination brought about the death and detention of thousands. World organizations such as the United Nations (UN) began publicly condemning apartheid and imposing economic and diplomatic sanctions against South Africa from 1977 to 1989; however, this did

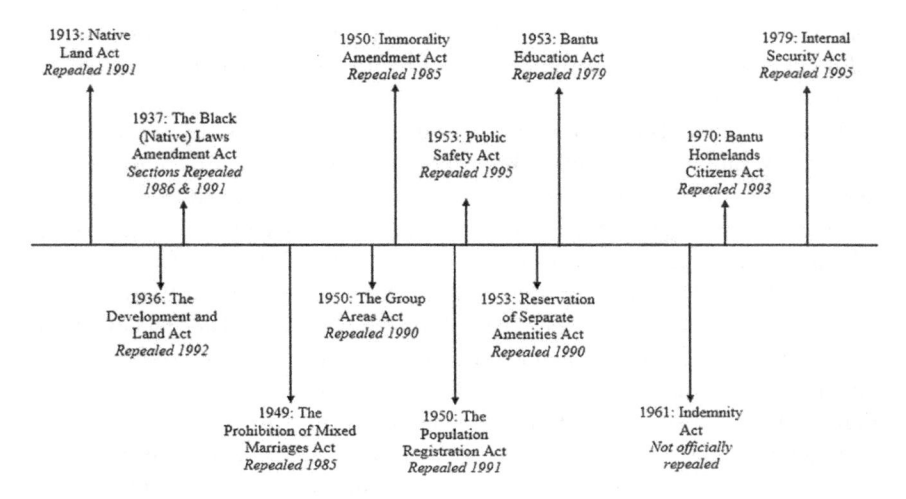

FIGURE 9.1 Timeline of Apartheid-Era Policies Adopted and Repealed.

little to influence change (Renner, 2014, p. 272). Figure 9.1 shows that some apartheid-era laws were repealed during this time, but many remained intact.

It was not until the early 1990s that South African government officials started confronting pervasive injustices related to race, ethnicity, gender, and class. With increasing international pressure and a rise in the level of social resistance, the apartheid system weakened. Negotiations began in earnest in 1990 when newly elected President F.W. de Klerk lifted the 30-year ban on anti-apartheid organizations, providing the political environment necessary for negotiations. Acting as the representative of the African National Congress (ANC), an organization formed in 1912 to promote the rights of Black South Africans and the current governing party, Nelson Mandela emerged as a leading figure in these negotiations.

The ANC and state representatives frequently met to establish and set the terms for the transition to a new democracy. Although this process was not seamless, a major transition came with the ratification of the Interim Constitution enfranchising all racial groups for the upcoming election. The political system of apartheid *formally* ended with these actions, meaning there was a democratic election that led to the inauguration of the country's first Black president, Nelson Mandela, in 1994. However, despite these advances, many *informal* effects remained embedded in South African society and institutions.

We conceptualize apartheid and the reckoning period that followed as a nervous area of government. After the election of Nelson Mandela, the state had to consider strategies for advancing public justice following decades of racial violence. Gooden (2014) notes that: "understanding how the organization effectively or ineffectively provides public justice requires an examination of four core areas ... the external environment; senior public administrators; public servants; and organizational values" (p. 5). We review each area to exemplify acknowledgment of nervousness associated with apartheid and racial segregation in this case.

First, the external environment triggered examination of equity-related issues. In this area, motivators originate from a political, legal, economic, or moral trigger (Gooden, 2014, p. 6). Increasing condemnation of apartheid from the UN, the United States, and other world organizations provided the moral trigger. The political trigger resulted from the negotiations in 1987–1993 between the anti-apartheid ANC and the ruling NP. The *Promotion of National Unity and Reconciliation Act, No 34 of 1995*, was the legal trigger, which mandated an honest and complete account be established for the causes and extent of gross violations of human rights emanating from the conflicts of the past and the fate of victims of these violations (Parliament of the Republic of South Africa, 1995).

Second, senior administrators responded to these external motivators. It is critical that administrators "…communicate important messages and allocate resources that influence the overall value of public justice and the administration of social equity … [and] operate as important translators of the external racial-equity triggers" (Gooden, 2014, pp. 7–8). President F.W. de Klerk set the tone for change in 1990 when he lifted the ban on anti-apartheid organizations. Through this action and the subsequent negotiations between the ANC and NP, de Klerk communicated to the members of his party and the South African public that he was serious about the transition to an inclusive democracy.

Relatedly, the TRC later interviewed public servants employed during apartheid to reconcile decades of unacceptable behavior committed on behalf of the state. Gooden (2014) notes that the "actions of public servants involve daily implementation decisions that affect life chances of the clients they serve and establish patterns of routine and service with important racial-equity consequences" (p. 8). Thus, perpetrator testimonies were critical in understanding the injustices and restoring humanity to Black and Coloured South Africans they had harmed.

The final TRC report found: "…the predominant portion of gross violations of human rights was committed by the former state through its security and law-enforcement agencies" ("Truth and Reconciliation Commission," 1998, p. 212). Those that testified discussed the reasoning behind their actions, such as being engaged in a war (which can elicit feelings of pride versus distress when committing violent actions) and acting on orders from, or with knowledge among, senior persons in authority. The latter reason, although mostly denied by senior officials, suggests an entrenched system to maintain power for the white minority population.

Finally, despite their limitations, the involvement of public servants shifted organizational values within South Africa's public sector. As Gooden (2014) emphasizes, organizational values are the single most important factor in understanding race equity as a nervous area of government (p. 9). From 1995 to

1998, the South African government prioritized human rights in general, and racial equity in particular, addressing the emotional, historical, and societal ramifications of apartheid. Looming in the nervousness of this time, the South African government attempted to facilitate a restorative justice process in the public arena.

A Promising Government Initiative: The TRC Model

Prior to the 1990s, TRCs had previously been adopted in Latin American and Eastern European nations where ruling regimes had been overthrown. Those models approached their TRC process with impunity and often sought vengeance. Unlike its predecessors, South Africa's transition to a new government came as a result of negotiations and consensus (Gibson & Gouws, 1999, p. 502). This led the South African TRC to uniquely apply a model based on *restorative justice*, which focused on the reconciliation between victims and perpetrators through acknowledgement of wrongs committed and shared rehabilitation.

Upholding these principles, the Government of National Unity established the TRC to facilitate open hearings where victims and perpetrators honestly shared their experiences of prior, state-sanctioned injustices. Its aim: "...was to combat impunity and recreate a culture of accountability, and most importantly to uncover [the] truth about gross human rights violations and assist families of the victims in getting closure" (South African History Online, 2017, para. 3). In other words, the primary goal of this process was to begin healing on a national scale.

The TRC was composed of 17 commissioners "selected through a country-wide nomination process and publicly interviewed by an independent selection panel comprising representatives of all the political parties, civil society, and the religious bodies in the country" (Tutu, 2019, para. 6). Archbishop Desmond Tutu was selected by President Nelson Mandela to chair the TRC. Prior to the commission, Archbishop Tutu was well-known for his anti-apartheid activism and received the Nobel Peace Prize for this work in 1984. His role as chair provided legitimacy to the work being undertaken by the newly established government.

The TRC aimed to promote national unity and a spirit of understanding through the work of three committees (South African History Online, 2018, para. 4). The Human Rights Violations (HRV) Committee investigated human rights abuses which occurred between 1960 and 1994; the Reparation and Rehabilitation (R&R) Committee was "...charged with restoring victims' dignity and formulating proposals to assist with rehabilitation"; and the Amnesty Committee reviewed applications for amnesty and accepted those that met three criteria: the action occurred between 1960 and 1994, the crimes were politically motivated, and the person seeking amnesty provided the whole truth ("Truth and Reconciliation," 2018, para. 2).

Approximately 21,000 victims testified to the TRC, and 2,000 were at public hearings (The United States Institute of Peace, 1995). Of the 7,112 amnesty applications submitted, 849 (12%) were granted (The United States Institute of Peace, 1995). The TRC believed that publicly sharing the abuses of apartheid would promote individual healing and provide victims with a sense of agency (Gobodo-Madikizela, 2015, p. 1092). Additionally, applying an invitational rather than adversarial approach, the TRC encouraged perpetrators to take ownership of their participation in the racist system of apartheid, permitting them to not only admit their guilt, but to feel it as well (Gobodo-Madikizela, 2016, p. 47).

In retrospect, limitations of the TRC are plentiful. Key government actors involved in the conflict refused to engage in the process, such as top military officials. Those involved in the liberation movement did not feel that they should be required to apply for amnesty given that they had conducted a "just war" (Tutu, 2019, para. 9). Prosecution was limited for the perpetrators who were not granted amnesty or did not apply, which disillusioned their victims (Tutu, 2019, para. 11).

The TRC also failed to produce reparations for land and livelihoods lost due to a lack of governmental funding (Bradshaw & Haines, 2014, p. 9). As demonstrated in Figure 9.2, farm and agricultural holdings represent one area in which such economic disparities remain. For example, although white South Africans accounted for less than 10% of the population in 2015, they owned more than 70% of farm and agricultural assets. Black Africans, who account for over 75% of the population, held only 4% of those assets.

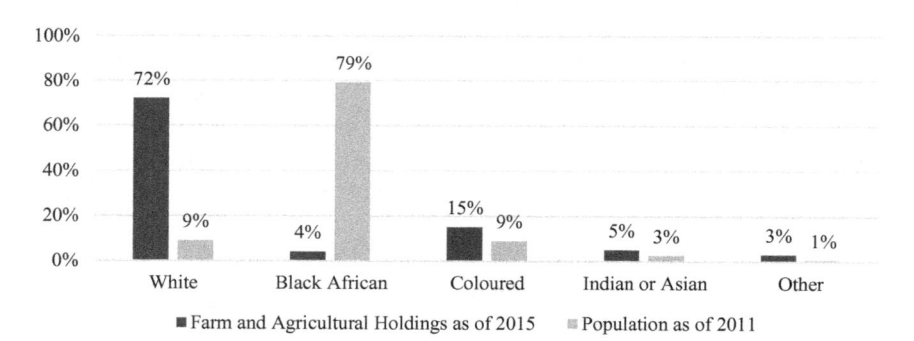

FIGURE 9.2 Comparison of Farm and Agricultural Holdings versus Population Demographics.

Population data was taken from the South African 2011 census ("Census," 2012). Farm and agricultural holding data came from the Land Audit Report (2017) as there are no comparable sources from the same year. Although there is a 4-year difference between the two data sets, they still serve to highlight persistent economic inequities operationalized as agricultural assets.

While the TRC body did not solve all racial inequities in South Africa, it "opened up a way to talk about the individual and systemic wrongs committed under 43 years of apartheid" (Magistad, 2017, para. 1). It is internationally recognized as a model for other post-conflict states. Despite its limitations, the South African TRC is generally regarded as successful in providing a mechanism to be heard and foster emancipation from historical trauma related to discrimination and violence (Meskell & Scheermeyer, 2008). In the next section, we explore these mixed claims more systematically.

Assessment and Evidence of Progress

Methods

To what extent did the TRC facilitate emotional processing and healing to advance greater racial equity in South Africa? Many studies have examined this general question since the TRC report was published in 1998. Yet, comprehensive evaluation of its effectiveness has not been conducted. The remainder of this chapter therefore conducts a systematic literature review to understand of the outcomes of the TRC process in South Africa. Systematic reviews assess the entirety of research-related publications on a given subject with well-defined parameters (Cronin, Ryan, & Coughlan, 2008). The methodological details are outlined below.

The literature search was conducted on the Web of Science Core Collection database. Other databases such as Google Scholar produce similar results (Martín-Martín, Orduna-Malea, Thelwall, & López-Cózar, 2018). However, Web of Science allows for enhanced reproducibility and reliability of publication results. Furthermore, Google Scholar is a search engine that includes a number of items, such as dissertations and citations. Conversely, Web of Science is curated and limited to documents that meet standards determined by qualified individuals.

Article selection was completed in four stages outlined by Moher, Liberati, Tetzlaff, and Altman (2009): identification, screening, eligibility, and included. First, articles were identified using standardized search criteria. Because the TRC launched in 1996, publication years from 1996 to 2018 were included. Keyword search of article titles included the phrases "Truth and Reconciliation Commission" and "South Africa." The initial search produced 190 articles.

Second, the screening process involved deleting duplicated articles. Then, articles were also excluded if they did not produce research findings. Additional articles were excluded because they focused on the TRCs of other countries, the psychology of healing and forgiveness among victims of violence, personality disorders among perpetrators, theology and religion in South Africa and the TRC, or consisted of book, theater, or film reviews.

After reading the articles and removing those that were ineligible, 63 articles were included in our analysis (see Appendix B). Figure 9.3 illustrates the journal

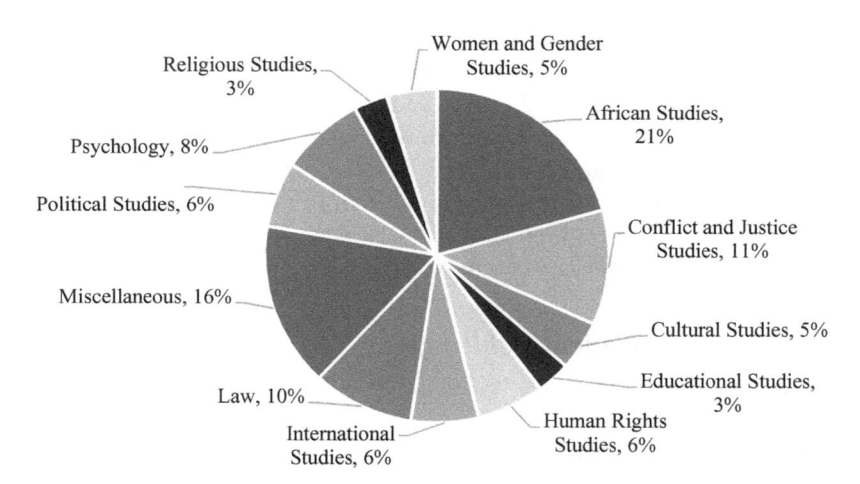

FIGURE 9.3 Percent of Articles Published by Journal Type.

types from which the articles were published. A majority of articles came from *African Studies* journals (21%). While 6% of articles came from *Political Studies* journals, none were published by any of the top 20 public administration journals as identified by Google Scholar Metrics – indicating a gap in examining this model as a practical governance approach to racial equity challenges.

Analysis Phase I: Deductive Approach with Preset Codes

The overarching goal of the analysis was to assess evidence of progress over the past 20 years. To do so, analysis of the articles was conducted in two phases. Phase I applied a deductive approach using present codes. It focused on two central questions. First, to what extent do article findings suggest that the South African TRC outcomes were *predominantly positive or negative*? Many articles suggested that outcomes of the TRC were mixed, noting that some good came of the process for restorative justice, but several inequities remained. Due to the high magnitude of mixed results, the authors selected two codes and identified whether the conclusion suggested a primarily positive or negative outcome.

The second question examined: to what extent did TRC articles focus on predominantly the South African *state* or *society*? Again, many articles spoke to impacts related to both state actors and the broader public. Many focused on how the TRC instituted a process in which healing and collective memory required both "victims" and "perpetrators" to participate in a reciprocal fashion. Due to the high number of such articles, we selected two codes and identified whether the conclusion primarily focused on (1) the state-sponsored process that involved public servants as perpetrators, or (2) the impacts that the process had on the South African public, including victims that testified, victims that did not testify, and broader society.

The authors followed a systematic process to establish intercoder agreement. Each author coded individual articles, discussed feedback, and reached agreement on the coding before moving onto the next set of articles following guidance of MacPhail, Khoza, Abler, and Ranganathan (2016). More specifically, the authors began by reading the same set of four articles independently. After each author had finished coding the articles, they compared codes and determined the percentage agreement. These meetings ensured that "errors relating to different allocations of codes were reduced considerably" (MacPhail et al., 2016, p. 8).

The first round produced 75% agreement on Code 1: Outcomes and 25% agreement on Code 2: Group Impacted. After discussing logic and code definitions, the authors coded four additional articles. The second round produced 50% agreement on Code 1: Outcomes (50%) and 75% agreement on Code 2: Group Impacted. After coding 12.5% of the articles, the authors found a primary reason for disagreement was due to a third category for each code that was labeled as "mixed." The authors removed the third category and changed the codes to "predominantly" positive or negative for Code 1 and "predominantly" state or South African society for Code 2. This enhanced agreement for all future articles. Initial findings are presented in Table 9.1. Out of 63 total articles, 25 articles (40%) were coded as *Predominantly Positive*. Of the articles that focused on positive outcomes, 12 articles emphasized impacts on the South African state, including examination of how the TRC model impacted government actors and restorative justice processes. The other 13 positive articles focused on South African society, emphasizing how the TRC offered a path forward for creating a collective memory of the past and communal healing in response to historical trauma.

The remaining 38 articles (60%) were coded as *Predominantly Negative*. Of those articles that critiqued the TRC process and emphasized negative outcomes, 17 identified issues within the South African state, such as issues with the processes and definitions of the TRC model itself. The other 21 negative articles placed predominant emphasis on South African society, especially the lack of economic justice that continues to plague the nation.

TABLE 9.1 Phase I Findings

Coding Category	C2: State	C2: Society	C1: Total Articles
C1: Positive	12	13	25 (40%)
C1: Negative	17	21	38 (60%)
C2: Total Articles	29 (46%)	34 (54%)	63 (100%)

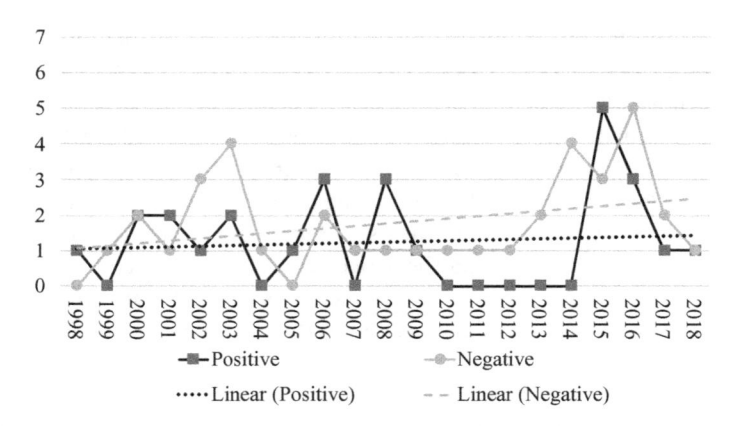

FIGURE 9.4 Publication Time Series Analysis: Predominantly Positive versus Negative Articles (1998–2018).

Code 2 findings were much closer in number. There were 29 (46%) *Predominantly State* focused articles. Many explicitly examined the TRC model and its relationship to transitional, restorative, and redistributive justice. Others investigated the role of public servants in apartheid and the amnesty seeking process. Conversely, 34 (54%) of the articles were *Predominantly Society* focused, emphasizing the impact on the South African public in terms of spiritual, symbolic, social, and economic justice and healing.

Examining the number of publications over the 20-year period reveals important code trends. There was a slight increase in the number of positive outcomes reported in articles over time. However, a greater number of articles emphasize negative outcomes, with marked growth from 2012 to 2016. Because scholarship is often focused on critique, this finding may be skewed toward negative outcomes because the intention of academics is to uncover limitations (Figure 9.4).

Further examination of Code 2 also illustrates slightly more articles focus on societal outcomes. Figure 9.3 presents the trends, showing greater emphasis on outcomes related to the South African state immediately following the TRC hearings. Greater opportunities to assess evidence of progress for society are possible as time goes on. Growing discontent with post-apartheid politics, enduring inequality, and violence may be one reason for the increasing attention to society as compared to the state (Figure 9.5).

Analysis Phase II: Inductive Approach of Emergent Themes

Three additional areas were examined. The first aimed to identify where progress had been achieved, if at all. The second assessed any remaining inequities that the articles identified. And the third focused on recommended strategies

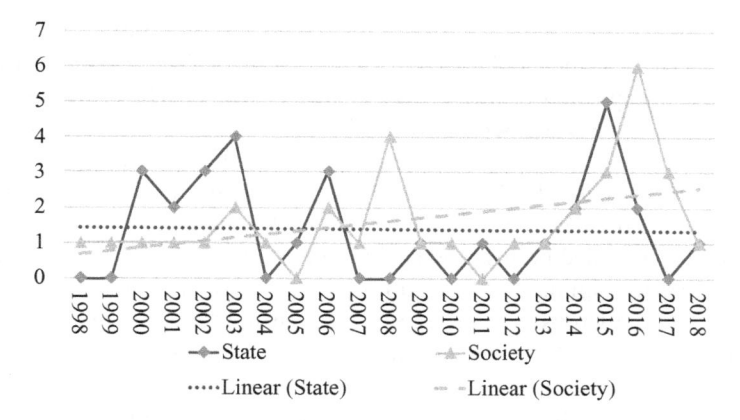

FIGURE 9.5 Publication Time Series Analysis: Predominantly State versus Society Articles (1998–2018).

that the articles suggested to future TRCs based on their findings. This was especially insightful as it provided understanding of areas in which the truth and reconciliation process may be enhanced when applied by other countries.

Phase II consisted of reviewing quotations from each article that aligned with those three areas of examination. This process was inductive. The authors did not begin with preset codes in mind. Rather, the themes emerged during content review. Articles were categorized based on common sentiment around the concepts of truth, reconciliation, and justice.

After categorized by theme, articles were further grouped into one of three thematic areas of justice. First, *transitional justice* "refers to the ways countries emerging from periods of conflict and repression address large-scale or systematic human rights violations so numerous and so serious that the normal justice system will not be able to provide an adequate response" ("What is Transitional Justice?" 2019, para. 1). Second, restorative justice, which:

> is an approach to justice that aims to involve the parties to a dispute and others affected by the harm (victims, offenders, families concerned and community members) in collectively identifying harms, needs and obligations through accepting responsibilities, making restitution, and taking measures to prevent a recurrence of the incident and promoting reconciliation.
>
> *(The Department of Justice and Constitutional Development, 2019, para. 1)*

Third, *redistributive justice* is defined as "those processes whereby resources are transferred from those who have them in abundance to provide for the social and economic needs of those with scant resources" (Turnier, Conover, & Lowery, 1995, p. 1277).

The number of articles that corresponds to each area of justice is presented in Figure 9.6. The remainder of Phase II highlights the extent to which the 63 articles in this review emphasized themes related to one of these three forms of justice.

Where has progress been achieved? The proportion of articles that related to each justice subtheme is presented in Figure 9.7. The pie chart includes an "NA" category for the 12 articles (19%) that did not provide any sense of progress. The greatest proportion of articles (43%) emphasizes how the South African TRC signaled progress by facilitating restorative justice.

Many articles highlighted how full disclosure in the public hearings aided healing for both victims and perpetrators, indicating: "Victims and their families could gradually release some of their rage and hatred toward the perpetrators and allow the healing process to begin to work" (Gordon, 2015, p. 502). The South African TRC thus offered a means for processing historical trauma founded on the spirit of forgiveness.

As an alternative to prosecutions, the TRC offered a "space for humanity to be restored, accounting for pain suffered" (Christodoulidis, 2000, p. 182).

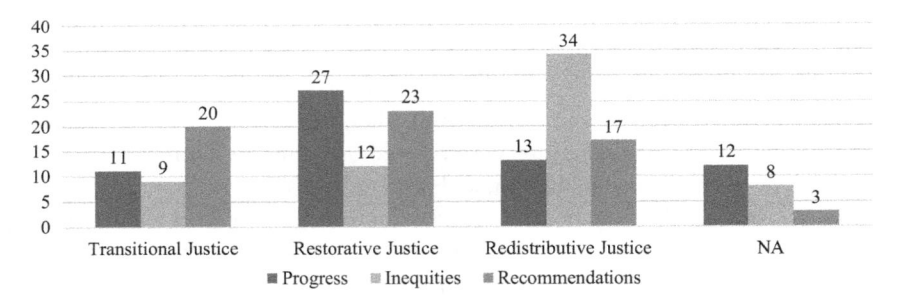

FIGURE 9.6 Total Articles by Area of Analysis and Justice Subtheme.

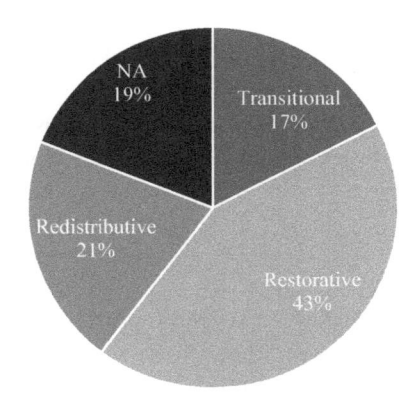

FIGURE 9.7 Proportion of Articles Relating Progress to Justice Subthemes.

Perpetrators took steps to seek forgiveness from their victims (Bhargava, 2002, p. 1304). In doing so, Kraft (2015) found that "perpetrators disengaged from their violence work, in some cases altering their ideologies and their self concepts" (p. 359). Moreover, Fourie (2000) found that victims illustrated deeper healing by interacting with those who had harmed them. One woman stressed her "perpetrator's gracious act of accepting my forgiveness and the healing for us all" (Fourie, 2000, p. 287).

The visceral emotional release signals acknowledgment and processing of nervousness about the acts committed under apartheid (Kagee, 2006). Many articles emphasized how the TRC relatedly created a collective memory, documenting the stories of the winners and the losers. This side effect of creating space for human connection with former enemies also brought untold histories of apartheid to light (Hook & Harris, 2000, p. 21). Creating a shared sense of the past was an important outcome of the TRC process (Nomfundo, 2003, p. 193). It also provides a playbook for future generations that did not experience apartheid firsthand, but can understand the past as a low point in their history that should remain in the past (Clark, 2012).

The other subthemes were less represented transitional justice appeared in 11 articles (17%). For instance, Eisikovits (2006) found that public hearings improved political stability and strengthened democratic institutions. Nation-building was seen as possible if "suffering is acknowledged, trauma ameliorated, and the legitimacy of the new states is founded" (Moon, 2009, p. 86). Moreover, the lack of democratic transition is partially attributable to the lack of redistributive justice noted in 13 articles (21%). The TRC recommended restitution and "the empowerment of the poor" (Nagy, 2006, p. 637), but little evidence of it was found in the research. Six articles noted implications for gender equity through Special Women's Hearings, giving Black women a voice (DeLaet & Mills, 2018; Grey & James, 2016). Like rich to poor, redistribution of power from men to women is also indicative of redistribution.

What inequities remain a challenge? The next focus of Phase II examined ways in which articles found the TRC did not adequately address specific inequities. The proportions are presented in Figure 9.7. Of the 63 articles, 8 (13%) did not report remaining inequities, and 34 (54%) suggested inequities remained due to the lack of redistributive justice (Figure 9.8).

Several articles pointed to the decision to narrow the focus to perpetrators that committed acts within the definition of the *Gross Violation of Human Rights*. For instance, because amnesty was only considered for those that committed *physical* acts of violence, the TRC could not address structural violence, chronic poverty, and racialized inequality (Stanley, 2001). Relatedly, the systemic consequences of apartheid were not discussed by the TRC (Tayler, 2002). Without reckoning of economic injustices, "black communities remain marked by violence, inequality, and poor service delivery rooted in the long-term impact of the past" (Abdullah, 2015, p. 49).

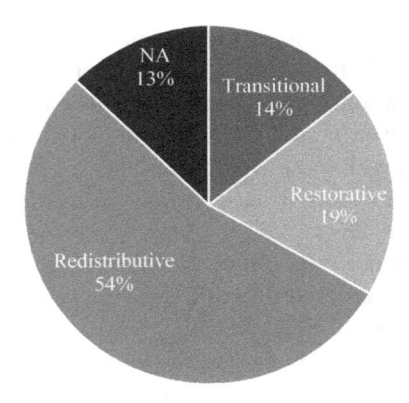

FIGURE 9.8 Proportion of Articles Relating Inequities to Justice Subthemes.

Nine articles (14%) indicated inequities related to transitional justice. Some state officials and members of South African society did not support the TRC, nor the nation-building process (Andrews, 2003). Many regarded it as a symbolic showcase of healing that overlooked internal histories and prior tensions (Meskell & Scheermeyer, 2008). The restorative justice process thus led to spiritual reparation, but not economic reparation (Norris, 2016).

Although the most progress was reported in restorative justice, 12 articles (19%) highlighted inequities of that component as well. For instance, the TRC was prepared to coordinate counseling for survivors, but few perpetrators were connected to support services (Fourie, 2000). There was also concern that the process retraumatized victims and perpetrators, creating "high potential for generating anger and revenge, because people had to relive those terrible events all over again" (Vora & Vora, 2004, p. 318).

Thus, the restorative justice process and the transition did not produce *economic policies* to address inherent inequities associated with

> rampant unemployment, high levels of violence and violent policing, high levels of political intolerance, the continued construction of political and racial difference, failures to address important issues such as the unresolved land question, and attacks on political freedoms; all of which collectively threaten such peace as does exist.
>
> *(Bradshaw & Haines, 2015, p. 4)*

Furthermore, 8 articles (13%) highlighted how women are especially limited to redistributive justice. The TRC was silent on the issue of harms suffered by women as a category (du Toit, 2017). They continue to struggle economically to a great extent (Graybill, 2001) and are arguably seen as second-class citizens as a result (Borer, 2009).

What recommendations are provided to improve success of future TRCs? Finally, articles were reviewed to determine recommendations that could improve the TRC model and process if applied by other countries. The distribution of articles was much more balanced in this subtheme, as pictured in Figure 9.9.

Recommendations for transitional justice were discussed in 20 articles (32%). One area emphasizes the need to focus on continuing beyond the work of the TRC to shift from merely symbolic actions. As Norris (2016) explains, "people must not demobilize, even when their champion is in office" (p. 527). This tends to occur after instances of punctuated progress, such as the election of Nelson Mandela.

Holding transnational corporations accountable, particularly those that profit from politically unjust systems such as apartheid, was another key recommendation. The Apartheid Reparation Litigation that commenced in 2002 is an example of one legal opportunity to seek public justice. South African plaintiffs brought suit against approximately 20 multinational corporations under the ATS [Alternative Tort Statute] (Simcock, 2011, p. 239). This is an important policy tool for other transitional democracies to consider. In the first article published after the TRC report was finalized, Minow (1998) explained:

> A truth commission could generate the evidence to support prosecutions. Or, when the fullest accounts and participation are sought in a nation marked by deep and historic divisions, a truth commission represents a potential alternative to prosecutions. Whether these implement or complement justice, they are worthy of human effort in the continuing struggles against mass atrocities.
>
> *(p. 347)*

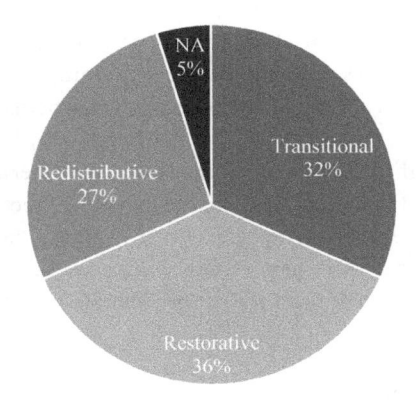

FIGURE 9.9 Proportion of Articles Relating Recommendations to Justice Subthemes.

Restorative justice was most reported in this systematic literature review (37%), so many recommendations are available for that process. Many articles described ways in which the TRC facilitated emotional processing. As Gobodo-Madikizela (2016) found,

> The TRC approach was unique in that, by adopting an invitational stance rather than an adversarial one, perpetrators were asked to 'give full disclosure' of the crimes they committed in exchange for amnesty … Without the threat of punishment, and with the promise of amnesty for truth telling, perpetrators were inspired to admit guilt rather than disown it. Thus, it was possible to face and, for some at least, to feel their guilt.
>
> *(p. 47)*

Truth can thus lead to reconciliation. Yet, several articles note that careful consideration must be taken to organize next steps for victims and perpetrators that participate in the TRC process. "Possible future reconciliation commissions may need to consider formalising their therapeutic processes in order to enhance opportunities not only for political peace-building but also for the psychological rehabilitation of survivors" (Kagee, 2006, p. 21). Rehabilitation of offenders is a critical component that is often overlooked.

Restorative justice processes must also acknowledge the gender disparities of state-sponsored violence. South Africa's TRC was an admirable effort at restorative justice, but it also drew attention to gaps where women's experiences were simplified or missing. Ephgrave (2015) and others have highlighted the importance of considering gender dimensions in the design of future truth commissions.

Finally, redistributive justice had the least amount of recommendations, with 17 articles (27%) including related strategies. A common lesson learned that restorative justice does not lead to redistributive justice. However, healing through the restorative justice process may be an antecedent. In other words, transitional justice and restorative justice are foundational to redistribution. But it takes ongoing work. Many articles emphasized the remaining need for reparations to communities of color. As Meskell and Scheermeyer articulated (2008):

> It is not enough to bolster state pageantry with heritage monuments, or spend billions of Rand in changing the names of streets, towns and airports or to say that heritage will pay and that ordinary citizens should market themselves and perform their 'ethnic' culture for their own socioeconomic uplift: the government must now provide more tangible benefits.
>
> *(p. 170)*

TRCs must broaden their conceptions beyond victims that suffered *physical* violence. As Walaza (2003) argues, "South Africans were denied an opportunity to hear the truth about the indignities of influx control, group areas act, separate amenities act, prohibition of mixed marriages act, racialized poverty and wealth, and unequal education (formally known as Bantu Education)" (p. 200). Each policy has economic implications. As Aiken (2016) proposes,

> additional efforts may still be required to bring attention to the impact of broader practices of structural violence on the daily lives of blacks, as well as the benefits these inequalities provided – and continue to provide – for the white minority.
>
> *(p. 200)*

Redistribution of capital from rich to poor relates to redistribution of power from men to women. Many articles emphasized that the TRC did not adequately consider gendered perspectives. As Russell (2008) reflected, "failure, at earlier stages, to involve women adequately in the framing of the Constitution or the legislation establishing the Commission and its mandate, left it with little option but to work retroactively to insert women into the Commission" (p. 50). This omission was problematic given the relationship between economic justice and women's rights. Durbach (2016) explains:

> A precursor to and component of such reparations is national acknowledgement of the impact of violence on women's lives. Failure to name the violence and recognize its debilitating impact on society, particularly on women victims, risks entrenching a destructive silence and facilitating a perception of violence as routine.
>
> *(p. 385)*

Violence against women primarily involved sexual assault, rape, and other abuses. Consequently, Grey and James (2016) note: "had more of an effort been made to address sexual violence at the Truth and Reconciliation Commission, debate around sexual violence in South Africa today might not be as cloaked in shame, normalcy, and denial" (p. 311). This ties back to acknowledging nervousness not only to racialized violence, but taking an intersectional lens to consider gender as well.

Conclusion

This chapter furthers understanding of nervousness in two ways. First, there are few instances in which a federal government has explicitly addressed inequitable policies. We contend that the South African TRC can foster understanding of such a model. Moreover, this chapter assesses evidence of progress of one process by which the administrative state attempts to collaborate with the public to acknowledge historical injustices. The TRC model is thus a worthwhile tool to consider when faced with fading confidence in facts in the post-truth era.

Based on a systematic review of the literature from 1998 to 2018, this chapter finds that the South African TRC was most effective at advancing restorative justice, which leads to healing. However, restorative justice immediately following apartheid did not lead to long-term redistributive justice for the disenfranchised communities of color. That is the next step. As previously discussed, many nervous areas of government remain in South Africa today related to economic injustice. As Sarkin (2015) contends: "Without continual fuel and without continual nurturing the process can easily falter" (p. 98). Those interested in applying this promising practice should therefore consider how to best source and expend their fuel in the long run.

References

Abdullah, S. (2015). Multicultural social work and national trauma: Lessons from South Africa. *International Social Work, 58*(1), 43–54.

Aiken, N. T. (2016). The distributive dimension in transitional justice: Reassessing the South African truth and reconciliation Commission's ability to advance interracial reconciliation in South Africa. *Journal of Contemporary African Studies, 34*(2), 190–202.

Andrews, M. (2003). Grand national narratives and the project of truth commissions: A comparative analysis. *Media, Culture, & Society, 25,* 45–65.

Bhargava, A. (2002). Defining political crimes: A case study of the South African truth and reconciliation commission. *Columbia Law Review, 102*(5), 1304–1339.

Borer, T. A. (2009). Gendered war and gendered peace: Truth commissions and post conflict gender violence: Lessons from South Africa. *Violence against Women, 15*(10), 1169–1193.

Bradshaw, G., & Haines, R. (2014). After Marikana: Rethinking conflict resolution in Africa: The South African case. *Stability: International Journal of Security & Development, 4*(1), 1–16.

Christodoulidis, E. A. (2000). 'Truth and reconciliation' as risks. *Social & Legal Studies, 9*(2), 179–204.

Clark, J. N. (2012). Reconciliation via truth? A study of South Africa's TRC. *Journal of Human Rights, 11*(2), 189–209.

Cronin, P., Ryan, F., & Coughlan, M. (2008). Undertaking a literature review: A step-by-step approach. *British Journal of Nursing, 17*(1), 38–43.

DeLaet, D. L., & Mills, E. (2018). Discursive silence as a global response to sexual violence: From title IX to truth commissions. *Global Society, 32*(4), 496–519.

du Toit, F. (2017). A broken promise? Evaluating South Africa's reconciliation process twenty years on. *International Political Science Review, 38*(2), 169–184.

Durbach, A. (2016). Towards reparative transformation: Revisiting the impact of violence against women in a post-TRC South Africa. *International Journal of Transitional Justice, 10,* 366–387.

Eisikovits, N. (2006). Rethinking the legitimacy of truth commissions: "I am the enemy you killed, my friend". *Metaphilosophy, 37*(3–4), 489–514.

Emanuelson Jr., E. (2018). Fake left, fake right: Promoting an informed public in the era of alternative facts. *Administrative Law Review, 70*(1), 210–232.

Ephgrave, N. (2015). Women's testimony and collective memory: Lessons from South Africa's TRC and Rwanda's *Gacaca* courts. *European Journal of Women's Studies, 22*(2), 177–190.

Fourie, J. A. (2000). The psychology of perpetrators of 'political' violence in South Africa-a personal experience. *Ethnicity & Health, 5*(3–4), 283–289.

Gibson, J. L., & Gouws, A. (1999). Truth and reconciliation in South Africa: Attributions of blame and the struggle over apartheid. *American Political Science Review, 93*(3), 501–517.

Gobodo-Madikizela, P. (2015). Psychological repair: The intersubjective dialogue of remorse and forgiveness in the aftermath of gross human rights violations. *Journal of the American Psychoanalytic Association, 63*(6), 1085–1123.

Gobodo-Madikizela, P. (2016). What does it mean to be human in the aftermath of mass trauma and violence? Toward the horizon of an ethics of care. *Journal of the Society of Christian Ethics, 36*(2), 43–61.

Gooden, S. (2014). Race and social equity: A nervous area of government. Armonk, NY: M.E. Sharpe.

Gordon, M. (2015). Between remembering and forgetting. *Studies in Philosophy and Education, 34*(5), 489–503.

Graybill, L. (2001). The contribution of the truth and reconciliation commission toward the promotion of women's rights in South Africa. *Women's Studies International Forum, 24*(1), 1–10.

Grey, S., & James, A. (2016). Truth, reconciliation, and "double settler denial": Gendering the Canada-South Africa analogy. *Human Rights Review, 17*(3), 303–328.

Hook, D., & Harris, B. (2000). Discourses of order and their disruption: The texts of the South African Truth & Reconciliation Commission. *South African Journal of Psychology, 30*(1), 14–22.

International Center for Transitional Justice. (2019). *What is Transitional Justice?* Retrieved from www.ictj.org/about/transitional-justice.

Kagee, A. (2006). The relationship between statement giving at the South African Truth and Reconciliation Commission and psychological distress among former political detainees. *South African Journal of Psychology, 36*(1), 10–24.

Kraft, R. N. (2015). The good intentions of violent perpetrators: A qualitative analysis of testimony from South Africa's truth and reconciliation commission. *Peace and Conflict: Journal of Peace Psychology, 21*(3), 359–377.

MacPhail, C., Khoza, N., Abler, L., & Ranganathan, M. (2016). Process guidelines for establishing intercoder reliability in qualitative studies. *Qualitative Research, 16*(2), 198–212.

Magistad, M. K. (2017, April 6). South Africa's imperfect progress, 20 years after the truth & reconciliation commission. *Public Radio International (PRI)*. Retrieved from www.pri.org/stories/2017-04-06/south-africas-imperfect-progress-20-years-after-truth-reconciliation-commission.

Martín-Martín, A., Orduna-Malea, E., Thelwall, M., & López-Cózar, E. D. (2018). Google scholar, web of science, and scopus: A systematic comparison of citations in 252 subject categories. *Journal of Informetrics, 12*(4), 1160–1177.

Meskell, L., & Scheermeyer, C. (2008). Heritage as therapy: Set pieces from the new South Africa. *Journal of Material Culture, 13*(2), 153–173.

Minow, M. (1998). Between vengeance and forgiveness: South Africa's truth and reconciliation commission. *Negotiation Journal, 14*(4), 319–355.

Moher, D., Liberati, A., Tetzlaff, J., & Altman, D. G. (2009). Preferred reporting items for systematic reviews and meta-analyses: The PRISMA statement. *Annals of Internal Medicine, 151*(4), 264–269.

Moon, C. (2009). Healing past violence: Traumatic assumptions and therapeutic interventions in war and reconciliation. *Journal of Human Rights, 8*(1), 71–91.

Nagy, R. (2006). Postapartheid justice: Can cosmopolitanism and nation-building be reconciled? *Law & Society Review, 40*(3), 623–652.

Norris, Z. (2016). Repairing harm from racial injustice: An analysis of the justice reinvestment initiative and the truth and reconciliation commission. *Denver Law Review, 94*, 515–535.

Parliament of the Republic of South Africa. (1995). *Promotion of National Unity and Reconciliation Act 34 of 1995*. Retrieved from www.justice.gov.za/legislation/acts/1995-034.pdf.

Renner, J. (2014). The local roots of the global politics of reconciliation: The articulation of 'reconciliation' as an empty universal in the South African transition to democracy. *Millennium: Journal of International Studies, 42*(2), 263–285.

The Department of Justice and Constitutional Development. (2019). *Restorative Justice*. Retrieved from http://www.justice.gov.za/rj/rj.html.

Russell, B. (2008). A self-defining universe? Case studies from the 'Special hearings: Women of South Africa's truth and reconciliation commission. *African Studies, 67*(1), 49–69.

Sarkin, J. (2015). Understanding the journey to reconciliation in transitional societies: Using the metaphor of a motor vehicle trip to understand South Africa's path (process) to political reconciliation. *International Journal of African Renaissance Studies, 10*(2), 87–103.

Simcock, J. (2011). Unfinished business: Reconciling the apartheid reparation litigation with South Africa's truth and reconciliation commissioner. *Stanford Journal of International Law, 47*, 239–263.

South African History Online. (2019). *The Native Land Act is Passed*. Retrieved from www.sahistory.org.za/dated-event/native-land-act-passed.

South African History Online. (2017). *The Truth and Reconciliation Commission (TRC) 1995*. Retrieved January 16, 2019 from www.sahistory.org.za/article/truth-and-reconciliation-commission-trc-1995.

South African History Online. (2018). *Truth and Reconciliation Commission (TRC)*. Retrieved from www.sahistory.org.za/article/truth-and-reconciliation-commission-trc-0.

Stanley, E. (2001). Evaluating the truth and reconciliation commission. *Journal of Modern African Studies, 39*(3), 525–546.

The United States Institute of Peace. (1995). Truth commission: South Africa. Retrieved from www.usip.org/publications/1995/12/truth-commission-south-africa.

Truth and Reconciliation Commission. (1998). *Truth and Reconciliation Commission of South Africa Report (Volume 5)*. Retrieved from www.justice.gov.za/trc/report/final-report/Volume5.pdf.

Turnier, W. J., Johnston Conover, P., & Lowery, D. (1995). Redistributive justice and cultural feminism. *American University Law Review, 45*, 1275–1322.

Tutu, D. (2019). *Truth and Reconciliation Commission, South Africa*. Retrieved February 19, 2019 from www.britannica.com/topic/Truth-and-Reconciliation-Commission-South-Africa.

Vora, J. A., & Vora, E. (2004). The effectiveness of South Africa's truth and reconciliation commission: Perceptions of Xhosa, Afrikaner, and English South Africans. *Journal of Black Studies, 34*(3), 301–322.

Walaza, N. (2003). Reconciling with partial truths: An assessment of the dilemmas posed by the reconciliation process in South Africa. *Smith Studies in Social Work, 73*(2), 189–204.

Oxford University Press. (2019). *Word of the Year 2016 is…* Retrieved from en.oxford-dictionaries.com/word-of-the-year/word-of-the-year-2016.

APPENDIX A

DESCRIPTION OF LAWS IN FIGURE 9.1 TIMELINE

All acts in the timeline were taken from a single source ("Apartheid Legislation 1850s–1970s," 2019). This list is not inclusive of all discriminatory laws enacted during apartheid, but it serves to highlight a sample of the most damaging to Black and Coloured South Africans.

Native Land Act, 1913 (also known as the Black Land Act): "prohibited Blacks from owning or renting land outside of designated reserves (approximately 7% of the land in the country)."

Development Trust and Land Act, 1936: Extended the reserves of land set aside for Black South Africans from 7% to 13%; however, this was never accomplished.

The Black (Native) Laws Amendment Act, 1937: Prohibited the purchase of land by Blacks from non-Blacks in urban areas unless granted permission from the government.

The Prohibition of Mixed Marriages Act, 1949: Prohibited marriage between whites and people of other race groups in South Africa.

The Group Areas Act, 1950: A set of three acts "that laid down legal provisions on specific areas where different populations could own property, reside and work." The Act "led to the evictions of thousands of Blacks, Coloureds and Indians."

The Immorality Amendment Act, 1950: "Prohibited adultery, attempted adultery or related 'immoral' acts such as sexual intercourse between White and Black people."

The Population Registration Act, 1950: Required "that all South Africans be racially classified in one of three categories: White, Black, or Coloured." Required Blacks to carry passbooks to access non-Black areas.

The Public Safety Act, 1953: Under this act, the British governor general had the authority to set aside all laws and declare a state of emergency, allowing for the detainment of individuals for reasons of public safety and detention without trial for any dissent.

The Reservation of Separate Amenities Act, 1953: Provided that there should be separate amenities for different racial groups that were not required to be of equal quality.

The Bantu Education Act, 1953 (aka the Black Education Act): "Provided for the establishment of a separate educational system ... to provide Blacks with skills to serve their own people in the homelands or to work in labouring jobs under Whites."

The Indemnity Act, 1961: Protected government officials from legal responsibility for acts carried out while preventing internal disorder and dissent, among other acts.

The Bantu Homelands Citizenship Act, 1970: Attempted to divide South Africa into separate states, requiring "all Black persons to become citizens of a self-governing territorial authority." This act would have denied Blacks nationality and the right to work in South Africa.

The Internal Security Act No 32, 1979: "Enabled the government to declare an organization unlawful and to control the distribution of publications."

APPENDIX B

ARTICLES INCLUDED IN SYSTEMATIC LITERATURE REVIEW

#	Article Citation	C1	C2
1	Abdullah, S. (2015). Multicultural social work and national trauma: Lessons from South Africa. *International Social Work, 58*(1), 43–54.	+	State
2	Aiken, N. T. (2016). The distributive dimension in transitional justice: reassessing the South African Truth and Reconciliation Commission's ability to advance interracial reconciliation in South Africa. *Journal of Contemporary African Studies, 34*(2), 190–202.	–	Society
3	Akpome, A. (2013). Ominous inevitabilities: Reflecting on South Africa's post-transition aporia in Achmat Dangor's bitter fruit. *Africa Spectrum, 48*(2), 3–24.	–	Society
4	Andrews, M. (2003). Grand national narratives and the project of truth commissions: A comparative analysis. *Media, Culture, & Society, 25*, 45–65.	+	Society
5	Backer, D. (2010). Watching a bargain unravel? A panel study of victims' attitudes about transitional justice in Cape Town, South Africa. *The International Journal of Transitional Justice, 4*, 443–456.	–	Society
6	Bhargava, A. (2002). Defining political crimes: A case study of the South African truth and reconciliation commission. *Columbia Law Review, 102*(5), 1304–1339.	–	State
7	Blyth, M. N. (2016). Re-imagining Restorative Justice: The Value of Forgiveness. *Oxford Journal of Law and Religion, 5*(1), 66–78.	+	Society
8	Borer, T. A. (2003). A taxonomy of victims and perpetrators: Human rights and reconciliation in South Africa. *Hum. Rts. Q., 25*, 1088.	–	State

#	Article Citation	C1	C2
9	Borer, T. A. (2009). Gendered war and gendered peace: Truth commissions and postconflict gender violence: Lessons from South Africa. *Violence Against Women, 15*(10), 1169–1193.	–	Society
10	Bradshaw, G., & Haines, R. (2014). After Marikina: Rethinking conflict resolution in Africa: The South African case. *Stability: International Journal of Security & Development, 4*(1), 1–16.	–	Society
11	Christodoulidis, E. A. (2000). 'Truth and reconciliation' as risks. *Social & Legal Studies, 9*(2), 179–204.	–	State
12	Clark, J. N. (2012). Reconciliation via truth? A study of South Africa's TRC. *Journal of Human Rights, 11*(2), 189–209.	–	Society
13	DeLaet, D. L., & Mills, E. (2018). Discursive silence as a global response to sexual violence: From title IX to truth commissions. *Global Society, 32*(4), 496–519.	–	Society
14	du Toit, F. (2017). A broken promise? Evaluating South Africa's reconciliation process twenty years on. *International Political Science Review, 38*(2), 169–184.	+	Society
15	Durbach, A. (2016). Towards reparative transformation: Revisiting the impact of violence against women in a post-TRC South Africa. *International Journal of Transitional Justice, 10*, 366–387.	–	Society
16	Eisikovits, N. (2006). Rethinking the legitimacy of truth commissions: "I am the enemy you killed, my friend". *Metaphilosophy, 37*(3–4), 489–514.	+	State
17	Ephgrave, N. (2015). Women's testimony and collective memory: Lessons from South Africa's TRC and Rwandans Gacaca courts. *European Journal of Women's Studies, 22*(2), 177–190.	–	Society
18	Fourie, J. G. (2000). The psychology of perpetrators of 'political' violence in South Africa-a personal experience. *Ethnicity & Health, 5*(3–4), 283–289.	+	Society
19	Gibson, J. L. (2006). The contributions of truth to reconciliation: Lessons from South Africa. *The Journal of Conflict Resolution, 50*(3), 409–432.	+	Society
20	Gibson, J. L., & Gouws, A. (1999). Truth and reconciliation in South Africa: Attributions of blame and the struggle over Apartheid. *American Political Science Review, 93*(3), 501–517.	–	Society
21	Gobodo-Madikizela, P. (2002). Remorse, forgiveness, and rehumanization: Stories from South Africa. *Journal of Humanistic Psychology, 42*(1), 7–32.	+	Society
22	Gobodo-Madikizela, P. (2008). Trauma, forgiveness and the witnessing dance: Making public spaces intimate. *Journal of Analytical Psychology, 53*(2), 169–188.	+	Society
23	Gobodo-Madikizela, P. (2015). Psychological repair: The intersubjective dialogue of remorse and forgiveness in the aftermath of gross human rights violations. *Journal of the American Psychoanalytic Association, 63*(6), 1085–1123.	+	Society

(Continued)

#	Article Citation	C1	C2
24	Gobodo-Madikizela, P. (2016). What does it mean to be human in the aftermath of mass trauma and violence? Toward the horizon of an ethics of care. *Journal of the Society of Christian Ethics, 36*(2), 43–61.	+	Society
25	Gordon, M. (2015). Between remembering and forgetting. *Studies in Philosophy and Education, 34*(5), 489–503.	+	State
26	Graybill, L. (2001). The contribution of the truth and reconciliation commission toward the promotion of women's rights in South Africa. *Women's Studies International Forum, 24*(1), 1–10.	+	Society
27	Grey, S., & James, A. (2016). Truth, reconciliation, and "Double Settler Denial": Gendering the Canada-South Africa analogy. *Human Rights Review, 17*(3), 303–328.	–	Society
28	Hook, D., & Harris, B. (2000). Discourses of order and their disruption: The texts of the South African Truth & Reconciliation Commission. *South African Journal of Psychology, 30*(1), 14–22.	+	Society
29	Jaising, S. (2014). Reconstructing apartheid, redefining racism: The South African truth commission and its representations. *Interventions, 16*(1), 117–134.	–	Society
30	Jolly, R. J. (2001). Desiring good (s) in the face of marginalized subjects: South Africa's Truth and Reconciliation Commission in a global context. *The South Atlantic Quarterly, 100*(3), 693–715.	+	State
31	Kagee, A. (2006). The relationship between statement giving at the South African Truth and Reconciliation Commission and psychological distress among former political detainees. *South African Journal of Psychology, 36*(1), 10–24.	–	Society
32	Khan, K. B. (2017). Confronting the horrors of Apartheid: The case of the documentary film night's journey into day: South Africa's truth and reconciliation (2000). *Journal of Literary Studies, 33*(4), 39–51.	–	Society
33	Koska, G. (2016). Corporate accountability in times of transition: The role of restorative justice in the South African Truth and Reconciliation Commission. *Restorative Justice, 4*(1), 41–67.	–	State
34	Kraft, R. N. (2015). The good intentions of violent perpetrators: A qualitative analysis of testimony from South Africa's truth and reconciliation commission. *Peace and Conflict: Journal of Peace Psychology, 21*(3), 359.	+	State
35	Leebaw, B. (2003). Legitimation or judgment? South's restorative approach to transitional justice. *Polity, 36*(1), 23–51.	+	State
36	Mamdani, M. (2002). Amnesty or impunity? A preliminary critique of the report of the truth and reconciliation commission of South Africa (TRC). *Diacritics, 32*(3/4), 32–59.	–	State

#	Article Citation	C1	C2
37	McEwan, C. (2003). Building a postcolonial archive? Gender, collective memory and citizenship in post-apartheid South Africa. *Journal of Southern African Studies, 29*(3), 739–757.	–	State
38	Meiring, P. (2018). Reformed spirituality and the spirit of reconciliation: A personal journey. *HTS Teologiese Studies/ Theological Studies, 74*(4), 1–7.	+	State
39	Meskell, L., & Scheermeyer, C. (2008). Heritage as therapy: Set pieces from the new South Africa. *Journal of Material Culture, 13*(2), 153–173.	+	Society
40	Minow, M. (1998). Between vengeance and forgiveness: South Africa's truth and reconciliation commission. *Negotiation Journal, 14*(4), 319–355.	+	Society
41	Moon, C. (2009). Healing past violence: Traumatic assumptions and therapeutic interventions in war and reconciliation. *Journal of Human Rights, 8*(1), 71–91.	+	State
42	Nagy, R. (2006). Postapartheid justice: Can cosmopolitanism and nation-building be reconciled? *Law & Society Review, 40*(3), 623–652.	+	State
43	Norris, Z. (2016). Repairing harm from racial injustice: An analysis of the justice reinvestment initiative and the truth and reconciliation commission. *Denver Law Review, 94*, 515.	–	State
44	Oboe, A. (2007). The TRC Women's hearings as performance and protest in the new South Africa. *Research in African Literatures, 38*(3), 60–76.	–	Society
45	O'Connell, S. (2015). Injury, illumination and freedom: Thinking about the afterlives of apartheid through the family albums of district six, Cape Town. *International Journal of Transitional Justice, 9*(297), 315.	–	Society
46	Renner, J. (2014). The local roots of the global politics of reconciliation: The articulation of 'reconciliation' as an empty universal in the South African transition to democracy. *Millennium: Journal of International Studies, 42*(2), 263–285.	–	State
47	Robins, S. (2014). The 2011 toilet wars in South Africa: Justice and transition between the exceptional and the everyday after apartheid. *Development and Change, 45*(3), 479–501.	–	State
48	Russell, B. (2008). A self-defining universe? Case studies from the 'Special Hearings: Women of South Africa's Truth and Reconciliation Commission. *African Studies, 67*(1), 49–69.	–	Society
49	Sarkin, J. (2015). Understanding the journey to reconciliation in transitional societies: Using the metaphor of a motor vehicle trip to understand South Africa's path (process) to political reconciliation. *International Journal of African Renaissance Studies, 10*(2), 87–103.	–	State

(*Continued*)

#	Article Citation	C1	C2
50	Simcock, J. (2011). Unfinished business: Reconciling the apartheid reparation litigation with South Africa's truth and reconciliation commissioner. *Stanford Journal of International Law, 47,* 239.	–	State
51	Southern, N. (2015). Conflict transformation and truth-seeking: The impact of South Africa's Truth and Reconciliation Commission on the National Party. *Nationalism and Ethnic Politics, 21*(3), 335–356.	+	State
52	Stanley, E. (2001). Evaluating the truth and reconciliation commission. *Journal of Modern African Studies, 39*(3), 525–546.	–	State
53	Stein, D. J., Seedat, S., Kaminer, D., Moomal, H., Herman, A., Sonnega, J., & Williams, D. R. (2008). The impact of the truth and reconciliation commission on psychological distress and forgiveness in South Africa. *Social Psychiatry and Psychiatric Epidemiology, 43*(6), 462.	+	Society
54	Swartz, S. (2006). A long walk to citizenship: Morality, justice and faith in the aftermath of apartheid. *Journal of Moral Education, 35*(4), 551–570.	–	State
55	Taylor, R. (2002). Justice denied: Political violence in KwaZulu-Natal after 1994. *African Affairs, 101*(405), 473–508.	–	State
56	Toit, A. D. (2005). Experiments with truth and justice in South Africa: Stockenström, Gandhi and the TRC. *Journal of Southern African Studies, 31*(2), 419–448.	+	State
57	Tovares, A. V. (2016). Going off-script and reframing the frame: The dialogic intertwining of the centripetal and centrifugal voices in the truth and reconciliation commission hearings. *Discourse & Society, 27*(5), 554–573.	+	Society
58	van der Walt, C., Franchi, V., & Stevens, G. (2003). The South African truth and reconciliation commission: 'Race', historical compromise and transitional democracy. *International Journal of Intercultural Relations, 27,* 251–267.	–	State
59	Vora, J., A., & Vora, E. (2004). The effectiveness of South Africa's truth and reconciliation commission: Perceptions of Xhosa, Afrikaner, and English South Africans. *Journal of Black Studies, 34*(3), 301–322.	–	Society
60	Walaza, N. (2003). Reconciling with partial truths: An assessment of the dilemmas posed by the reconciliation process in South Africa. *Smith Studies in Social Work, 73*(2), 189–204.	–	Society
61	Wilson, R. A., Borneman, J., Griffiths, A., James, D. A., Merry, S. E., Nader, L., & Wilson, R. A. (2000). Reconciliation and revenge in post-apartheid South Africa: Rethinking legal pluralism and human rights. *Current Anthropology, 41*(1), 75–98.	–	State

#	Article Citation	C1	C2
62	Worby, E., & Ally, S. (2013). The disappointment of nostalgia: Conceptualising cultures of memory in contemporary South Africa. *Social Dynamics, 39*(3), 457–480.	–	State
63	Wright, T. (2017). Justice, silence, complexity: Recent forays into the reconstitution of apartheid experience. *African Studies, 76*(1), 163–176.	–	Society

PART III
Religion & Community

10

RECONCILIATION PROGRAMING AND DISCOURSE IN NORTHERN IRELAND SINCE THE GOOD FRIDAY AGREEMENT OF 1998

Brendan F. Burke and John Barry

A Nervous Area of Government in Northern Ireland

How does a system reorient itself from centuries of enduring inequity toward a fairer society in the present day, and for future generations? This chapter assesses efforts to reconcile a cultural divide between two long-dominant identities in Northern Ireland, ostensibly linked, on the one hand, by loyalty toward rule by the UK and generally of the Protestant faith, contrasted, on the other, with those who support unity with the Irish republic, predominantly consisting of Roman Catholics. After centuries of unrest between these groups, in the form of revolution, civil war, and more recently a 30-year terrorist conflict, progress has been made toward ending the violent conflict and moving towards the reconciliation between its peoples, mediated by a reformed governance system. But with enduring bitterness and the legacy of the past to be overcome, Northern Ireland is not changing without some growing pains.

Gooden's (2014) introduction of 'nervous areas of government' focuses on racial dynamics and their impact on social inequity in the United States. The findings of Gooden's work are important within other identity-based differences and to other nations. But these differences and their equity impacts are nuanced when applied in other settings. First, it is important to Gooden's argument that racism and other injustice-producing differences include a very important unspoken and institutionalized nature, such that governments and organizations tend to accept inequity as *a condition to be managed* rather than as a *problem to be resolved and transformed*. The American civil rights movement advanced fairness in American society, but its legalistic focus placed the resolution of inequities into the adversarial forum of the courts and legal system in many cases, rather than into voluntary, cultural, and other extra-institutional-cum-legal cooperative settings for the resolution of differences and their impacts. In Northern Ireland, the American civil rights movement was an inspiration for republican and Catholic protesters in the late 1960s and early 1970s as they attempted to redress their historical subjugation, but when neither the unionist- and Protestant-dominated Northern Ireland government nor the UK government were moved by the demonstrations (or rather the latter was motivated to act too little, too late, and in a problem exacerbating manner), the protest moved to an active, terrorist war for approximately 30 years. The need to overcome the conflict and resolve differences did prompt a set of 'peace' agreements and acts to reduce inequity; appearances were that resolution was ready for action by 1998, when the Belfast/Good Friday Agreement was signed. Second, in the case of race in America, differences are visible but frequently underanalyzed. In Northern Ireland, an island with very little racial diversity throughout its history, the differences on which we focus are internal; there is no racial difference between the 'two communities,' and limited ethnic difference. Religious and political differences are unclear until the participants reveal them through discussion or questioning. But this contrast between Protestant/loyalists and Catholic/republicans created "knife-edge times" in Northern Irish society at least until the end of the 20th century (Burns 2018). It is only with the softening of this tense situation that other inequities have come onto the Northern Irish political agenda. Third, statistics reveal an ongoing inequity in American public policies, based on the distribution of different benefits that are affected by government action in some cases, intransigence in others (Gooden 2014, 28–39). In Northern Ireland, some surface differences are being resolved quite quickly since 1998, but with other gaps in the policy response just under way (Brennan 2017; Long 2018). Fourth, the tone of discussion in resolving differences in the two nations is different. In the United States, the central "nervous" discussion component is a lack of acknowledgement that racism still persists; in Northern Ireland, the difficulty is the passion that arises over politics and faith once the discussion starts. It is very hard for individuals and communities in Northern Ireland to get over previous wrongdoing by one side, aimed at the other. This may undergird Northern Ireland's greatest contribution to resolution of 'nervous' areas: lessons in how to move dialogue from bitterness toward productive and shared (even if disputed) memories, grieving and loss, and then moving on to (sometimes uneasy and unstable) mutual accommodation and then power sharing as necessary steps on the road to (perhaps) reconciliation and a 'positive peace.'

This chapter moves through four sections: First, it displays the history of group difference and conflict in Northern Ireland, with the impact of governmental discrimination on communities, policies, and work force. Second, it highlights the innovative peace process that was brokered in 1998, and its offshoots to enhance fairness in civil service hiring and provision of community services. These were not perfect processes, but they did move Northern Ireland forward in dramatic and important ways. Third, the government's current process for deliberation on policy equity is outlined. This process is more holistic with regard to inequality in Northern Ireland, a movement beyond just the main historical division addressed in the first efforts after the Peace Accords. And finally, it discusses the relevant lessons from Northern Ireland to enhance how other states and communities can confront other areas and sources of inequity.

Why Faith Difference Is a Nervous Area of Government

Ireland's history is dominated by invasions and conflicts of varying intensity to create, sustain, and protect an Irish identity. Romans, Vikings, Normans, and the British provided a consistent line of war and struggle for control of the island, until the partition of Ireland in 1922. This created an Irish Free State (in the south) in 1922—with an overwhelming Catholic Irish majority, and Northern Ireland, with a Protestant British majority. But that was the beginning of an internal conflict over external rule based on colonization by Britain, first in a civil war across the island, then concentrated within the newly created 'statelet' or province of Northern Ireland. The Norman and British invasions had populated the island in earlier centuries, and provide the roots for conflict over Celtic identity among several different subpopulations. For simplicity's sake, these are expressed as those loyal to the UK, predominantly of the Protestant faith, and those who support an independent and united Irish republic, mostly claiming the Catholic faith. This is an oversimplification of sorts, as faith does not appear to be central to dispositions in an ongoing violent and bloody battle. Rather religious affiliation should be viewed as a convenient 'badge' of political identity and aspiration for the island in whole (united) or part (continuation of Northern Ireland as part of the UK). The two groups are captured in governmental discussions through the shorthand expression of 'community background.'

Among other characteristics of the Irish peoples is an affinity for folklore and storytelling, through its literature, song, and visual arts. The Irish playwright Brian Friel tells of British surveyors who roamed the Irish countryside early in the 19th century, converting Irish place names from their Gaelic to English expressions ('Baile Beag' converted to 'Ballybeg,' for example) in his play, *Translations*. Elizabeth Bowen tells the story of *The Big House*, the symbolic estate home of the Protestant landlords before Irish independence. The socialist Sean O'Casey, in *The Plough and the Stars*, tells of the folly of violent conflict in the Easter Uprising of 1916, which prompted active revolution and did lead to Irish independence, but did not focus on class differences and socio-economic injustice. Indeed, the play itself led to violence, a riot at the Abbey Theatre in

1926 over its class-based critique of the independence movement. This line of literature highlights in different ways the suppression and subjugation of a fully Irish identity in favor of colonial overlords from the UK.

It was the 1922 treaty to end conflict between the UK and Irish republican forces (the original Irish Republican Army as it were), and the partition of Ireland, that planted the seed for ongoing conflict in Northern Ireland, erupting into the decades-long armed conflict known as 'the Troubles,' which erupted in 1968–1969 and ended in 1998. The Anglo-Irish Treaty of 1922 gave Irish independence to most of the southern three provinces (Leinster, Munster, and Connacht) as long as they pledged loyalty to the Crown (constitutionally the 'Irish free state' or *Saorstát Éireann* as it was known, which was established as a Dominion of the British Commonwealth much like Canada or Australia). This condition would be dropped in time as the Irish state moved to full independence when Ireland's Dominion status was terminated with the passage of the Republic of Ireland Act 1948, which declared that the state was a republic. But one aspect of the Treaty endured and maintained a bitter divide. Most of Ulster (six of the nine counties that made up this fourth Irish province) remained with the UK, as a gerrymandered border was drawn to exclude Catholic-dominated counties of Ulster (Cavan, Monaghan, Donegal) from the newly created Northern Ireland. The simplest part of the boundary leaves these three predominantly Catholic counties to the Irish state, but smaller pockets along the border were included or excluded from Northern Ireland based on political loyalty and faith differences.

The artistic expression of loyalist/republican differences is clearest in murals, seen throughout Belfast in segregated neighborhoods. A popular and informative lesson can be gleaned from the 'Black Taxi Tour.' When one drives up the Falls Road, murals on this republican side commemorate the Easter 1916 Uprising and its republican heroes, as well as other pioneers of civil rights movements like Nelson Mandela and the freed African American slave and abolitionist Frederick Douglass. One of the most famous murals on the Falls Road side is of Bobby Sands, a member of the Irish Republican Army who was elected to the UK's Parliament on the night that he died (5 May 1981), from participation in a hunger strike in the Maze prison. The Falls Road flag is clearly the tricolor of the Republic of Ireland, on display on many businesses and homes. When crossing over to the loyalist side, the murals change dramatically, to commemorations of King William of Orange's 1690 victory to preserve Britain's place in Ireland, and prevent a Catholic, King James, from being Monarch; quotes from the early 20th century such as "Ulster will fight, and Ulster will be right"; and memorials to paramilitaries from the Ulster Defence Association or Ulster Volunteer Force, killed in conflict with the IRA or the British Army. The flag of the Shankhill neighborhood is, without question, the Union Jack. Memories are very long of the fights between groups, and this line of history is well documented (Barry 2019; Bew 2010; McGarry 2019). Over 3,500 people, at least 1,700 of them civilians, died in the conflict between 1969 and 1998, before the peace talks of the 1990s moved forward to their eventual conclusion, under the chairpersonship of US Senator George Mitchell in 1998.

The prevailing nature of life in Northern Ireland involves ongoing tension between these two 'sides.' When one takes the Black Taxi tour through West Belfast, one of the most impressive icons is the 'peace wall,' an approximately 30 foot high, dull green structure with gated access points between the Protestant/loyalist and Catholic/republican neighborhoods. Now, this wall is a symbol of peace, with colorful, spraypainted images and artistic expressions along its base; anyone can write their message of hope, remembrance, and peace on the wall's surface (including the Dalai Lama, who left his message in 2000). But historically, the wall served the function of closing off and separating violent factions of youths when the conflict grew heated. The wall, and over one hundred others like it around Northern Irish cities, is tall enough so that youths could not throw Molotov cocktails—gasoline bombs—from one neighborhood to the other.

But day-to-day life in Belfast was tense as well, with ongoing fear of violence and reprisal between the two sides in the conflict. The hair-trigger anxiety within this split is recorded effectively in *The Milkman*, Anna Burns's Man Booker Prize-winning novel about Belfast in the 1970s. The wry humor within the novel captures sad tensions that loyalist or republican residents of Belfast could become conflictual over the other 'side's' names, schools, workplaces, sports teams, church hymns, newspapers, and more. The protagonist in the novel claims that there is "the tea of allegiance (and) the tea of betrayal," with wit—but only marginally (Burns 2018). Tension between these segregated groups was constant, especially because of the higher level of direct violence that could quickly arise. This was not true everywhere in Northern Ireland; tensions were reduced in rural areas. But in the dense regions of the two main cities of Derry (also called Londonderry, by loyalists) and Belfast, these constraints on daily life prevailed until recently, and have not eased completely.

This conflict between political and religion-based factions steadily stunted virtually any form of progress in Northern Ireland, until the end of the 20th century. When the Good Friday Agreement was crafted and negotiated in 1998, political leadership within Northern Ireland was ready for an innovative movement toward peace; alongside of this, it was clear that some equalization of access to positions within the civil service would help to move toward equality for the disadvantaged minority within the territory—the Catholic republicans. Figure 10.1 shows the disparity over time between the overall Catholic population and the presence of Catholics in the Irish civil service, which has been corrected through some reform efforts especially since 1998. In the next section, the Peace Accord and its implementation are discussed.

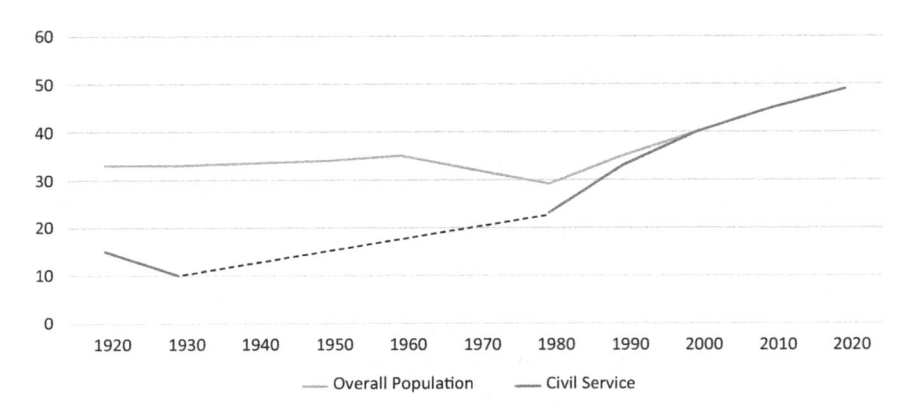

FIGURE 10.1 Catholics in Northern Ireland Civil Service, 1920–2018.

Missing Civil Service data from 1930s to 1980s. Sources: The 1981 Northern Ireland Census Report, Religion Report; Northern Ireland Statistics and Research Agency; Northern Ireland Equality Commission.

Promising Government Initiatives: The Good Friday Agreement, the Patten Act, and Section 75 of the Northern Ireland Act

Ever after the Anglo-Irish Accords of 1922, equity in the civil service was addressed by the Northern Ireland government, but with some indifference on both sides. The civil service was supposed to be allotted with a goal of one-third Catholics as job holders, which would match the ratio of Catholics in the overall population. Within the police force, the Royal Ulster Constabulary (RUC), only one-sixth of positions were pursued by Catholics, at the outset. Leadership within the civil service was limited to Protestants. At times, the Northern Ireland executive, under leaders like James Craig, pressed for Catholic inclusion in the civil service, but bowed easily in the face of local Protestant opposition (Patterson 2007). At other times even 'reformist' and 'progressive' unionist leaders such as the ill-fated Terrence O'Neill betrayed a deep misunderstanding and sectarian (quasi-racist) view of Catholic nationalists as when he stated the following in 1969 as Prime Minster of Northern Ireland:

> It is frightfully hard to explain to Protestants that if you give Roman Catholics a good job and a good house, they will live like Protestants because they will see neighbours with cars and television sets; they will refuse to have eighteen children. But if a Roman Catholic is jobless, and lives in the most ghastly hovel, he will rear eighteen children on National Assistance. If you treat Roman Catholics with due consideration and kindness, they will live like Protestants in spite of the authoritative nature of their Church.
>
> *(Quoted in Kane, 2019)*

The sharing of civil service positions completely stopped when the UK government took control of Northern Ireland out of the state's hands, with rule from Westminster, in 1972, as a result of widespread gerrymandering, police brutality, and outbreak of lawlessness. Local governance and administration returned, almost three decades later, when the Good Friday Accord was put in place.

Gradual movement toward peace between loyalists and republicans proceeded throughout the 1990s. Rapprochement occurred between political parties in Northern Ireland (most notably, the Social Democratic and Labour Party or SDLP under John Hume and Sinn Fein leader Gerry Adams in the early part of the decade), as well as between executive leadership of the Republic of Ireland and the UK (Ireland's Taoiseach Bertie Ahern and the UK's Prime Minister Tony Blair, respectively). Leading the negotiation was retired US Senator George Mitchell. The theme of all discussions was reestablishment of local governance and the creation of an inclusive power-sharing executive so that there would be the return of a democratically elected Northern Ireland Assembly, the institution of an Irish-British Conference for those two governments, and a committee to handle cross-border issues. Two referenda helped to bring the agreement to fruition; first was a referendum within Northern Ireland on accepting the Accord (passed with 71% support), and a vote in the Republic giving up its constitutional claim to Northern Ireland (passed with 94% support). However, while overwhelmingly supported, there were significant differences between unionists and nationalists. As Hayes and McAllister note: "Although the Agreement was formally ratified by 71 percent of voters in the referendum held on 22 May 1998, only a narrow majority of Protestants voted to support it" (Hayes and McAllister 2001: 73). The reality is that in Northern Ireland while over 90% of Catholics voted for the Agreement, only 57% of Protestants did, and the now largest party in Northern Ireland, the Democratic Unionist Party (DUP) campaigned against the Agreement.

It should be pointed out that while the Republic's government went along with this policy, it did include a provision that the people of Northern Ireland could revisit the unification of the island under the Republic's government if supported in a future referendum. Under the provisions of the Agreement the UK Secretary of State for Northern Ireland—currently Brandon Lewis—has to call a vote if it appears likely there would be a majority for a united Ireland.

Implementation of the Good Friday or Belfast Agreement would follow over the next decade. One of the most important components politically was the involuntary power-sharing agreement between loyalist and republican leadership. In 2007 Ian Paisley, the leader of the Democratic Unionist Party, and Martin McGuinness, the Sinn Fein leader in Northern Ireland (and former IRA commanding officer in Derry), came together to serve as First Minister and Deputy First Minister in the capital building of Stormont, establishing a coalition to unite the two sides, based in large part on supplanting their two more moderate rivals—the SDLP and the Ulster Unionist Party (UUP) who had established power sharing since 1998. This was an impressive achievement, given the vitriol that Paisley had spread in earlier days against Catholics, from the pulpit as a Free Presbyterian minister, only equaled by McGuinness's violent opposition to the partition of Ireland and the Northern Ireland statelet while he served as an IRA commander. The power-sharing agreement would last until January 2017, but fell when McGuinness resigned as Deputy First Minster and collapsed the government. The Northern Ireland Assembly or government has barely met since then. But the symbolism of this alliance, while it held, was clear: Even the most extreme of rivals could work together, with the goal of establishing peace between the sides.

Since 1972, the center of the UK's rule in Northern Ireland has come with few breaks from the civil service. Three different reforms affecting the civil service were central to the implementation of the Belfast Agreement, with the goal of bridging divides within communities. In 1998, the UK Parliament passed the Fair Employment and Treatment Order for Northern Ireland, which prioritized the elimination of Catholic/Protestant disparities in the Northern Ireland Civil Service (NICS). Affirmative or 'positive' action was integrated into workforce review and development for all public authorities, and has met with broad success. The analytic arm of the NICS was able to track a steady progression during the first decade of this century toward parity between Catholics and Protestants in the civil service, in aggregate. The UK government rarely collected data on this demographic within the civil service during the first several decades of the existence of the NICS (Buckland 1979; Irish Times 2010). Some public authorities would lag in this movement. The toughest conversion to a fair and equitable civil service resides in the public safety realm; in 1999, British politician Christopher Patten was tasked with convening the Independent Commission on Policing for Northern Ireland. Their product was titled 'A New Beginning: Policing in Northern Ireland' (1999). The commission and report both adopted the name of its chair. Police experts from around the world served on the Patten Commission, offering the best in policing philosophy and practice in the writing of the Patten Report. Several dramatic changes emerged from the Report's recommendations, and while these were resisted by portions of either side from the earlier conflicts, most have been implemented and have proven successful. The third reform is known as Section 75 of the Northern Ireland Act of 1998; it is the mechanism by which ongoing assessment of the equity within Northern Irish policy and administration receives due consideration. The rest of this section treats the affirmative action and Patten Report reforms that created much progress by 2010. The following section will treat Section 75 in a deeper analysis.

As mentioned previously, Northern Ireland's border with the Republic of Ireland was very intentionally drawn to include Protestant/loyalist communities within the Northern Irish border, and to exclude Catholic/republican populations. This gerrymandering process gave Protestants a tenuous majority within Northern Ireland, until this decade. At the time of the Belfast Agreement, the overall population in Northern Ireland was 49% Protestant and 47% Catholic. But the civil service was dominated by Protestants at that time, with a 60–40% split between Protestants and Catholics. The Fair Employment and Treatment Order finally instituted consistent data collection on this disparity across Northern Irish public agencies (including the central government, local governments, and public authorities) and authorized "appropriate and practical" affirmative action programs to eliminate agency disparities. These included movement toward quotas in hiring and promotion, as well as analysis of the impact of workforce reduction plans or redundancies. Marketing dynamics were important to the Order's implementation, as the NICS moved to make it clear that Catholics were a welcome and important part of the workforce for agencies. Management was encouraged to identify "chill factors" that especially discouraged Catholic participation in the public workforce, particularly in functions like public safety and corrections.

The focus of review and action under the Fair Employment and Treatment Order was managerial; data gathering, review, and strategies were to be carried out by agency leadership. On the whole this was a successful tactic, as the Catholic/Protestant disparity was steadily reduced. By 2011, 49.1% of the NICS was Catholic, 50.9% Protestant (while the economically active portion of the overall population was 47% Catholic, 52% Protestant) (NISRA 2018). So the achievement of 'community background' fairness and equity within the civil service workforce was relatively steady during this period, with some exceptions. For instance, the prison services remained unequal, with prison grades of employment displaying as nearly 85% Protestant. Here, part of the explanation was reluctance among Catholics to work in this service, dominated by the interests and needs of the British military during the Troubles. Unfortunately, prison services were not a part of the Patten Commission's focus, whose policing reforms were explicitly targeted at addressing both historical difficulties and future service needs.

The Fair Employment and Treatment Order is a fine case example of the ways that expert-led, parliamentary government programing can be reformed in short order, under the right conditions. The Patten Report's efforts addressed the broader issue of community acceptance and feasibility within its reform agenda. The tense community relations especially within Belfast and Derry would require more than just marketing and hiring consideration, to make up for the militaristic nature of policing during the Troubles. The Patten Commission specified the need for a new kind of policing, detached from the past practices; linkage and meshing with the interests of community residents; and a movement from the organizational structure, symbols, and emblems prominent of policing in the past. So for example, the RUC was restructured and renamed the Police Service of Northern Ireland (PSNI) with new badges, uniforms, etc., aimed at creating a neutral and inclusive police force. All of these would enhance the fairness as well as the feasibility of the resulting statewide policing organization.

Within policing services, the history was especially contentious, as several different constabulary forces had provided law enforcement until the 1960s, including the Protestant-dominated RUC police force, and the even more unrepresentative quasi-military Ulster Defence Regiment and the B Specials. But by 1969, the fragmented law enforcement units were replaced by para-military forces on both sides of the conflict and the deployment of the British Army in August 1969 (Barry 2019). A movement back toward peace would require the disbanding and disarmament of all paramilitary forces, and the reinstatement of a more equitable and representative police service, accept-able to Catholic-nationalists. The Patten Report recommended an overhaul in policing tactics and training. Rapid response to paramilitary activities would rarely be needed; now police response would center on community crimes like vandalism, drugs, and domestic incidents. Training would correspond to new needs, focusing less on militaristic drilling and counter-insurgency/terrorist activities and more on developing positive community relations.

The Patten Report provides an eloquent statement about the conversion in policing, necessary in Northern Ireland and elsewhere around the world. Instead of a focus on the expertise and discretion, for better or worse, among police of-ficers, policing for the 21st century would require ownership and buy-in from community residents. A sharing and mutuality between police and the citizenry would go further in sustaining safe communities and positive perception of po-lice services. This was the rationale for creating a police service that mirrored the community through the affirmative action-based hiring processes of the Fair Employment and Treatment Order. The numbers of woman and Catholic police officers were to be enhanced, not necessarily through hiring quotas, but in equal or proportional admissions to the police academy. The best of these candidates would be hired in the end, but at the start of the training process, equal access to policing jobs would be established. But for this community orientation to take hold, it would be important to communicate the changes to police strat-egy. Work in the police services held a stigma for many Catholics, because of the RUC's former role in upholding British rule and often violent repression of the Catholic minority. The old police force fought against both Protestant and Catholic paramilitaries, but in general was seen as having a more solid alignment with Protestant communities, less attachment to Catholic ones. A 'new' inclu-sive and impartial police services would need to be developed and marketed to the public in general. "So we see our approach as restorative, not retributive—restorative of the values of liberty, the rule of law, and mutual respect, values that have sometimes been casualties of the years of violence" (Commission 1999: 4). The report reflected a solid movement to a new values base.

The Patten Commission recognized the significance of symbols and artifacts as a contentious base for political and organizational cultures (Schein 1992). Old symbols with their tensions would need to be replaced with new ones that could be considered more inclusive, or at least not exclusive of formerly conflicting sides. The RUC, considered to be a one-sided title for the police, was replaced with the more progressive Police Services of Northern Ireland. Badges and emblems for the new PSNI did not include symbols such as the crown or other linkages to the UK. But nor would the logos and images of the PSNI include any Celtic or Irish references. Police facilities around Northern Ireland would not fly the Union Jack at their fronts, instead opting for a specific flag of the PSNI. But the police services did not entirely dismiss a committed history to law enforcement; memorials to fallen police officers were retained, as they were emblematic of a commitment to a policing mission. The color of police uniforms was retained from the past, but the functional style was updated. A balance to the look and feel of the PSNI was maintained, generally favoring the continuation of good policing but now in a manner acceptable to and effective for the entire community.

The Patten Report was widely praised following its publication in 1999. Over the following years, loyalists and republicans found reasons to oppose some of the implementation specifics that emerged from the Report, but within the decade, the well-crafted particulars had been enmeshed in the new police force (Shearing 2010). The image and practices of the reformed police agency have become well established. Nevertheless, the PSNI would be one of the Northern Irish public functions that struggled with equity in hiring over time. Where the overall balance between Protestants and Catholics in the NICS is 51%–49%, the Catholic make-up of the PSNI is approximately 31%, as some of the historical stigma remains regarding policing. Law enforcement is likely the most contentious discipline in Northern Ireland's civil service, so this can still be considered a relatively progressive reform since the Belfast Agreement.

Successes in diversifying the civil service and establishing a relatively diverse and much more community-oriented police service are highlights in Northern Ireland's progression from its violent past. But there is still potential for advancement at the community level, as residential areas and schools are still segregated in Northern Ireland's largest urban areas. As many as 95% of Northern Ireland schoolchildren attend a public school that matches with their either Protestant or Catholic faith identity. The focus of equality-based reforms has moved away from 'community background' in the second decade of the 21st century, toward previously neglected concerns of the disabled, gender, LGBTQ issues, race, and ethnicity. The mechanism whereby other equality advancements have been made is worth studying in the next portion of this chapter. With more practice, the Section 75 screening and assessment procedures may be up to tackling the education and housing segregation issues, in time.

Assessment and Evidence of Progress

The Good Friday/Belfast Agreement was the negotiated peace settlement signed by the political leaders of the Republic of Ireland and the UK; the parliamentary act that rendered the specifics for the UK government was the Northern Ireland Act of 1998. The legislation included human rights protections, the formation of the Equality Commission of the Northern Ireland government, and 'equality mainstreaming' guidance known commonly as 'Section 75' of the Northern Ireland Act. Donaghy (2004) defines mainstreaming as "a strategy that aims to promote an equity perspective throughout the policymaking process, from conception to implementation to review, and all stages in between" (393). Mainstreaming efforts may be aimed at single affected groups, such as women, or as in the case of Section 75, they may affect the spectrum of inequalities. These efforts also contrast between expert-driven internal processes and more widely consultative processes. In the case of Section 75, deliberation in the screening and assessment of policy impacts is central to the implementation of the law, and thus provides an important area to carry out potentially 'nervous' dialogues about fairness in policymaking (Donaghy 2004; Egan and Murray 2007) (Table 10.1).

Section 75 promotes a focus on two aspects of policy setting within all of the activities of Northern Ireland public authorities (government agencies, local governments, and other commissions and organizations). The first statutory duty under Section 75 is the promotion of equality of opportunity for nine potentially affected equality groups: those of different religious belief, political alignments, race, age, marital status, sexual orientation, gender, disability status, and parenting situations for those with or without dependents. Second, public authorities are required to promote good relations between affected groups (including religion, political opinion, and racial group). The Equality Commission of Northern Ireland picked up the duties to implement Section 75 in 1998. It provides an information clearinghouse of equality statistics as well as annual reporting from public authorities; offers training sessions on Section 75 and the analytic, deliberative, and consultation processes to carry out the law; and investigates complaints from citizens who feel they have been adversely affected by policies carried out by public authorities.

Section 75 adopted a holistic approach to equality protection from the outset, as the list of nine affected groups has been consistent from the writing of the legislation. Analysts were largely supportive of the recognition of all forms of inequality within the definition of affected groups, negating any elevation of especially protected identities, as well as recognizing the potential for the meshing of these group identities (Donaghy 2004). 'Community background,' as mentioned previously, tends to combine religious (Protestant/Catholic) and political (loyalist/republican) factors. As with the Fair Employment and Treatment Order, many public authorities met the new self-analytic requirements of Section 75 with enthusiasm, but early progress was inconsistent across the Northern Ireland government. The Equality Commission standardized the implementation process and reporting in 2010, through its "Guide for Public Authorities." Agency dialog and public consultation included structured

TABLE 10.1 Equality Reform Steps and Actions in Northern Ireland, 1998–Current

Action	Focus	Participants	Mechanisms	Assessment
Good Friday Agreement (1998)	Initiation of peace between Northern Ireland factions	UK and Irish governments; Northern Ireland Political Parties	Acceptance of national identities and "Power Sharing" of political leadership	Cornerstone of Northern Ireland governance since its signing; but Power Sharing" collapsed in 2017
Fair Employment and Treatment Order (1998)	Integration of Catholics into the Northern Ireland Civil Service (NICS)	UK Parliament and NICS	'Affirmative Action' in NICS hiring; data collection tracking disparities	Since 1998, the 60–40 split between Protestants and Catholics in NICS has been virtually equalized
Patten Report (1999)	Policing reform, from fighting terrorism and armed conflict to community policing	Public safety leadership and experts from around the world, led by Sir Christopher Patten	Careful definition of community policing; enhanced recruitment of women and Catholics into policing; formation of the Police Services of Northern Ireland	"Rebranding" of PSNI and retraining focus is a worldwide model; Catholic representation in PSNI and corrections still lags at 30% of Catholic population
Section 75 of Northern Ireland Act of 1998	Analysis and resolution of 'community background' and other inequities in Northern Irish society	UK Parliament; newly formed Equality Commission of Northern Ireland; all statewide and local government organizations	Standardized screening and implementation assessment of potential inequitable government decisions	Annual reporting through the Commission offers numerous "best cases" of inequity reduction for disabled, LGBTQ, ethnic, gender, and other groups

screening and impact assessment procedures, based on the following questions applied to existing and new policy initiatives and applied to each of the nine equity groups in turn:

- What is the likely impact on equality of opportunity for those affected by (enacted) policy, for each of the Section 75 equality categories?
- Are there opportunities to better promote equality of opportunity for people within the...categories?
- To what extent is the policy likely to impact on good relations between people of a different religious belief, political opinion, or racial group?
- Are there opportunities to better promote good relations between people of different religious belief, political opinion, or racial group? (Section 75 Guide, 54)

Through this systematized screening process, a given policy might be 'screened out,' meaning that it would not affect any group inequitably, or it might be 'screened in' and need some form of adjustment to maintain equitable treatment of affected groups if possible. Those policies that were screened in would be further analyzed through an impact assessment procedure, to track equality protections for the affected groups. For example, at the local government/council level, the 2016 Local Government Regulations permit any council decision or strategy could be 'called in' by 15% of councillors if they think the decision will disproportionately and negatively affect a section of the local community. The Regulations state that the following grounds must be met "(a) the section of the inhabitants of the district that would be affected by the decision; and (b) the nature and extent of the disproportionate adverse impact." This call in procedure thus offers another protective mechanism against discrimination and inequality.

While the reporting process under the "Guide's" new design requires annual review, there are no sanctions or penalties for failing to file reports. However, if an authority does file, there is a 50% rate of discussing policy accommodation focuses (Commission 2018). Mainstreaming under the revised guidance focuses on at least the following four themes, between 2015 and 2018:

- *Disabilities access.* The Department of Education has enhanced its focus to serve children with autism and spectrum disorders through increased screening and coordinated training with the Department of Health. Autism and Asperger's syndrome have been identified as rapidly growing health conditions, and treatment of the issue within primary schools is the next step after an overall Autism Strategy within health services. One of the main workforce development programs, "Steps 2 Success" or S2S, has recruited consultants to review disabilities access to both its web portal and to the specific program initiatives. For example, since one of the protected groups under Section 75 is people with dependents, the inclusion of child care within the training program has been funded. In another use of affected consultants, elderly volunteers have been involved in testing the City of Belfast's infrastructure development plan.

– *Awareness education*: The Health and Education Departments are expanding educational programs and modules around a wide range of affected groups and issues. In 2017 alone, designated panels and sessions were formed around issues for new immigrants to Northern Ireland, LGBTQ educational focuses, autism awareness, single parenting, and mental health disparities. Specific groups have had their issues highlighted by Northern Ireland and City of Belfast governments including Deaf Awareness Week, Belfast Pride Day, Transgender Day of Remembrance, the Women in Business NI Leadership Conference, and DisabledGo training days.

– *Expanded culture and arts access*: The City of Belfast has expanded its criteria for arts grants and programing to include diversity focuses, including support for the Outburst Queer Arts Festival, Belfast Pride, the Belfast Children's Festival, the Bounce! Disabilities Arts Festival, and Exhibitions at the Chinese Welfare Association and the Northern Ireland Community of Refugees and Asylum Seekers.

– *Hate crimes and anti-bullying*: The PSNI and Department of Education collaborate on educational programing and increased enforcement of hate crimes, as protections for new immigrant populations, the disabled, and LGBTQ youths. In November 2017, over 800 organizations participated with the Department of Education in 'Anti-bullying Week,' with the theme, 'All equal, All different, All together.' PSNI's policy changes have especially emphasized the protection of victims of hate crimes over conviction of the perpetrators.

The Section 75 reports database inventories the impacts of policy changes across the nine affected groups, but the collaboration across public authorities is striking. While the focus specifies more impacts within peoples with disabilities, immigrants, and LGBTQ communities within the past three years, there is an interesting collaboration on the long-standing 'community background' issue. For centuries, Protestant communities have celebrated victories such as William of Orange's triumph with parades and bonfires on the anniversary day. July 11 and August 8 are the major bonfire days across Belfast, and have long been flash points for violence. But the PSNI, City of Belfast, and other agencies have pursued an effort to convert the bonfire commemorations to more inclusive celebrations, better-managed sites (keeping fires under better control), and even substitution of the bonfires for other activities. A positive interpretation could be that Northern Ireland is reaching the point where it can get beyond the violent earlier conflict underlying the Troubles, and move toward larger transformations with regard to broader equality.

Conclusion

This study of predominantly faith- and politics-based inequity in Northern Ireland expands on Gooden's work in predictable or consistent ways, as well as in some varied and unexpected ones. To the first point, inequity and the historical abuse of power is ubiquitous in our world. But a sort of awakening comes to many states and their communities; government deliberation and action may develop appropriate legal responses to the institutional inequity that emerged. Along the way, the tension in having the discussion about difference and inequity is difficult to initiate and daunting to pursue, at the outset. But it can be transforming for our vision of a fair and just public service contribution.

What were the differences between the racial inequity case developed in Gooden's initial study, and the political and faith-based divide in Northern Ireland? The reconciliation between the depths of the inequity, involving slavery in the United States and colonialism in Ireland/Northern Ireland, ended many years ago in both places (in 1865 and 1922, respectively), but the unrest, deep distrust, and constant tensions between groups was especially violent and concentrated in Northern Ireland (nicely captured in the title of one of the many books about Northern Ireland, Jonathan Powell's *Great Hatred, Little Room*), which led to a very specific second reconciliation in 1998 with the Good Friday Agreement. This is meant by no means to dismiss any of the violence in the engagement of Reconstruction and civil rights in the United States, only to highlight the concentration of conflict in the two Northern Irish cities of Belfast and Derry, especially. Affirmative action is a policy used to address inequity in both places, but is much more contentious in the United States than in Northern Ireland. It appears that the latter state was far more willing to accept the need for the policy, following 1998.

In Northern Ireland, the dialogue about religious and political contrasts starts differently and maybe more contentiously. The 'community background' differences are unseen until the verbal cues highlight the difference. So the initial dialogue can be where the contentiousness starts. It appears that the resolution, since 1998, has been a smoother discussion. This may arise from a shared sense on both 'sides' that the violence that can erupt does need to be quelled if possible. And more to the point that public policies and institutional changes and initiatives are needed to address some of the underlying causes of that conflict, not least discrimination, unequal treatment, and experiencing public services as non-neutral and partial towards one side of the community. So this chapter has highlighted that 'nervousness' might have a cultural difference, within the history, intensity, and concentration of the divisions between peoples, including the 'long memory' of the legacy of unstable, contested, and often violent relations between the two communities.

The policy differences that emerge in the United States and Northern Ireland are interesting. Gooden lays out very effectively how government-endorsed housing discrimination segregated American society, and the "saturation" led to further unfairness. Predominantly African American communities suffer from lagging economic development because of discriminatory support from the banking industry; and thus property values in African American communities are lower. Since the dominant tax source for municipalities in the United States is the local community's property tax, there are consequently less financial resources in these communities. Local services suffer—with the most dominant local service in American communities being their school system. And thus opportunity for African Americans, within this saturated system, is societally constrained. Some cities and states in the United States have implemented separate structures to enhance equity in funding for school systems, but these have a long way to go.

Funding is not the issue in Northern Irish communities, but the segregation is. As mentioned above, over 95% of Northern Irish children study in schools with other children of their shared faith. Interestingly, Catholic children now have higher attainment to college and university studies than Protestant children; so the inequity has almost reversed on this dimension, but at the expense of shared schooling as enhancing reconciliation and creating positive community relations. All that said—cultural dispositions lead to a different form of nervousness, and at the margins, different ways to initiate and proceed through the conversation to overcome it.

Northern Ireland has made progress since its 1998 Peace Agreement on addressing discrimination and inequality including the creation of a more peaceful society and, at first, a more consensual governance system. It has an impressive policy architecture for monitoring and delivering equality in public services and government decision-making, yet more needs to be done, not least in tackling its still segregated primary and secondary education system and encouraging more Catholics to join the police and prison services. But there are three additional 'nervous areas of government' or sources of nervousness with which we conclude. These relate to important issues to do with the past, the present, and the future of and for Northern Ireland. It is perhaps a testament to the success of the post-1998 political and policy system in Northern Ireland in dealing with and addressing inequalities between the two communities, that one of the major political issues still unresolved in Northern Ireland is the legacy of the past conflict. How to deal with the past was not addressed in the 1998 Agreement but has risen up the political agenda in recent years as victims and survivors of paramilitary and state violence seek truth, justice, compensation, or some combination of all three. While the UK government has suggested a way forward (NIO 2018), and these proposals are currently out for consultation, the issue and the proposal has caused deep divisions within Northern Ireland between victims and survivors, between the Northern Irish political parties, and between the British and Irish governments. But everyone agrees that a way to deal with the past is absolutely vital if Northern Ireland is to move from a 'peace process' and conflict management to reconciliation and conflict transformation.

The issue relating to the present is one that is a great threat to the peace process and the post-1998 political settlement. That issue is Brexit, the decision by referendum in 2016 that the UK leaves the European Union. The fact that Northern Ireland voted to remain and that those parties pushing for Brexit are mostly unionist ones (DUP, UUP, TUV) has added an additional set of tensions to the already fragile relations between unionist and nationalist political parties and communities. Not least is the fact that Brexit has been used as an opportunity by the largest nationalist party, Sinn Fein, to call for a border poll for a United Ireland. This has predictably caused concern and anxiety among large sections of the unionist population and political parties who are nervous about their status in any future reunified Ireland when they would be a minority on the island, and related to the latter that the demographic trends within Northern Ireland are such that there will be a Catholic majority within the next decade. An example of the changed status for the once dominant group is that since the 2018 Assembly election, unionist parties are, for the first time in Northern Ireland's history, not long the majority in the Assembly. Brexit has not only been seized opportunistically to call for a border poll, but has at one and the same time also raised the prospect or specter of return to a 'hard border' in Ireland. Not least among those pushing for a 'hard Brexit' i.e. cutting all links with the European Union, an impact of a hard Brexit might be the return of physical infrastructure along the border. This would undermine the progress since 1998 of there being no guards or border posts along the border which has both symbolically and empirically reduced tensions and normalized relations between communities in the two jurisdictions and lessened tensions between communities within Northern Ireland, especially those in border counties. As we write Brexit has still not been resolved with the UK government and Parliament completely divided and unable to come up with and deliver a Brexit deal. These divisions mirror the deep divisions Brexit has exposed within UK society, and it has done nothing but increases tensions within Northern Ireland.

While also a current issue, climate breakdown and ecological degradation will dominate politics and policy for decades to come, and as such is as much a future issue to consider as it is a current pressing one. Whether as a result of the remarkable school strike for climate movement of school children led by the Swedish teenager Greta Thunberg, the more non-violent direct action of the Extinction Rebellion movement, the remarkable success of David Attenborough's Blue Planet program and others to popularize the plastic pollution crisis in our oceans and his prominence in public debates on climate breakdown, it does seem that a 'tipping point' has been reached on our climate and ecological crises. So, while like other societies Northern Ireland will have to face these and find responses (and here given its unique status one could say it should benefit from the fact that both the UK and Irish Parliaments have recently declared 'Climate and Ecological Emergencies'), Northern Ireland is burdened not only by dealing with these global and existential threats, but has to look backward as well as forward as it were to deal with the legacy of the past; the current chaos caused by Brexit; and the even greater chaos and devastation that climate and ecological breakdown heralds unless radical and transformative changes are made quickly and in all areas of life (from our food system, the energy system, transportation options, building systems, and others). But perhaps oddly Northern Ireland and its uneven peace process have something to offer in responding to climate and ecological breakdown. This has to do with the often overlooked fact that the transformations required to adequately deal with the climate emergency will produce winners and losers. And therefore conflict management and transformation strategies should be seen as central elements of any transition from 'actually existing unsustainability' (Barry 2012), for example how to create processes for those who will lose from the transition to a climate resilient and low carbon economy (such as workers, communities, and companies involved in the fossil fuel energy sector). And here, on this issue of finding compromise, negotiating a fair agreement on a way out of the climate and ecological crisis, Northern Ireland might have something to offer, such that its name begins to be associated with something other than its past history of violence and division.

References

Barry, J. (2012). The politics of actually existing unsustainably: Human flourishing in a climate-changed, carbon-constrained world. Oxford University Press.

Barry, J. (2019). *The outbreak and development of the 'troubles'.* Belfast: Island Publications.

Bew, P. (2010). *Ireland. The politics of enmity.* Oxford: Oxford University Press.

Bolman, L., and Deal, T. (2013). *Reframing organizations: Artistry, choice and leadership.* Fifth Edition. San Francisco, CA: Jossey Bass.

Brennan, S. (2017). *Ulster's uncertain menders?: The challenge of reintegration and reconciliation for Ulster Loyalists in a post-ceasefire society,* unpublished PhD thesis. Belfast: Queen's University Belfast.

Buckland, P. (1979). *The factory of grievances: Devolved government in Northern Ireland, 1921–1939.* Dublin: Gill Macmillan.

Burns, A. (2018). *The milkman.* London: Faber & Faber.

Donaghy, T.B. (2004). Applications of mainstreaming in Australia and Northern Ireland. *International Political Science Review 25*(4), 393–410.

Egan, S., and Murray, R. (2007). A charter of rights for the Island of Ireland: An unknown quantity on the Good Friday/Belfast Agreement. *International and Comparative Law Quarterly 56,* 797–836.

Equality Commission for Northern Ireland. (2010). *Section 75 of the Northern Ireland Act of 1998: A guide for public authorities.* Belfast: Equality Commission.

Equality Commission of Northern Ireland. (2018). *Section 75 statutory equality and good relations duties acting on the evidence of public authority practices.* Belfast: Equality Commission.

Gooden, S. (2014). *Race and social inequity: A nervous area of government.* Armonk, NY: ME Sharpe.

Hayes, B., and McAllister, I. (2001). Who voted for peace?: Public support for the 1998 Northern Ireland Agreement. *Irish Political Studies 16*(1), 73–93.

Independent Commission on Policing in Northern Ireland. (1999). *A new beginning: Policing in Northern Ireland.* London: H.M.S.O.

Irish Times (Editorial). (2010, May). Civil service in North short on Catholics. *Irish Times*, 10.

Kane, A. (2019). Half-a-century on, we've still to learn lessons of Terrence O'Neill. *Belfast Telegraph* (https://www.belfasttelegraph.co.uk/opinion/columnists/halfacentury-on-weve-still-to-learn-lessons-of-terence-oneill-30905355.html, accessed May 26, 2019)

Long, S. (2018). *The politics of misrecognition: An insider analysis of political loyalism and its 'place in the peace'*, unpublished PhD thesis. Belfast: Queen's University Belfast.

McGarry, F. (2019). Reframing Ireland's revolution. In McGarry, F., and Delaney, E. (eds). *The Irish revolution 1919–21: A global history.* (8–12). Dublin: History Publications Ltd.

McMahon, S. (1996). *A short history of Ireland.* Chester Springs, PA: Dufour Editions.

Northern Ireland Office. (2018). *Addressing the legacy of Northern Ireland's past* (https://www.gov.uk/government/consultations/addressing-the-legacy-of-northern-irelands-past, accessed May 31, 2019)

Northern Ireland Statistics and Research Agency. (2018). *Equality statistics for the Northern Ireland Civil Service.* Belfast, NI: NISRA.

Patterson, H. (2007). *Ireland since 1939: The persistence of conflict.* London: Penguin Books.

Schein, E. (1992). *Organizational culture and leadership.* Second Edition. San Francisco, CA: Jossey-Bass.

Shearing, C. (2010). The curious case of the Patten Report. In Doyle, J. (ed). *Policing the narrow ground: Lessons from the transformation of policing in Northern Ireland.* (27–38). Dublin: Royal Irish Academy.

11

ISLAMOPHOBIA IN FRANCE

Intersectoral Collaborations to Advance Social Equity

Sean A. McCandless and Angela Kline

In the consciousness of many, "France" and "Islamophobia" can go hand in hand. The complicity of the state in perpetuating and exacerbating these inequities is well documented in that it is in public institutions where many acts of Islamophobia take place, often in the name of maintaining secularism (*laïcité*). Problems of Islamophobia have only heightened in the wake of several deadly terrorist attacks from 2015 onward (Najib & Hopkins, 2018).

French Islamophobia is not merely a 21st-century phenomenon. It is undergirded by an "acceleration of history" (Nora, 1989) marked by the upheavals of war, immigration, globalization, colonization, and decolonization as well as debates of "What does it mean to be a French citizen?" There is no set answer, with some answering that to be French, one must look, act, and speak French and with others arguing that France needs to adopt a more diverse, inclusive definition of citizenship that allows multiple ways to be French. Minorities, especially Muslims, are often caught in the middle. Islamophobia becomes a nervous area of government.

This chapter focuses on these dimensions by providing a brief historical perspective of key events and changes that have served as catalysts for the present-day situation in France. It then reviews practices adopted by the French government to address Islamophobia, and special attention herein is paid to how government dialogue and collaboration with Muslim organizations show promise at addressing inequities.

A Nervous Area of Government in France

Governments across the world have created, perpetuated, and exacerbated inequities, and addressing these issues often makes people nervous. Nervousness about social inequities, while understandable, merely stifles the steps needed to foster justice, and it is not until those throughout a society, but especially those serving in government, learn to manage and overcome nervousness that true progress toward improving equity can occur (Gooden, 2014).

Islamophobia is one such nervous area of government. Gallup defines Islamophobia as "An exaggerated fear, hatred, and hostility toward Islam and Muslims that is perpetuated by negative stereotypes resulting in bias, discrimination, and the marginalization and exclusion of Muslims from social, political and civic life" (Gallup, n.d.). Many scholars attribute the advent of the term "Islamophobia" to a report from 1997 from the Runnymede Trust, a British independent research center (Runnymede Trust, 1997). This seminal report categorized Islamophobia as *prejudice, discrimination, exclusion*, and *violence*. *Prejudice* manifests in both everyday conversation and the media. *Discrimination* can take multiple forms, whether in employment practices or in the provision of services, which are particularly acute in education and health. *Exclusion* can result in politics and government, employment, and from management and responsibility. Finally, *violence* can manifest in physical assaults, vandalizing property, and verbal abuse (Runnymede Trust, 1997). In a 20th anniversary report, the Runnymede Trust expanded its definition of Islamophobia as

> any distinction, exclusion or restriction towards, or preference against, Muslims (or those perceived to be Muslims) that has the purpose of effect of nullifying or impairing the recognition, enjoyment or exercise, on an equal footing, of human rights and fundamental freedoms in the political, economic, social, cultural or any other field of public life.
>
> *(Runnymede Trust, 1997)*

Islamophobia in France is well documented in scholarly, governmental, and popular presses. According to the Pew Research Center, France has the largest percentage of Muslims in Western Europe with an estimated 5.7 million Muslims, or 8.8% of France's total population. This population is expected to double by 2050 due to the young age of Muslims, high fertility rates among the Muslim population, and continued migration across Europe (Hackett, 2017).

With a changing population, France has historically adopted a model of integration and emphasis on universalist ideals promoting the unity of the people (Bleich, 2005). This has a distinctly nationalist character in that to many, to be French, one must look, act, and speak French (Bell, 2003). This conception has often excluded many from full "Frenchness" on the basis of race, ethnicity, religion, and the intersections therein, and the government has had varying success in modifying this approach to address implicit and overt acts of Islamophobia.

Why Islamophobia Is a Nervous Area of Government

As established in a representative survey of 1,000 French Muslims, the *Fondation Jean Jaurès* (2019) found that reported acts of bias—whether use of injurious language, threats of assault, physical assaults, and attacks on property—remain common. Such prejudices evidence intersectional dimensions with women and those outside of non-Arabic origins disproportionately experiencing inequities (Collectif Contre L'Islamophobie en France [CCIF], 2019).

Hate crime data collected by French government institutions, such as the Ministry of Justice and the police, can help give a picture of why Islamophobia is a nervous area of government. Figure 11.1 summarizes police-reported data collected by the Organization for Security and Cooperation in Europe (OSCE), which operates the Office for Democratic Institutions and Human Rights (ODIHR) that annually reports on hate crimes and bias acts (see OSCE-ODIHR, 2018).

As shown above, anti-Muslim bias in France since 2012, the first year of data offered by the OSCE, has fluctuated. In 2012, for instance, police recorded 2,358 hate crimes. Of these, 287 were against Muslims, including threats or threatening behavior ($n = 149$), attacks against places of worship ($n = 84$), and physical assaults ($n = 54$). In 2017, there were 95 police-reported instances, which included damage to property ($n = 59$), threats or threatening behavior ($n = 23$), arson ($n = 7$), and physical assault ($n = 6$). Perhaps not surprisingly, the year with the most instances was 2015 during which two major terrorist incidents occurred—the *Charlie Hebdo* attack and the attacks of November 13, 2015 (discussed in detail below). While the overall number of racist incidents reported to police has gone down, recorded attacks against Jews and Muslims began to climb again after 2016, although data sources differ on the exact

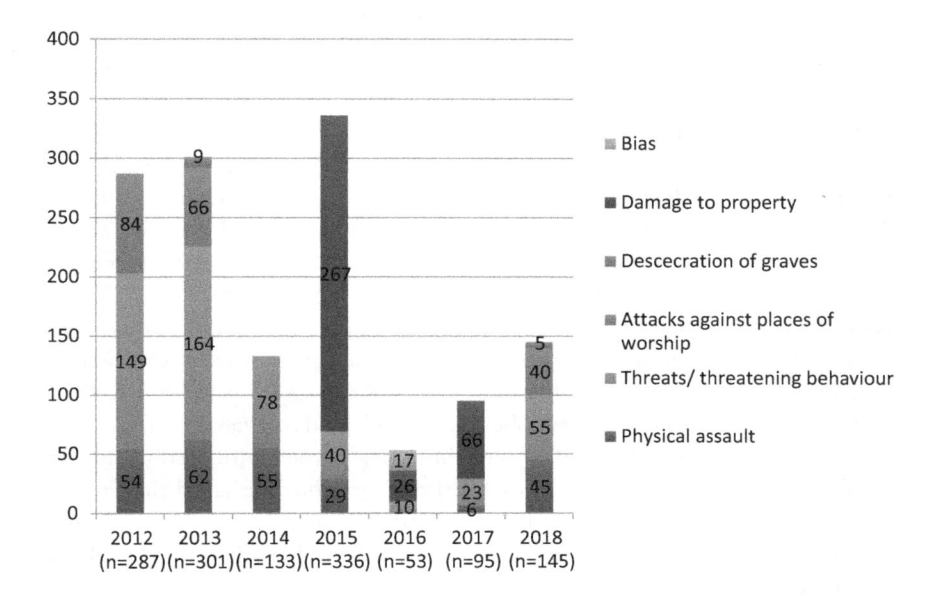

FIGURE 11.1 Police-Documented Anti-Muslim Hate Crimes: 2012–2018.

numbers (Radio France Internationale, 2018). Other organizations report higher rates of Islamophobia. The French National Human Rights Commission (CNCDH) reported 429 anti-Muslim threats and attacks in 2015, and the CNCDH attributes the increase from earlier years to a response to the 2015 terror attacks on *Charlie Hebdo*, namely extremism that leads to exclusion of and discrimination toward French Muslims (Glasser, 2016).

As context, many assaults documented by police concerned racism/ xenophobia, anti-Semitism, bias against Christians and members of other religions, and bias against sexual orientation and gender identity. Given that hate crimes tend to be underreported (see Pezzella et al., 2019), the actual numbers may be much higher. While data collection leaves much room for improvement (especially in terms of accounting for overlaps and distinctions between "racist attacks" and attacks on Jews and Muslims, and tracking types of incidents) and while data sources can and do differ in terms of the exact numbers of reported incidents, the data clearly show how Muslims experience many types of instances of bias, often on a daily basis.

An historical perspective is needed to understand the current state of affairs. From World War II onward, France has grappled with both its world position and self-identity. It struggled with diplomatic relations among its current and former colonies, most notably Algeria. To help readers understand this historical progression, this chapter reviews this context using presidential administrations as signposts.

De Gaulle: "Mon Général" and Father of France

Charles de Gaulle was elected as the head of the provisional government following the Liberation of France in November 1945. De Gaulle resigned in January 1946 after a series of frustrations including being considered a figurehead without real power and disputes among the political parties (Thody, 1998). The Fourth Republic (1946–1958) was marked by foreign conflicts as the French attempted to maintain colonies in Indochina and Algeria. These external tensions were compounded by internal political struggles between the French Communist Party and the Socialist Party. Vincent Auriol was elected as President in January 1947. Auriol espoused socialist beliefs and was described by Anatole de Monzie, a former minister, as "*un fanatique de la tolerance* [a fanatic of tolerance]" (Thody, 1998). Then, President Rene Coty served as the final leader of the French Fourth Republic until it collapsed in 1958.

Gopnik writes that de Gaulle "had three rendezvous with history, in the old-fashioned sense he loved [...] on all three occasions, he saved the French state by sheer theatricality and élan" (Gopnik, 2018). Charles de Gaulle returned as President in 1958 with the creation of the French Fifth Republic. This marked the beginning of de Gaulle's quest to strengthen France economically and contend with global superpowers, including the United States and

Great Britain (Moravcsik, 2012). Notably, de Gaulle's presidency was marked by the Algerian War (1954–1962), which resulted in Algeria's independence from France. The war unofficially commenced in 1945 with an independence protest in Sétif, Algeria, that turned deadly when protesters murdered more than 100 *pieds-noirs* (i.e., "black feet," or European residents). The French military responded by killing between 1,000 and 45,000 Algerians at the protest, depending upon the estimate (Hitchens, 2006). With continued tension between the Algerians and the French government, de Gaulle visited Algeria in 1958 and asserted that "self-determination" is necessary for Algeria's future. After armed conflicts and thousands of casualties among Algerians and French troops, Algerian citizens affirmatively voted for independence in 1962 (Hitchens, 2006). Many of the *pieds-noirs* returned or came to France following the vote, whose absorption into France likely contributed to France's economic prosperity in the 1960s (Thody, 1998).

However, the early 1960s also saw a significant number of migrants from former French colonies like Mali, Senegal, and Mauritania move to France in search of employment opportunities. The French government adopted strategies of extreme surveillance and monitoring of these migrants, which contributed to their intelligence for colonial policy formation. The goals of these surveillance operations were focused on controlling these populations based on French anxieties around the racial and ethnic identities of the migrants. While French leaders publicly praised the benefits of labor migration, the Ministry of Interior monitored African migrants because of the French government's view of migrants as "less likely to fit into French society and problematic for the social and political order" (Glaes, 2010).

The 20 years following World War II were characterized by rebuilding the country and France reclaiming its national identity (Scheinman, 1969). Post-war nationalism served to help unify and rebuild France as a nation-state. Gaullists espoused a strong nationalist ideology in foreign affairs. However, post-war nationalism included right- and left-wing varieties. Whereas this era's nationalism of the left is characterized by proselytizing a French identity, the nationalism of the right focused on "the enemy within" (Scheinman, 1969).

Pompidou: The Heir Apparent

De Gaulle lost a referendum in April 1969, and as Thody writes, "[De Gaulle] could not, in April 1969, tell the French that it was a choice between him and chaos" as de Gaulle had previously served as a unifying and centering figure during the previous two decades (1998, p. 34). Georges Pompidou had a close relationship with de Gaulle with Pompidou serving as the treasurer of de Gaulle's philanthropic foundation for children with Down's Syndrome. Pompidou served as a principal negotiator with the initial negotiations with the Algerian *Front de Libération Nationale* in 1961 and was appointed as the

Prime Minister under de Gaulle in 1962. His close relationship with de Gaulle and instrumental position during important events like the Algerian Crisis lead to Pompidou's victory in the presidential elections in 1969. As a moderate President, Pompidou is credited with ensuring the survival of the French Fifth Republic; he served until his death in 1974 (Thody, 1998).

Giscard d'Estaing and Mitterrand: Looking for Middle Ground

Valery Giscard d'Estaing's presidency (1974–1980) was characterized by *le moins d'état* ("the least state," or small but better government). This "smaller government" movement mirrored others in England and the United States, all of which sought to scale back government in the name of efficiency. Giscard d'Estaing's conservative administration differed from de Gaulle and Pompidou, and attracted attention from the right-wing populist party, *Le Front National* (The National Front), founded by Jean-Marie Le Pen.

Le Pen's *Front National* gained momentum during the following presidential administration of Francois Mitterrand when the party won seats in the *Assemblée nationale* ("National Assembly," or the lower house of France's legislature). This shift is notable given description of *Front National* being "overtly racist" and supporting policies that require individuals to prove that they are "ethnically French" (Thody, 1998, p. 143). Despite the party's momentum during the Mitterrand administration (1981–1995), Mitterrand as a President responded and changed the political landscape of France to the left when he formed a coalition with the French Communist Party. The focus of his efforts was to unite the Socialist and Communist Parties to address the right-wing coalitions of Le Pen's National Front Party.

Chirac: "La Girouette" (The Weathervane)

Throughout the periods above, currents of Islamophobia began to take shape, especially by raising the issue of Muslims' place in France to a national question and character it previously had not had (Alouane, 2019). By the end of the 20th century and beginning of the 21st century, it became increasingly evident that many French questioned whether Islam is incompatible with French society and values. The issue, to many, often comes down to a question of integration, namely whether someone, especially from a traditionally non-French background, is "French enough." This situation is acute for immigrants: To be considered a citizen, they must give evidence of being integrated (Megherbi, 2018).

It was during the presidency of Jacques Chirac that issues of Islamophobia as a nervous area of government rapidly developed. Chirac's political career included positions in the government starting in the early 1970s as the Minister of Agriculture, Interior Minister, Prime Minister, Mayor of Paris; and, finally, as President (1995–2007).

Chirac struggled throughout his administration to embrace France's Muslim population. Upon his election, he sought to "reinforce secular Islam at the expense of fundamentalism" and "promote reform in Algeria without openly undercutting the government" (Laird, 1996, p. 236). Chirac spearheaded initiatives to reinforce immigrants' assimilation, which aligned with the classical French model of the citizen as French in character, dress, custom, and especially language (Megherbi, 2018). As discussed later, in 2003, the then-Interior Minister Nicolas Sarkozy helped create a national, elected *Conseil* ("Council") to represent the estimated 5 million French Muslims, half of whom were citizens. One catalyst for creating such a body was increasing anti-Muslim sentiments in France following the terror attacks on September 11, 2001, in the United States. Critics of the *Conseil* felt that its structure being under the tutelage of the French government merely repackaged colonialism for the 21st century (Sciolino, 2003).

In 2003, Chirac supported a proposal that would have banned the Islamic headscarf or hijab from public schools for the sake of French secularism. Chirac defended the proposal by including the Jewish kippa and displays of the cross as also being banned in public schools ("Chirac backs hijab ban," 2003).

Further, prior to his election, Chirac expressed anti-immigration sentiments, noting: "If there were fewer immigrants, there would be less unemployment, fewer tensions in certain towns and neighborhoods, a lower social cost" (Chirac, 1985, p. 165). When pressed to the validity of his claims about unemployment, Chirac stated,

> This means that we must not accept any new immigration and that we must severely curb illegal immigrants, rigorously apply the laws of the Republic, systematically expel those whose status is irregular and doubtless promote a policy of encouraging return migration.
>
> *(Chirac, 1985, p. 165)*

Sarkozy: Greater (But Still Limited) Dialogue

It was in this context that Nicolas Sarkozy, first Interior Minister (2002–2004 and 2005–2007) under Chirac and later President (2007–2012), sought to improve the French government's relationships with Muslims. As part of his duties as Interior Minister, Sarkozy was also the Minister of Public Worship, a Napoleonic era position meant to oversee relations between the state and religions. Part of Sarkozy's portfolio was enforcing the "Loi du 9 décembre 1905 concernant la séparation des Eglises et de l'Etat" (Law of December 9, 1905, Concerning the Separation of Church and State), which mandates free exercise of religion and state neutrality and that limits how taxes can be used for and allocated toward religious institutions.

Sarkozy saw some of the provisions of this law as impediments toward better reaching out to (and integrating) Muslims. Relatedly, he opined that loosening the law's strictures could make French mosques less reliant on outside money, which Sarkozy argued made radicalization of Muslims in France easier. Sarkozy was never successful in amending this law. However, he expressed his vision in *La République, Les religions, l'espérance* (The Republic, Religions, and Hope). He argued the young should not be raised solely with secular values, despite that France (especially since the Revolution) had historically endeavored to be constitutionally secular (Sarkozy, Collin, & Verdin, 2004). He also asserted that the government should reduce separations between religions and the state, and argued that government subsidies for mosques could encourage greater Muslim integration into French society (Sarkozy et al., 2004).

These broad visions were embodied in Sarkozy helping to create nonprofit organizations that facilitated dialogues between French Muslims and the government. As noted earlier, in 2003, he helped create the "French Council of the Muslim Faith" (*Conseil Français du Culte Musulman*) (Etchegoin, 2006; Boubakeur, 1995). Modeled on other religious French outreach institutions that fostered outreach with, for instance, French Protestants and French Jews, these organizations' goals, as expressed by Sarkozy, were "to fight against the danger of an Islam of cellars and garages" ("Pour lutter contre le danger d'un Islam des caves et garages") (Zeghal, 2005, p. 98; see also Etchegoin, 2006). More simply, the goals of these organizations were to foster dialogue, encourage integration, and combat extremism.

Organizations like the *Conseil* have had no special legal status but, rather, are associations with the explicit approval of the state in fostering integration. The *Conseil* is a national, elected body consisted of 25 regional councils (*Conseil Regional du Culte Musulman*). This body resides in a complex landscape of similar Muslim organizations—such as *Union des organisations islamiques en France* (1983–1989), later *Union des organisations islamiques de France* (1989–2017), and now *Musulmans de France* (2017–present), among many others—that act (contentious) as umbrellas to promote integration and the creation of an Islam allegedly compatible with the French context (Boubakeur, 1995; Etchegoin, 2006; Moussaoui, 2020; Zeghal, 2005). For instance, the National Gathering of French Muslims (*Le Rassemblement des musulmans de France*), which is complementary to yet independent from the *Conseil*, seeks to "contribute to the emergency of a moderate Islam, tolerant and respectful of the laws of the Republic, an Islam of the golden mean" ("Contribuer à faire émerger un islam modéré, tolérant et respectueux des lois de la République, un islam du juste milieu") ("Un nouveau mouvement musulman français," 2006).

While these associations have varied and at times conflicting goals, they all share missions in common to combat Islamophobia. Still, Sarkozy's record on improving relations with Muslims was mixed. While spearheading the creation of structures to help French Muslims interact with the government, which in principle embodied significant changes in outreach, he was also criticized for noting that veils were oppressive to women and not welcome in France

(BBCNews, 2019). Further, critics charged that such organizations are simply attempts by the state to co-opt Islam. Thus, Sarkozy's goal of creating a representative council of French Muslims failed to gain support of the majority of French Muslims.

Hollande: Terrorism Strikes France

The presidency of Francois Hollande saw greater skepticism of Sarkozy's tactics of reaching out to French Muslims. Hollande led France during several terrorist attacks, which shaped policies toward Muslims, fueled concerns about radicalization of Muslims, and reignited debates over integration (Kepel, 2017). For instance, attacks in 2014—such as the Joue-les-Tours knife attack, 11 pedestrians being run over in Dijon, and a vehicular attack at a Nantes Christmas market—prefaced more widely known attacks like those on *Charlie Hebdo*, the attacks of November 13, 2015, and the Nice terrorist incident, all of which significantly harmed Muslims' place in French society (Kepel, 2017).

The *Charlie Hebdo* attacks occurred between January 7–9, 2015, and 17 were killed. The target was the headquarters of the satirical newspaper *Charlie Hebdo*. The gunmen—Cherif and Said Kouachi who the press described as "perfect targets for recruiters of jihad" in that they were "orphan French brothers from an immigrant family, virtually along in the French capital with almost no resources"—said that the newspaper had published cartoons mocking Islam, particularly Prophet Muhammad (Bronstein, 2015). The gunmen shot and killed persons working at *Charlie Hebdo*, and on January 9, took hostages at a Jewish grocery store in Dammartin-en-Goele. Four persons, all Jews, were killed in this portion of the attacks. In the national press, a Muslim shop owner earned praise by hiding people from the gunmen. Police later shot and killed the attackers. In response to these attacks, on January 14, the cover of *Charlie Hebdo* featured the Prophet Muhammad holding a sign with "Je Suis Charlie" ("I am Charlie") and "Tout est Pardonné" (i.e., "All is Forgiven"). This image as well as the related hashtag *#jesuischarlie* became popular on social media, although many opined that the earlier and January 14 images merely insulted Muslims, many of whom expressed condemnation of the attacks (Roy, 2015).

These attacks were followed by more deadly attacks on November 13, 2015, a series of inter-related incidents in Paris and Saint-Denis (a northern suburb of Paris) ("Paris attacks," 2015). Perpetrators detonated a suicide bomb at the *Stade de France* (France's national stadium) plus committed mass shootings at an Eagles of Death Metal concert in Paris's Bataclan Theater. The attack killed 130 people. The Islamic Republic of Iraq and Syria (ISIS) claimed responsibility. Muslim organizations strongly condemned attacks, arguing that such attacks were contrary to the spirit of Islam. Still, the country did not see the same call for solidarity with Muslims as had been evident after earlier attacks ("Paris attacks," 2015).

These attacks were followed by the July 14, 2016, attack in Nice. Occurring during a celebration of Bastille Day, Mohamed Lahouaiej-Bouhlel (a Tunisian immigrant) drove a truck through a crowd gathering on the *Promenade des Anglais*. After 86 people were killed, Lahouaiej-Bouhlel was killed in a shoot-out with police (Rubin & Breeden, 2017).

To Hollande and many others, these events were attacks on France's soul, and the French government responded in numerous ways (Hume & Said-Moorhouse, 2016; Schofield, 2016). These included declaring a state of emergency, the central features of which included temporarily closing borders, posting police and military to sensitive public spots, shutting down selected metro stations, temporarily closing some state schools and universities, banning public demonstrations and closing mosques with allegedly extremist ties (Kaplan, 2015), and significantly expanding police powers to search without warrant and engage in house arrests (Schwarzenbach, 2018; Serhan, 2016). Still, Hollande reaffirmed an earlier arrangement to let in 30,000 Syrian refugees over the next two years. Simultaneously, Interior Minister Bernard Cazeneuve spearheaded closing what were described as 20 radicalized mosques and preachers the state claimed incited violence (Schwarzenbach, 2018).

France's political climate turned decidedly anti-Muslim. For instance, Marine Le Pen, the head of *Le Front National*, opined in December 2015, during the start of the upcoming presidential election campaign, that she wanted much more punitive security, that the attacks were due to an influx of immigrants, and that Islam was incompatible with French society. At the same time, Francois Fillon, Sarkozy's Prime Minister as well as one time presidential candidate, published *Vaincre le totalitarisme islamique (Defeating Islamic Totalitarianism)* (Fillon, 2016). Fillon argued for more pervasive surveillance of Muslim communities and that the recent attacks represented an attack of French identity. Perhaps not surprisingly, anti-Muslim and racist rhetoric increased in this period, including charges in the press that Islam and French values are incompatible. French Muslims also experienced a rise in hate crimes (El Karoui, 2016).

Hollande named Islamic terrorism as a threat to the French state. The internal security measures came in tandem with the launching of *Operation Chammal*, the French military campaign against ISIS. Many persons, especially Muslims of North African descent, were identified as radicals and threats to state security and were arrested or placed under house arrest. More mosque closures followed, and Hollande expressed concern about whether some schools connected to mosques glorified the terrorists (Schwarzenbach, 2018).

A Promising Government Initiative: Promoting Awareness and Collaboration

Many used the terrorist incidents of 2015 and 2016 to question if France's Muslims were sufficiently assimilated, despite that most French Muslims were against the attacks. An incident that became a symbol of the assimilation debate was an April 2018 occurrence in which an Algerian Muslim woman refused to shake hands with a French immigration official. She was denied citizenship because, to officials, not shaking hands suggested she was not integrated and did not respect French values (Conseil d'État, 2018). Further, issues of integration compound and overlap with Muslims facing employment discrimination (Adida, Laitin, & Valfort, 2017) and over-representation in the criminal justice system (Moore, 2008).

Still, the news has not been entirely negative, and as showcased below, the French government has initiated several interrelated campaigns to address prejudice. These include government information pages, social media campaigns, and an anti-racism and anti-Semitism campaign for 2018–2020. As also argued below, it is intersectoral dialogue between the government and Muslim community organizations that showcase the most potential to address Islamophobia. Such dialogues have promoted awareness and collaboration in ways not previously seen in relations between French Muslims and the state.

Macron's Promise: Greater Attention to Islamophobia

Despite Muslims facing extensive prejudice, some research suggests that many non-Muslim French hold favorable views of Muslims. A Pew Research Center survey conducted during the height of terrorist attacks in France found that 72% of the French held favorable views of Muslims (Sahgal & Webster, 2015). Further, the 2018 World Cup provided opportunities for the French to reflect on the positives of diversity and inclusion. The French national team ("*Les Bleus*") won, prompting many on social media to highlight how several of the players are Muslims (Hamdani, 2018). A popular Tweet by the American author Khaled Beydoun, when congratulating France on winning the World Cup, noted: "80% of your team is African, cut out the racism and xenophobia. 50% of your team are Muslims, cut out the Islamophobia. Africans and Muslims delivered you a second World Cup, now deliver them justice" (Hamdani, 2018).

Still, between the Pew survey conducted above and the elation of France's 2018 World Cup victory thanks to its largely African and majority Muslim team, issues of Islamophobia again expressed themselves in the 2017 presidential election. By 2016, it had become obvious to many that Hollande would not be re-elected, so he opted not to run. The 2017 presidential election became in many ways a referendum on Hollande's policies and evidenced a desire among many French for change. Further, it was also a referendum, at least in part, on the place of France's Muslims. For instance, the 2017 election was held under the state of emergency still in effect after the November, 2015, Paris attacks. It also saw Emmanuel Macron, running under a new reformist party label *En Marche!*, effectively competing for the presidency against Marine Le Pen, running for *Le Front National* and whose campaign often featured decidedly anti-immigrant rhetoric. Macron won in the second round with 66.1% of the vote.

Macron campaigned on reformist agenda, and his platform included proposals meant to promote Muslim outreach. For one, unlike Le Pen, Macron noted that migration crises were not as acute in 2017 as they had been in 2015. For another, he expressed desires to spearhead greater dialogue between French Muslims and the government. Yet, Macron's record on and statements about Muslim outreach is mixed. While supporting greater dialogue, he called for the removal of verses from the *Quran* that allegedly incite violence against Jews, Christians, and nonbelievers, and his comments caused significant consternation in Muslim communities who see the *Quran* as the literal and unalterable word of God ("Manifeste 'Contre le Nouvel Antisémitisme,'" 2018).

While advocating outreach, Macron simultaneously argued for stricter anti-terrorism laws, one of which was easily passed in the French parliament. This law makes permanent aspects of the 2015 state of emergency declaration, including expanded police powers to establish security zones in vulnerable areas, engage in expanded stop-and-search operations of pedestrians and motorists (which critics charge would simply lead to harassment of Muslims in particular), expand house arrest powers, allow easier access to search homes of people suspected of terrorist links, dismiss suspected radicalized public servants, approve intelligence agencies to magnify wiretapping phones and emails, close religious centers promoting radicalism, enhance intelligence gathering in prisons, as well as establish programs to help youth in predominantly immigrant (and, thus, largely impoverished) areas from being tempted to join extremist groups. The apparent need for such laws was in part influenced by the concerns among some of a "parallel society" of French Muslims, or the fear of some Muslims who being insufficiently integrated into French society and who could increasingly be under the sway of extremist ideologies (Byrne, 2017; Gattengno, 2018; "Macron Urges French Police," 2017).

Contextualizing the situation was the assertion among many Muslims that previous governments merely interfered with religious matters without consulting Muslims themselves (Randall, 2018), raising legitimacy crises in attempts at Muslim outreach like Sarkozy's *Conseil* (Piser, 2018). Macron couched promises as the need to explore what French secularism (*laïcité*) means in the 21st century, arguing that France's government is secular but that its society is not and that if taken too far, there is a "risk of a 'radicalization of secularism'" ("[un] risque d'une 'radicalisation de la laïcité'") (Bloch, 2018). As described by one commentator, Macron's objective has been "to place the Muslim faith in a peaceful relationship with the state and other religions – and thus to associate it fully with the fight against fundamentalism" ("inscrire le culte musulman dans une relation apaisée avec l'Etat et les autres religions - et, partant, l'associer pleinement à la lutte contre le fondamentalisme") (Gattengno, 2018).

Islam de France and Intersectoral Dialogues

Macron resurrected the idea of restructuring Islam in France to ideally ameliorate internal division in the country and to create an *Islam de France* (Islam of France) (Bloch, 2018). Early into his presidency, Macron noted he wanted to curb foreign influence, create a national organization to replace Sarkozy's *Conseil*, possibly help create a "Grand Imamate" of France, and implement a plan to counter Islamist radicalization in part by increasing security but also providing greater economic and educational opportunities for youth living in deprived areas (Randall, 2018).

These plans came on top of government campaigns, especially in terms of e-outreach, that sought to raise public awareness of inequities. These included *#lescompetencesdabord* campaign ("Competencies First") ("#LesCompétencesDabord," 2016), a popular hashtag, social media campaign, and public awareness project featured on public transportation billboards that showcased differential outcomes in employment opportunities for persons based upon name and national origin. Other campaigns included public information pages supporting visions of Muslim outreach ("Islam de France," 2018), and government statements issued jointly with Muslim organizations supporting secularism, living together in a spirit of non-discrimination, and combatting attempts to highjack Islam to make it intolerant ("Communiqué de l'Observatoire de la laïcité," 2014).

Further, in 2018, the French government launched a broad anti-racism and anti-Semitism campaign. This campaign came on the heels of a similar 2015 plan promoted by former Prime Minister Manuel Valls that had only half of its proposals put into action (Cross, 2018). Among the 2018 plans many initiatives include proposing European legislation to limit hate speech on the internet, amending national legislation to target hate speech, creating a national rapid response team to fight racism, promoting education against racism, launching programs to help victims and ensure effective punishment for offenders, improving public sector training on these topics, among others (Premier Ministre, 2018). However, the plan specifically mentions anti-Muslim acts only once (p. 11).

Something that may not be, at first, an obvious candidate for a promising strategy concerns growing dialogic collaborations between the government and so-called moderate voices in the Muslim community. In particular, the Macron administration has engaged in collaborative geneses with the liberal think tank, *Institut Montaigne*, which has published several reports on the possibilities and needs for an *Islam de France* both before and concurrent with Macron's administration. This collaboration has ultimately provided much of the intellectual fuel to combat Islamophobia in France. Three reports, all authored by Hakim El Karoui, a senior fellow of the *Institut* and a former public servant, are particularly important in shaping dialogue.

The first report, revealingly titled *A French Islam Is Possible* (*Un islam français est possible*), is based on results of a survey of over 1,000 Muslims in France (a process the author admitted was rooted in the reality that sociological and demographic data on French Muslims were unreliable and incomplete). The report warns how hostility toward Muslims in France threatens national unity and how radical Muslims have disproportionately dominated integration discourses. Most importantly, the report finds that French Muslims largely fall into three groups. The first is "the silent majority," making up 46% of respondents who believe that their beliefs are compatible with living in French society. The second are "the conservatives," making up 25% and who El Karoui argues fuel political and ideological struggles regarding Muslim identity in France. The final group is "the authoritarians," who make up 28% and are primarily young, low-skill, largely unemployed youth and who see Islam as a way to rebel against French society. These findings have led to several recommendations being co-developed with the French government, especially creating a new Muslim Association for Islam in France (*l'Association musulmane pour un islam français*, or AMIF), the royalties of which would be from the sale of *halal* products (i.e., those meeting Muslim dietary requirements), the election of a Grand Imam of France to guide the intellectual and theological basis of an Islam of France, giving local governments the tools to support recognizing Islam better, and a proposal to create a new government position, a Secretariat of Religious and Secular Affairs, who would report to the Prime Minister and who would be directly responsible for better informing the government of issues faced by the Muslim community, including Islamophobia (El Karoui, 2016).

The second report, *A New Strategy for France in a New Arab World* (*Nouveau monde arabe, nouvelle "politique arabe" pour la France*), added to the previous report by examining France's foreign policy with Arab countries (El Karoui, 2017). The analysis centers on better understanding patterns in French foreign relations, and suggestions largely pertain to the need for the French government to improve its narrative with Arab countries through emphasizing greater cooperation on common interests but, perhaps most importantly, acting as a force to counter Islamist influences (El Karoui, 2017).

The third, and perhaps the most widely known, report is *The Islamist Factory* (*La fabrique de l'islamisme*) that detailed, on the one hand, the supposed need to limit foreign influence, especially financial, of Arab countries like Saudi Arabia on French Muslims, and, on the other hand, to reform French Muslim institutions to bring them under the umbrella of the French state (Young, 2018). El Karoui, again authoring the report, noted how young Muslims seemingly increasingly fell under the sway of social media, including disproportionately from influential and Islamist Saudi clerics (El Karoui, 2018).

Assessment and Evidence of Progress

Many in France see Islamophobia as something that can no longer be ignored (Riemer, 2019), and tactics to address Islamophobia are needed more than ever as hate crimes against Muslims occur regularly and with great visibility (Chrisafis, 2019). Yet, as noted by Cross (2019), it can often be difficult to judge the efficacy of France's anti-prejudice initiatives. For instance, while the numbers of racist incidents have fallen in past years, assaults, especially on Jews and Muslims, have risen. And French government anti-racism plans may barely distinctly touch on Islamophobia. Thus, a purely quantitative examination of the efficacy of outreach can be unrevealing. However, as shown in Table 11.1, qualitatively, practices show promise.

In such an environment, almost any dialogue promoting tolerance is a positive. Given that the specific campaigns above may not specifically address Islamophobia or insufficiently parse racism and Islamophobia (although they clearly overlap), often, the only consistent discussion of Islamophobia occurs most meaningfully in intersectoral dialogue and collaboration.

The history of relations between the state and French Muslims helps showcase the promise of dialogues. Prior to the 1990s, the management of Islam was often not a public issue in that the organization of Islam was largely centered around local mosques. From Chirac onward, French governments simultaneously adopted incompatible approaches. On the one hand, officials sought to create national umbrella organizations to facilitate dialogue between Muslims and the French state, yet those same officials often placed greater emphasis

TABLE 11.1 Types of French Government Practices Targeting Prejudice

Practice	Specifics and Intended Effects
Government information pages	• Raising awareness of anti-Muslim bias • Reinforcing secularism but also Muslim community outreach
Social media campaigns	• Showcasing employment discrimination based on race and gender • Encouraging awareness of bias and workplace techniques to combat it
Anti-Racism Plan (2018–2020)	• Proposing laws, education, trainings, and more to combat racism and anti-Semitism in particular • Advancing more action taken against particularly online hate speech
Intersectoral Dialogues	• Showing most Muslims as "moderate" majority • Creating a national umbrella organization for Muslims • Keeping Islamophobia as a named issue • Changing dialogue around anti-Muslim bias

on security crackdowns, removing foreign influences (especially financial) and legislating certain cultural styles of dress as incompatible with French society. Even several high-ranking government figures, such as Fillon and Valls, referred to Islam a problem for France. These dynamics mean that many French Muslims feel disaffected, vulnerable, and persecuted (Alouane, 2019; Yasar, 2019). While to many Macron's *Islam de France* is just another attempt to control Muslims, the dialogues undergirding this plan show potential in that such dialogues have allowed the government to be better aware that French Muslims must be financially independent of other powers, that they are not homogeneous, and that there is enormous benefit in working with them in a spirit of collaboration (Alouane, 2019; El Karoui, 2016, 2017, 2018).

Such dialogues and outreach have helped lead to changes in French government rhetoric in recent years, including several government officials' recognition of and use of government resources to promote the message that French Islamists appear to be a minority among French Muslims yet that this minority dominates images of and discourses about Islam in France and that members of government need to resist far-right attempts to highjack conversations about inclusion (France24, 2019). Macron's collaboration with El Karoui, for instance, has shaped the former's language by providing further knowledge of how social networks have offered platforms for Islamist figures to influence French Muslim youth and that these figures cast news stories and societal issues affecting French Muslims as ideological struggles. Further, dialogues have encouraged the French government to promote messages that the so-called silent Muslim majority must disseminate counter-narratives to Islamist figures. Additionally, government-led collaborations with Muslim community organizations have facilitated discussions of how the French state should consider reinventing its discussion of republican and secular values so that it can still promote itself as open and value driven but also not strictly bound by a rigid conception of secularism (Kilickaya, 2019; Randall, 2019; see also BBCNews, 2019).

A major step in the potential for further collaborations occurred in early 2019 when El Karoui founded the Muslim Association for Islam in France (*l'Association musulmane pour un islam français*, or AMIF) (Rhouma, 2019). The Sarkozy-supported *Conseil* had been facing numerous crises, especially regarding legitimacy, so AMIF's founding showcased the potential for it to be a trusted third party for Muslims and their interactions with the French state ("L'essayiste Hakim El Karoui," 2019). The dialogues influencing AMIF's creation placed Macron in a position to succeed where others had failed. Whereas Sarkozy's *Conseil* largely failed due to internal divisions within the Muslim community and concerns that it merely co-opted Islam to the French state, El Karoui argued that an organization with a broad, representative base could help limit the influence of foreign countries funding mosque construction and even raise capital through being a way to ensure that food products in Muslim stores are *halal* ("L'essayiste Hakim El Karoui," 2019).

The positives of government outreach in consulting Muslims when the government was to take action were on display in an early 2019 meeting between Macron and officials of the French Council of Muslim Worship (FCMW). The meeting was to ensure that proposed changes to the 1905 secularism law that would allow for greater government action in framing and organizing Islam would not be "against Islam." In making these assurances, Macron noted that the intentions were manifold, including "to prevent and punish jihadist speeches" ("prévenir et sanctionner les discours djihadistes"), "ensure transparency of religious funding" ("assurer la transparence sur les financements du culte"), and "empower and strengthen mosque management associations" ("responsabiliser et conforter les associations gestionnaires de mosques"), all of which are meant to "stop stigmatizing Muslims" (…arrêter de stigmatiser les musulmans). While critics charged that Macron and other officials had intentionally dismissed some officials, those present, such as FCMW President Ahmet Ogras, were encouraged (Sautreuil, 2019).

Such outreach has helped shape the recognition among many in government that government bodies should prioritize better planning for future security needs, engage in neighborhood-level outreach, encourage moderate Muslims to help change the narrative on Islam, and even reach out to Maghreb and Gulf states in matters of religious cooperation to identify common interests in religious domains (Riemer, 2019; see also El Karoui, 2018). As Macron noted, it is incumbent upon the current generation to understand principles of the separation of church and state through "pacifying the relationship with Islam" yet in ways that "[do not weaken] the 1905 law and without compromising [French values]" ("pacifier la relation avec l'islam", sans "affaiblir la loi de 1905 et sans transiger") ("Loi de 1905," 2019). Still, while Macron has not always been responsive and demonstrates quite a mixed record on combatting Islamophobia, dialogue means that Islamophobia remains on government's radar.

Despite AMIF's official founding, the government is limited in its powers to engage Muslim communities in more expansive ways due to the strictures of the 1905 law. There is widespread recognition that the government must act more ardently to combat Islamophobia by backing moderate strains of Islam, addressing foreign financing, improving youths' economic and education opportunities, offering Arabic lessons in school, and engaging in related tactics (El Karoui, 2018). Historically, the French government has been strongly reliant on Muslim community organizations to develop solutions, yet such initiatives depend upon having the support of the majority of Muslims, many of whom do, in principle, support some type of national organization that can lead, represent, and advocate for Muslims (Marsi, 2019).

Further, dialogues face issues by having detractors on all sides. On the one side are often powerful French elites arguing that even admitting that Islamophobia is an issue is problematic. As but one example, the French philosopher Pascal Bruckner charged that Islamophobia is tantamount to "imaginary racism," political extremism, and silencing criticism of religion (Bruckner, 2018). On the other side, while many Muslims support some national organization to advocate on their behalf, they often view government-led attempts as illegitimate and unrepresentative of their interests (Burgat, 2018; "Control Muslims in France," 2019). Again, most promise lies not yet in specific programs but, rather, in dialogue leading to smaller gains.

However, societal tensions in 2019 have stalled Macron's plans to help support initiatives like El Karoui's (Randall, 2019), particularly the crisis caused by the *Mouvement des gilets jaunes* ("Yellow Vests Movement"). Participants in this movement charge that the working and middle classes disproportionately face economic injustices, such as high fuel prices, costs of living, and inequitable tax reforms. The protests have resulted in significant disruptions, including deaths and widespread arrests and detentions (Ozcan, 2019). The movement is overwhelmingly White with many supporters appearing to espouse racist ideologies, including both Islamophobia and anti-Semitism (Kantor, 2019). Thus, as of the time of this writing, Macron has remained largely silent on El Karoui's plans. However, AMIF has started financing training imams, yet it is not uncommon to see claims that AMIF members are merely radicals in disguise (Randall, 2019). In the absence of explicit French government support, those like El Karoui have looked to the United Arab Emirates, which El Karoui argues has not exported extremism, to counter so-called Saudi influences (Kilickaya, 2019). Macron has not been entirely silent on Islamophobia, however, and in the light of a wave of anti-Muslim prejudice in late 2019, he has stressed how Muslims should not be stigmatized and that it was improper to link fights against terrorism with the Islamic religion (BBCNews, 2019). He has urged members of his own political party not to let far-right groups dominate conversations about these topics (France24, 2019).

Thus, in the issue of Islamophobia in France, one step forward is often met with two steps backward. The promises of government programs combatting prejudice often remain unfulfilled (Cross, 2018). Given this low bar, any step away from seeing Muslims merely as threats is a positive. Government-led discussions on the need to resist stereotypes in tandem with the government both being made aware of the issues France's Muslims face through intersectoral dialogue and in promoting awareness of Islamophobia, however limited, are the most promising strategies proposed to date.

Gooden's (2014) *naming, blaming, claiming* framework can help put these dynamics in better context. She argued that achieving social equity should proceed through three stages. In the first, *naming*, a government agency identifies a specific practice, policy, or action that is unjust, especially racially. Second, after *naming*, a government agency should identify what as well as who is responsible for the social injustice. Third, or *claiming*, an agency must replace an inequitable practice, policy, or action with those that are equitable (Gooden, 2014).

When using Gooden's framework, it is clear that the French government has made progress in *naming* Islamophobia as a problem, but it has room for improvement. For one, the government acknowledges that racism, anti-Semitism, and Islamophobia are issues. However, in official government plans, the focus on race and anti-Semitism, while entirely appropriate, infrequently specifically mentions Muslims (see Premier Ministre, 2018), thus running the risk that anti-Muslim bias is named albeit not to the extent required to fully address bias.

From Sarkozy onward, it has been more common to see government officials discussing Islamophobia and *naming* it as a societal ill. More problematically, however, is that the French government has sought to name the issue of Islamophobia on its own terms. For instance, as seen above, while, on the one hand, often arguing that policies toward Muslims need to be improved, government officials have, on the other hand, often cast Islamophobia as an issue of integration. The issue, these officials opine, is not with Muslim identity, *per se*, but rather that Muslims are given the burden of proving they are integrated. Further, the government has often acknowledged that French Muslim youths are vulnerable to the influences of radicalization given their relatively poorer economic situations and dearth of educational opportunities. By naming educational inequities and employment discrimination as societal problems, the French government has made significant advancements in acknowledging diversity in ways that it historically has not done. Further, the French government has historically responded to charges that it must better treat its Muslim population by referencing the constitutional value of *laïcité*, the 1905 secularism law, and the need for greater Muslim integration. However, while French political figures like Sarkozy and Macron have called for somewhat more malleable interpretations of these principles, overwhelmingly French Muslims find themselves in a situation in which other religions, including other minority religions like Judaism, find themselves in somewhat better positions with respect to support of, interactions with, and acknowledgment by the state (although, as a reminder, anti-Semitic violence is quite high in France). Thus, when issues of Muslims' positions in France are discussed, the government, while admitting some inequities, often shifts the issue to foreign capital supporting French mosques rather than by identifying and understanding inequities perpetrated by the French government itself, especially segregation, outright racism, and attempts to make one national, unified French identity. Further, issues of race and religion are often insufficiently parsed (Premier Ministre, 2018), thus giving an incomplete picture of how intersectional violence against Muslims and against non-Whites can be.

The situation is even more complex when accounting for how the French government stacks up in terms of *blaming* and *claiming*. Very often, French officials blame not their own actions but Muslims for allegedly not better integrating and relying too much on foreign powers. By placing the definition of social inequity as a burden of the Muslim populations and outside influences, the French government has never fully *blamed* and *claimed* its own roles. Consequently, the "solutions" developed by the French government are literally Napoleonic, namely by, on paper, treating Islam as another religion and represented in part under the aegis of the state, to make it compatible with French values and to make it an Islam of France.

Further, while it can be debated whether an *Islam de France* is actually an attempt by the government to co-opt Muslim identity, the basic principle of basic outreach, especially intersectoral collaboration with organizations like the *Institut Montaigne* and AMIF, shows evidence of progress. The French government, as seen above, has historically treated Muslim populations as homogeneous when, in reality, they are anything but. Previous government attempts to create umbrella organizations, such as Sarkozy's *Conseil*, faced legitimacy and representativeness crises. Organizations like AMIF, themselves supported by more liberal think tanks and that seek to play to the so-called "hidden majority" of France's Muslims, have showcased how with receptive politicians, the French government can change its understanding of Islamophobia and change the discourse. By the French government, and Macron in particular, receiving and even adopting the recommendations of reports calling for better relations with France's Muslim population (see El Karoui, 2016), it is making significant strides. Such collaborations also come in tandem with evermore government officials calling out anti-Muslim bias when it occurs (see Chrisafis, 2019).

While more remains to be seen whether AMIF can deliver on the promises of its founder, it is clear that the type of outreach and intersectoral collaboration evidenced thus far are steps in the right direction, but in order to improve, the French government must more fully *name* the problem and *blame* its role in perpetrating social inequities. These include, for instance, not only identifying supposed issues of Muslims' failure to integrate and the influence of foreign capital but also admitting roles played by extensive racism in the economic and education situations of France's Muslims, especially youth.

As suggested by Johnson and Svara (2011), governments must make fairness a greater priority and measure progress. This requires not only continuing its outreach and collaboration with moderate Muslim organizations like AMIF but also expanding those collaborations. More (and better) data are needed on the demographics and requirements of Muslim populations, which very often has been inspired by Muslims organizations themselves (see CCIF, 2019 as an example). From there, the government can engage in the type of on-the-ground outreach long recommended by moderate voices. Given France's unique institutional arrangements, enhancing the power and oversight of organizations like AMIF, especially over matters of *halal* food, education, and financing of mosques, might give a place for the "silent majority" of French Muslims, provide greater economic and education opportunities for disaffected youth, curtail the voices of authoritarians, but do so in ways that do not merely co-opt Islam as an arm of the state but, rather, have a new respect for diversity and inclusion without the strictures of full integration.

Conclusion

Islamophobia will likely remain a nervous area of government in France well into the future. The French state and underlying attitudes of racism, segregation, and a strict commitment to secularism unequally applied to Muslim persons all contribute. The history of Islamophobia is one in which the government has tried to make the religion and its practitioners into something the state can understand—an organized group represented in the mechanisms of the state itself. It was precisely this desire to transform Islam from a character oriented around local mosques to something needing national representation that has helped lead to issues of Islamophobia (Alouane, 2019). This re-organization demonstrates a double-edged sword: the potential to address Islamophobia but also co-opt the religion to the state. Not surprisingly, organizations created top-down by the state have suffered legitimacy crises. And the attempt to create an *Islam de France* is likely fraught with many dangers.

Still, it is precisely in this attempt to create an *Islam de France* that there are some positives concerning intersectoral collaboration and using technology to advance social equity. The mere fact that such collaborations have led to politicians and community leaders talking to and learning from one another suggests progress. It showcases how Muslim communities, in small steps, are not passive agents merely affected by government policy but, rather, can be active agents representing the interests of their communities vis-à-vis the state. Issues remain regarding how truly representativeness these collaborations are, and an *Islam de France* can legitimately be criticized as an attempt to co-opt the religion, but using state resources to dialogue about Muslims' place in France and seeing Muslims as a group to be incorporated and not just legislated against are steps in the right direction.

References

Adida, C., Laitin, D., & Valfort, M.-A. (2017). Les Français musulmans sont-ils discriminés dans leur propre pays? Une étude expérimentale sur le marché du travail. *French American Foundation*, 1–20.

Alouane, R.-S. (2019, May 1). Islam, made in France? Debating the reform of Muslim organizations and foreign funding for religion. Retrieved November 17, 2019, from Brookings website: https://www.brookings.edu/blog/order-from-chaos/2019/05/01/islam-made-in-france-debating-the-reform-of-muslim-organizations-and-foreign-funding-for-religion/

BBCNews. (2019, October 17). Macron warning on stigmatising Muslims amid France veil row. Retrieved from https://www.bbc.com/news/world-europe-50079997

Bell, D.A. (2003). *The cult of the nation in France: Inventing nationalism, 1680–1800.* Cambridge, MA: Harvard University Press.

Bleich, E. (2005). The legacies of history? Colonization and immigrant integration in Britain and France. *Theory and Society, 34*(2), 171–195. doi:10.1007/s11186-005-7016-7

Bloch, M. (2018, January 10). Laïcité : en fait, le discours de Emmanuel Macron a déjà eu lieu [Newspaper]. Retrieved November 17, 2019, from Le Journal du Dimanche website: https://www.lejdd.fr/Politique/laicite-en-fait-le-discours-de-emmanuel-macron-a-deja-eu-lieu-3542279

Boubakeur, D. (1995). *Charte du Culte Musulman en France.* Paris: Editions du Rocher.

Bronstein, S. (2015, January 14). Cherif and Said Kouachi: Their path to terror - CNN. Retrieved November 17, 2019, from CNN website: https://www.cnn.com/2015/01/13/world/kouachi-brothers-radicalization/index.html

Bruckner, P. (2018). *An imaginary racism: Islamophobia and guilt* (Trans. S. Rendall). New York: Polity Books.

Burgat, F. (2018, December 14). The dead-end politics of exclusion: Islam in France according to Hakim el-Karoui [Newspaper]. Retrieved November 17, 2019, from Middle East Eye website: http://www.middleeasteye.net/opinion/dead-end-politics-exclusion-islam-france-according-hakim-el-karoui

Byrne, C. (2017, October 4). French anti-terror bill explained: How emergency powers are now law - The Local [Newspaper]. Retrieved November 17, 2019, from The Local website: https://www.thelocal.fr/20171004/french-anti-terror-bill-explained-how-emergency-powers-are-now-law

Chirac backs hijab ban. (2003, December 17). Retrieved May 31, 2019, from https://www.aljazeera.com/archive/2003/12/200841015515714139.html

Chirac, J. (1985). Jacques Chirac on French Population Issues. *Population and Development Review, 11*(1), 163–164. doi:10.2307/1973399

Chrisafis, A. (2019, October 28). Police arrest 84-year old man over gun and arson attack at French mosque. Retrieved from https://www.theguardian.com/world/2019/oct/28/two-injured-in-arson-and-gun-attack-at-french-mosque

Collectif Contre L'Islamophobie en France. (2019). *CCIF Report 2019.* Retrieved from http://www.islamophobie.net/wp-content/uploads/2019/09/ccif-report-2019.pdf

Communiqué de l'Observatoire de la laïcité : « Convention citoyenne des Musulmans de France pour le vivre ensemble ». (2014, June 11). Retrieved November 17, 2019, from Gouvernement.fr website: https://www.gouvernement.fr/communique-de-l-observatoire-de-la-laicite-convention-citoyenne-des-musulmans-de-france-pour-le

Conseil d'État, 2ème -7ème chambres réunies, 11/04/2018, 412462, No. 412462 (Conseil d'État November 4, 2018).

Cross, T. (2018, March 19). France targets online hate in new anti-racism campaign. Retrieved from http://www.rfi.fr/en/20180319-france-targets-online-hate-new-anti-racism-campaign

El Karoui, H. (2016). *Un Islam Francais est Possible* [Institute Report]. Retrieved from L'Institut Montaigne website: https://www.institutmontaigne.org/ressources/pdfs/publications/rapport-un-islam-francais-est_-possible.pdf

El Karoui, H. (2017). *Nouvelle Monde Arabe, Nouvelle "Politique Arabe" pour la France.* Retrieved from Institut Montaigne website: https://www.institutmontaigne.org/ressources/pdfs/publications/nouveau-monde-arabe-nouvelle-politique-arabe-pour-la-france.pdf

El Karoui, H. (2018). La Fabrique de l'islamisme [Think Tank]. Retrieved November 17, 2019, from Institut Montaigne website: https://www.institutmontaigne.org/ressources/pdfs/publications/la-fabrique-de-islamisme.pdf

Etchegoin, M.-F. (2006, February 2). Sarkozy, L'Islam et la Laicite. *Le Nouvel Observateur*. Retrieved from: http://vigilance-laique.over-blog.com/article-3480367.html

Fillon, F. (2016). *Vaincre le Totaliarisme Islamique*. Paris: Albin Michel.

Fondation Jean Jaurès. (2019). *Etat des lieux des discriminations et des agressions envers les Musulmans de France*. Retrieved from https://jean-jaures.org/sites/default/files/redac/commun/productions/2019/1106/116663_presentation_ifop_dilcrah_2019.11.06.pdf

France24. (2019, November 11). Macron and Islam: French president weighs in on new headscarf row. Retrieved from https://www.france24.com/en/debate/20191031-macron-and-islam-french-president-weighs-in-on-new-headscarf-row

Gallup. (n.d.). Islamophobia: Understanding anti-muslim sentiment in the West. Retrieved May 26, 2019, from Gallup.com website: https://news.gallup.com/poll/157082/islamophobia-understanding-anti-muslim-sentiment-west.aspx

Gattengno, H. (2018, February 11). Islam de France: Ce que veut faire Macron. Retrieved November 17, 2019, from Le Journal du Dimanche website: https://www.lejdd.fr/Politique/islam-de-france-ce-que-veut-faire-macron-3571067

Glaes, G. (2010). Policing the post-colonial order: Surveillance and the African immigrant community in France, 1960–1979. *Historical Reflections/Reflexions Historiques, 36*(2). doi:10.3167/hrrh.2010.360208

Glasser, A. (2016, May 6). New French Report shows rise in attacks on Muslims, sustained targeting of Jews. Retrieved May 26, 2019, from Human Rights First website: https://www.humanrightsfirst.org/blog/new-french-report-shows-rise-attacks-muslims-sustained-targeting-jews

Gooden, S. (2014). *Race and Social Equity: A Nervous Area of Government*. New York: M.E. Sharpe.

Gopnik, A. (2018, August 13). *How Charles de Gaulle Rescued France*. Retrieved from https://www.newyorker.com/magazine/2018/08/20/how-charles-de-gaulle-rescued-france

Hackett, C. (2017, November 29). 5 facts about the Muslim population in Europe. *Pew Research Center*. Retrieved from https://www.pewresearch.org/fact-tank/2017/11/29/5-facts-about-the-muslim-population-in-europe/

Hamdani, K. (2018, July 16). Beautiful diversity: Football to Spur social reform as Muslim Players Shine for France at World Cup. *The Express Tribune*. Retrieved from https://tribune.com.pk/story/1759560/7-football-catalyst-change-seven-muslim-players-win-world-cup-france/

Hitchens, C. (2006, November 1). A chronology of the Algerian war of independence. Retrieved May 26, 2019, from The Atlantic website: https://www.theatlantic.com/magazine/archive/2006/11/a-chronology-of-the-algerian-war-of-independence/305277/

Hume, T., & Said-Moorhouse, L. (2016, September 8). Francois Hollande: "Islam of France" needed to beat terror threat. Retrieved November 17, 2019, from CNN website: https://www.cnn.com/2016/09/08/europe/france-hollande-islam-secularism/index.html

Is 'French Islam' an attempt to control Muslims in France? [Newspaper]. (2019, April 3). Retrieved November 17, 2019, from TRT World website: https://www.trtworld.com/europe/is-french-islam-an-attempt-to-control-muslims-in-france-25522

Islam de France: Adapter la loi de 1905 au monde de 2018. (2018, December 10). Retrieved November 17, 2019, from Gouvernement.fr website: https://www. gouvernement.fr/islam-de-france-adapter-la-loi-de-1905-au-monde-de-2018

Johnson, N. J., & Svara, J. H. (2011). *Justice for All: Promoting Social Equity in Public Administration.* New York: M.E. Sharpe.

Kantor, A. (2019, January 28). Why are France's yellow vest protests so white? Retrieved from the *Al Jazeera* website: https://www.aljazeera.com/indepth/features/france-yellow-vest-protests-white-190127223757928.html

Kaplan, M. (2015, November 25). French Muslim leaders want extremist mosques closed, Islamic preachers to be licensed, following Paris terror attacks. Retrieved November 17, 2019, from International Business Times website: https://www. ibtimes.com/french-muslim-leaders-want-extremist-mosques-closed-islamic-preachers-be-licensed-2200224

Kepel, G. (2017). *Terror in France: The Rise of Jihad in the West.* Princeton: Princeton University Press.

Kilickaya, B. (2019, September 16). French Islam: How France and UAE partners to create a state-approved religion. Retrieved from https://thenewturkey.org/french-islam-how-france-and-the-uae-partners-to-create-a-state-approved-religion

Laird, R. (1996). France, Islam and the Chirac presidency: Strategic choices and the decision-making framework. *European Security, 5*(2), 219–239. doi:10.1080/0966283960 8407265

#LesCompétencesDabord : Lutter contre les discriminations à l'embauche. (2016, April 19). Retrieved November 17, 2019, from Gouvernement.fr website: https:// www.gouvernement.fr/argumentaire/lescompetencesdabord-lutter-contre-les-discriminations-a-l-embauche-4409

L'essayiste Hakim El Karoui présente son Association musulmane pour l'islam de France. (2019, January 22). Retrieved November 17, 2019, from Europe 1 website: https:// www.europe1.fr/societe/lessayiste-hakim-el-karoui-presente-son-association-musulmane-pour-lislam-de-france-3843212

Loi de 1905: La laïcité selon Emmanuel Macron lors du débat avec les intellectuels. (2019, March 18). Retrieved November 17, 2019, from France Culture website: https://www.franceculture.fr/politique/la-laicite-selon-emmanuel-macron

Loi du 9 décembre 1905 concernant la séparation des Eglises et de l'Etat. | Legifrance. (n.d.). Retrieved November 16, 2019, from https://www.legifrance.gouv.fr/affich-Texte.do?cidTexte=LEGITEXT000006070169&dateTexte=20080306

Macron urges French police to make full use of draconian anti-terror powers. (2017, October 19). Retrieved November 17, 2019, from The Local France website: https:// www.thelocal.fr/20171019/macron-urges-police-to-use-new-emergency-powers

Manifeste "Contre le Nouvel Antisémitisme." (2018, April 21). Retrieved November 17, 2019, from Le Parisien website: http://www.leparisien.fr/societe/manifeste-contre-le-nouvel-antisemitisme-21-04-2018-7676787.php

Marsi, F. (2019, January 23). New association aspires to reorganise Islam in France. Retrieved from https://www.thenational.ae/world/europe/new-association-aspires-to-reorganise-islam-in-france-1.817221

Megherbi, F. (2018, April 17). Refus d'une poignée de main, rejet de la nationalité française. Retrieved November 16, 2019, from Juritravail website: //www.juritravail.com/Actualite/nationalita-franaaise-mariage/Id/282924

Moore, M. (2008, April 29). *In France, Prisons Filled With Muslims - washingtonpost.com.* Retrieved from http://www.washingtonpost.com/wp-dyn/content/story/2008/04/28/ST2008042802857.html?noredirect=on

Moravcsik, A. (2012). Charles de Gaulle and Europe: The new revisionism. *Journal of Cold War Studies*, *14*(1), 53–77. doi:10.1162/JCWS_a_00192

Moussaoui, M. (2020, February 18). Mohammed Moussaoui : «Les musulmans de France ne veulent pas d'un ghetto communautaire». Retrieved April 18, 2020 from Le Monde website: https://www.lemonde.fr/idees/article/2020/02/18/mohammed-moussaoui-les-musulmans-de-france-ne-veulent-pas-d-un-ghetto-ommunautaire_6029906_3232.html

Najib, K., & Hopkins, P. (2018, April 13). Islamophobia in Paris and London – how it differs and why. Retrieved November 16, 2019, from The Conversation website: http://theconversation.com/islamophobia-in-paris-and-london-how-it-differs-and-why-94793

Nora, P. (1989). Between memory and history: Les Lieux de Mémoire. *Representations*, *26*, 7–24. doi:10.2307/2928520

Organization for Security and Cooperation in Europe, Office for Democratic Institutions and Human Rights. (2018). *France*. Retrieved from the Hate Crime Reporting website: http://hatecrime.osce.org/france?year=2018

Ozcan, Y. (2019, April 26). "Political Islam" seeks secession from France: Macron. Retrieved from https://www.aa.com.tr/en/europe/political-islam-seeks-secession-from-france-macron/1462978

Paris attacks: What happened on the night. (2015, December 9). *BBC News*. Retrieved from https://www.bbc.com/news/world-europe-34818994

Pezzella, F.S., Fetzer, M.D., & Keller, T. (2019). The dark figure of hate crime underreporting. *American Behavioral Scientist* [OnlineFirst article]. doi:10.1177/0002764218823844

Piser, K. (2018, March 29). A new plan to create an "Islam of France" [Newspaper]. Retrieved November 17, 2019, from The Atlantic website: https://www.theatlantic.com/international/archive/2018/03/islam-france-macron/556604/

Premier Ministre. (2018). *National plan against racism and anti-Semitism* (2018–2020). Retrieved from https://www.gouvernement.fr/sites/default/files/contenu/piece-jointe/2018/06/national_plan_against_racism_and_anti-semitism_2018-2020.pdf

Radio France Internationale. (2018, January 2). Racist incidents down in France but assaults rise. Retrieved from http://www.rfi.fr/en/20180201-france-racist-incidents

Randall, C. (2018, May 30). Emmanuel Macron to tackle France's troubled relationship with organised Islam. Retrieved November 17, 2019, from The National website: https://www.thenational.ae/world/mena/emmanuel-macron-to-tackle-france-s-troubled-relationship-with-organised-islam-1.735450

Randall, C. (2019, August 14). French Muslim association to forge ahead with imam training plans despite Macron reticence. Retrieved from https://www.thenational.ae/world/europe/french-muslim-association-to-forge-ahead-with-imam-training-plans-despite-macron-reticence-1.898120

Rhouma, H. B. (2019, April 10). La naissance de l'Association musulmane pour l'islam de France est officiellement actée. Retrieved November 17, 2019, from SaphirNews.com website: https://www.saphirnews.com/La-naissance-de-l-Association-musulmane-pour-l-islam-de-France-est-officiellement-actee_a26223.html

Riemer, N. (2019, November 14). France's left is finally fighting Islamophobia. Retrieved from https://jacobinmag.com/2019/11/france-left-islamophobia-macron-melenchon-bayonne-attack-marine-le-pen

Roy, S. (2015, March 11). #JeSuisCharlie? No, I'm Not Charlie Hebdo: Here's Why. Retrieved November 17, 2019, from HuffPost website: https://www.huffpost.com/entry/jesuischarlie-no-im-not-charlie-hebdo_b_6447258

Rubin, A. J., & Breeden, A. (2017, July 14). France remembers the nice attack: 'We Will Never Find the Words.' *The New York Times*. Retrieved from https://www.nytimes. com/2017/07/14/world/europe/nice-attack-france-bastille-day.html

Runnymede Trust / Publications & Resources. (1997). Retrieved May 26, 2019, from https://www.runnymedetrust.org/companies/17/74/Islamophobia-A-Challenge-for-Us-All.html.

Sahgal, N., & Webster, B. (2015, January 14). French have positive views of both Jews, Muslims [Think Tank]. Retrieved November 17, 2019, from Pew Research Center website: https://www.pewresearch.org/fact-tank/2015/01/14/french-have-positive-views-of-both-jews-muslims/

Sarkozy, N., Collin, T., & Verdin, P. (2004). *La Republique, Les Religions, L'esperance* (cerf). Paris: Les Ed. du Cerf.

Sautreuil, P. (2019, January 1). Emmanuel Macron « rassure » les musulmans de France. *La Croix*. Retrieved from https://www.la-croix.com/Religion/Islam/ Emmanuel-Macron-rassure-musulmans-France-2019-01-07-1200993684

Scheinman, L. (1969). The politics of Nationalism in contemporary France. *International Organization*, *23*(4), 834. doi:10.1017/S0020818300025686

Schofield, H. (2016, October 20). Hollande's political bombshell detonates. *BBC News*. Retrieved from https://www.bbc.com/news/world-europe-37702917

Schwarzenbach, A. (2018). Fighting the "Threat from Within": France and Its Counter-Radicalization Strategy. In L. Vidino (Ed.), *De-radicalization in the Mediterranean: comparing challenges and approaches* (First edition). Retrieved from https://www. ispionline.it/sites/default/files/pubblicazioni/mediterraneo_def_web.pdf

Sciolino, E. (2003). French officials and Muslims celebrate New Islamic Council. *New York Times*, https://www.nytimes.com/2003/01/15/world/french-officials-and-muslims-celebrate-new-islamic-council.html.

Serhan, Y. (2016, August 1). France Has Shut Down 20 Mosques Since December Over Alleged Radical Islam Sermons. Retrieved November 17, 2019, from The Atlantic website: https://www.theatlantic.com/news/archive/2016/08/french-mosques-islam/493919/

Thody, P. (1998). *The fifth French republic presidents, politics and personalities*. New York: Routledge.

Un nouveau mouvement musulman français. (2006, June 20). *La Croix*. Retrieved from https://www.la-croix.com/Archives/2006-06-20/Un-nouveau-mouvement-musulman-francais-_NP_-2006-06-20-265856

Yasar, A. A. (2019, February 18). French anti-terror law primarily targets mosques [Newspaper]. Retrieved November 17, 2019, from TRT World website: https://www. trtworld.com/europe/french-anti-terror-law-primarily-targets-mosques-24202

Young, Z. (2018, September 10). Macron to review report calling for reform of Islam in France.RetrievedNovember17,2019,fromPOLITICOwebsite:https://www.politico. eu/article/macron-islam-france-muslim-review-report-calling-for-reform/

Zeghal, M. (2005). La constitution du Conseil Français du Culte Musulman: Reconnaissance politique d'un Islam français? *Archives de sciences sociales des religions*, *50*(129), 97–113.

12

ACCESS TO HEALTHCARE IN THE NETHERLANDS

Erna Ruijer and Jelena Arsenijevic

A Nervous Area of Government in the Netherlands

After the Second World War, the desire to equalize society became a deep drive of modern European culture (Mead, 2013; Rostilla, 2013). The rise of the new modern welfare states across Europe promoted this idea through different policy measures, guaranteeing several social protection services (De Beer & Koster, 2009; Zarrinkhameh & Doorten, 2013). Social protection services are provided to everyone in need, irrespectively of their ability to pay (Schmid & Siemsen, 2015). They include equal access to education and basic healthcare services. Although welfare states differ in their welfare regimes (liberal, socio-democratic or corporate regimes), they all aim to redistribute wealth in order to secure social justice. The Netherlands, one of the wealthiest countries in Europe, is no exception. After the Second World War, inequalities between classes, sexes and elites and mass were no longer considered accepted. However, that does not mean that inequalities are obsolete (Becker, 2000). The inequalities that still exist in modern welfare states are inequalities in health and inequalities in healthcare (Mackenbach, 2012). Graph 1 shows that the difference in life expectancy between people with high and lower education for a period 2011–2014 (at the age 25) was 2.1 years, while the same difference for a period 2015–2018 was 2.9. The gap in life expectancy between the low and high educated has widened. These findings are in accordance with a general increase in social stratification along educational lines in Dutch society (Bovens & Wille, 2017) (Figure 12.1).

It is also worth mentioning that socioeconomic inequalities in health are persistent but not always negative – for example, female babies have less weight at birth than boys or incidence of prostate cancer is higher among men (females

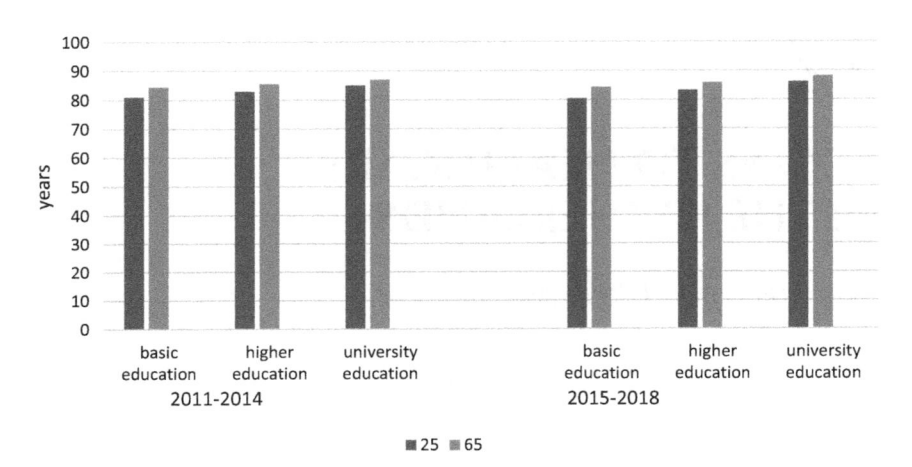

FIGURE 12.1 Life Expectancy for Periods 2011–2014 and 2015–2018.
Source: CBS for year 2011–2018: https://opendata.cbs.nl/statline.

do not have prostates) (Jansen et al., 2018). These examples show that inequalities in health are not necessarily negative and that they can occur as a result of biological factors (Marmot, 2005). However, when inequalities are systematic and related to specific social groups, they become inequities. This means they are imposed by unfair social factors, and it is a role of welfare states to tackle them (Whitehead, 1991). Designing and implementing policy measures that provide basic healthcare services to all population groups is one solution. Among the EU welfare states, the concept of universal healthcare coverage is almost achieved. However, it seems not enough to decrease inequities in healthcare. The Netherlands is a wealthy country that has a long tradition on equity towards disadvantaged groups such as ethnical minorities, people with lower income status, single parents and lower educated people. Yet also the Netherlands faces health inequities (Droomers, 2009).

In this chapter we will examine how inequity in access to healthcare became a nervous area in the Netherlands (Gooden, 2014). Additionally, we will analyze how a local government attempts to reverse healthcare inequities. We focus on the local level because of the Dutch context. After the healthcare reforms in the Netherlands in 2006, the responsibility for some healthcare services, such as help to disabled people or household help for older adults, shifted from the national to the local government level. National government still has a regulatory role, but local municipalities are responsible for the decision on who is eligible for services, and for how the services are funded. The aim of our study is twofold. First, this study aims to further build the concept of nervousness in government by examining nervousness in the context of an EU welfare state. Justice is context based: determining what is fair depends on understanding a complex array of historical, political and social trajectories (Gooden, 2014). We propose that in the Dutch case, nervousness does not arise from an enduring history of inequality such as race in the US (Gooden, 2014). Nervousness in the Dutch case might in fact arise from more recent societal developments leading to inequity, which are at odds with historical deeply engrained societal values of solidarity and justice. Second, this study aims to contribute to the literature on inequalities and inequities in healthcare by analyzing how nervousness can be managed in order for local government agencies to proactively address health inequities.

In the first part of the chapter we will provide an overview of the historical and political context of healthcare within the Dutch welfare state. Based on a secondary data analysis of CBS for 2017, we show how the reform in the Dutch healthcare system affected the use of healthcare services among socially disadvantaged groups in four cities in the Netherlands. In the second part of the chapter we zoom in on a municipality. The municipality observes and measures possible health inequities of her citizens and is aiming to reduce these inequities (Utrecht, 2015). We study nervousness in the municipality from the perspective of (senior) public administrators and assess how they are trying to reverse inequities in access to healthcare and promote equity, thereby taking into account organizational values. We used a mixed method analysis consisting of a document analysis of 18 documents including the municipality's vision, policies and procedures, and three interviews with (senior) public administrators and street level bureaucrats. The documents and interviews were analyzed using NVIVO 12. A thematic analysis was conducted thereby using the elements of the nervousness framework (Gooden, 2014) as themes (Bryman, 2012). Finally, we draw conclusions for the concept of nervousness and provide practical implications for government organizations aiming to conquer health inequities as a nervous area.

Why Access to Healthcare Is a Nervous Area of Government

Conceptualizing Access to Health Care

Before turning to the Dutch context we will first conceptualize equity in healthcare. Equity and justice are fundamental concerns of public administrators (Gooden, 2014; Guy, 2012). Equity in health is an ethical and normative concept (Whitehead, 1991). It is defined as the absence of systematic disparities in health status among population groups with different status in social hierarchy (Braveman & Gruskin, 2003). Inequities in health are always unfair, unjust and unnecessary (Marmot, 2005). This means that they should be distinguished from inequalities – systematic inequalities do exist, and they are not necessary negative (Whitehead, 1991). For example, the general health status among young population groups is better than among older adults.

However, when younger adults with migrant backgrounds have lower health status than younger adults with non-migrant background, we speak about inequities (Whitehead, 1991). Inequities put people with already disadvantaged social status (in terms of lack of power, and lack of prestige or wealth) into more disadvantaged position by lowering their health status (Braveman & Gruskin, 2003). This is why inequity in health is strongly associated with society and governance. These inequities can be considered a nervous area for EU welfare states, which promote social justice towards all population groups. Good policy measures that take into account specific needs of disadvantaged population groups can decrease inequities in health (Alleyne, 2000).

As an ethical and normative concept, equity in health is grounded in different philosophical theories. The two well-known concepts are egalitarian and libertarian theories (Alleyne, 2000). Since equity in health is a philosophical concept, equity in healthcare is used as a better operationalization for understanding the implications from the theories (Whitehead, 1991). Egalitarian theories describe health and access to basic healthcare as human rights. In libertarian theories, access to healthcare services is a state reward and it should be given only to those who are poor. In the early 1970s, John Rawls developed a libertarian approach in his theory: "Theory of Justice" (Rawls, 2009). He claims in one of his two main principles that if inequities exist policies should be in favor of most disadvantaged groups. Most European welfare states have accepted the egalitarian approach, and their healthcare policies are strongly designed to secure social and distributive justice. Additionally, in most EU welfare states the basic healthcare services are provided to everyone in need and according to their ability to pay.

Equity in healthcare is a broad concept and refers to equity in access (psychological access, time access, physical and spatial access), equity in financing and equity in quality of received care (Van Doorslaer et al., 2000; Wagstaff & Van Doorslaer, 2000). Equity in accessing healthcare services and equity in financing are the two concepts that are most often examined (Wagstaff & Van Doorslaer, 2000). The most common way to assess inequity in healthcare is to look at income distribution among population and their utilization of healthcare services (Wagstaff & Van Doorslaer, 2000). This approach was criticized because utilization does not say anything about need. What if people do have a need for healthcare services but do not access them for financial reasons? In most EU welfare states, however basic services are covered and universal health coverage is achieved. Psychological acceptability or understanding the rights to use care can also play a role. Previous scientists have gone one step forward and distinguish vertical and horizontal equity in healthcare (Van Doorslaer et al., 2000). Vertical equity means that people with different needs are treated differently, while horizontal equity means that people with the same needs receive the same care (Van Doorslaer et al., 2000). Many different methodological approaches are developed to assess both vertical and horizontal equities in healthcare, while focusing on physical, psychological or financial access. In this chapter we assess access to health care as a Nervous Area of Government. We will focus on the Dutch context and start by outlining the historical and political context.

Historical and Political Context of Healthcare in the Netherlands

In European countries, including the Netherlands, there is a widespread belief that healthcare systems should be based on the value of equity: the basic healthcare services should be provided to anyone in need irrespectively to their ability to pay. This is in accordance with the egalitarian tradition that welfare states adopted after the Second World War. European welfare states use different funding mechanisms to achieve this goal. Countries with corporatist welfare regimes such as Germany, Italy or France have introduced a social insurance scheme, which implies that everyone is eligible for insurance but people pay according to their abilities (Esping-Andersen, 2013). Similarly, Sweden (Nordic welfare state) also uses a social insurance scheme – only here insurance is free of charge. The most known representative of the liberal welfare state is the UK which has introduced a tax-based free of charge national healthcare system. This system also offers the possibility to use private healthcare services that should be paid out-of-pocket (Rostilla, 2013).

The Netherlands with its cultural background and geographical position has always been considered in-between liberal and corporate welfare states (De Beer & Koster, 2009). This is reflected in the financing and funding of the Dutch healthcare system. In accordance with Dutch cultural heritage – healthcare systems should be based on solidarity, i.e., those who are better off support those who are more disadvantaged (Houtepen & Ter Meulen, 2000; Lindenberg, 2014; Zarrinkhameh & Doorten, 2013). These solidarity-based arrangements were built by Christian Democratic and Social Democratic Parties, which ruled the political system after the Second World War (Becker, 2000; Houtepen & Ter Meulen, 2000). They favored the egalitarian approach towards healthcare. In the early 1960s, a generous healthcare system was established. This system was based on a social insurance fund that covered people with low and moderate income. People eligible for the social insurance fund were paying small monthly premiums and out-of-pocket payments for certain services. People with high income had to buy private insurance – most of them usually stayed non-insured. The long-term care was organized through the 'Algemene Wet Bijzondere Ziektekosten' (AWBZ) or the Dutch Health Care Law and was available to each Dutch citizen (Kolnaar, 2001). The generosity of the welfare state and material equality reached a peak in the 1970s. However, financial problems in the 1980s led to a shift aimed at liberalizing the welfare state. The main problem with the social insurance fund was pooling of the funds – people with the highest income did not participate in the insurance scheme

(Enthoven & van de Ven, 2007). Furthermore, the healthcare system became inefficient – long waiting lists and low quality of care were the factors that raised dissatisfaction among citizens (Kolnaar, 2001). During this time individual responsibilities were emphasized and the concept of solidarity changed in nature (Zarrinkhameh & Doorten, 2013). Solidarity was no longer considered to be formal and delivered by the state but rather informal and the personal responsibility of each citizen (Veen, 2005).

These developments led to a change in the concept of the welfare state; the state incorporated a more libertarian concept. The responsibility shifted from the national to the local level based on the idea that decentralization would empower citizens. Furthermore, administrative workers in municipalities can better recognize the needs of their community. The change in the welfare state concept, the lack of financial resources and the inefficient provision of services eventually led to the Dutch healthcare reform: The new Health Insurance Act (HIA, known as Zvw act in Dutch) which was introduced in 2006 and the Social Support Act (WMO) which was introduced in 2015 (van de Ven et al., 2009). The WMO obliges municipalities to provide (long term) care (e.g. home care) and social support. It is designed as a more efficient "replacement" for AWBZ (Putman, 2015). Within AWBZ individuals were entitled to a right to care while the WMO provides individuals the right to compensation. This is best illustrated with the example of an old man 75, who becomes a widow and has rheumatoid arthritis. His main problem is to wash the dishes and to maintain the household. In 1999, he would talk to his GP and he would get a household helper – a person who comes and helps with domestic issues. In 2016, he would need to go to his local municipality. A street level bureaucrat would listen to his complaints, and based on this he/she would fill in the "tree" form. Based on the result of the form the old man would be assigned a personal budget (PGB). With the PGB he can buy a washing machine and find someone to help him with domestic work. With these changes, municipalities were obliged to make new units, and educate workers how to fill in the tree form and how to identify to what extent each individual is eligible for care (Arsenijevic & Groot, 2018). The challenge of these reforms was to make healthcare more innovative, patient-oriented and more efficient without compromising the welfare state values of solidarity, universal access, affordability and quality of care (Maarse & Paulus, 2011). However, the reforms were controversial from the beginning (Maarse & Paulus, 2011).

First of all, several empirical studies (Heijmans, Waverijn, Rademakers, van der Vaart, & Rijken, 2014; Rademarkers, Nijman, Brabers, de Jong, & Hendriks, 2014) indicate that the expectation of active choice by patients leads to inequity (Maarse & Paulus, 2011). Based on the reforms, patients are expected to be in charge of their health and to make active and well-informed choices for a specific healthcare provider (Brabers, Rademakers, Groenewegen, van Dijk, & de Jong, 2017; Rademarkers, Nijman, Brabers, de Jong, & Hendriks, 2014;

Wetenschappelijke Raad voor het Regeringsbeleid, 2017). It is associated with autonomy and self-determination, a means to enhance competition between providers and thus increasing the quality of care (Rademarkers et al., 2014). The reforms require health literacy: social and communication skills that enable people to obtain and understand and use health information in ways that enhance their health and well-being (Brabers, Rademakers, Groenewegen, van Dijk, & de Jong, 2017; Heijmans et al., 2014, p. 41). People with chronic diseases and disabilities, who need long-term care, are increasingly expected to manage their own health (Jansen, Rademakers, Waverijn, Verheij, Osborne, & Heijmans, 2018; Wetenschappelijke Raad voor het Regeringsbeleid, 2017). Second, Rademakers et al. (2014) show that educational level is the strongest predictor of active choice, with people with low education being less active. They argue that social capital, education, social background, location of residences and professional status may affect whether patients feel comfortable making active choices, eventually possibly leading to receiving suboptimal care and the likelihood of inferior health outcomes (Rademarkers et al., 2014; Rostilla, 2013). Third, a recent report conducted by the Ombudsman (Tuzgöl-Broekhoven, Stam, & Atalikyayi, 2018) shows that access to healthcare remains a concern. It is unclear for people where to go with a request for care (physical access), they complain about red tape (time access), insufficient professional expertise and a lack of continuity in care (adequate access) (Tuzgöl-Broekhoven et al., 2018). Studies indicate that either people in lower activation levels (Rademarkers et al., 2014) or people with less health literacy (Jansen et al., 2018) have to get help in the search for information, regarding the formation of the questions they might have and help with where to look for understandable and reliable information. While in the past income was a cornerstone for inequalities in access to healthcare, nowadays it is knowledge. Finally, the WMO 2015 is based on the assumption that municipalities are able to provide better care support at lower costs because they know their communities and citizens better (Rekenkamer Utrecht, 2016; van der Ham, 2018). The main aim of the WMO is to provide the option for citizens to stay at home longer and to participate in society by supporting independence and participation. The target groups of the WMO are, for instance, people with chronic, psychological or psychosocial problems and people with disabilities (Gemeente Utrecht, 2014–2019). Yet a recent study showed that municipalities only "somewhat know" their target groups and less than half indicated that they know the different WMO target groups in their city well (Sociaal Cultureel Planbureau, 2014).

A Promising Government Initiative: The City of Utrecht

In this part of the chapter we focus on the city of Utrecht. Before examining Utrecht in-depth we will first compare Utrecht with three other big cities in the Netherlands: Amsterdam, Rotterdam and the Hague. Compared to the other three cities Utrecht has more people with a higher education: 52% of the citizens of Utrecht. However, Utrecht has more elderly with a lower education than the other cities. Finally, 35% of the citizens of Utrecht have a migration background (Gemeente Utrecht, 2018). Table 12.1 shows how social services related to WMO, such as household help, residential care, support in the house and use of medical devices and healthcare services, are used between migrants and non-western migrants in the four big cities in the Netherlands. Non-western migrants (usually with Moroccan or Turkish background) are considered to have less social capital and less administrative knowledge in order to manage their healthcare needs within the current WMO arrangements. Most of them that are now in their age of retirement came in the late 1960s to the Netherlands to perform low-paid simple works such as household cleaning or to work as bricklayers. Their knowledge of the Dutch language is limited, and they usually have only basic education.

The table shows that use of WMO services by migrants with non-western background is more frequent in Rotterdam than in the other three cities. However, this is expected – Rotterdam is the city with highest number of non-western migrants in the country. Unlike the other cities, in Utrecht all four services are about equally used by non-western migrants – from residential care (29.6%) to use of medical devices (19.9%). In Amsterdam, for example, we can observe that services such as support and help in the household (45.23% and 29.06%) are more often used than residential care (22.9%). If we look at the number of migrants who used residential services as a percentage of the total amount of immigrants, we see that numbers in Den Hague (4.23%), Amsterdam (0.24%) and Rotterdam (8.74%) are lower in comparison with Utrecht – 14.85%. The results from Amsterdam, Rotterdam and Den Hague are in accordance with previous studies – traditionally immigrants use residential care less often than native Dutch inhabitants (de Graaff & Francke, 2002; Denktas et al., 2009; Verhagen et al., 2014). The reasons for low use can vary – most often this is a lack of knowledge about administration related to residential care, but also different cultural perception and financial barriers play a role (Denktas et al., 2009; Verhagen et al., 2014). Very often elderly migrants need more support from administrative workers. On the other side, residential care is more expensive – this is why approving the eligibility for administrative care is also more difficult (Denktas, 2011). As a consequence, the older immigrants rather rely on more cultural sensitive informal help – from family members than on residential care (Suurmond et al., 2016). Although the case of Utrecht is more optimistic with a higher average level of use of residential care among immigrants (14.85%), the results might also be due to higher demand within Utrecht municipality.

In Table 12.2 we present the use of different financial mechanisms related to WMO services. One of the biggest changes that WMO has introduced is the shift from right to care towards right to compensation. Within the former AWBZ everyone in need would receive care such as household help or

TABLE 12.1 Use of WMO Service by Non-Western Migrants and Non-Migrants in Four Dutch Cities

		Support in the House	Household Help	Residential Care	Healthcare Services and Medical Devices
Amsterdam Total number of inhabitants = 844 947	Total number of users	13785 (100%)	19935 (100%)	370 (100.00%)	49960 (100.00%)
	Non-migrant users	5985 (43.42%)	11870 (59.54%)	245 (66.21%)	27780 (55.60%)
Total number of migrants = 34 581	Migrant non-western	6235 (45.23%) 18.03%	5795 (29.06%) 16.75%	85 (22.97%) 0.24%	16630 (33.28%) 48.08%
Den Hague Total number of inhabitants = 524 882	Total number of users	12 805 (100%)	12 895 (100%)	2300 (100%)	
	Non-migrant users	6245 (48.77%)	7110 (55.14)	1300 (56.52)	14265
Total number of migrants = 17 242	Migrant non-western	5305 (41.42%) 30.76%	4605 (35.7%) 26.71%	730 (31.74%) 4.23%	7580 43.96%
Rotterdam Total numbers of inhabitants = 634 660	Total number of users	15980 (100%)	17530 (100%)	2295 (100%)	34280 (100%)
	Non-migrant users	6330 (39.61%)	10780 (61.5%)	880 (38.34%)	24730 (72.14%)
Total number of migrants = 13 436	Migrants non-western	8335 (52.15%) 62.03%	5390 (30.7%) 40.11%	1175 (51.19%) 8.74%	6915 (20.17%) 51.46%
Utrecht Total numbers of inhabitants = 343 038	Total number of users	2355 (100%)	6320 (100%)	2415 (100%)	14100 (100.00%)
	Non-migrant users	1470 (62.42%)	4465 (70.64%)	1495 (61.90%)	10085 (71.52%)
Total numbers of migrants = 4814	Migrant non-western	640 (27.17%) 13.29%	1320 (20.88%) 27.42%	715 (29.6%) 14.85%	2810 (19.92%) 58.55%

Source: CBS for year 2017: https://opendata.cbs.nl/statline.

TABLE 12.2 Different Financing Mechanisms for WMO Services

	Receiving Financial Support based on PGB	Receiving Financial Support based on Zorg in Natura	Receiving Financial Support Based on Combination between Two Financial Options
Amsterdam (n = 61925)	2150 (3.47%)	54920 (88.68%)	4855 (7.84%)
Den Hague (n = 36070)	1145 (3.17%)	33590 (93.12%)	1340 (3.71%)
Rotterdam (n = 51290)	2775 (5.41%)	43345 (84.50%)	5170 (10.07%)
Utrecht (n = 19105)	550 (2.87%)	17545 (91.8%)	1010 (5.28%)

residential care (Arsenijevic & Groot, 2018). Based on this change, users are eligible to receive PGB and they can organize their care. Another option is called Zorg in Nature – the municipality organizes and does administration work in order to provide the care to the users. Zorg in Nature is similar to the former AWBZ, only with limited resources. Although it was assumed that PGB will give personal freedom to users and that it will be widely used, our data show that most of the users still prefer the Zorg in Nature, which is similar to the old model. It implies that users of WMO services prefer that complicated administration is done by municipalities instead of being able to make personal choices (van Loghum, 2011). Also, a small proportion of users have opted for mixed model – combination of PGB and Zorg in Nature.

Now we zoom in on data provided by municipality of Utrecht for year 2018. The municipality collects these data in order to better understand the needs of users. Here, we present two graphs – Figures 12.2 and 12.3. In Figure 12.2 we present the use of WMO services by migrants and non-migrants, but also by non-migrants with lower education. The data show that older migrants use some services (help with administration and personal hygienic services) more often than non-migrants in general. However, the older non-migrants with lower education use these services more often than migrants. This is in accordance with previous research – older people with lower education sometimes need help regarding the information about healthcare services (Schellingerhout, 2004). Moreover, sometimes they forgo use of services due to lack of information (Joung et al., 2000).

In Figure 12.2, we present the data related to use of WMO services among people with different educational level, irrespectively of their migrant status. People with the lowest education use some of the WMO services more often than people with higher education. This is particularly observed for administration and personal hygienic issues.

If we compare results from Figures 12.2 to 12.3, we see that not only migrant status but also level of education can act as precursors for disparities in healthcare. On the other side, if we compare data from national level (Table 12.1)

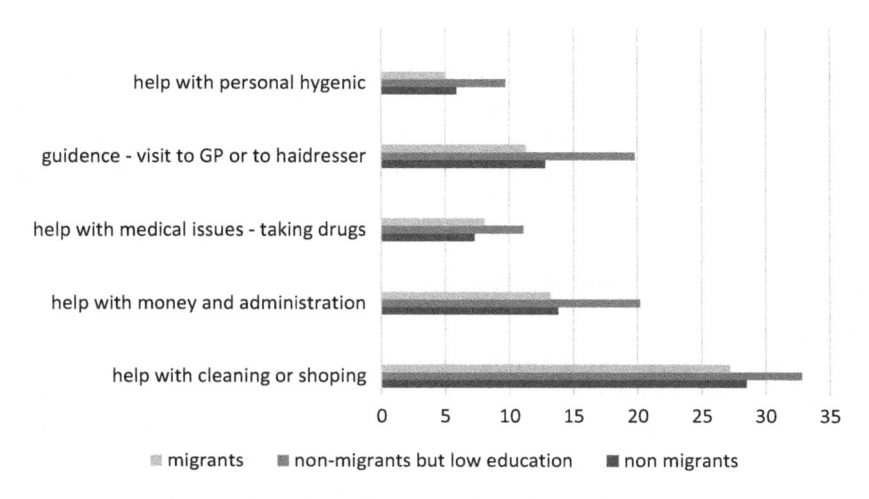

FIGURE 12.2 The Number of People in Utrecht Who Used Social Services Provided by Municipality in 2018, based on their Ethnical Background.

Source: This data is obtained from: https://www.volksgezondheidsmonitor.nl/.

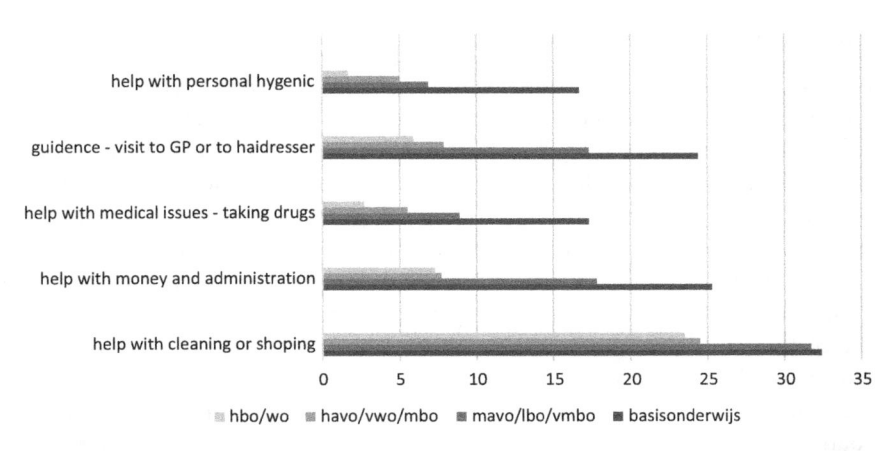

FIGURE 12.3 Use of Different WMO Services in Municipality Utrecht among Population Groups with Different Education Level for 2018.

Source: This data is obtained from: https://www.volksgezondheidsmonitor.nl/.

with data from local level (Figures 12.2 and 12.3), we see that on the national level immigrants use some services less often (residential care), while on the local level some services are used more often among migrants than among non-migrants. This can be explained by the fact that Utrecht municipality is better able to manage the disparities related to migrant status. However, this can also be explained by a difference in demand – there might be more need for residential care in Utrecht. In our analysis we also observed that there is a lack of data available at the national level that allows us to combine the level of education and migrant status. In addition, data about people who need care but do not get it (unmet need) are also not available. As Starfield (2011) points out, there is need to collect more data on inequities among groups in the population to be able to observe possible hidden inequity.

Assessment and Evidence of Progress

In this section, we will describe how the city of Utrecht promotes, distributes, examines and evaluates healthcare regarding vulnerable groups such as the lower educated, migrants and the elderly, with a specific focus on the WMO. We will do this based on the conceptual framework of nervousness developed by Gooden (2014). This framework consists of four areas that influence nervousness in an organization: the external environment, organizational values, senior public administrators and public servants involved in daily implementation decisions. In addition, we examined the outcomes and more specifically how the city monitors and evaluates results.

External Environment

For the city of Utrecht the motivator from the external environment for focusing on healthcare and vulnerable groups is mainly triggered by the national developments; the legal shift of the responsibility of the WMO from the national to the local level due to an increase in healthcare costs. Based on the WMO municipalities have to develop integrative policy regarding support services. But under the WMO municipalities have the freedom to develop health support policies in line with local needs (Sociaal Cultureel Planbureau, 2014). The policies are influenced by coalition agreements. In the Netherlands elections take place at the local level every four years. The winning political parties form a coalition and describe their vision in a coalition agreement. During the WMO transformation three different political coalitions took office in the city of Utrecht. The three coalitions consisted of different combinations of political parties. In general these parties can be positioned at either the left or middle of the Dutch political landscape. The WMO reform took place during three coalition timeframes: 2010–2014, 2014–2018 and 2018 until 2022. The first two coalition agreements emphasized the importance of health equity. The 2010–2014 coalition agreement states that all citizens of Utrecht should be healthy for which it is among others important that the city provides accessible, affordable care for everyone who needs it. Additionally, it states that special attention is needed for the elderly and for migrants, and it recognizes that there is a difference in health based on socio-economic status that requires attention. The 2014–2018 coalition agreement explicitly states that the political parties are aiming to reduce health inequity in the city and state that the 2015 healthcare reform should not have a negative effect on those who need care but does not explicitly refer to different target groups such as the elderly and migrants are people with a low socio-economic status. Remarkably, the current coalition agreement of 2018–2022 does not explicitly refer to health equity but does state that the coalition would like to take measures in order to increase the accessibility of care by enhancing the visibility of the community services. A respondent explained that the term "health inequity" is used within the public health discourse of the city but not so much in the department responsible for the WMO, where the focus is on inclusiveness. They prefer to emphasize, in line with the national WMO, *"That everyone should be able to participate"* (Respondent 1). The respondent also indicated that in practice it is not always possible for people to be in charge of their own health. Therefore, Utrecht has nuanced the national WMO policy approached: they emphasize, *"You have to support someone in order for the person to be in charge. It is not always feasible for a person life and therefore you have to be able to anticipate this [with your policy]"* (Respondent 1).

Hence, in terms of external motivators it can be observed that legal, economic and political triggers played a role. Moreover, we can observe a change in discourse from equity to inclusiveness, in line with the national discourse.

Organizational Values

Based on the documents and the interviews the following values can be identified that are central to the Utrecht policy approach in relation to vulnerable groups: a community-based approach in which the needs of the clients are at the forefront, innovation and learning from practice, participation and collaboration.

The Utrecht policy approach is characterized by three tracks: a strong social base that is focused on self-organizing abilities of citizens, basic care provided by community-based organizations and additional care by healthcare providers. The access to the WMO is organized via the community-based centers across the city, which are accessible for all citizens in their own neighborhood. These centers will help with questions regarding social and practical healthcare support. The aim is that citizen of Utrecht can function independently, despite their problems and disabilities. If additional healthcare or long-term care is needed, the community center will refer to other specialized organizations. The needs of the client are according to the respondents, central to this approach. One respondent indicated that the organizational chart was literally turned upside down, with the client at his or her needs at the top, supported by the teams, and the rest of the organization facilitates the client and teams. *"This is not common in the social domain"* (Respondent 2).

The city of Utrecht started four years before the WMO went into effect with experimenting and learning (Gemeente Utrecht, 2013; Gemeente Utrecht, 2014–2019). The city started with two pilots, consisting of two community-based centers. Through the community-based pilots the city learned on how to best organize the WMO transition. Currently, there are 18 teams spread out over the city. The city made an initial assessment of the different neighborhoods of the city based on the complexity of the different neighborhoods thereby taking into account, among others, social assistants benefits, education and the number of people who are socially isolated (Gemeente Utrecht, 2013). Based on this assessment more community centers in high complex areas of the city were opened and less community-based centers in neighborhoods with less complexity:

> In areas with a high degree of vulnerability, the intensity of community-based centers increases, the capacity increases as well. The demand is also higher in these areas and there are more complex problems.
>
> *(Respondent 1)*

The documents analyzed emphasize that the reform requires constant change, innovation and experimentation, which is confirmed by the respondents. Organizational learning is considered important. The community-based centers perceive themselves as pioneers. There is a constant need for adaption and reflection on what works and what does not work. After the reform of 2015 the city continued to experiment with new approaches such as pilots in mental health and household help (Buurtteam organisatie sociaal, 2018), and an innovative approach was used in one of the complex neighborhoods in Utrecht: Utrecht Overvecht, which has a high degree of migrants and lower educated (Roosenboom, Makkes, & van Wezel, 2018).

The city collaborates with a separate independent organization that is specialized in healthcare and the social domain. The new organization allowed for a new start as was pointed out by one of the respondents. The organization is co-responsible for the implementation of the community centers. The city is both contractor and co-creator:

> This means that the assignment each year is always in close collaboration. You are together designing a new model instead of having the traditional contractor-client relationship.
>
> *(Respondent 2)*

The city, together with the organization, co-created the implementation of the WMO based on practice and is perceived as one of the success factors (Smid, Verhoef, & Simons, 2016). One respondent indicated that there were no protocols at the start but these were developed in practice. The experience of practice feeds into policy (Smid, Verhoef, & Simons, 2016): a bottom-up approach. In addition, the city emphasizes the importance of collaboration with (migrant) citizen's initiatives and (migrant) NGO's, between formal and informal care and between formal care organizations. (Gemeente Utrecht, 2018). Moreover, there is close collaboration with general practitioners and community nurses, and regular meetings are held with citizens and clients (Gemeente Utrecht, 2014–2019). The community-based centers organize an activity for or together with citizens once a month, in order to get to know the citizens better and to learn what is happening in the neighborhood (Incluzio, 2015).

Hence, these values show how resources are distributed in light of public justice: there are more community-based centers in areas where there is more need. In addition, it shows how experimenting and organizational learning, allowing for continuous self-improvement in close collaboration with different partners, advances the values.

Senior Public Administrators and Frontline Workers

The senior public manager interviewed expressed the importance of quarterly meetings with the community-based centers to discuss the results so far and the integrated policy approach to health and health care. The integrative approach consists of collaboration with domains responsible for youth, poverty, employment, sports, culture and living (Gemeente Utrecht, 2018). People with health problems might need social support, but other underlying factors such as having debts might also influence their health:

> Now that the responsibility of help in the household is part of the community-based center we always visit the people. The biggest advantage is that we are visiting people's homes. From the moment we ring the doorbell we are observing how someone lives. Often times the person needs more than household help (…) There might be other problems such as loneliness or addiction.
>
> *(Respondent 3)*

Furthermore, it prevents that one family, for instance, is dealing with several frontline workers depending on the issue. Therefore, the community workers are educated as all-round professionals, with a specialization. This according to the interviewees was challenging and sometimes frustrating for workers who were used to working in a certain way before the WMO reform.

> The frontline workers were for instance first [before the reform] mental health worker and now they also had to know something about debt. This took time but has now been achieved.
>
> *(Respondent 1)*

The frontline workers have a high degree of autonomy and discretion. The idea is that the needs of vulnerable persons are the point of departure and not the organizational process. The vision of the city is based on the idea that frontline workers know best what is necessary for a vulnerable person.

> As an organization you have to trust the front-line workers, in that they will do what is necessary. You cannot do that right away. But by giving them the freedom, we noticed that they did take that responsibility or ownership.
>
> *(Respondent 2)*

That according to one of the respondents is also one of the success factors of the Utrecht approach. In addition, the community centers work with experience experts in reaching out to vulnerable groups with different cultural backgrounds (Gemeente Utrecht, 2018). According to the 2017 annual report of the community-based centers, diversity has been high on the agenda since 2015. The vision of the WMO of the City of Utrecht states that Utrecht is characterized by a rich "diversity of cultural backgrounds, lifestyles, age, disabilities, sexual orientation and world views" (Gemeente Utrecht, 2014–2019). This according to the vision requires a culturally sensitive attitude and cultural knowledge. Consequently, the city is stimulating a representative workforce and asked all frontline workers to participate in a cultural sensitivity training.

> I thought it was a very interesting training. It teaches you to reflect on where you are coming from and what your norms and values are. This is very important when you approach a client.
>
> *(Respondent 3)*

Hence, the example of the diversity training reflects the socialization of the organization in what they stress is important for frontline workers.

Assessment and Evidence of Progress

The city of Utrecht is using a data-driven policy approach for monitoring and evaluation, combined with "in-depth stories in order to learn and to continuously improve the approach" (Gemeente Utrecht, 2018, p. 18). The stories are considered important to contextualize the data and to hear client stories. The city conducts an annual public health monitor among its citizens and also pays attention to health differences between different groups. The health monitor is available as open government data on the website of the city and includes, for instance, statistics on the access of healthcare for lower educated and people with a migration background and the number of people reached by the community centers related to education and migration. In both cases a clear difference between the groups can be observed in the 2014 and 2016 monitor, with access being lower for the lower educated and migrants compared to the higher educated and non-migrants (www.volksgezondheidsmonitor.nl). Not all statistics are available as open data yet according to a respondent. The reason for this is that some data concerns pilot data, but the expectation is that more data will be available online for everyone to use without restrictions. The city works with account managers that hold quarterly meetings based on data with their partners. They have a dashboard that shows the trends of inflow and outflow, for instance. It can also be observed how the different community centers are performing compared to one another. If there are outliers then there is a joined conversation in order to find an explanation. The intention is not to judge or to assess in terms of wrong or right, but the intention is to improve.

The community-based centers also use a monitoring tool to assess the progress that clients make. However, the idea is to keep registration minimal and as simple as possible for frontline workers (Buurtteam Sociaal, 2016). Background variables such as education and migration are not part of the community-based registration system. According to one respondent this is not desirable and not necessary because these statistics are available at a more general level for each neighborhood. Furthermore, the respondent indicated that frontline workers know their citizens and their problems, and there are issues of privacy that need to be taken into account. Differences however are explicitly talked about even though it is not registered as such. The 2018 WMO vision of the city indicates that the city will not ask more registration of the community-based centers, but that they will make better use of existing datasets and aim to further analysis whether indicators can be included that allow for zooming in on citizens with a low education and a low economic status (Gemeente Utrecht, 2018, p. 18).

Monitoring is used to improve policy. For example, an independent review report (Rekenkamer Utrecht, 2016) stated that more customization is necessary in the support and information provided and to improve the quality of care. The city provided information regarding household help mainly via the Internet. Yet a substantial amount of the clients are elderly and lower educated, and do not possess digital skills. These clients prefer face-to-face and information on paper (Rekenkamer Utrecht, 2016). Consequently, the vision of the city refers to these results and indicates that they will increase the support for the community-based centers (Gemeente Utrecht, 2018). In addition, the community-based centers enhanced the face-to-face contact and are working in close collaboration with general practitioners and visit clients at their home.

In terms of outcomes, the interviewees indicate that the Utrecht approach is working, that it is within budget and that it can be considered as a best practice. Other cities also have an interest in the model. Furthermore, the 2018 annual report of the community centers indicated that in general satisfaction by customers with the provided support and care has risen, waiting lists have been reduced and citizens are better able to find the community-based centers.

In addition, more people than the year before are able to independently move being helped by the community-based center. Thus, no distinction is made between groups. However, based on experiences in some community-based centers, the presence of frontline workers with diverse cultural backgrounds is perceived to contribute to the outreach of a broad variety of groups in the neighborhood (Gemeente Utrecht, 2014–2019). Moreover, a survey among frontline workers showed that they themselves consider inclusiveness and cultural sensitive working as important (Buurtteam organisatie social, 2018). Finally, an assessment was conducted in one of the most complex neighborhoods in Utrecht: Utrecht Overvecht. This neighborhood has a high degree of people with a migrant background and lower education. The results showed that the approach in this neighborhood has likely improved the sustainability of the quality of healthcare, and the use of care has been reduced, while the use of care in the control group increased and the approach has led to cost-savings. This approach is used as a best practice (Roosenboom, Makkes, & van Wezel, 2018).

Nevertheless, there are also challenges. One challenge that was pointed out by the respondents and documents (Gemeente Utrecht, 2016) is fragmentation. There are many organizations active in Utrecht, and therefore, it is sometimes difficult for the community workers to know which client to refer to which organization. There are many professional organizations but also citizens' initiatives sometimes subsidized by the city. One respondent indicated that due to the fragmentation contradictory information is sometimes provided and another indicated this sometimes leads to competition instead of collaboration between initiatives and confusion for clients. The respondents also indicated that not all citizens are reached by the community based-centers. The community centers conduct outreach activities, collaborate and have partnerships with many organizations, including general practitioners. Additionally, not all people are able to articulate their health question. Furthermore, the danger of the success of the community-based centers is that they might get too many tasks and become a victim of its own success. Finally, the respondents at the community-based center emphasized the importance of an integrated approach, but they also experienced this approach sometimes as a challenge in their contact with the city, where different departments are responsible for, e.g., public health, health care, and employment and benefits. Even though information is exchanged all respondents indicate that this could be improved across silos; the city is planning to work on a joined agenda in order to integrate activities and use the same discourse.

Hence, in Utrecht a data-driven approach in combination with face-to-face conversations with stakeholders, citizens and clients is used to monitor results. The Utrecht case implies that progress is made, but that challenges remain.

Conclusion

This chapter focused on healthcare inequity as a Nervous Area of Government in the Netherlands. In European countries, including the Netherlands, there is a widespread historical belief that healthcare systems should be based on the value of solidarity: those who are better off support the less advantaged. The generosity of the welfare state and material equality reached a peak in the 1970s. However, financial problems in the 1980s led to a shift aimed at liberalizing the welfare state. During this time, individual responsibilities were emphasized and the concept of solidarity changed in nature. This eventually led to the Dutch healthcare reform: the new HIA of 2006 and the WMO in 2015. We used the conceptual model of the Nervous Area of Government (Gooden, 2014) to analyze how a city in the Netherlands is trying to advance access healthcare equity. It showed that legal and political triggers in the form of elected officials started the navigation of nervousness. It also showed the importance of organizational values: a community-based approach, innovation and learning from practice, participation and collaboration. It showed the role of frontline workers and their degree of autonomy and discretion. In line with the model, we found the importance of data as a way of continuously adapting policies and procedures. This fits within the idea that data can serve the goal of improved decision-making, by continuous evaluation in the policy cycle (Hochtle, Parycek, & Scholhammer, 2016). Data provides an opportunity to learn; however, the city stressed the importance of contextualizing data by discussing the data with stakeholders, citizens and clients. These face-to-face conversations give meaning to the data. However, the Utrecht approach also showed challenges including fragmentation, silos and the fact that not all respondents can articulate their health needs. The conceptual model of the Nervous Area of Government (Gooden, 2014) turned out to be valuable to assess the Dutch case. What the Dutch cases contributed to the model is that not an enduring history of inequality lead to nervousness, but nervousness might also arise from more recent societal developments, which are at odds with historical deeply engrained societal values of solidarity and justice.

In addition, our findings provide an indication of so-called "hidden inequity." This means that official numbers presented by the national Dutch statistical office show positive values such as migrants use of GP services even more than native Dutch. However, the numbers that might act as potential "disrupting effects" are not clearly visible. For example, data about use of particular services among migrants or to what extent migrants with different educational levels use certain services are not available. Also, data related to unmet needs – people who needed services but did not get them are also not available. These findings are in line with previous studies that showed that descriptive statistics such as a "mean" can hide potential inequity (Alonge & Peters, 2015).

In other words, examining the unmet needs within different subpopulation groups (migrants or low educated people) will provide a more accurate picture. Finally, we would like to address that this study also has some limitations. We zoomed in on one case in the Netherlands: the city of Utrecht. This provided us an in-depth understanding of how they approached healthcare equity. However, we did not in-depth compare the Utrecht approach with other municipalities in the Netherlands. Further research might be conducted in which different approaches can be compared in order to further distill success factors in dealing with healthcare equity. Furthermore, healthcare equity is complex and is influenced by many factors. It was not our intention to assess healthcare equity or the WMO in itself but to assess a promising practice in dealing with inequities.

References

Arsenijevic, J., Pavlova, M., & Groot, W. (2013). Measuring the catastrophic and impoverishing effect of household health care spending in Serbia. *Social Science and Medicine, 78*, 17–25.

Becker, U. (2000). Welfare state development and employment in the Netherlands in comparative perspective. *Journal of European Social Policy, 10*(3), 219–239.

Bovens, M., & Wille, A. (2017). *Diploma Democracy.* Oxford: Oxford University Press.

Brabers, A. E., Rademakers, J. J., Groenewegen, P., van Dijk, L., & de Jong, J. D. (2017). What role does health literacy play in patients' involvement in medical decision-making. *PLoS One, 12* (3).

Bryman, A. (2012). *Social Research Methods* (pp. 1–12) (4th edition ed.). Oxford: Oxford University Press.

Buurtteam organisatie sociaal. (2018). *Het verslag van 2018. Buurtteam organisatie sociaal.* Utrecht.

Buurtteam organisatie Sociaal. (2016). *Het verslag 2016. Buurtteamorganisatie Sociaal.* Utrecht. Retrieved from incluzio.nl

De Beer, P., & Koster, F. (2009). *Sticking Together or falling apart. Solidarity in an Era of Individualization and Globalization.* Amsterdam: Amsterdam University Press.

Droomers, M. (2009). Tackling health inequalities in the Netherlands. *Eurohealth, 15*(3), 16–18.

European Patients Forum. (2016). *Access to healthcare EPF's survey -final report.* European Patients Forum. Brussels: European Patients Forum.

Gemeente Utrecht. (2013). *Meedoen naar Vermogen. WMO uitvoeringsplan eerste fase: van kaders stellen tot uitvoeren.* Retrieved from www.utrecht.nl

Gemeente Utrecht. (2014–2019). *Bijlagen Meedoen naar Vermogen tweede fase 2014–2019.* Utrecht: Gemeente Utrecht.

Gemeente Utrecht. (2016). *Samen verder werken aan een zorgzame en toegankelijke stad.* Utrecht.

Gemeente Utrecht. (2018a). *Utrecht Gezondheidsprofiel 2018.* volksgezondheidmonitor.nl.

Gemeente Utrecht. (2018b). *Utrecht voor iedereen. Visie versterken sociale basis (WMO).* Utrecht.

Gemeente Utrecht. (2019). *Gezondheid voor iedereen. Volksgezondheidsbeleid Utrecht 2019–2022.* Utrecht.

Gold, M. (1998). Beyond coverage and supply: Measuring access to health care in today's market. *Health Services Research, 33*, 625–652.

Gooden, S. (2014). *Race and Social Equity. A Nervous Area of Government.* New York: Taylor & Francis.

Guy, M. (2012). Social equity: Its legacy, its promise. *Public Administration Review, 72*(1), 5–13.

Heijmans, M., Waverijn, G., Rademakers, J., van der Vaart, R., & Rijken, M. (2014). Functional, communicative and critical healt literacy of chronic disease patients and their importance for self-management. *Patient Education and Counseling, 98*, 41–48.

Hochtle, j., Parycek, P., & Scholhammer, R. (2016). Big data in the policy cycle: Policy decison making in the digital era. *Journal of Organizational Computing and Electronic Commerce, 26*(1–2), 147–169.

Houtepen, R., & Ter Meulen, R. (2000). New types of solidarity in the European welfare state. *Health Care Analysis, 8*, 329–340.

Incluzio. (2015). *Jaarverslag Buurtteams Utrecht.* Utrecht.

Jansen, T., Rademakers, J., Waverijn, G., Verheij, R., Osborne, R., & Heijmans, M. (2018). The role of health literacy in explaining the association between educational attainment and the use of out-fo-hours primary care services in chronically ill people: a survey study. *BMC Health Services Research, 18*, 1–13.

Lindenberg, S. (2014). Solidarity: Unpakcing the social brain. In A. Laitinen, & A. Pessi (eds), *Solidarity - Theory and Practice* (pp. 30–54). Lexington Books. New York: London

Maarse, H., & Paulus, A. (2011). The politics of health-care reform in the Netherlands since 2006. *Health Economics, Policy and Law, 6*, 125–134.

Mackenbach, J. (2012). The Persistence of health inequalities in modern welfare states: the explanation of a paradox. *Social Science and Medicine, 75*(4), 761–769.

Mead, L. (2013). The universities: Avatars of modernity. *Society, 50*, 167–175.

Rademarkers, J., Nijman, J., Brabers, A., de Jong, J. D., & Hendriks, M. (2014). The relative effect of health literacy and patient activitaon on provider choice in the Netherlands. *Health Policy, 114*, 200–206.

Rekenkamer Utrecht. (2016). *Hulp bij Maatwerk. Een onderozek naar de hulp bij het huishouden in het kader van de WMO 2015.* Utrecht.

Rekenkamer Utrecht. (2016). *Hulp bij maatwerk. Een onderzoek naar de hulp bij het huishouden in het kader van de WMO 2015.* Utrecht: Rekenkamer Utrecht.

Roosenboom, M., Makkes, N., & van Wezel, P. (2018). *Krachtige basiszorg. Overzicht resultaten.* Utrecht.

Rostilla. (2013). *Social capital and health inequality in European welfare states.* London: Springer.

Schmid, A., & Siemsen, P. G. (2015). Keeping an eye on IRIS: Risk and income solidarity in OECD Health care systems. In W. M., B. T., & L. S. (eds), *Welfare state transformations and inequality in OECD Countries. Transformations of the state* (pp. 111–129). London: Palgrave Macmillan.

Smid, E., Verhoef, M., & Simons, H. (2016). *Een positief verhaal. Visitatie; over visie, vertrouwen en volwassen relatie.*

Sociaal Cultureel Planbureau. (2014). *De WMO in beweging. Evalutie Wet maatschappelijke ondersteuning 2010–2012.* Den Haag: Sociaal Cultureel Planbureau.

Starfield, B. (2011). The hidden inequity in health care. *International Journal for Equity in Health, 10*(15), 1–3.

Tuzgöl-Broekhoven, A., Stam, J., & Atalikyayi, R. (2018). *Zorgen voor burgers. Onderzoek naar knelpunten die burgers ervaren bij de toegang tot zorg.* Nationale Ombudsman.

Utrecht, C. o. (2015). *Bouwen aan een Gezonde toekomst. Een uitnodiging aan de stad. Volksgezondheidbeleid 2015–2018.* City of Utrecht.

van der Ham, L. (2018). Bedoelingen van de Wet maatschappelijke ondersteuning 2015. In M. Kromhout, N. Kornalijnslijper, & M. de Klerk (eds), *Veranderende zorg en ondersteuning voor mensen met een beperking. Landelijke evalutie van de Hervorming Langdurige Zorg.* Den Haag: Sociaal Cultureel Planbureau.

Veen, R. (2005). *Nieuwe vormen van solidariteit. Sociaal Democratische Beginselen en de verzorgingsstaat.* Den Haag: Wiardi Beckman Stichting.

Wetenschappelijke Raad voor het Regeringsbeleid. (2017). *Weten is nog geen doen. Een realistisch perspectief op redzaamheid.* Den Haag: Wetenschappelijke Raad voor het Regeringsbeleid.

Zarrinkhameh, A., & Doorten, I. (2013). *LETS CARE- Hoe andere vormen van solidariteit de wederkerigheid bevorderen.* Raad voor de Volksgezondheid en Zorg aan de staatssecratris van Volksgezondheid, Welzijn en Sport.

13

PRINCIPLES FOR CONQUERING NERVOUSNESS IN GOVERNMENT

Susan T. Gooden

Principle 1

All countries have a responsibility to operate in the nervous area of government.

The nervous area of government is how an organization considers, examines, promotes, distributes, and evaluates the provision of public justice in areas such as race, ethnicity, gender, religion, sexual orientation, and ability status. This area is "nervous" because examination of such areas has an emotional context. It is "of government" because public administrators are responsible for providing services to the public at large and countries have an equity record, shaped by history, as well as current policies and practices. Measures of equity in government involve dimensions of procedural fairness, access, quality, and outcomes.

Article I of the United Nations Charter details its primary purpose which includes "encouraging human rights and fundamental freedoms for all without distinction as to race, sex, language, or religion" (United Nations Charter, 1945). All countries have the responsibility to continuously improve the alignment between equity in principle and equity in action. This is essential for all humankind and also critical to the promotion and sustainability of world peace.

Principle 2

The legal history of social discrimination is an important context that cannot be minimized, but rather offers instructive guidance.

As each of these chapters reveals, nervous areas of government operate within an important historical, political, and societal context. Contemporary saturations of social inequities are not randomly distributed, but rather are largely shaped by their historical context. The context of China is different from that of India, India is different from Germany, Germany is different from Cyprus, and so forth. Understanding this history is important in detecting and countering embedded vestiges of social inequities. It is also critical to affirmatively promoting policies that provide redress to discriminated groups. For example, as detailed in the Mexico chapter, the long history of discrimination against indigenous women is complex and dates back to the country's colonization as well as the engrained culture of machismo. Regardless of the specific country, these historical social inequities are understandably a source of embarrassment, particularly for democratic nations on an international stage. But successfully navigating the nervous area of government requires learning from this history and correcting it, rather than avoiding or minimizing it.

Principle 3

Initial motivators to begin navigation of nervousness typically include some combination of political, moral, legal and/or economic triggers.

Motivators to begin navigation of nervousness vary from country to country, but their origins can be traced back to specific triggers. For example, while Rwanda, South Africa, and Northern Ireland all developed and implemented important reconciliation efforts, in the case of Rwanda, this was motivated by the end of the Rwandan genocide. In the case of South Africa, it was motivated by the end of apartheid. And, in the case of Northern Ireland, it was a negotiated peace settlement. In the political arena, social equity motivation is largely shaped by political leaders and/or pressure from the international community. Motivators in the legal area include laws, regulations, court decisions, and/or litigation. Economic triggers advance social equity issues based on monetary terms, such as cost-benefit analysis or improved organizational dimensions. Moral motivators are largely the result of shifts in societal pressures that wield organizational pressure. Importantly, these motivators are not mutually exclusive and when operating in tandem can often result in the greatest opportunity for significant social equity progress.

Principle 4

Senior leadership is a critically important factor in realizing sustained progress.

Leaders within countries, by virtue of their position, formal authority, perceived and real power, and influence, routinely articulate strong messages about what is important, what is unimportant, and what resides in the zone of indifferences. Larger values of social equity are affirmed or moderated by leadership action and behavior. Practically speaking, actions of senior leaders largely influence the parameters of operations with the nervous area of government. In the case of France, analyzing presidential administrations reveals very different presidential approaches to Islamophobia. Across the world, elections and leadership matter.

Principle 5

At the individual level, actors must recognize and eliminate behaviors that impede social equity progress.

Conversations, dialogues, and meetings about social equity and the administration of public services offer individuals an opportunity to have an increased understanding of the role that social identity and group membership play in the provision, administration, and delivery of public services. In Germany, for example, despite the fall of the Berlin Wall in 1989, the question of German identity remains uncertain today. This directly impacts the educational opportunities for Turkish-origin Germans.

Principle 6

At the organizational level, governments should evaluate their socialization boundaries and extend them to accommodate a wider range of social equity work.

Through the socialization process, organizations provide boundaries on social equity activities that are required, permitted, discouraged, or prohibited. These boundaries include two key dimensions: public boundaries and real boundaries. Often, in order to perform social equity work, the externalities of the "real" boundaries need expansion in order to include activities that reside in the nervous area. This results in a cultural redefinition of acceptable boundaries and more easily accommodates social equity work through a reduction of fear. For example, the government of Cyprus is trying to extend its boundaries by endorsing a pro-LGBT framework, as part of its desire to demonstrate a stronger connection to the values held by other members of the European Union.

Principle 7

There are no perfect solutions; however, solutions that embody a social equity approach most directly facilitate structural equity solutions.

Like all aspects of government and public policy, perfection is impossible to achieve. There will be challenging aspects, conflicting values, ineffective approaches, expenditures of political capital, important trade-offs, and difficult moments. Navigating a nervous area of government often involves significant turbulence and is not for the faint-hearted. Beginning social equity work is often the most difficult and nervousness peaks here. Normalizing discussions with the area of social equity, whether the topic is race, gender, sexual orientation, ability status, class, or religion, is an early indicator of progress. Importantly, however, the engagement of solutions designed to counter social inequities must directly confront the equity issue. As detailed in the Brazil analysis, where educational quotas have been established to redress previous state-caused inequities, their implementation is challenging in determining the criteria for *preto* designation.

Principle 8

Social equity needs to operate in a context of accountability.

In order to appropriately access social equity progress, performance goals should be developed, measured, evaluated, and updated. Governments should be invested in analyzing social equity dimensions of their services from an intrinsic goal to demonstrate high performance and accountability. This will lead to the clear identification of best practices and offer instructive guidance relative to return on policy investments. An examination of data trends since the implementation of China's universal two-child policy and their "Care for Girls" campaign reveals very promising trends along such factors as declining gender imbalance at birth and increased access to education for females.

Principle 9

If legal barriers to social equity have been largely eliminated, leadership, policies, practices, and innovations form the foundation of essential social equity work.

While many countries have eliminated legal barriers to inequities, particularly in the areas of gender, race, and religion, the realization of social equity requires an examination of the broader structural inequities in public agency systems and making needed improvements. Emblematic of this, while India has made many positive legal improvements to the status of women through their Constitution as well as through legislative policies, serious challenges remain relative to female access to education, gender-based violence, and gender bias more generally. A seemingly straightforward solution, such as providing mid-day lunches in schools, can offer important innovations to serve as the foundation of important social equity work. By contrast, the experience of healthcare in the Netherlands suggests that countries without a history of discrimination based on race or gender are not immune from important equity challenges relating to more recent social changes and developments.

Principle 10

Significant social equity progress in government can be achieved.

A core contribution of this book is offering concrete examples of substantial social equity work across multiple country contexts. While they do not constitute a "one size fits all approach" by any means, these examples underscore how social equity can and does occur. All countries are imperfect and have their societal shortcomings, embedded in their particular historical context. Yet, as the authors of these chapters demonstrate, countries can also work effectively in the nervous area of government in improving their social equity record. It may not be easy, but it is also not impossible. As Nelson Mandala reminds us, "It always seems impossible until it's done."

References

Gooden, Susan T. 2015. *Race and Social Equity: A Nervous Area of Government*. Abingdon: Routledge.

United Nations. n.d. About Us. https://www.un.org/en/about-un/

INDEX

Note: **Bold** page numbers refer to tables; *Italic* page numbers refer to figures and page numbers followed by 'n' refer to notes.